Hopes and Prospects

Hopes and Prospects

Noam Chomsky

HAMISH HAMILTON
an imprint of
PENGUIN BOOKS

HAMISH HAMILTON

Published by the Penguin Group
Penguin Books Ltd, 80 Strand, London WC2R ORL, England
Penguin Group (USA) Inc., 375 Hudson Street, New York, New York 10014, USA
Penguin Group (Canada), 90 Eglinton Avenue East, Suite 700, Toronto, Ontario, Canada M4P 2Y3
(a division of Pearson Penguin Canada Inc.)
Penguin Ireland, 25 St Stephen's Green, Dublin 2, Ireland (a division of Penguin Books Ltd)
Penguin Group (Australia), 250 Camberwell Road, Camberwell, Victoria 3124, Australia
(a division of Pearson Australia Group Pty Ltd)
Penguin Books India Pvt Ltd, 11 Community Centre, Panchsheel Park, New Delhi – 110 017, India
Penguin Group (NZ), 67 Apollo Drive, Rosedale, North Shore 0632, New Zealand
(a division of Pearson New Zealand Ltd)
Penguin Books (South Africa) (Pty) Ltd, 24 Sturdee Avenue, Rosebank, Johannesburg 2196, South Africa

Penguin Books Ltd, Registered Offices: 80 Strand, London WC2R ORL, England

www.penguin.com

First published in the USA by Haymarket Books 2010
First published in Great Britain by Hamish Hamilton 2010

1

Copyright © Noam Chomsky, 2010

The moral right of the author has been asserted

Printed in Great Britain by Clays Ltd, St Ives plc

A CIP catalogue record for this book is available from the British Library

HARDBACK ISBN: 978-0-241-14475-6

TRADE PAPERBACK ISBN: 978-0-241-14501-2

www.greenpenguin.co.uk

Penguin Books is committed to a sustainable future
for our business, our readers and our planet.
The book in your hands is made from paper
certified by the Forest Stewardship Council.

CONTENTS

Preface

The essays collected here had their origin in a series of lectures in Chile in October 2006, published in Spanish in 2009 by EDUFRO Universidad de la Frontera (Temuco) with the title *Neoliberalismo y Globalización*. I had intended to prepare them for publication in English, but was unable to do so for some time. They appear here as the first three chapters, updated to early 2010 and considerably expanded. Chapter 4, completing Part I, is based on a videoconference at the VII Social Summit for Latin American and Caribbean Unity in Caracas, on September 24, 2008, also updated and expanded. The primary focus of Part I is Latin America and U.S. relations with the subcontinent.

Part II consists of expanded and revised talks and articles from 2008 to 2009, also updated to early 2010, concerned with a variety of interrelated themes of domestic U.S. and international affairs. Earlier versions of chapters 5, 9, and 11 appeared in *Z Magazine*, and chapter 7 in *International Socialist Review*. Chapter 12 draws on talks in October to November 2009, in the United Kingdom and Ireland, and at Boston College (November 30), a commemoration of the assassinations of November 16, 1989.

PART I

Latin America

ONE

Year 514: Globalization for Whom?

Human affairs proceed in their intricate, endlessly varied, and unpredictable paths, but occasionally events occur that are taken to be sharp turning points in history. There have been several in recent years. It is a near platitude in the West that after September 11, 2001, nothing will be the same. The fall of the Berlin wall in 1989 was another event accorded this high status. There is a great deal to say about these two cases, both the myth and the reality. But in referring to the 514th year I of course have something different in mind: the year 1492, which did, undoubtedly, direct world history on a radically new course, with awesome and lasting consequences.

As we know, the voyages of Columbus opened the way to the European conquest of the Western hemisphere, with hideous consequences for the indigenous population, and soon for Africans brought here in one of the vilest episodes of history. Vasco da Gama soon opened the way to bring to Africa and Asia the "the savage injustice of the Europeans," to borrow Adam Smith's rueful phrase, referring primarily to Britain's terrible crimes in India, plain enough even in his day. Also in 1492, Christian conquerors extended their barbaric sway over the most advanced and tolerant civilization in Europe, Moorish Spain, forcing Jews to flee or convert to the civilization of the Inquisition and initiating the vast ethnic cleansing of the Muslim population ("Moors"), while also destroying much of the

rich record of classical learning that they had preserved and developed—
rather like the Mongol invasion of Iraq two centuries earlier, or the even
worse destruction of the treasures of civilization in the course of the U.S.-
British invasion of Iraq that continues to take a terrible toll.[1] The conquest
of most of the world by Europe and its offshoots has been the primary
theme of world history ever since.

The basic reasons for Europe's remarkable military successes are well
understood. One was European filth, which caused epidemics that deci-
mated the much healthier populations of the Western hemisphere.[2] Apart
from disease, "It was thanks to their military superiority, rather than to
any social, moral or natural advantage, that the white peoples of the world
managed to create and control, however briefly, the first global hegemony
in history," military historian Geoffrey Parker observes.[3] From America
to Southeast Asia, he continues, the population was astonished by the savagery of the Europeans and "equally appalled by the all-destructive fury
of European warfare." The victims were hardly pacifist societies, but European savagery was something new, not so much in technology as in
spirit. Parker's phrase "however briefly" might turn out to be correct, in
a much more grim sense than he meant. Some of the most prominent
and judicious strategic analysts in the United States warn of "ultimate
doom" or even "apocalypse soon" if the government persists in its aggressive militarism[4]—and looming not too far in the distance is the threat
of anthropogenic environmental catastrophe.

Today's gap between North and South—the rich developed societies
and the rest of the world—was largely created by the global conquest.
Scholarship and science are beginning to recognize a record that had been
concealed by imperial arrogance. They are discovering that at the time of
the arrival of the Europeans, and long before, the Western hemisphere was
home to some of the world's most advanced civilizations. In the poorest
country of South America, archaeologists are coming to believe that eastern
Bolivia was the site of a wealthy, sophisticated, and complex society of perhaps a million people. In their words, it was the site of "one of the largest,
strangest, and most ecologically rich artificial environments on the face of
the planet, with causeways and canals, spacious and formal towns and

considerable wealth," creating a landscape that was "one of humankind's greatest works of art, a masterpiece." In the Peruvian Andes, by 1491 the Inka had created the greatest empire in the world, greater in scale than the Chinese, Russian, Ottoman, or other empires, far greater than any European state, and with remarkable artistic, agricultural, and other achievements.[5]

One of the most exciting developments of the past few decades is the revival of indigenous cultures and languages, and the struggles for community and political rights. The achievements in South America have been particularly dramatic. Throughout the hemisphere and elsewhere there are indigenous movements seeking to gain land rights and other civil and human rights that have been denied them by repressive and often murderous states. This is happening even where the indigenous communities barely survived the conquest, as in the United States, where the pre-contact population of perhaps seven million or more was reduced to a few hundred thousand by 1900. I need hardly mention that the issues are very much alive right here in Temuco, at the frontier with the Mapuche.

My own department at MIT has played a significant role in the revival, thanks to the extraordinary work of the late Kenneth Hale. Apart from working on human rights issues for indigenous populations in the Americas and Australia, and fundamental contributions to the study of their languages and to linguistic theory, he also brought people from reservations who had had few educational opportunities and devoted great effort to helping them gain doctoral degrees in a very demanding program, with dissertations on their own languages that surpassed anything in the literature in depth and sophistication. They returned to their homes, and have established educational and cultural programs, several of which have flourished, revitalizing marginalized communities and helping them to gain broader rights. I will mention only one really spectacular achievement. One of the major languages of New England before the conquest was Wampanoag. The people themselves were mostly expelled or murdered, with a bounty offered for their heads, while those who surrendered and did not want to fight were sold into slavery—men, women, and children—by the early English colonists.[6] The last known speaker died a century ago. Hale and some of his students were able to reconstruct the language from textual and comparative evidence. Hale's primary collaborator was a Wampanoag woman, Jesse Little Doe, who helped reconstruct the language and then learned it. At a memorial for Hale, she paid her tribute to him in fluent Wampanoag, and also brought her two-year-old daughter, the first native speaker of the language in a century. There is a good chance that the culture and community will flourish and find a proper place in the larger society, a model for what might be achieved elsewhere.

On the other side of the world, at the time of the European conquests, China and India were the world's major commercial and industrial centers, well ahead of Europe in public health and probably sophistication and scale of market systems and trading areas. Life expectancy in Japan may have been higher than in Europe.[7] England was trying to catch up in textiles and other manufactures, borrowing from India and other countries in ways that are now called "piracy," and are banned in the international trade agreements imposed by the rich states under a cynical pretense of "free trade."

The United States relied heavily on the same mechanisms of "piracy" and protectionism, as have other states that have developed. Britain also engaged in actual piracy—now considered among the most heinous of international crimes. The most admired of English pirates was Sir Francis Drake. The booty that he brought home "may fairly be considered the fountain and origin of British foreign investments," John Maynard Keynes concluded.[8]

England finally adopted a form of "free trade" in 1846, after centuries of protectionism and state intervention in the economy had given it an enormous advantage over competitors, while it destroyed Indian manufacture by high protective tariffs and other means, as it had done before in Ireland. The United States adopted free trade a century later, for similar reasons. But in both cases the "free trade" commitments were carefully hedged, matters to which we return. In general, with extensive state intervention and violence at home, and barbarism and imposed liberalization in conquered areas, Europe and its offshoots were able to become rich developed societies, while the conquered regions became the "third world," the South. While history is too complex to be reduced to just a few factors, these have been salient ones.

The effects are dramatic, sometimes startling. Consider the poorest country in the Western hemisphere: Haiti, which may not be habitable in a few generations; it was probably the richest colony in the world, the source of much of France's wealth. By 1789, it was producing 75 percent of the world's sugar and was the world leader in production of cotton— the "oil" of the early industrial revolution—as well as other valued commodities. The plantation slave economy set in motion the processes of destroying arable land and forests that have been carried forward since, regularly enhanced by imperial policies. French ships returning from delivery of slaves brought back Haitian timber. The destruction of the forests by the French rulers, later poverty-driven, caused erosion and further destruction. After a brutal and devastating struggle against the armies of France and Britain, backed by the United States, the colony finally won its freedom in 1804, becoming the first free country of free men in the hemisphere, twenty years after the slave society that now dominates the world had liberated itself from England. Haitians were made to pay a bitter price for the crime of liberation. The United States refused to recognize this dangerous free society until 1862, when it also recognized Liberia for the same reason: slaves were being freed, and there was hope that the country could be kept free of contamination by non-whites by exporting them to where they belonged. The project withered when means were found to reinstitute a new form of slavery through criminalization of Black life, a major contribution to the American industrial revolution, continuing until World War II, when "free labor" was needed for military industry. France imposed a huge indemnity on Haiti as punishment for liberating itself from vicious French rule, a burden it has never been able to overcome. The civilized world agreed that France's punishment of Haiti was just, and still does. A few years ago, Haitian president Jean-Bertrand Aristide politely asked France whether the time had not come to compensate Haitians for this crushing debt, at least slightly. France was outraged, and soon joined Washington in overthrowing the democratically elected government of Haiti in 2004, instituting yet another reign of terror in the battered society.[9]

The immediate consequences were investigated by the University of Miami School of Law, which found "that many Haitians, especially those living in poor neighborhoods, now struggle against inhuman horror [as] [n]ightmarish fear now accompanies Haiti's poorest in their struggle to survive in destitution [in] a cycle of violence [fuelled by] Haiti's security and justice institutions." In August 2006, the world's leading medical journal, the *Lancet*, released a study of human rights abuses from the February 2004 overthrow of the government until December 2005. The researchers found that some eight thousand individuals (about twelve per day) were murdered during the period, and sexual assault was common, especially against children, with the data suggesting thirty-five thousand women and girls were raped in the Port-au-Prince area alone. The atrocities were attributed primarily to criminals, the Haitian National Police, and UN peacekeepers. They found very few attributed to the pro-Aristide Lavalas forces. The study passed without notice in the United States, very little elsewhere.[10]

Perhaps the most extreme of the many disasters visited upon Haiti since its liberation was the invasion by Woodrow Wilson in 1915, restoring virtual slavery, killing thousands—fifteen thousand according to Haitian historian Roger Gaillard—and opening up the country to takeover by U.S. corporations. The shattered society was left in the hands of a murderous, U.S.-trained National Guard serving the interests of the Haitian elite, mulatto and white, who are even more predatory and rapacious than is the norm in Latin America and who regularly appropriate the aid sent to the country. This is one of the many triumphs of what has passed down through history as "Wilsonian idealism."

The takeover of Haiti by U.S. corporations was accomplished by disbanding the Parliament under U.S. Marine guns when it refused to accede to the U.S. demand that it accept a U.S.-written Constitution that permitted these "progressive" measures. True, the U.S. occupiers did conduct a referendum, in which its demands received 99.9 percent approval with 5 percent of the population participating. That the measures were progressive was widely accepted. As the State Department explained, Haitians were "inferior people" and "It was obvious that if our occupation was to be beneficial to Haiti and further her progress it was necessary that foreign capital should come to Haiti…[and] Americans could hardly be expected to put their money into plantations and big agricultural enterprises in Haiti if they could not themselves own the land on which their money was to be spent." Thus it was out of a sincere desire to help suffering Haitians that the United States forced them at gunpoint to allow U.S. investors to take over their country in an "unselfish intervention" carried out in a "fatherly way" with no thought of "preferential advantages, commercial or otherwise" for ourselves (*New York Times*).

The terror and repression increased under the rule of the National Guard and the Duvalier dictatorships while the elite prospered, isolated from the country they were helping to rob. When Reagan took office, USAID and the World Bank instituted programs to turn Haiti into the "Taiwan of the Caribbean" by adhering to the sacred principle of comparative advantage: Haiti was to import food and other commodities from the United States while working people, mostly women, toiled under miserable conditions in U.S.-owned assembly plants. As the World Bank explained in a 1985 report, in this export-oriented development strategy domestic consumption should be "markedly restrained in order to shift the required share of output increases into exports," with emphasis placed on "the expansion of private enterprises," while support for education should be "minimized" and such "social objectives" as persist should be privatized. "Private projects with high economic returns should be strongly supported" in preference to "public expenditures in the social sectors," and "less emphasis should be placed on social objectives which increase consumption." In contrast, the Taiwanese developmental state, free from foreign control, pursued radically different policies, targeting investment to rural areas to increase consumption and prevent the flow of peasants to miserable urban slums, the obvious consequence of the progressive policies dictated for Haiti—which remained Haiti, not Taiwan. Subsequent disasters, including the earthquake of January 2010, are substantially man-made, the consequences of these policy decisions and others like them since the U.S. invasion of 1915 exacerbating the disasters set in motion by France as it enriched itself by robbing and destroying its richest colony.

The Reagan administration was particularly pleased by an "encouraging step forward" in Haiti in 1985: the legislature passed a law requiring
that every political party must recognize president-for-life "Baby Doc"
Duvalier as the supreme arbiter of the nation, outlawing the Christian
Democrats, and granting the government the right to suspend the rights
of any party without reasons. This achievement of Reagan's "democracy
enhancement" programs enabled the administration to keep providing
military aid to the vicious and venal dictator who was democratizing the
country so successfully. And the Reaganite judgment about the progress
of democracy was not entirely with merit. The law was passed by a
99.98 percent majority, not very different from the 99.9 percent under
Wilsonian idealism. Cynics might say that the divide reflects the spectrum of approved choices for our dependencies as domestic politics veers
from one extreme to the other.

Haiti's first free election, in 1990, threatened the rational programs
imposed by Washington and the international financial institutions. The
poor majority entered the political arena for the first time and, by a two-
thirds majority, elected their own candidate, the populist priest Jean-
Bertrand Aristide—to the surprise and shock of observers, who had been
paying little attention to the extensive grassroots organizing in the slums
and hills and took for granted that U.S.-backed candidate Marc Bazin, a
former World Bank official who monopolized resources and had the full
support of the wealthy elite, would win easily; Bazin received 14 percent
of the vote. During Aristide's brief tenure in office, the refugee flow reversed: instead of refugees fleeing from terror and repression, and being
turned back by the U.S. Coast Guard (or sometimes dispatched to Guantánamo) in violation of international conventions on refugees, Haitians
were returning to their homeland in this moment of hope. U.S. refugee
policy shifted accordingly: though they were few, refugees were now
granted asylum, since they were fleeing a democratic government that
the United States opposed, not vicious dictatorships that the United
States supported. Aristide's success in controlling finances and cutting
down the bloated bureaucracy was praised by international lending institutions, which accordingly provided aid. The situation was dangerous:

Haiti was moving toward democracy, drifting from the U.S. orbit, and adopting policies oriented to the needs of the impoverished majority, not the rich U.S. allies.

Washington instantly adopted standard operating procedures in such a case, shifting aid to the business-led opposition and moving to undermine the Aristide regime by other devices labeled "democracy promotion." A few months later, in September 1991, came the anticipated military coup, with probable CIA participation, confirmed by Emmanuel Constant, the leader of the terrorist organization FRAPH (Front pour l'Advancement et le Progès Haitien) which killed thousands of Haitians; he was later protected from extradition to Haiti by the Clinton administration, very likely because he had too much to say. Probably for similar reasons, the U.S. forces sent to restore the president in 1994 confiscated 160,000 pages of documents that the Clinton administration refused to provide to the democratic government—"to avoid embarrassing revelations" about Washington's support for the military junta and efforts to undermine democracy, Human Rights Watch speculated. The junta instituted a vicious reign of terror, which was backed by Bush senior and even more fully by Bill Clinton, despite pretenses. U.S.-Haiti trade increased in violation of an OAS (Organization of American States) embargo, and the Texaco oil company was quietly authorized to deliver oil to the military junta in violation of presidential directives. Now that Haiti was in the hands of a murderous dictatorship serving the wealthy, refugee policy returned to the norm.[11]

By 1994 Clinton apparently decided that the population was sufficiently intimidated and that Aristide had been "civilized" by his U.S. instructors, and sent U.S. forces to restore the elected president to a few more months in office. But on strict conditions: that he accept a harsh neoliberal regime, pretty much the program of the U.S.-backed candidate he had defeated handily in the 1990 election (who had been installed in office by the junta and their rich supporters in 1992). Aristide's efforts to disband the army, which had been the bitter enemy of Haitians since its institution, were barred. Haiti was also barred from providing any protection for the economy. Haitian rice farmers are efficient, but cannot compete with U.S. agribusiness that relies on huge government subsidies, thanks largely to Reagan, anointed as the high priest of free trade with little regard to his record of extreme protectionism and state intervention in the economy. Other small businesses were destroyed by U.S. dumping, which Haiti was powerless to prevent under the imposed conditions of economic rationality.

There is nothing surprising about what followed: a 1995 USAID report observed that the "export-driven trade and investment policy [that Washington mandated will] relentlessly squeeze the domestic rice farmer," accelerating the flight to miserable slums that reached its hideous denouement in the catastrophe caused by the January 2010 earthquake—a class-based catastrophe, like many others, striking primarily at the poor whose awful conditions of existence render them particularly vulnerable (the rich escaped lightly). Meanwhile neoliberal policies dismantled what was left of economic sovereignty and drove the country into chaos, accelerated by Bush II's blocking of almost all international aid on cynical grounds, guaranteeing that there would be chaos, violence, and even more suffering. Then came the return of the two traditional torturers of Haiti, France and the United States, which overthrew the government in 2004, kidnapping the elected president (in the guise of "rescue") and dispatching him to Central Africa; the United States has since sought to bar Aristide not just from Haiti, but from the hemisphere. Haiti had by then lost the capacity to feed itself, leaving it highly vulnerable to food price fluctuation.[12]

In early 2008 riots broke out around the world in reaction to sharply rising food prices. The first were in Haiti and Bangladesh, a significant coincidence for those with historical memory. The desperate plight of the poor gained a few moments of attention, but without such historical memory. A year later, the London *Financial Times* reported an announcement by the UN World Food Program that it would be "cutting food aid rations and shutting down some operations as donor countries that face a fiscal crunch at home slash contributions to its funding": victims included Ethiopia, Rwanda, Uganda, and others. The severe budget cut came as the toll of hunger passed a billion, with over 100 million added in the preceding six months, while food prices rose, and remittances declined as a result of the economic crisis in the West.

In Bangladesh, the newspaper *New Nation* observed that

> It's very telling that trillions have already been spent to patch up leading world financial institutions, while out of the comparatively small sum of $12.3 billion pledged in Rome earlier this year, to offset the food crisis, only $1 billion has been delivered. The hope that at least extreme poverty can be eradicated by the end of 2015, as stipulated in the UN's Millennium Development Goals, seems as unrealistic as ever, not due to lack of resources but a lack of true concern for the world's poor.

The WFP report of the sharp reduction in the meager Western efforts to address the growing catastrophe merited 150 words in the *New York Times* on an inside page, under "World Briefing."[13]

The reaction is not unusual. At the same time the UN released an estimate that desertification is endangering the lives of up to a billion people, while it announced World Desertification Day. Its goal is "to combat desertification and drought worldwide by promoting public awareness and the implementation of conventions dealing with desertification in member countries."[14] The effort to raise public awareness passed without mention in the national press. As in the case of repeated catastrophes in Haiti, of increasing ferocity, these are not just natural disasters. There is a human hand, commonly close to home, but concealed by what has aptly been termed "intentional ignorance."[15]

At about the same time, the secretary-general of Amnesty International, the Bangladeshi human rights activist Irene Khan, published a book entitled *The Unheard Truth*, describing the poverty that afflicts three billion people, half the world's population, as the most severe of the many human rights crises.[16] Human rights crises involve human agency, both in creating them and in adopting, or rejecting, measures that might mitigate or end them. Poverty is no exception, and Haiti is a striking illustration. The poverty is largely a human creation, ever since the French occupation (putting aside Columbus and the other murderers who quickly wiped out the indigenous population with indescribable savagery). So is the refusal to mitigate the disaster. After the January 2010 earthquake, a donor's conference was held in Montreal. The participants refused to consider two of the most urgent requirements for ameliorating the grim conditions of Haiti: writing off Haiti's completely illegitimate debt—"odious" debt for which the population bears no responsibility (to borrow the concept invented by the United States, referring to Cuba's "debt" to Spain, which the United States did not want to pay after taking Cuba over in 1898)—and reducing the agricultural subsidies of the rich countries that have been a lethal blow to the agricultural system and a major spur to the urbanization that is largely responsible for the colossal death toll of the earthquake.

Two countries were not invited to the Montreal conference: Cuba and Venezuela, two of the leading participants in the aid effort, particularly Cuba, which had hundreds of doctors working in Haiti for many years and sent others immediately, one example of its remarkable record of genuine internationalism over many years. Unlike the participants at Montreal, Venezuela immediately cancelled Haiti's quite substantial debt for the oil that Venezuela had been providing at reduced cost. As the conference opened, Haitian prime minister Bellerive specifically thanked Cuba, Venezuela, and the Dominican Republic (invited to attend), which "came immediately to help our people affected by the quake."[17]

We may recall an observation of Francis Jennings, who played an important part in unearthing the true story of the destruction of the indigenous population of the United States from the depths to which it had long been consigned: "In history, the man in the ruffled shirt and gold-laced waistcoat somehow levitates above the blood he has ordered to be spilled by dirty-handed underlings."[18] One of the enduring principles of intellectual history.

Turning to the opposite side of the world, British conquerors were astonished at the wealth, culture, and sophisticated civilization of Bengal, which they regarded as one of the richest prizes in the world. The conqueror was Robert Clive—whose statue greets visitors to the Victoria museum in Kolkata (Calcutta), a memorial to British imperial violence and degradation of its subjects. Clive was amazed at what he found. He described the great textile center of Dacca, now the capital of Bangladesh, as "extensive, populous and as rich as the city of London." After a century of British rule its population had fallen from 150,000 to 30,000, and it was reverting to jungle and malaria. Adam Smith wrote that hundreds of thousands die in Bengal every year as a result of British regulations that even forced farmers to "plough up rich fields of rice or other grain for plantations of poppies" for opium production, turning "dearth into a famine." In the words of the rulers themselves, "The misery hardly finds a place in the history of commerce. The bones of the cotton-weavers are bleaching the plains of India." Bengal's own fine cotton became extinct, and its advanced textile production was transplanted to England. Bangladesh may soon be wiped out by rising sea levels, unless the industrial societies act decisively to control and reverse the likely environmental catastrophe they have been creating, joined now by China and other developing societies.

Haiti and Bangladesh, once the sparkling jewels in the crown of empire, are now the very symbols of misery and despair, facts that must escape the view of "the man in the ruffled shirt and gold-laced waistcoat."

So the story continues around the world, with only a few exceptions. The best-known is Japan, which managed to avoid colonization—and is the only country of the South to have developed and industrialized during this era, a correlation that tells us quite a lot about political and economic history. A well-documented conclusion is that sovereignty, hence ability to control internal economic development and to enter international market systems on one's own terms, is a crucial prerequisite to economic development.

It should be added that colonization extended in a different way to the societies of the conquerors as well, and continues to do so today. "European societies were also colonized and plundered, less catastrophically than the Americas but more so than most of Asia," historian Thomas Brady wrote. His point was that the profits of empire were privatized, but the costs socialized. The empire was a form of class war within the imperial societies themselves. The basic reason was explained by Adam Smith, who observed that the "merchants and manufacturers" of England were "the principal architects" of state policy, and made sure that their own interests "were most peculiarly attended to," however "grievous" the effects on others, including the people of England.

Smith was referring to the mercantilist system, but his observation generalizes, and in that form stands as one of the very few authentic principles of the theory of international relations, alongside another fundamental principle, the maxim of Thucydides that the strong do as they wish, and the weak suffer as they must. These two principles are not the end of wisdom, but they carry us a long way toward understanding the world. They also enlighten us about what must be done if we are to move toward a more decent society—or even one that has a chance to survive.

Another pervasive principle is that those who hold the clubs can carry out their work effectively only with the benefit of self-induced blindness: the principle of intellectual history that Francis Jennings formulated with unfortunate precision, which we can take to be a corollary to the maxims of Thucydides and Smith. That includes selective historical amnesia and a variety of devices to evade the consequences of one's actions (in contrast, it is permissible, indeed obligatory, to posture heroically about the crimes of enemies, lying freely if it helps the story, particularly when we can do nothing about the crimes so that the exercise is costless). To mention only one of innumerable illustrations, a conventional version of the Columbian era at the time of the quincentennial celebration in 1992 was that "For thousands of centuries—centuries in which human races were evolving, forming communities and building the beginnings of national civilizations in Africa, Asia, and Europe—the continents we know as the Americas stood empty of mankind and its works." Accordingly, the story of Europeans in the empty New World "is the story of the creation of a civilization where none existed." The quote is from the standard high school textbook of the day, written by three prominent U.S. historians.[19]

It was recognized that there were some savages wandering through these empty spaces, but that was a matter of little moment. As the national poet Walt Whitman explained, our conquests "take off the shackles that prevent men the even chance of being happy and good." With the conquest of half of Mexico in mind, he asked rhetorically, "What has miserable, inefficient Mexico…to do with the great mission of peopling the New World with a noble race?" His thoughts were spelled out by the leading humanist thinker of the period, Ralph Waldo Emerson, who wrote that the annexation of Texas was simply a matter of course: "It is very certain that the strong British race which has now overrun much of this continent, must also overrun that trace, and Mexico and Oregon also, and it will in the course of ages be of small import by what particular occasions and methods it was done."

It had of course been understood that not all would benefit from the just and necessary task of opening the wilderness for the superior race arriving to claim it. Nonetheless, the ideas were conventional, and remained so. As recently as 1969, the leading scholarly history of U.S. diplomacy explained that after liberating themselves from British rule, the united thirteen colonies were able to "concentrate on the task of felling trees and Indians and of rounding out their natural boundaries" (Thomas Bailey). Little if any notice appears to have been taken in the profession or mainstream discourse.

The United States is, I suppose, the only country that was founded as an "infant empire," in the words of the father of the country. After liberation from England, George Washington observed that "the gradual extension of our settlements will as certainly cause the savage, as the wolf, to retire; both being beasts of prey, though they differ in shape." We must "induce [the Aborigines] to relinquish our Territories and to remove into the illimitable regions of the West"—which we were to "induce" them to leave later on, for heaven. The Territories became "ours" by right of conquest as the "Aborigines" were regularly instructed.

Washington's colleagues agreed. The most libertarian of the Founding Fathers, Thomas Jefferson, predicted that the newly liberated colonies would drive the indigenous population "with the beasts of the forests into the Stony Mountains," and the country will ultimately be "free of blot or mixture," red or Black (with the return of slaves to Africa after eventual ending of slavery). What is more, it "will be the nest, from which all America, North and South, is to be peopled." In 1801 he wrote to James Monroe that we should "look forward to distant times, when our rapid multiplication will expand...& cover the whole northern if not the southern continent, with people speaking the same language, governed in similar forms, and by similar laws." "In other words," historian R. W. van Alstyne summarizes, "he pictured the United States as the homeland for teeming millions who would emigrate and reproduce their kind in all parts of North and South America, displacing not merely the indigenous redmen but also the Latin populations to the south," creating a continent that would be "American in blood, in language and habits, and in political ideology." It was expected that it would be easier to achieve this end in Canada after the conquest of the country that Jefferson and his associates anticipated and attempted to implement several times by force—and that may yet take place, by means of contemporary forms of subjugation.

All of this was suffused with love and concern for our wards. James Madison orated that we must "carry on the benevolent plans which have been so meritoriously applied to the conversion of our aboriginal neighbors from the degradation and wretchedness of savage life to a participation of the improvements of which the human mind and manners are susceptible in a civilized state.... With our Indian neighbors, the just and benevolent system continued toward them has also preserved peace and is more and more advancing habits favorable to their civilization and happiness." How this was to happen after they were expelled and exterminated, as frankly acknowledged by the perpetrators, he did not say.[20]

It could be argued that citations from eminent historians a few years ago are misleading. After all, there had by then been only five hundred years of savagery and destruction, not yet enough time for proper understanding to have been gained. And it is true, and very important, that the common rhetoric of a few years ago, even in scholarship, would be condemned as vulgar racism today in substantial circles. That is one of many indications of the success of the popular activism of the 1960s in civilizing Western societies. But there is a long way to go.

To illustrate the scale of the task ahead, we may turn to one the world's leading intellectual journals, the *New York Review of Books*. In mid-2009, liberal political analyst Russell Baker records what he learned from the work of the "heroic historian" Edmund Morgan: namely, that Columbus and the early explorers "found a continental vastness sparsely populated by farming and hunting people…In the limitless and unspoiled world stretching from tropical jungle to the frozen north, there may have been scarcely more than a million inhabitants." Virtually repeating the quincentennial celebration, the calculation is off by many tens of millions, and the "vastness" included advanced civilizations. But no matter. The exercise of genocide denial with a vengeance again merits little notice, presumably because it is so unremarkable and in a good cause.[21]

It is worth remembering that the perpetrators themselves had few illusions about what they were doing. Revolutionary War hero General Henry Knox, the first secretary of war in the newly liberated American colonies, described "the utter extirpation of all the Indians in most populous parts of the Union [by means] more destructive to the Indian natives than the conduct of the conquerors of Mexico and Peru," as proved to be the case. He warned that "a future historian may mark the causes of this destruction of the human race in sable colors." In his later years— long after his own contributions to the crimes—President John Quincy Adams lamented the fate of "that hapless race of native Americans, which we are exterminating with such merciless and perfidious cruelty, among the heinous sins of this nation, for which I believe God will one day bring [it] to judgement."[22] Earthly judgment is nowhere in sight.

There was, to be sure, a more convenient and conventional version, expressed for example by Supreme Court Justice Joseph Story, who mused that "the wisdom of Providence," inscrutable to mere mortals, caused the natives to disappear like "the withered leaves of autumn" even though the colonists had "constantly respected" them. In the same years, as the groundwork was being laid for Andrew Jackson's programs of Indian removal (today called "ethnic cleansing" when carried out by enemies), President Monroe explained that "We become in reality their benefactors" by expelling the natives from their homes. Their successors carried forward the humane mission of extirpation and extermination of the natives, for their own good. A century ago, President Theodore Roosevelt informed a group of white missionaries that "The expansion of the peoples of white, or European, blood during the past four centuries…has been fraught with lasting benefit to most of the peoples already dwelling in the lands over which the expansion took place." In short, we are "in reality their benefactors," despite what Native Americans, Africans, Filipinos, and other beneficiaries might mistakenly believe.[23]

Such versions of history are not unusual, nor unique to the United States. They are standard themes of imperial conquest. The belief in the essential humanity of the resort to force by the powerful has a resonance in what today is termed the "emerging international norm that recognizes the 'responsibility to protect' innocent civilians facing death on a mass scale" (President Obama's UN ambassador Susan Rice).[24] That there is such a responsibility should be uncontroversial, and has long been recognized by the UN and individual states. But the occasional resort to this principle by powerful states is a different matter, as history more than amply reveals. In its real world form, the norm is not "emerging." Rather, it is venerable, and has consistently been a guiding imperial doctrine, invoked to justify the resort to violence when other pretexts are lacking, and regularly ignored when great power interests so dictate. The prospect of mass starvation just mentioned is one of a great many current examples, striking because there is no need for any form of intervention, just simple humanity, and because the harrowing news was released only weeks before diplomats and intellectuals were solemnly intoning their dedication to the "emerging international norm" at the UN, including highly respected figures who had been at the forefront of crushing any thought of such norms when they held political office, and journals expert in denying the crimes of their own states.[25]

Just keeping to the conquest of the hemisphere, the Spanish conquistadors in the early sixteenth century were careful to instruct the natives that if you "acknowledge the Church as the Ruler and Superior of the whole world," then we "shall receive you in all love and charity, and shall leave you, your wives, and your children, and your lands, free without servitude," and even "award you many privileges and exemptions and will grant you many benefits," fulfilling our responsibility to protect. But those who are protected also have responsibilities, the Spanish humanitarians sternly admonished: "If you do not [meet your obligations in this way, then] we shall powerfully enter into your country, and shall make war against you in all ways and manners that we can…and we protest that the deaths and losses which shall accrue from this are your fault, and not that of their Highnesses, or ours, nor of these cavaliers who come with us"—sentiments that resonate to the present.

The Requerimiento of the Spanish conquerors, just quoted, had a counterpart a century later among the English colonists settling North America. To this day, the United States is reverentially admired, at home at least, as "a city on a hill." In April 2009, British historian Geoffrey Hodgson was criticized by *New York Times* columnist Roger Cohen for describing the United States as "just one great, but imperfect, country among others." Hodgson's error, Cohen explained, is his failure to realize that unlike other states, "America was born as an idea," as a "city on a hill," an "inspirational notion" that resides "deep in the American psyche." The crimes that Hodgson reviews—accurately, Cohen agrees—are merely unfortunate lapses that do not tarnish the essential nobility of America's abiding "transcendent purpose"; they are merely "the abuse of reality," not "reality itself," to borrow the terms of the eminent scholar Hans Morgenthau, to which we return.[26]

Like the Spanish, the early English colonists were guided by Rice's "emerging humanitarian norm." The inspirational phrase "city on a hill" was coined by John Winthrop in 1630, outlining the glorious future of a new nation "ordained by God." A year earlier, his Massachusetts Bay Colony received its charter from the king of England and established its Great Seal. The seal depicts an Indian holding his spears pointing downward in a sign of peace, with a scroll coming from his mouth with a plea to the colonists to "Come over and help us." The charter states that conversion of the population is "the principal end of this plantation." The British colonists were thus benevolent humanists, responding to the pleas of the miserable natives to be rescued from their bitter pagan fate.[27]

The Great Seal is a graphic representation of "the idea of America" from its birth. It should be exhumed from the archives and displayed on the walls of every classroom. It should certainly appear in the background of all the Kim Il-Sung–style worship of the grand murderer and torturer Ronald Reagan, whose "spirit seems to stride the country, watching us like a warm and friendly ghost," so we learn from Stanford University's Hoover Institution, and who blissfully described himself as the leader of a "shining city on the hill" while orchestrating the ghastly crimes of his years in office, leaving not only slaughter and destruction in much of the world but also major threats of nuclear war and terror, and as an extra benefit, a major contribution to global jihadism.[28]

The conquest and settling of the West did indeed show individualism and enterprise, as Cohen observed. Settler-colonialism, the cruelest form of imperialism, regularly does. The outcome was hailed by the respected and influential senator Henry Cabot Lodge in 1898. Calling for intervention in Cuba, Lodge lauded our record "of conquest, colonization, and territorial expansion unequalled by any people in the 19th century," and urged that it was "not to be curbed now," as the Cubans too were pleading with us to come over and help them.[29]

Their plea was answered. The United States sent troops, thereby preventing Cuba's liberation from Spain and turning it into a virtual colony, as it remained until 1959.

The "American idea" is illustrated further by the remarkable campaign, initiated almost at once, to restore Cuba to its proper place: economic warfare with the clearly articulated aim of punishing the population so that they would overthrow the disobedient government; invasion, terror, and other crimes continuing to the present, in defiance of nearly unanimous world (and American) opinion.[30]

There are to be sure critics who hold that our efforts to bring democracy to Cuba have failed, so we should turn to other ways to "come over and help them." How do these critics know that the goal was to bring democracy? There is evidence: so our leaders proclaim. There is also counter-evidence: the rich internal record of planning and the events themselves, but all of that can be dismissed as just more of the "the abuse of reality."

American imperialism is often traced to the takeovers of Cuba, Puerto Rico, and Hawaii in 1898. But that is to succumb to what historian of imperialism Bernard Porter calls "the salt water fallacy," the idea that conquest only becomes imperialism when it crosses salt water. Thus if the Mississippi were as wide and salty as the Irish Sea, Western expansion would have been imperialism. From Washington to Lodge, those engaged in the enterprise had a clearer grasp.

After the success of humanitarian intervention in Cuba in 1898, the next step in the mission assigned by Providence was to confer "the blessings of liberty and civilization upon all the rescued peoples" of the Philippines (in the words of the platform of Lodge's Republican party)—at least upon those who survived the murderous onslaught and the large-scale torture and other atrocities that accompanied it. These fortunate souls were left to the mercies of the U.S.-established Philippine constabulary within a newly devised model of colonial domination, relying on security forces equipped with the most advanced technology and trained in sophisticated modes of surveillance, intimidation, and violence. Similar models were adopted in many other areas where the United States imposed brutal National Guards and other client forces, with consequences that should be well known, and significant applications at home as well, as historian Alfred McCoy reveals in his magisterial history of the century-long colonial/neocolonial enterprise in the Philippines.[31]

To illustrate the value of historical amnesia with an example of great contemporary significance, consider the first scholarly work on the roots of George W. Bush's preventive war doctrine, issued in September 2002 in preparation for the invasion of Iraq—which was then already under way, as we now know, and as Bush and his accomplice Tony Blair knew well when they were pretending to be seeking a diplomatic settlement. The study was written by the distinguished Yale University historian John Lewis Gaddis, and has been much admired in the general and scholarly literature. The core principle of the Bush doctrine, Gaddis writes approvingly, is that "expansion, we have assumed, is the path to security." Gaddis traces this doctrine to "the lofty, idealistic tradition of John Quincy Adams and Woodrow Wilson," the New York Times explained. Adams developed the "lofty idealistic tradition" in justification of the conquest of Florida in "defense" against runaway slaves and lawless Indians, as they were called, offering the ludicrous pretext that these renegades were threatening the United States, serving as agents of the feared great power, Britain. In reality, as Adams knew well, Britain was posing no threat beyond deterrence of the plans to conquer Cuba and Canada, and in fact was seeking peace with its former colonies. It is painfully easy to think of modern analogues.[32]

Gaddis cites the right historical sources, but scrupulously avoids what they say. They vividly describe the cynical and brutal act of aggression that established the "lofty idealistic" doctrines of the great grand strategist JQA. To quote Gaddis's primary source, the conquest was an "exhibition of murder and plunder" that was just a phase in the project of "removing or eliminating native Americans from the southeast," and incorporating conquered territory within the expanding American empire, as it was frankly described. The conquest of Florida in 1818 was also the first executive war in violation of the Constitution, by now routine practice.[33]

Gaddis observes, quite rightly, that the doctrine that expansion is the path to security has prevailed from the founding fathers to the present moment. In Gaddis's words, when President George W. Bush warned on the eve of the full-scale invasion of Iraq "that Americans must 'be ready for preemptive [sic] action when necessary to defend our liberty and to defend our lives,' he was echoing an old tradition rather than establishing a new one," reiterating principles that presidents from Adams to Woodrow Wilson "would all have understood...very well."

Those who followed also would have understood, among them Bush's immediate predecessor. The Clinton doctrine, presented to Congress, was that the United States is entitled to resort to "unilateral use of military power" to ensure "uninhibited access to key markets, energy supplies and strategic resources." Clinton too was echoing a familiar theme. In the early post–World War II years, the influential planner George Kennan explained that in Latin America "the protection of our raw materials" must be a major concern—"our raw materials," which happen by accident to be somewhere else, just as the "Aborigines" were illegitimately living in "our Territories," as George Washington explained. An astute analyst, Kennan understood that the main threat to our interests is indigenous, not the terrifying foreign enemies invoked when intervention is packaged for the public. Accordingly, "the final answer might be an unpleasant one," Kennan concluded: "police repression by the local government." "Harsh government measures of repression" should cause us no qualms, he continued, as long as "the results are on balance favorable to our purposes." In general, "it is better to have a strong regime in power than a liberal government if it is indulgent and relaxed and penetrated by Communists." The term "communist" has a technical sense in planning circles, as in media and commentary, referring to labor leaders, peasant activists, human rights workers, priests reading the Gospels with peasants and organizing self-help groups based on their radical pacifist message, and others with the wrong priorities—matters that require no elaboration here in Chile.[34]

Kennan's personal views were articulated in official policy, which saw U.S. interests as threatened by "radical and nationalistic regimes" that are responsive to popular pressures for "immediate improvement in the low living standards of the masses" and development for domestic needs, tendencies that conflict with the need for "a political and economic climate conducive to private investment," with adequate repatriation of profits (NSC 5432/1, 1954).

A major concern of policy makers from World War II was what a State Department official called "the philosophy of the New Nationalism, [which] embraces policies designed to bring about a broader distribution of wealth and to raise the standard of living of the masses." That was true all over the world, and had to be combated strenuously, but particularly in Latin America, where people are deluded into believing that "the first beneficiaries of the development of a country's resources should be the people of that country," and that Latin America should industrialize. In contrast economic rationalism dictates that the first beneficiaries should be U.S. investors while Latin America fulfills its service function, refraining from "excessive industrial development" that infringes on U.S. interests. The "Economic Charter for the Americas" imposed on Latin America at the Chapultepec (Mexico) hemispheric conference in February 1945 declared that economic nationalism must be barred "in all its forms"— with the unspoken exception of the United States, where it was upheld even more forcefully than from the early days of the republic. Elsewhere, it was also necessary to discipline countries tempted to "go berserk with fanatical nationalism" and try to control their own resources, to borrow the rhetoric of the editors of the *New York Times*, praising the U.S.-UK overthrow of the parliamentary government of Iraq and installation of the rule of their favored tyrant.[35]

With changes of names and terminology, these themes resound through American history, and the United States is of course no innovator in that regard.

The divine right of aggression and other forms of intervention to ensure "uninhibited access to key markets, energy supplies and strategic resources" is, of course, unilateral. The privileged and powerful, and their dependencies, must be immune to such assaults. I mentioned at the outset the platitude that after 9/11, nothing will ever be the same. The murderous acts of terror on September 11, 2001, were bitterly condemned throughout the world, even within the jihadi movements, as revealed by Fawaz Gerges, the leading scholar of these movements[36]—facts that suggest what would have been a constructive reaction, had the goal been to reduce terrorism. But in the South the condemnations were often accompanied by a qualification: "Welcome to the club. This is the kind of atrocity the West has been carrying against us for centuries."

For the United States, this was the first attack on national territory of any consequence since 1814, when the British burned down Washington, D.C. Pearl Harbor is often cited as a predecessor, but that is inaccurate. The Japanese attacked military bases in U.S. territories, virtual colonies, which had been conquered not long before by violence and guile. And by U.S. official standards, the Japanese crimes were a legitimate exercise of "anticipatory self-defense," the doctrine that Gaddis traces approvingly back to John Quincy Adams. Japan's leaders were well aware that the United States was deploying B-17 Flying Fortresses to these military bases with the intent "to burn out the industrial heart of the Empire with fire-bomb attacks on the teeming bamboo ant heaps of Honshu and Kyushu," as the plans were described by their architect, Air Force General Chennault, with the enthusiastic approval of President Roosevelt, Secretary of State Cordell Hull, and Army Chief of Staff General George Marshall.[37]

Vile as the atrocities on 9/11 were, one can easily imagine worse. Suppose that al-Qaeda had been supported by an awesome superpower intent on overthrowing the government of the United States. Suppose that the attack had succeeded: al-Qaeda had bombed the White House, killed the president, and installed a vicious military dictatorship, which killed some fifty thousand to one hundred thousand people, brutally tortured seven hundred thousand, set up a major center of terror and subversion that carried out assassinations throughout the world, and helped establish neo-Nazi "National Security States" elsewhere that tortured and murdered with abandon. Suppose further that the dictatorship brought in economic advisers—call them "the Kandahar boys"—who within a few years drove the economy to one of its worst disasters in U.S. history while their proud mentors collected Nobel Prizes and received other accolades. That would have been vastly more horrendous than 9/11.

And as everyone in Chile knows, it is not necessary to imagine, because it in fact did happen, right here: on "the first 9/11," September 11, 1973. The only change above is to per capita equivalents, an appropriate measure. But the first 9/11 did not change history, for good reasons: the events were too normal.

Mention of these truisms would elicit incomprehension in the West, in some educated circles outright fury—not over the facts, but for mentioning them. Another tribute to the validity of Jennings's maxim.

The prevailing doctrine that "expansion is the path to security," like official doctrine generally, should be interpreted in the light of Adam Smith's principle of international affairs, which I quoted earlier. The phrase "security" does not refer to the security of the population; rather to the security of the "principal architects of policy"—in Smith's day "merchants and manufacturers," in ours megacorporations and great financial institutions, nourished by the states they largely dominate.

There are numerous current illustrations of the real meaning of the term "security," including two that are of transcendent importance, because they have to do with threats to survival: nuclear war and environmental catastrophe. Both threats are being enhanced, knowingly, by the principal architects of policy and the states they dominate, not of course because they want elimination of any hope for decent existence, but because of higher priorities: short-term profit and power, priorities that are rooted in deeper features of prevailing socioeconomic and political systems. The same is true of lesser though quite serious threats, among them the threat of terror, which is not slight. Many strategic analysts, joined by U.S. intelligence, regard nuclear terror in the United States within the next few years as "inevitable," or at least with too high a probability to countenance, if policies continue on their present course. These policies are, consciously, enhancing the threat of terror. The invasion of Iraq is a telling recent illustration. It was undertaken with the expectation that it would probably enhance terror and nuclear proliferation, as it did, far beyond what intelligence agencies and specialists had predicted. In an analysis of quasi-official data, terrorism specialists Peter Bergen and Paul Cruickshank found that the "Iraq effect"—the consequence of the Iraq invasion—was a seven-fold increase in terror, hardly a slight effect. Again, it is not that Rumsfeld, Cheney, and others wanted terror. Rather, it is not a high priority as compared with control over the world's energy resources, which provides Washington with "veto power" and "critical leverage" over industrial rivals, as high-level planners have advised from George Kennan in the early postwar years to Zbigniew Brzezinski today, commenting on reasons for invading Iraq. The 2006 U.S.-Israeli invasion of Lebanon, on pretexts that do not withstand a moment's examination, is a similar example. It may create new generations of jihadis, inspired by hatred of the United States and its regional client.[38]

Similar calculations are pervasive in policy. With great reluctance, the Bush administration permitted the formation of a high-level commission to investigate ways to improve security after 9/11. As the commission directors have bitterly reported, their recommendations were mostly ignored. To cite one example, the commission recognized the importance of securing borders, particularly the long and easily penetrated Canadian border. The Bush administration responded by reducing growth of the number of agents patrolling borders, and shifting them to the Mexican border, which was not a concern for the 9/11 commission, but is important to prevent a flood of immigrants fleeing the predicted effects of neoliberal reforms.[39]

Like borders generally, the Mexican border is artificial, the result of conquest. Historically it had been quite open, with people moving fairly freely in both directions, sometimes just to visit friends and relatives. That changed in 1994, when Clinton instituted Operation Gatekeeper, militarizing the border. As he explained, "we will not surrender our borders to those who wish to exploit our history of compassion and justice."[40] He had nothing to say about the compassion and justice that created the conditions impelling those ingrates to exploit our benevolence, and neither he nor others explained how the enthusiasts for neoliberal globalization deal with the observation of Adam Smith that "free circulation of labor" is a foundation stone of free trade.

Nineteen ninety-four was also the year of the enactment of NAFTA, the so-called North American Free Trade Agreement, which, like others, has only a limited relation to free trade and is not an "agreement," at least if citizens are part of their countries. It was anticipated by rational analysts that opening Mexico to a flood of highly subsidized U.S. agribusiness production would sooner or later undermine Mexican farming, and that Mexican businesses would not be able to withstand competition from huge U.S. corporations that must be allowed to operate freely in Mexico under the treaty. One likely consequence would be flight to the United States, joined by those fleeing the countries of Central America, which had been ravaged again by Reaganite terror in the 1980s. Therefore, the border had to be militarized. The imperative of protecting the country from the consequences of NAFTA and other such economic measures is far higher than protection from the threat of terror.

It is of interest that in 2004 the Bush electoral campaign was able to focus on their dedication to protecting the country from terror, while in reality consciously enhancing the threat. The success in misleading the public, which is quite impressive, illustrates another serious threat to American society. It is one element of a growing deterioration in the functioning of democratic institutions—a threat to the world generally, given the enormous power in the hands of the principal architects and the interests they represent.

Still more ominous is the fact that to a significant extent, the policy choices that are undermining democracy at home, while often contributing to suffering abroad and potential disaster everywhere, are institutionally based and hence do not vary greatly across the narrow planning spectrum—though it is important to be aware that they are often opposed by public opinion, sometimes large majorities. It is no great secret that the economy is overwhelmingly in the hands of private corporations. As far back as 1890 it was estimated that three-fourths of the wealth of the nation was in their hands. Two decades later corporate control over the economy and society was so vast that Woodrow Wilson described "a very different America from the old…no longer a scene of individual enterprise…individual opportunity and individual achievement," but an America in which "comparatively small groups of men," corporate managers, "wield a power and control over the wealth and the business operations of the country," becoming "rivals of the government itself"[41]—increasingly its masters, in accord with the maxim of Adam Smith, very much in force.

Furthermore, the masters are bound by law to Smith's maxim in their business lives. A core doctrine of corporate law is that the directors are legally obligated to pursue only material self-interest. They are permitted to do "good works," but only if that has a favorable impact on image, hence profit and market share. The courts have sometimes gone beyond, warning corporations that unless they support charitable and educational causes, an "aroused public" may take away the privileges granted to them by state power. And those privileges are indeed extraordinary. The founding principle of corporate law, limited liability, is in itself an example: it allows corporations to commit serious crimes while the shareholders remain largely immune.[42]

A century ago, these "collectivist legal entities," as legal historian Morton Horwitz calls them, came to be considered "natural entities" by legal theorists and the courts, and were granted the rights of persons. This radical attack on the principles of classical liberalism was sharply condemned by the vanishing breed of conservatives as "a menace to the liberty of the individual, and to the stability of the American States as popular governments" (Christopher Tiedeman). And as the courts determined further, they are obligated to act in a way that we would regard as pathological among real persons, who would require therapy or institutionalization to protect society from their destructive rampages.[43]

Over the years, the privileges granted to these state-created private tyrannies have been extended, primarily by courts, though sometimes by treaties. One example is the provision of today's "free trade agreements" that grant corporations the right of "national treatment" abroad. If General Motors invests in Mexico, it must be granted the rights of a Mexican business. If a Mexican of flesh and blood were to arrive in New York and demand "national treatment," he would be lucky if he did not end up in Guantánamo. The example is not frivolous. While corporations are legally persons under the law, with rights far beyond those of human beings, non-resident aliens are not persons, so the courts have determined.[44] Therefore they did not have the protections of persons under the law when they were shipped to Guantánamo, presumably one of the reasons the United States stored prisoners there rather than in a perfectly secure facility in the United States—incidentally, in violation of the grotesque treaty that Cuba was forced to sign under military occupation, granting the United States the right to use Guantánamo as a coaling station and naval base.

These legal principles sometimes lead to coincidences that are quite startling. In 2009, for example, the two political parties were competing to see which could proclaim more fervently its dedication to the sadistic doctrine that "illegal aliens" must be denied health care. Their stand is consistent with the legal principle, established by the Supreme Court, that these creatures are not "persons" under the law, hence are not entitled to the rights granted to persons. And at the very same moment, Chief Justice Roberts cut short the Court's summer break to consider the question whether the right of corporations effectively to buy elections should be restricted, in accord with a century of precedents[45]—a complex constitutional matter, because the courts had determined that, unlike undocumented immigrants, corporations are real persons under the law, indeed with rights far beyond those of persons of flesh and blood. The law is indeed a solemn and majestic affair.

On January 21, 2010, the Supreme Court reached its decision. The four Court reactionaries (misleadingly called "conservatives") were joined by Justice Anthony Kennedy in a 5–4 decision. The decision is "breathtaking in its scope," Michael Waldman writes: "It overturns doctrine dating back a century and laws upheld in 1990, that banned corporate managers from directly spending shareholder money in elections." And from doing so without shareholder approval, he observes; under the law, management needs no such approval to engage in such "free speech," just as the nanny state permits CEOs to select the panels that fix their salaries and bonuses without shareholder interference.[46]

Waldman does not exaggerate when he writes that this exercise of the radical judicial activism that the right wing claims to deplore "matches or exceeds Bush v. Gore in ideological or partisan overreaching by the [Supreme] court. In that case, the court reached into the political process to hand the election to one candidate. Today it reached into the political process to hand unprecedented power to corporations." Chief Justice Roberts selected a case that could easily have been settled on narrow grounds, and maneuvered the Court into using it for a far-reaching decision that, in effect, permits corporate managers to buy elections directly, instead of using more complex indirect means, though it is likely that to avoid negative publicity they will choose to do so through trade organizations. It is well known that corporate campaign contributions, sometimes packaged in complex ways, are a major factor in determining the outcome of elections, and the same is sure to be true of the virtually unlimited advertising for candidates now permitted by the Court. This alone is a significant factor in policy decisions, reinforced by the enormous power of corporate lobbies and other conditions imposed by the very small sector of the population that dominates the economy.[47]

A very successful predictor of government policy over a long period is political economist Thomas Ferguson's "investment theory of politics," which interprets elections as occasions on which segments of private sector power coalesce to invest to control the state.[48] These means for undermining democracy are sure to be enhanced by the Court's dagger blow at the heart of functioning democracy.

The editors of the New York Times also did not exaggerate when they wrote that the decision "strikes at the heart of democracy" by having "paved the way for corporations to use their vast treasuries to overwhelm elections and intimidate elected officials into doing their bidding"—more explicitly, for permitting corporate managers to do so.[49]

In his majority decision, Justice Kennedy argued that the First Amendment prohibits Congress from punishing "citizens, or associations of citizens, for simply engaging in political speech." The "associations of citizens" in question are corporate management, who control vast wealth and are unaccountable to the public or to "stakeholders" (workers, communities), and need not even consult the shareholders whose money they spend in political campaigns.

Kennedy's opinion also held that there is no principled way to distinguish between media corporations and other corporations, a most remarkable position. Kennedy is saying that there is no principled way to distinguish between corporations that are bound by law to restrict themselves to gaining profit and market share, and others that are granted the rich array of corporate rights by the state to fulfill a public trust: to provide news and opinion in an unbiased fashion.

Media corporations have indeed been criticized for violating the public trust, but never have they been condemned so severely as by Justice Kennedy in this argument.

Some legislative remedies are being proposed, for example, requiring managers to consult with shareholders. At best, that would be a minor limit on the corporate takeover of the political system, given the very high concentration of ownership by extreme wealth and other corporate institutions. Any legislation would have been difficult to pass even without this new weapon provided by the Court to unaccountable private concentrations of power. The same holds, even more strongly, for a constitutional amendment that Waldman and others think might be necessary to restore at least the limited democracy that prevailed before the decision, an unattainable goal in today's business-run sociopolitical system without large-scale mass mobilization of the kind that made New Deal legislation possible, curbing business power and guaranteeing some basic human rights.

In his dissent, Justice Stevens acknowledged that "we have long since held that corporations are covered by the First Amendment." That traces back to the period when the 1907 Tillman Act banned corporate contributions, the earliest of the precedents overturned by the Court. As noted above, by the early twentieth century legal theorists and courts were coming consistently to adopt and implement the Court's 1886 (Santa Clara) principle that these "collectivist legal entities" have the same rights as persons of flesh and blood,[50] rights since expanded far beyond those of persons, notably by the mislabeled "free trade agreements."

The conception of corporate personhood evolved alongside the shift of power from shareholders to managers, and finally to the doctrine that "the powers of the board of directors…are identical with the powers of the corporation."[51] As corporate personhood and managerial independence were becoming established in law, the control of corporate management of the economy had reached the stage that elicited Woodrow Wilson's description of the "very different America" that was taking shape, cited above. Corporate control over the political system has now been given even greater scope by the Roberts Court, another triumph for George W. Bush and the Republican far right.

The steady shift of the Court to the right reflects broader tendencies in neoliberal/financialized American political economy and society. As the *Wall Street Journal* explains, contemporary Republicans use their tenure in power to select Justices with a "provocative philosophical profile" who are dedicated to "a conservative approach to legal interpretation"— euphemisms for an ultranationalist, extreme pro-business, and socially reactionary posture, reflecting the shift of the party since Reagan to a unified far-right stance, eliminating Republican moderates. The Democrats, also drifting toward the right ("New Democrats"), keep away from candidates with a "sharp liberal record," "trailblazing liberals like the late Justices William Brennan and Thurgood Marshall," preferring uncontroversial centrist liberals like Obama's appointment Sonia Sotomayor. The result is that "the court is getting this completely skewed internal debate about how to think about constitutional law," skewed to the right (University of Chicago law professor Geoffrey Stone).[52]

January 21, 2010, will go down in history as a dark day for what remains of functioning democracy. It is hard to overestimate the severity of this blow by the right-wing Justices, though it could be argued, as just noted, that their reasoning is consistent with the original attack on basic classical liberal principles a century earlier.

Even this very brief sketch of the half millennium of conquest illustrates its major mechanisms: abroad, imposed liberalization along with violence when needed; and at home, state-supported economic policy combined with massive, dedicated, and unremitting efforts to undermine limits to rule by virtually unaccountable private tyrannies (corporate management), created and protected by a powerful state of which they are largely the masters.

The current version is called "globalization." Like most terms of political discourse, this term has two meanings: a literal meaning and a technical meaning employed for doctrinal warfare. In the literal sense, "globalization" means international integration. Its leading advocates are those who meet annually at the World Social Forum, coming from countries all over the world and all walks of life, working together to craft and debate forms of international integration—economic, cultural, political—that serve the interests of people: real people, of flesh and blood. But in the doctrinal system, their commitments are called "anti-globalization." The description is correct if we use the term "globalization" in its technical sense, referring to a particular form of international economic integration, with a mixture of liberal and protectionist measures and many related to investor rights, not trade, all designed to serve the interests of investors, financial institutions, and other centers of concentrated state-private power—those granted the rights of super-persons by the courts.

The likely impact of globalization in the technical sense has not been obscure. One goal of NAFTA, for example, was to "lock Mexico in" to the so-called reforms of the 1980s, which created billionaires at about the same rate as they enhanced poverty. These "reforms" are of great benefit to U.S. owners, managers, and investors, though not to working people. Studies undertaken a few years later revealed that NAFTA was one of those rare treaties that managed to harm the working populations in all of the countries participating: Canada, the United States, and Mexico.

The U.S. labor movement had proposed alternatives that would have benefited the workforce in all three countries. Similar proposals were developed by Congress's own research bureau, the Office of Technology Assessment (since disbanded). These proposals never entered the political agenda, and were even barred from the media, a dramatic example of how existing state capitalist democracy really functions.[53]

The attraction of NAFTA for North American elites, the business press reported, was "precisely that it would tie the hands of the current and future governments" of Mexico with regard to economic policy. In that way, NAFTA might fend off the danger that was detected by a Latin America Strategy Development Workshop at the Pentagon in 1990. Its participants found U.S. relations with Mexico to be "extraordinarily positive," untroubled by stolen elections, massive corruption, death squads, endemic torture, scandalous treatment of workers and peasants, and so on. Participants in the workshop did, however, see one cloud on the horizon: "a 'democracy opening' in Mexico could test the special relationship by bringing into office a government more interested in challenging the United States on economic and nationalist grounds." The grim threat of democracy and economic nationalism could be averted by a treaty that would "lock Mexico in" to the neoliberal policies of the 1980s and would "tie the hands of the current and future governments" of Mexico with regard to economic policy, as the business press explained. In brief, NAFTA, duly imposed by executive power, in opposition to the public will.[54]

More generally, Clinton administration analysts concluded that "globalization of the world economy" will lead to a "widening economic divide" along with "deepening economic stagnation, political instability, and cultural alienation," hence unrest and violence among the "have-nots," much of it directed against the United States. Planners recognized that the United States must therefore be prepared for appropriate military action, including "precision strike from space [as a] counter to the world-wide proliferation of [Weapons of Mass Destruction]" by unruly elements, a likely consequence of the recommended programs of U.S. aggressive militarism, just as a "widening divide" is the anticipated consequence of the specific version of international integration that is misleadingly called "globalization" and "free trade" in the doctrinal system.[55]

Control of Latin America was the earliest goal of U.S. foreign policy, and remains a central one, partly for resources and markets, but also for broader ideological reasons. If the United States could not control Latin America, it could not expect "to achieve a successful order elsewhere in the world," Nixon's National Security Council concluded in 1971 while considering the paramount importance of destroying Chilean democracy, finally achieved on the first 9/11. "In the view of the Nixon White House," David Schmitz writes, Allende "threatened American global interests by challenging the whole ideological basis of American Cold War policy.... It was the threat of a successful socialist state in Chile that could provide a model for other nations that caused concern and led to American opposition"—in fact direct participation in establishing and maintaining the brutal torture state and international terrorist center.[56]

The internal record makes it clear that throughout the Cold War, a primary concern of U.S. policy makers has been what Oxfam called "the threat of a good example," referring to Washington's dedication to destroying Nicaraguan democracy and independence in the 1980s. The fear that successful independent development might appeal to others motivated U.S. terror and aggression against Guatemala, Cuba, Vietnam, and a sordid list of others, and was a leading theme of the Cold War, which provided pretexts for aggression and violence much as the junior partner in world control appealed to the threat of the West when it crushed popular uprisings in East Berlin, Hungary, and Czechoslovakia.

Washington's concerns about the threat of a good example were not original. In earlier years, the czar and Metternich had expressed similar concerns about "the pernicious doctrines of republicanism and popular self-rule" spread by "the apostles of sedition" in the former colonies that had cast off the British yoke.

The answer to the question, globalization for whom? depends on which meaning of the term we choose: the literal meaning or the technical meaning that is standard in public discourse. If we mean "globalization" in the technical sense, then the doctrines of Adam Smith and Thucydides give the basic answer: it will be globalization in the interests of the principal architects of policy. The interests of people may be helped or harmed, but that is incidental.

But there is no reason to subjugate ourselves to the doctrines of the powerful. U.S. courts are quite right to warn that an "aroused public" may restrict or even entirely dismantle power concentrations and their privileges, and work to construct a domestic and global society that is more free and more just. That has often happened in the past. Latin America, today, is the scene of some of the most exciting developments in the endless struggle for freedom and justice. At last, the region is moving to overthrow the legacy of the conquests and the external domination of the past centuries, and the cruel and destructive social forms they have helped to establish.

In the past, Latin America has often led the world in progress toward social justice and human rights. The Universal Declaration of Human Rights of 1948 is a landmark in the progress of civilization. Though it is far from being implemented or even formally accepted, its influence should not be ignored. Nor should we ignore the fact that much of its inspiration was right here in Chile. The declaration crucially incorporates social, economic, and cultural rights, assigning them the same status as civil and political rights. That achievement is substantially based on Latin American initiatives. The Chilean delegate Hernán Santa Cruz stressed that "if political liberalism does not ensure the economic, social, and cultural rights of its citizens, then it cannot achieve an enduring progress.... Democracy—political as well as social and economic—comprises, in my mind, an inseparable whole," he wrote. Franklin Delano Roosevelt's New Deal also drew from the Latin American tradition of liberal jurisprudence and rebellion against imposed authority. Historian Greg Grandin writes that some of FDR's initiatives were literally "plagiarized" from Latin American jurists. Today, popular struggles in Latin America show real promise of serving as an inspiration to others worldwide, in a common quest for globalization in a form that should be the aspiration of decent people everywhere.[57]

TWO

Latin America and U.S. Foreign Policy

There is a very clear doctrine on the general contours of U.S. foreign policy in Latin America—and elsewhere. It reigns with little challenge in Western commentary and most scholarship, even among critics. The major theme is what is called "American exceptionalism": the doctrine that the United States is unlike other great powers, past and present, because it has a "transcendent purpose": "the establishment of equality in freedom in America," and indeed throughout the world, since "the arena within which the United States must defend and promote its purpose has become world-wide."

The particular version of the doctrine that I quoted is not unusual. I selected it because it is the formulation by one of the most distinguished scholars, and an unusually honorable person and independent thinker, written in the glow of Camelot: Hans Morgenthau, founder of the tough-minded realist school of international relations, which avoids sentimentality and keeps to the hard truths of state power in an anarchic world. An honest and competent scholar, Morgenthau recognized that the historical record is radically inconsistent with America's "transcendent purpose." But he explains that we should not be misled by the sharp contradiction. In his words, we should not "confound the abuse of reality with reality itself." Reality itself is the unachieved "national purpose" revealed by "the evidence of history as our minds reflect it." The actual historical record is merely the "abuse of reality," which is of only secondary interest. Morgenthau goes on to say that those who confuse "reality" with "the abuse of reality" are committing "the error of atheism, which denies the validity of religion on similar grounds." His analogy is apt, if not in the manner he intended.[1]

Sometimes the august character of America and its "purpose" is raised to the level of pure logic. Thus in Harvard University's prestigious journal *International Security*, the Eaton Professor of the Science of Government at Harvard, Samuel Huntington, explains that the "national identity" of the United States is "defined by a set of universal political and economic values," namely "liberty, democracy, equality, private property, and markets." Hence the United States has a solemn duty to maintain its "international primacy" for the benefit of the world. And since this is a matter of definition, so the Science of Government teaches, we may dispense with the tedious work of empirical confirmation— which, in fact, would be absurd, rather like seeking empirical confirmation for the thesis that $2+2 = 4$. And in any event, empirical inquiry would only deal with the "abuse of reality."[2]

These are, naturally, very welcome doctrines—at least to those who wield the clubs. In one or another form, the doctrines are quite commonly adopted, explicitly or tacitly. And for good reasons, which are surely familiar here in Chile and in much of the rest of the world.

A variant of these prevailing concepts is that it is the very nobility of our ideals that leads us to violate them regularly. Our lofty values lead to what political scientist Michael Desch calls "America's Liberal Illiberalism."[3] As he explains, "Indeed, it is precisely American Liberalism that makes the United States so illiberal today." The reason is America's zeal in bringing to others the values that define its national identity, which sometimes leads to excess. He offers grand theses about the principles that inspire American action in the world, and lists some cases where they have allegedly been applied, but he too appears to recognize that evidence is superfluous; at least he provides none. Fortunately, because even the most superficial examination reveals that his own examples also fall under "the abuse of reality." Like others, Desch argues that these ideals must be sincerely held, because they are articulated in internal discussion—as in the Soviet Union, fascist Japan, and other equally impressive cases, so we learn from released internal documents.

Other scholars routinely adopt the same perspective. Citing examples is unfair, because the practice is virtually reflexive, hardly more than the product of a good education, which, as George Orwell observed with regard to England, instills a "general tacit agreement that 'it wouldn't do' to mention" certain unacceptable facts; or even to allow them to enter into consciousness. To pick one example of great current significance, the fine historian David Schmitz recently published his second major book on Washington's policies of undermining democracy and its support for vicious monsters, including Mussolini and Hitler, and a postwar record that I need not mention. His scholarship is careful and accurate. His final conclusion is that "throughout most of the twentieth century, the United States supported right-wing dictatorships [in] violation of America's political ideals" and its commitment to "the promotion of democracy and human rights." He says "most" of the twentieth century because he begins in 1921 and believes that Carter was an exception, a judgment that is partially true but not easy to sustain if we attend to "the abuse of reality," including Suharto, Somoza, Chun, and the shah, among notable examples.[4]

If we turn to the years before 1921, we find the same pattern: Woodrow Wilson's depredations in the Caribbean, the murderous conquest of the Philippines that slaughtered hundreds of thousands, and much else. Practice in the nineteenth century need not be reviewed.

In short, throughout its history, the United States has consistently acted in violation of its ideals. But the doctrine that leaders are committed to these ideals is an unchallengeable article of faith, sacrosanct, holy writ. What happened is simply "abuse of reality." With regard to Bush II, a minor problem in upholding the faith is that his dedication to the mission of "promoting democracy" was grandly declared in November 2003, when a new pretext was needed for the invasion of Iraq after the wrong answer was provided to what had been the "single question": will Saddam abandon his programs of development of weapons of mass destruction (and for the really dedicated true believers, like Dick Cheney, his alliance with al-Qaeda)? While the "single question" was being upheld, references to democracy did not go beyond routine boilerplate, but as soon as they were enunciated, "scholars jumped on the democratization bandwagon," as Middle East specialist Augustus Richard Norton observed, joining others—though not everyone: among Iraqis, 99 percent dismissed the newly discovered project, while 95 percent denied that the goal had been "to assist the Iraqi people"—views that were generally sustained as the tragedy of Iraq proceeded on its grim course.[5]

To be sure, U.S. intellectual culture is breaking no new ground. There are two problems with the conventional phrase "American exceptionalism." First, to sustain a belief in "exceptionalism," one must scrupulously dismiss major parts of what actually happened as the mere "abuse of reality." And second, the stance is not peculiarly "American"; rather, it is close to a historical universal among powerful states.

The same perspective guides major scholarship on current foreign policy. The most extensive scholarly article on "the roots of the Bush doctrine" opens with these words: "The promotion of democracy is central to the George W. Bush administration's prosecution of both the war on terrorism and its overall grand strategy." In one of Britain's leading journals of international affairs, the major article on the same topic extends the scope of the thesis. The author writes that "promoting democracy abroad" has been a primary goal ever since Woodrow Wilson endowed U.S. foreign policy with a "powerful idealist element," which gained "particular salience" under Reagan and has been taken up with "unprecedented forcefulness" under George W. Bush. Such doctrines are standard in scholarship. In journalism and intellectual commentary they are generally taken to be the merest truisms.[6]

There are prominent critics, who argue that it is important not to go too far in our idealism. New York Times diplomatic correspondent Thomas Friedman cautioned that our policy of "granting idealism a near exclusive hold on our foreign policy" may lead us to neglect our own legitimate interests in our dedicated service to others. In the second national daily, the veteran commentator of the Washington Post, David

Ignatius, former editor of the *International Herald Tribune*, warned that the man he calls the "idealist-in-chief" of the Bush administration might be "too idealistic—his passion for the noble goals of the Iraq war might overwhelm the prudence and pragmatism that normally guide war planners."[7] He is referring to Paul Wolfowitz, who was soon removed from Washington as an embarrassment and sent off to head the World Bank with the mission of curtailing corruption—briefly, until he had to resign because of his involvement in a scandal. The many accolades to Wolfowitz at the time of his appointment scrupulously evaded his record, which is one of utter contempt for democracy and human rights, including strong support for General Suharto of Indonesia, one of the worst mass murderers and torturers of the modern era, and also the easy winner in the international ranking of most corrupt leaders. But Suharto offered great profits to the foreign investors to whom he opened Indonesia's rich resources for plunder, and was therefore very popular in the West, along with many other monsters past and present, as long as they obey the rules.

The tributes to the "idealist-in-chief" managed to overlook not only his general record but even his behavior in 2003 during a highly revealing escapade that is one of the clearest examples on record of contempt for democracy: Donald Rumsfeld's distinction between "Old Europe" and "New Europe," taken up by many others. The criterion distinguishing the two categories was sharp and clear. "Old Europe" consisted of the governments that followed the will of the overwhelming majority of their populations and refused to join the Bush-Blair invasion of Iraq. "New Europe" consisted of the governments that ignored an even larger majority of the population and took their orders from Bush's ranch in Crawford, Texas. Therefore "Old Europe" was bitterly condemned (sometimes in infantile ways that reveal quite strikingly the ranking of democracy in comparison with abject obedience to the master, for example, the rechristening of French fries as "freedom fries" in the Senate cafeteria), and "New Europe" was hailed as the hope for democracy. The favorite democrats of New Europe were Italy's Berlusconi, honored with a visit to the White House, and Spain's Aznar, who was even invited to the summit to join Bush and Blair in announcing the war—with the support of 2 percent of the Spanish population, polls showed.

Easily winning the prize for hatred of democracy was the "idealist-in-chief." To everyone's surprise, Turkey followed the will of 95 percent of its population and refused to join the invasion. The Turkish government was bitterly condemned by Colin Powell and others. Wolfowitz was the most outraged. He denounced the Turkish military for not compelling the government to follow Washington's orders, and demanded that Turkey apologize and recognize that it is their responsibility to help America, whatever the ridiculous population believes.[8]

The most interesting feature of this episode was that it passed virtually unnoticed in the West, and indeed the Rumsfeld–Old/New Europe distinction became conventional. The episode did not in the least tarnish the reverence for Bush's "messianic mission" to "promote democracy," the "noble goal" lauded by the liberal press.

The reverence continues no matter how dramatic the refutation. To select just one of many cases, in January 2006, the population of Palestine voted in an election that was recognized to be free and fair—apart from the Bush administration's intervention in an effort to gain victory for its favored candidate, Mahmoud Abbas. But the wrong side won. Instantly, the United States and Israel turned to severe punishment of the population for their democratic errors, with Europe toddling politely along. Israel even cut off water to Gaza, where water shortages are severe, and a few months later, as Israeli terror increased, it bombed and destroyed power plants that provide electricity for pumping and sewage removal. Always with firm U.S. support, all further demonstrations of Bush's "messianic mission" to promote democracy. As always, there were pretexts; as usual, they collapse under even superficial examination.[9]

U.S.-Israel goals were not at all concealed: the goal was to impose suffering on the population to induce them to shift their support to Washington's favorite. The dramatic demonstration of hatred and contempt for democracy was reported frankly, while right alongside the Bush administration was praised for dedicating itself to promoting democracy, or criticized because its excess of idealism might be harmful to ourselves.

Easy tolerance of contradiction is an important talent to acquire, the talent for Orwell's "doublethink": the ability to hold two contradictory beliefs in one's mind simultaneously, while accepting both of them.

It might be observed that Gazans are protected people under the Geneva Conventions, and any harm done to individuals except in response to their personal criminal acts is a severe crime. Furthermore, the High Contracting Parties that are signatories to the conventions are obligated to apprehend and punish those who are responsible for these breaches of its provisions, including their own leaders. These observations would be relevant in a world of law-abiding states. But they are scarcely even intelligible in this one.

We find similar conclusions when we turn to the most serious scholarship that deals specifically with democracy promotion. The most prominent scholar-advocate of the cause is Thomas Carothers, who was director of the Democracy and Rule of Law Project at the Carnegie Endowment. He identifies himself as a neo-Reaganite, agreeing with general scholarship that Wilsonian idealism took on particular "salience" under Reagan's leadership. After Bush's dramatic declaration of the suddenly discovered mission of democracy promotion, Carothers published a book reviewing the record of democracy promotion by the United States since the end of the Cold War. He finds "a strong line of continuity" running through all administrations, including Bush II: democracy is promoted by the U.S. government if and only if it conforms to strategic and economic interests. All administrations are "schizophrenic" in this regard, he concludes, a strange and inexplicable malady.[10]

Carothers also wrote the standard scholarly work on democracy promotion in Latin America in the 1980s, in part from an insider's perspective. He was serving in the Reagan State Department in the programs of "democracy enhancement." Carothers regards these programs as sincere, but a failure. He too is an honest scholar, and points out that the failure of the programs was systematic. Where U.S. influence was least, in South America, progress toward democracy was greatest, despite Reagan's attempts to impede it by embracing right-wing dictators. Where U.S. influence was strongest, in the regions nearby, progress was least. The reason, he explains, is that Washington would tolerate only "limited, top-down forms of democratic change that did not risk upsetting the traditional structures of power with which the United States has long been allied [in] quite undemocratic societies."[11]

In short, the strong line of continuity goes back well before Bush II, to the Reagan years, when the "powerful idealist element" in traditional U.S. policy gained "particular salience," according to scholarship. Nonetheless, the dedication of our leaders to the principle is beyond question, throughout history and today, particularly under Reagan and Bush II.

In fact, the strong line of continuity goes back much farther. Democracy promotion has always been proclaimed as a guiding vision, but it is not even controversial that the United States regularly overthrew parliamentary democracies, often installing or supporting brutal tyrannies: Iran, Guatemala, Brazil, Chile, a long list of others. There were Cold War pretexts, but they regularly collapse upon investigation. I will not insult your intelligence by recounting how Reagan brought democracy to Central America by terrorist wars that left hundreds of thousands of corpses and three countries in ruins, a fourth tottering.

The paradoxical character of policy is also recognized at the liberal extreme of the policy spectrum, where it elicits regret but is felt to be unavoidable. The basic dilemma facing policy makers was expressed by Robert Pastor, a liberal Latin America scholar who was President Carter's national security adviser for Latin America. He explains why the administration had to support the murderous and corrupt Somoza regime in Nicaragua, and when that proved impossible, to try at least to maintain the U.S.-trained National Guard even as it was massacring the population "with a brutality a nation usually reserves for its enemy," in his words, killing some forty thousand people. The reason was straightforward: "The United States did not want to control Nicaragua or the other nations of the region," he writes, "but it also did not want developments to get out of control. It wanted Nicaraguans to act independently, *except* when doing so would affect U.S. interests adversely."[12]

The Cold War was scarcely relevant, but once again we find the dominant operative principle, illustrated copiously throughout history: policy conforms to expressed ideals only if it also conforms to interests. It is important to stress again that that term "interests" does not refer to the interests of the domestic population, but the interests of the concentrations of power that dominate the domestic society. The truism—essentially Adam Smith's maxim—is often derided by respectable opinion as a "conspiracy theory," or "Marxist," or some other epithet, but it is readily confirmed when subjected to inquiry. In a rare and unusually careful analysis of the domestic influences on U.S. foreign policy, Lawrence Jacobs and Benjamin Page find, unsurprisingly, that the major influence on policy is "internationally oriented business corporations," though there is also a secondary effect of "experts," who, they point out "may themselves be influenced by business." Public opinion, in contrast, has "little or no significant effect on government officials," they find. As they observe, the results should be welcome to "realists" such as Walter Lippmann, the leading public intellectual of the twentieth century, who "considered public opinion to be ill-informed and capricious [and] warned that following public opinion would create a 'morbid derangement of the true functions of power' and produce policies 'deadly to the very survival of the state as a free society,'" in Lippmann's words. The "realism" is scarcely concealed ideological preference. One will search in vain for evidence of the superior understanding and abilities of those who have the major influence on policy.[13]

Let us turn to the founder of the noble ideals that have always animated the policies that consistently violate them. Wilsonian idealism was practiced most directly in Hispaniola, where Washington was carrying "the white man's burden, the duty of the big brother," as Wilson's military governor explained. Meanwhile, the idealists who invaded Haiti and the Dominican Republic were taking over the valuable land and resources, and when that was accomplished, they left the country in good hands—the brutal National Guard in Haiti, and in the Dominican Republic, the self-proclaimed "Benefactor of the Fatherland," Rafael Trujillo, the grand killer and torturer who was described by President Kennedy's ambassador to the OAS as the "man responsible for the great work of Dominican progress, the man who brought trade between the

Republic and the other American nations to a peak." The enemy from whom Wilson's marines were defending the inhabitants was not the Russians in this pre-Bolshevik intervention; rather the Huns, who were also blamed for the insurgency that sought to disrupt the idealistic venture. Dominican president Henríquez went to the Versailles Conference in 1919 to request that his country be included among the oppressed nationalities whose cause President Wilson claimed to champion in his famous Fourteen Points. But Henríquez failed: Wilson barred any consideration of the Western hemisphere. Among his other notable achievements at the Versailles conference, Wilson refused even to speak to a gentleman asking politely whether Vietnam might merit some limited form of self-determination; he later became famous under the name Ho Chi Minh.

In Hispaniola itself, Wilson's vicious treatment of the Dominican Republic was relatively benign, because its inhabitants had "a preponderance of white blood and culture," the State Department explained, while the Haitians "are negro for the most part" and "are almost in a state of savagery and complete ignorance." There is no need to review the events or the aftermath.[14]

More generally, Wilson's dedication to self-determination, he explained, did not apply to people "at a low stage of civilization," who must be given "friendly protection, guidance, and assistance" by the colonial powers that had tended to their needs in earlier years. His famous Fourteen Points held that in questions of sovereignty, "the interests of the populations concerned must have equal weight with the equitable claims of the government whose title is to be determined," the colonial ruler. At home his idealism took the form of a "Red Scare" that was the worst attack on elementary civil rights in American history.[15]

As noted earlier, among the many reasons for regarding the fabled "American exceptionalism" with some skepticism is that the doctrine appears to be close to a historical universal, including the worst monsters: Hitler, Stalin, the conquistadors—it is hard to find an exception. Aggression and terror are almost invariably portrayed as self-defense and dedication to inspiring visions. Japanese emperor Hirohito was merely echoing a broken record in his surrender declaration in August 1945 when he told his people that "we declared war on America and Britain out of Our sincere desire to ensure Japan's self-preservation and the stabilization of East Asia, it being far from Our thought either to infringe upon the sovereignty of other nations or to embark upon territorial aggrandizement." If Asians have a different picture, it shows that they are backward and uncivilized people. They too are "naughty children who are exercising all the privileges and rights of grown ups" and require "a stiff hand, an authoritative hand," the description of Latin Americans by Secretary of State John Foster Dulles, though he advised President Eisenhower that to control the naughty children more effectively, it may be useful to "pat them a little bit and make them think that you are fond of them." The Kennedy administration relied more on academic intellectuals, who were more respectful. Kennedy's Latin American adviser, historian Arthur Schlesinger, recommended to the president that he should address Latin Americans with "a certain amount of high-flown corn" about "the higher aims of culture and spirit, [which] will thrill the audience south of the border, where metahistorical disquisitions are inordinately admired." Meanwhile we'll take care of the serious business.[16]

In the internal planning record, the guiding principles of policy are often articulated without illusion. The basic principles are revealed by the oldest concern of U.S. policy in Latin America: Cuba. In 1823, the Monroe Doctrine declared Washington's right to rule the hemisphere, but it was not powerful enough to exercise that right because of the British deterrent. The British did not try to impede the murderous conquest of Spanish Florida in 1818 and could not prevent the conquest of half of Mexico or the remainder of the national territory. But British forces did bar the conquest of Canada and Cuba. The intellectual father of Manifest Destiny, John Quincy Adams, predicted that Cuba would eventually drop into U.S. hands by the laws of "political gravitation" just as "an apple severed by a tempest from its native tree cannot but choose to fall to the ground." By the end of the century, the laws of political gravitation had come to apply, as Adams had anticipated. The

British deterrent was overcome, and the United States was able to intervene to bar Cuba's liberation from Spain, turning it into a "virtual
colony" until 1959, to quote historians and policy analysts Ernest May
and Philip Zelikow.[17]

The propaganda of 1898 held that the United States intervened to
liberate Cuba from Spanish terror, a noble "humanitarian intervention"
fulfilling what is now solemnly called "the responsibility to protect." The
power of U.S. propaganda is so great that it has prevailed in most of the
world until quite recently. By now, it has been torn to shreds by serious
scholarship, primarily the work of Louis Pérez, which reveals that Cubans
were on the verge of defeating the Spanish armies when the United States
intervened. Furthermore, had it not been for the valiant efforts of Cuban
forces, the U.S. military campaign might have ended in a "military disaster," even a "humiliating withdrawal." In Pérez's words, it was "war ostensibly against Spain, but in fact against Cubans.... The intervention
changed everything, as it was meant to. A Cuban war of liberation was
transformed into a U.S. war of conquest." Some recognized reality at the
time. The distinguished statesman Elihu Root, then secretary of war, declared bluntly that "we intend to rule and that is all there is to it." The
Cuban commanders were not even permitted to attend Spain's surrender,
and along with other Cubans, were treated with racist contempt, from
the first moments.[18]

What happened after Cuba's actual liberation in 1959 is highly instructive.[19] Within a few months, the Eisenhower administration resolved
to overthrow the government. Support for military operations began,
later extended to a major terrorist war by Kennedy. Responsibility for the
war was assigned to the president's brother, Robert Kennedy, whose highest priority was to bring "the terrors of the earth" to Cuba, according to
his biographer, Arthur Schlesinger. The terrorist war was no slight affair;
it was also a major factor in bringing the world to the verge of nuclear
war in 1962, and was resumed as soon as the missile crisis ended. And it
continued through the century, from U.S. territory, though in later years
Washington no longer initiated and supported terrorist attacks on Cuba,
but only tolerated them, and continues to provide haven to some of the

most notorious international terrorists who have been involved in these and other crimes: Orlando Bosch, Luis Posada Carriles, and numerous others. Commentators are polite enough not to recall the Bush doctrine that those who harbor terrorists are as guilty as the terrorists themselves, and must be treated accordingly: by bombing and invasion.

It is not that Washington lacks the means to punish those guilty of true crimes. Its capacity to do so was revealed when Cuban agents infiltrated the Miami-based terrorist networks that Washington was harboring, to try to expose and deter their terrorist operations. They gained substantial information. In 1998, high-level FBI officials were invited to Havana, where they were given thousands of pages of documentation and hundreds of hours of videotape about terrorist actions organized by cells in Florida. The FBI was not slow to react: it arrested the informants who provided the information, including a group now known as the Cuban Five.

The arrests were followed by a show trial in Miami. The Five were convicted, three to life sentences (for espionage; and the leader, Gerardo Hernández, also for conspiracy to murder). Since no punishment can be severe enough for those who exposed U.S.-based terror to the FBI, Hernández has even been denied the right to a visit from his wife. In July 2009, the Obama administration issued the tenth such visa denial, reportedly on grounds that she "constitutes a threat to the stability and national security of the United States." Meanwhile, people regarded by the FBI and Justice Department as dangerous terrorists live happily in the United States, enjoying their freedom and privilege.[20]

The Eisenhower administration initiated the economic warfare against Cuba that was also sharply escalated by Kennedy. In internal documents, high officials explained that "the Cuban people are responsible for the regime." Therefore the U.S. has the right to punish them because "if [the Cuban people] are hungry, they will throw Castro out." Kennedy agreed that the embargo would hasten Fidel Castro's departure as a result of "rising discomfort among hungry Cubans." The punishment of the people of Cuba intensified when Cuba was in dire straits after the collapse of the Soviet Union. The author of the 1992 measures to tighten the blockade proclaimed that "my objective is to wreak havoc in Cuba" so that the people will suffer and force government policy to change (liberal Democrat Robert Torricelli). The basic thinking was expressed by a high State Department official in 1960: Castro would be removed "through disenchantment and disaffection based on economic dissatisfaction and hardship [so] every possible means should be undertaken promptly to weaken the economic life of Cuba [in order to] bring about hunger, desperation and [the] overthrow of the government"—a policy which, as you all know, was applied successfully here in Chile, with consequences that we need not review.

The punishment of Palestinians for voting the wrong way, already discussed, was no innovation. Rather, it is common and is considered acceptable across the political spectrum, with rare exceptions.

It should, again, not be thought that this form of savagery is somehow unique to the United States and its clients. Like other elements of "American exceptionalism," it is probably close to a historical universal, routinely adopted by systems of power, though naturally most visible and destructive in the case of the most powerful states.

Also close to a historical universal, as far as I know, is the unwillingness of educated classes to perceive what they are doing: the Jennings corollary, once again. There was a revealing illustration a few days after the Palestinian elections of January 2006. The New York Times published a review of a collection of Osama bin Laden's pronouncements. The reviewer, constitutional lawyer Noah Feldman, described Osama's descent to greater and greater evil over the years, finally reaching the absolute lower depths, when "he put forth the perverse claim that since the United States is a democracy, all citizens bear responsibility for its government's actions, and civilians are therefore fair targets." Ultimate evil—and quite acceptable practice, as the Times reported two days later, when the United States and Israel announced that all Palestinians bear responsibility for the government they had just elected, so that they are all fair targets for terror and economic strangulation. Like Cubans.[21]

In one case, it is ultimate evil; in the other, it is noble idealism. The determining factor is agency. And unsurprisingly, the long record of similar practices received no more notice than the pairing of Osama's doctrines with our own.

The reasons Cuba must be tortured were frankly explained in the internal record, particularly when the attack escalated under Kennedy. The basic reason was Cuba's "successful defiance" of U.S. policies going back 150 years; not Russians, but rather the Monroe Doctrine. Then come the usual reasons for intervention: the concern that the Cuban example might infect others with the dangerous idea of "taking matters into their own hands," an idea with great appeal throughout the continent because "the distribution of land and other forms of national wealth greatly favors the propertied classes and the poor and underprivileged, stimulated by the example of the Cuban revolution, are now demanding opportunities for a decent living." That was the warning given to incoming President Kennedy by his Latin America adviser Arthur Schlesinger, along with the suggestions about how to handle Latin Americans that I quoted earlier. A few months later the analysis was confirmed by the CIA, which observed that "the extensive influence of 'Castroism' is not a function of Cuban power.... Castro's shadow looms large because social and economic conditions throughout Latin America invite opposition to ruling authority and encourage agitation for radical change," for which Castro's Cuba might provide a model.[22]

The basic themes prevail with little change. When Washington reacted with fear and fury to the democratic election that brought Allende to office, the concern was not just the threat to corporate interests: rather, his election was perceived as a challenge to the whole ideological basis of U.S. global policy. As discussed in the previous lecture, policy makers feared that if the United States could not control Latin America, it could not expect "to achieve a successful order elsewhere in the world." Similar concerns appear to have motivated Clinton's bombing of Serbia, which was also guilty of "successful defiance," so we learn from the highest sources in the Clinton administration, who inform us that "it was Yugoslavia's resistance to the broader trends of political and economic reform—not the plight of Kosovar Albanians—that best explains NATO's war." The necessary "reforms" are the neoliberal policies that Clinton sought to impose on the world—though in the traditional manner, exempting elites at home, where he carried forward the

Reagan-Thatcher project of constructing a powerful state for the rich
and privileged, a "conservative nanny state," as it is described by economist Dean Baker in a revealing study.[23]

Before World War II, although the United States was by far the
world's leading economy, it was not a major player in world affairs. Its
domination was restricted to its own region, apart from forays into the
Pacific: conquering Hawaii and the Philippines along with Pacific islands, part of the race of the industrial countries to exploit the riches of
China during the years when it had lost its capacity to defend itself from
conquest and robbery. The one major exception was the campaign to
control energy resources, as the world began to shift to an oil-based
economy after World War I. The United States was the greatest producer,
but wanted to ensure control of resources elsewhere—the charge now
leveled against China today. Wilson therefore expelled the British from
Venezuela, which by 1928 had become the world's leading oil exporter,
with U.S. companies now in charge. To achieve the goal, Washington "ac-
tively supported the vicious and venal regime of Juan Vicente Gómez,"
violating its Open Door policy to achieve "U.S. economic hegemony in
Venezuela" by pressuring its government to bar British concessions—
more abuse of reality in the service of Wilsonian idealism.[24] Meanwhile
the United States continued to demand—and secure—oil rights in the
Middle East, where the British and French were in the lead.

By the end of World War II, everything had changed. U.S. industrial
production more than tripled during the war, while industrial rivals were
severely damaged or destroyed. The United States had literally half of the
wealth of the entire world, along with incomparable security and military
power, including nuclear weapons. U.S. planners had no doubt that they
could now implement the Monroe Doctrine for the first time, and could
also go on to dominate most of the world. High-level planners and foreign policy advisers determined that in the new global system the United
States should "hold unquestioned power" while ensuring the "limitation
of any exercise of sovereignty" by states that might interfere with its
global designs, while developing "an integrated policy to achieve military
and economic supremacy for the United States" throughout most of the

world, all if possible. Since then, fundamental policies have changed more in tactics than in substance.[25]

It was particularly important to control Middle East oil, which was recognized to be "a stupendous source of strategic power" and "one of the greatest material prizes in world history," in the words of internal documents of the 1940s. The influential planner A. A. Berle held that control of Middle East oil would yield "substantial control of the world."[26] France was expelled from the region by legal chicanery, and the British were gradually reduced to a junior partner. In Latin America, repeated efforts to follow an independent path elicited violence or economic warfare in ways I need not recount. Until recently, there was only a single survivor. Hence the seemingly irrational passion of the continuing assault against Cuba, in virtual isolation from world opinion as regular votes at the General Assembly show. And also in defiance of U.S. public opinion, which for decades has favored entering into normal relations with Cuba. And even in defiance of major segments of business, which is an unusual sign of a driving state interest: the Mafia doctrine—the Godfather does not easily tolerate disobedience, which could spread—an underappreciated principle of international order, to be added to the doctrines of Smith and Thucydides and the Jennings corollary.[27]

The conventional version of the Mafia doctrine is the "domino theory": if we allow them to survive where they are, they'll topple dominoes nearby, and will soon be a direct threat to us. So by the standard principles of preventive war, we must stop them at once, far from our shores. This version of the theory is regularly abandoned, often ridiculed as exaggerated, once the occasion for invoking it has passed. But the rational version of the doctrine persists, unchallenged, because it is quite plausible. Several examples have already been cited, and there are many others, including the U.S. invasion of South Vietnam, later all of Indochina. The Godfather's concerns are valid.

We should not, however, underestimate the element of genuine fear, which is deeply rooted in American culture. The basic theme was expressed plaintively by President Lyndon Johnson, speaking to troops in Asia. "There are 3 billion people in the world and we have only 200 million of them," he warned. "We are outnumbered 15 to 1. If might did make right they would sweep over the United States and take what we have. We have what they want." So we have to stop them in Vietnam. Similar fears were voiced by Ronald Reagan when he strapped on his cowboy boots and declared a national emergency in 1985, warning that the fearsome Nicaraguan army was only "two days driving time" from Harlingen, Texas, an imminent terrorist threat if we don't stop them in Managua. And when he bombed the nutmeg capital of the world, Grenada, because the Russians might use it to bomb the United States, if they could find it on a map.

It is a mistake to ridicule these fears because of the manifest absurdity. In Johnson's case, at least, they were probably sincere, drawn from a long tradition. Literary critic Bruce Franklin has shown that a leading theme of popular literature since colonial days is that we are about to be destroyed by monsters, but are saved at the last moment by a superweapon or a superhero. And as he also shows, the monsters are commonly those we are crushing. This fear of *them* reveals itself in mobilization for aggression and violence abroad, and at home in the hatred of the next generation of immigrants that has been a pervasive feature of this immigrant society, and is once again taking ugly forms today. It is an element of the periodic outbursts of so-called populism: the idea that *they* are taking our country away from us, poisoning our culture and society, stealing our hard-earned money, particularly salient now with a growing recognition that whites are becoming a minority—a persecuted minority, as many see it. One doesn't have to keep to rabid talk-show hosts to perceive the sentiment. A version appears in more mainstream commentary and even in scholarly literature, and plays no slight role in foreign and domestic politics.[28]

The end of the Cold War brought some changes, but more in pretexts and tactics than in principle. The "war on drugs" was redeclared by Bush I with a huge government-media propaganda campaign just in time to provide a pretext for the invasion of Panama to kidnap a thug who was convicted in Florida for crimes mostly committed when he was on the CIA payroll—incidentally killing unknown numbers of poor people in the bombarded slums, thousands according to Panamanian human rights investigators, but there was no U.S. inquiry: "We don't do body counts," as explained by General Tommy Franks, the conqueror of Iraq. The "war on drugs" also had an important domestic component. Much like the "war on crime," it served to frighten the population into obedience as domestic policies were being implemented to benefit extreme wealth at the expense of the large majority, one part of broader processes to which we return.

The alleged threat was later transmuted from drugs to narcoterrorism, exploiting opportunities offered by 9/11. By the end of the millennium, total U.S. military and police assistance in the hemisphere already exceeded economic and social aid. That is a new phenomenon. Even at the height of the Cold War, economic aid far exceeded military aid. Predictably, the policies "strengthened military forces at the expense of civilian authorities, exacerbated human rights problems and generated significant social conflict and even political instability," according to a study by the Washington Office on Latin America. From 2002 to 2003, the number of Latin Americans troops trained by U.S. programs increased by more than 50 percent, and has probably increased since. Police are trained in light infantry tactics. The Southern Military Command (SOUTHCOM) by then had more personnel in Latin America than most key civilian federal agencies combined. The new focus is on street gangs and "radical populism": there is no need to tarry on what that phrase means in the Latin American context. Military training is being shifted from the State Department to the Pentagon. That frees military training from human rights and democracy conditionalities under congressional supervision, never very strong, but at least a deterrent to some of the worst abuses.[29]

The U.S. Fourth Fleet, disbanded in 1950, was reactivated in 2008. Its responsibility extends to the Caribbean, Central and South America, and the surrounding waters. The official announcement defines its "various operations" to "include counter-illicit trafficking, Theater Security Cooperation, military-to-military interaction and bilateral and multinational training." The reactivation of the fleet understandably elicited protest and concern from the governments of Brazil, Venezuela, and others.[30]

Impediments to U.S. militarization of Latin America continue, however, including the decision of Ecuador's president Rafael Correa to terminate Washington's use of the Manta military base, the last one open to the United States in South America. But that does not end the story.

In July 2009, as the United States terminated its operations in Ecuador, the United States and Colombia concluded a secret deal to permit the United States to use seven military bases in Colombia—"one of the few places left in the Americas where the Yanqui military is welcome," *Time* magazine observed.[31] In Honduras, the United States uses the Palmerola military base, called the "unsinkable aircraft carrier" when it served as a major base for Reagan's terrorist war against Nicaragua, possibly a factor in Obama's isolated stance in accepting the 2009 Honduran elections under military rule after the president was expelled (see pp. 67–68). After the United States endorsed the Honduran elections, Honduras signed a security pact with Colombia, adding another piece to the U.S.-run project of remilitarization of the region.[32] The United States also has access to bases in the Dutch islands Curaçao and Aruba, regarded as threats particularly by Venezuela, close by.

The officially highlighted purpose of the Colombian bases is to counter narcotrafficking and terrorism, "but senior Colombian military and civilian officials familiar with negotiations told the Associated Press that the idea is to make Colombia a regional hub for Pentagon operations," AP reported. There are reports that the agreement provides Colombia with privileged access to U.S. military supplies. Colombia had long before become the leading recipient of U.S. military aid (apart from Israel-Egypt, a separate category). Colombia has had by far the worst human rights record in the hemisphere since the Central American wars of the 1980s wound down. The correlation between U.S. aid and human rights violations has long been noted by scholarship (see p. 261).[33]

AP also cited an April 2009 document of the U.S. Air Mobility Command. This study proposes that the Palanquero base in Colombia could become a "cooperative security location" (CSL) from which "mobility operations could be executed." From Palanquero, the authors observe, "Nearly half the continent can be covered by a C-17 (military transport) without refueling." This could form part of "a global en route strategy," which "helps achieve the regional engagement strategy and assists with the mobility routing to Africa." For the present, "the strategy to place a CSL at

Palanquero should be sufficient for air mobility reach on the South American continent," the document concludes, but it goes on to explore options for extending the routing to Africa with additional bases, all of which are to form part of the U.S. system of global surveillance, control, and intervention, a remarkably ambitious construction with no historical parallel.[34]

In May 2009 the air force submitted a budget request to Congress, explaining that the Palanquero base would provide "full spectrum operations" over most of the hemisphere and thus "increase our capability to conduct Intelligence, Surveillance and Reconnaissance (ISR), improve global reach, support logistics requirements, improve partnerships, improve theater security cooperation, and expand expeditionary warfare capability." Among the tasks is to counter the "threat from narcotics funded terrorist insurgencies [and] anti-U.S. governments."[35]

On August 28, 2009, the newly formed Union of South American Nations, UNASUR, met in Bariloche (Argentina) to consider the military bases. The final declaration stressed that South America must be kept as "a land of peace," and that foreign military forces must not threaten the sovereignty or integrity of any nation of the region. It instructed the South American Defense Council to investigate the document of the Air Mobility Command. Problems of implementation were left to subsequent meetings.[36]

A month after the UNASUR meeting, the Panamanian press reported that Obama-Clinton had arranged for two new air and naval bases in Panama for U.S. operations, again near Venezuela.[37]

Bolivian president Evo Morales was particularly bitter about the plans for military bases. Drawing on his background in a coca growers union, he said he had witnessed U.S. soldiers accompanying Bolivian troops who fired at his union members. "So now we're narcoterrorists," he continued. "When they couldn't call us communists anymore, they called us subversives, and then traffickers, and since the September 11 attacks, terrorists." He warned that "the history of Latin America repeats itself."[38]

Morales observed that the ultimate responsibility for Latin America's violence lies with U.S. consumers of illegal drugs: "If UNASUR sent troops to the United States to control consumption, would they accept it? Impossible!"

Morales's rhetorical question can be extended. Suppose that UNA-SUR, or China, or many others claimed the right to establish military bases in Mexico to implement programs to eradicate tobacco in the United States: by aerial fumigation in North Carolina and Kentucky, interdiction by sea and air forces, and dispatch of inspectors to the United States to ensure it was eradicating this poison—which is turned into products far more lethal than cocaine or heroin, incomparably more than cannabis. The toll of tobacco use, including "passive smokers" who are seriously affected though they do not use tobacco themselves, is truly fearsome, overshadowing the lethal effects of other dangerous substances (even the second largest killer, alcohol, which like tobacco causes great harm to non-users).

The idea that outsiders should interfere with the production and distribution of these lethal substances is plainly unthinkable. The fact that the U.S. justification for its drug programs abroad is accepted as plausible, even regarded as worthy of discussion, is yet another illustration of the deep roots of the imperial mentality in Western culture.

Even if we adopt the imperial premises, it is hard to take seriously the announced goals of the "drug war," which persists without notable change despite extensive evidence that other measures—prevention and treatment—are far more cost-effective, and despite the persistent failure of the resort to criminalization at home and violence and chemical warfare ("fumigation") abroad—at least, with regard to the announced goals.[39]

In February 2009, the Latin American Commission on Drugs and Democracy issued its analysis of the U.S. "war on drugs" in past decades. The commission, led by former Latin American presidents Fernando Cardoso (Brazil), Ernesto Zedillo (Mexico), and César Gavíria (Colombia), concluded that the drug war had been a complete failure and urged a drastic change of policy, away from forceful measures at home and abroad and toward much less costly and more effective measures. Their report had no detectable impact, just as earlier studies and the historical record have had none. That again reinforces the natural conclusion that the "drug war"—like the "war on crime" and "the war on terror"—is pursued for reasons other than the announced goals.[40]

To determine the reasons, we may adopt a procedure familiar in the legal system, which takes predictable consequences to be evidence of intent, particularly when the consequences are so clear over a long period, along with the predictable failure to reach the announced purposes.

The consequences have always been clear. The programs underlie counterinsurgency abroad, with particularly harsh effects in the main target, Colombia; and at home serve as "population control," in part by frightening the population, a standard mode of imposing discipline, in part by removing a superfluous population, mostly Black and Latino, by sending huge and growing numbers to prison—the civilized counterpart to Latin American "social cleansing" (*limpieza social*). This neoliberal phenomenon has led to by far the highest incarceration rate in the world since the programs took off thirty years ago, adding another dark chapter to the history of African Americans, to which we return.

The "war on drugs" was a centerpiece of President Nixon's domestic policies, though unlike his successors he included prevention and treatment as significant components. The reasons for his large-scale revival of the "war on drugs" were not obscure.[41] Nixon and the right, joined by elite sectors quite generally, faced two crucial problems in the early 1970s. One was the rising opposition to the Vietnam War, which was beginning to cross a boundary that must be zealously guarded: some were even charging Washington with crimes, not merely errors committed in an excess of benevolence and naiveté, as liberal commentators insisted. A related problem was activism, particularly among young people, which was bringing about an "excess of democracy," liberal intellectuals warned while calling for restoration of obedience and passivity, along with measures to overcome the failure of the institutions responsible for "the indoctrination of the young"—schools, university, churches—to perform their tasks, and perhaps even government control of the media if self-censorship did not suffice. And in Nixonian hands, much harsher measures.[42]

The drug war was a perfect remedy. With the enthusiastic participation of the media, a tale was concocted of an "addicted army" that would bring down domestic society as the shattered troops returned home, all part of an insidious communist plot. "The Communists [in Vietnam] are battling American troops not only with firepower but with drugs," the respected liberal commentator Walter Cronkite proclaimed, while his colleagues lamented that the "worst horror to have emerged from the war" is the plague of addiction of American troops (Stewart Alsop). Others chimed in as well, with little skepticism, and little reaction even to horrifying statements like these. Though drug use appears to have been roughly on the order of the youth culture generally, there was indeed extremely serious addiction: alcohol and tobacco.

The ideological construction fulfilled these functions admirably. The United States became the victim of the Vietnamese, not the perpetrator of crimes against them, and the sacred image of the "city on the hill" was preserved. Furthermore, the basis was laid for a "law and order" campaign at home to discipline those who were straying beyond the bounds of subordination to power and doctrine. Successes were impressive. By 1977, President Carter could inform the country that we owe the Vietnamese no debt, because "the destruction was mutual." For Reagan the war was a "noble cause." The first President Bush was able to go on to inform the Vietnamese that of course we can never forgive them for the crimes they have committed against us, "but Hanoi knows today that we seek only answers without the threat of retribution for the past," and being an unusually compassionate people, we will agree to let them join the world if they show good faith in dealing with the only moral issue remaining from the noble cause: dedicating themselves to finding the bones of American flyers shot down while flying over North Vietnam on their missions of mercy.[43]

All this passed with no detectable criticism or even comment, another impressive tribute to the culture of imperialism. But though the successes have indeed been substantial, they were far from complete. Activism not only continued but expanded, with significant civilizing effects on the general society.

Militarization of South America is a component of much broader global programs, as the "global en route strategy" indicates. In Iraq, there is virtually no information about the fate of the huge U.S. military bases. Reports from the contractors in charge—effectively mercenary forces—

indicate that they are still under construction despite formal commitments to withdraw. The immense city-within-a-city "embassy" in Baghdad not only remains, but its cost is also to rise under Obama to $1.8 billion a year, from an estimated $1.5 billion in Bush's last year. The Obama administration is also constructing mega-embassies in Pakistan and Afghanistan that are completely without precedent. Throughout the Gulf region, billions of dollars are being spent to develop "critical base and port facilities," along with military training and arms shipments expanding the U.S. global system of militarization. The United States and UK are demanding that the U.S. military base in Diego Garcia, used heavily in recent U.S. wars after Britain expelled the inhabitants, be exempted from the planned African nuclear weapons–free zone (NWFZ), just as U.S. bases are exempted from similar efforts in the Pacific to reduce the nuclear threat. Not even on the agenda, of course, is a NWFZ in the Middle East, which would mitigate, perhaps end, the alleged Iranian threat. The enormous global support for this move, including a large majority of Americans, is not considered relevant.[44]

Meanwhile global military expenses continue to rise, though with a setback caused by the 2008 financial crisis (but not in the United States). The annual Yearbook of the Stockholm International Peace Research Institute reports that for 2008, the United States accounted for over 40 percent of global military expenses, eight times as much as its nearest rival, China. The United States is of course alone in having a vast network of military bases around the world and a global surveillance and control system, and in regularly invading other countries (with impunity, given its power). From 1999 to 2008, global military spending increased 45 percent, with the United States accounting for 58 percent of the total. Since 2002, the value of the top one hundred arms sales industries, primarily U.S.-based, increased by 37 percent in real terms, until the recession. The United States is also the world's largest arms supplier, with $23 billion in receipts in 2007 and $32 billion in 2008, including the small arms and light weapons that are used in most of the conflicts around the world—twenty out of twenty-seven of the world's major wars, according to the report by the New America Foundation, which released these figures. A congressional study found that in 2008 the United States signed weapons agreements valued at $37.8 billion in 2008, amounting to over 68 percent of the global total, a sharp increase from $25.4 billion in 2007. Italy was second, with $3.7 billion in worldwide weapons sales in 2008. Russia was slightly below Italy, its sales having dropped by two-thirds, from $10.8 billion in 2007. "The growth in weapons sales by the United States last year was particularly noticeable against worldwide trends," the press reported, noting that global arms sales in 2008 had dropped by 7.6 percent from 2007 and reached the lowest level since 2005. The United States opposes international regulation of arms sales. In the winter 2008 UN session, Washington voted against a global treaty regulating the arms trade, though it was not alone: it was joined by Zimbabwe.

Obama is "on track to spend more on defense, in real dollars, than any other president has in one term of office since World War II," according to independent monitors, and "that's not counting the additional $130 billion the administration is requesting to fund the wars in Iraq and Afghanistan next year, with even more war spending slated for future years." In January 2010, Congress passed his Pentagon budget with supplemental funding for Afghanistan pending. The $708.3 billion budget (with another $33 billion expected for Afghanistan) is not only a record, but also amounts to almost half the deficit, which is also reaching post–World War II highs, largely as a result of the tax cuts for the rich and lavish spending of the Bush administration. A major contributory factor was the "efficient market" theology touted by the economics profession, which prevented the Federal Reserve from attending to an $8 trillion housing bubble. The huge bubble, along with the consumer spending based on this mirage, sustained the economy until the inevitable crash—much as the Clinton economy was sustained by a tech bubble, though the extravagance and the crash were much less severe than under Bush.

The deficit is arousing huge concern among the right wing and the media, a concern with perhaps some merit, even though running deficits is an appropriate policy to help stimulate an economy in deep recession. A lead story in the *New York Times*, for example, is headlined "A Red-Ink Decade" and warns of two "stunning" numbers in the president's budget proposal: the deficit for the coming year and the long-term deficit projection. The article praises the president for recognizing that it may be necessary to cut entitlement programs and increase taxes—which means letting Bush-era tax cuts for corporations and the rich expire. There is no reference to another "stunning" number: the military budget, untouchable and virtually unmentionable.[45] What the *Times* and other commentators project is cutbacks in programs that serve people rather than concentrations of power—and surely not the military. That is particularly likely after "health care reform" has turned into another giveaway to the insurance companies and Big Pharma, in violation of the public will, and without the obvious steps to reduce costs in the manner of other industrial societies, critical matters to which we return.[46]

In short, moves toward "a world of peace" do not seem likely to fall within the "change you can believe in," to borrow Obama's campaign slogan.

A crucial question is what Obama's position will be on "missile defense"—understood on all sides to be, in effect, a first-strike weapon—and militarization of space. On the latter, he has called for "a worldwide ban on weapons that interfere with military and commercial satellites," which would mean that the U.S. project of the weaponization of space—so far in isolation and over global objections, spearheaded at the UN by China—would remain undisturbed, while there would be a ban on any interference with satellites, including those essential for the militarization of space. He has also called for a space weapons ban, a very welcome step, but presented in a way that leaves "a lot of wiggle room" (Victoria Samson at the Center for Defense Information). More disturbing are the remarks of Michael McFaul (special assistant for National Security Affairs and senior director for Russian and Eurasian affairs at the National Security Council) on the eve of Obama's first trip to Russia. McFaul informed the press that "we're not going to reassure or give or trade anything with the Russians regarding NATO expansion or missile defense," referring to U.S. missile defense programs in Eastern Europe (to which we return) and NATO membership for Russia's neighbors Ukraine and Georgia. Obama has spoken about eventual abolition of nuclear weapons, in accord with the legal obligation of signers of the Non-Proliferation Treaty, but again in rather vague terms. And as longtime antinuclear activist Joseph Gerson has observed, Mikhail Gorbachev and others have recognized that "Russia will not be able to embrace serious efforts to achieve abolition unless space is demilitarized—something which is not discussed in Washington's agenda."[47]

Obama's approach may be an improvement over Bush, and offers prospects for popular movements that seek to rid the earth of these threats to survival of the species. But a lot of work will be needed.

Returning to Latin America, Washington planners are now facing a broad range of new and unexpected problems. Although Central America was largely pacified by Reaganite terror at least temporarily, the region from Venezuela to Argentina is falling out of control. And the traditional mechanisms—violence and economic warfare—are losing their effectiveness. Bush and associates did try to resort to the traditional means in Venezuela in 2002, backing a military coup to overthrow the democratically elected government—another illustration of the "strong line of continuity" in democracy promotion. But the effort failed. After a popular uprising restored the elected government, Washington immediately turned to funding groups of its choice within Venezuela while refusing to identify recipients: $26 million by 2006 for the new program after the failed coup attempt, all under the guise of supporting democracy. When the facts were reported by wire services, law professor Bill Monning at the Monterey Institute of International Studies in California said, "We would scream bloody murder if any outside force were interfering in our internal political system."[48]

Monning is of course correct: such actions would never be tolerated for a moment, but the imperial mentality allows them to proceed, even with praise, when Washington is the agent.

In a second coup attempt, the United States and France succeeded in eliminating the elected government of Haiti, as already discussed.

The third military coup was in Honduras in 2009, a class-based coup ousting left-leaning President Zelaya. The U.S. reaction was unusual in that Washington joined the OAS in criticizing the coup, though tepidly, not withdrawing its ambassador in protest as Latin American and European countries did. Meanwhile, the United States continued to train Honduran officers, and the IMF, largely U.S.-controlled, provided a $150 million loan to the coup regime—after having withdrawn loans to the democratically elected Zelaya government because of disagreement with his economic policies. In an unprecedented move, the IMF had also provided immediate offers of aid to the coup regime in Venezuela in 2002.[49]

Amnesty International released a long and detailed account of serious human rights violations by the Honduran coup regime. If such a report were issued concerning a official enemy, it would be front-page news. In this case it was scarcely reported, consistent with the downplaying of human rights violations by governments to which U.S. political and economic power centers are basically sympathetic, as in this case.[50]

Soon Obama ended the limited deviations from the normal track. He separated the United States from almost all of Latin America and Europe by accepting the military coup, which his administration refused to describe in those terms. Virtually alone, the United States recognized the subsequent elections held under military rule. Obama's ambassador to Honduras, Hugo Llorens, called the elections "a great celebration of democracy"—echoing Kennedy-Johnson ambassador to Brazil Lincoln Gordon after the U.S.-backed military coup in 1964, which instituted the first of the neo-Nazi national security states that spread through the continent, the worst plague of repression in its history. The goal of these national security states, as described by Latin America scholar Lars Schoultz, was "to destroy permanently a perceived threat to the existing structure of socioeconomic privilege by eliminating the political participation of the numerical majority...[the] popular classes."[51] Gordon exulted that the Brazilian coup was "the most decisive victory for freedom in the mid-twentieth century," adding that the "democratic forces" now in charge should "create a greatly improved climate for private investment." Like Honduras, "a great celebration of democracy."

Ties between the Pentagon and the Honduran military are so close, and U.S. aid is so decisive for this virtual client state, that the United States could easily have joined Latin America and Europe in defending democracy. But Obama chose to keep to the tradition: democracy is fine, if and only if it accords with U.S. state and corporate power interests. So it is fine in Eastern Europe, up to a point. But not in our own domains, unless it meets the Reaganite conditions already quoted. The vast majority of U.S. aid to Honduras was never suspended. In contrast, after recent military coups in Mauritania and Madagascar aid was suspended immediately. The United States also blocked an OAS resolution that would have refused to recognize Honduran elections carried out under the dictatorship—elections that Washington quickly applauded. After the election, Arturo Valenzuela, Obama's State Department official in charge of Western hemisphere affairs, told the press that "the issue is not who is going to be the next president.... The Honduran people decided that"—choosing between two coup supporters while the elected president was holed up in the Brazilian Embassy. Meanwhile Lewis Anselem, Obama's representative to the OAS, instructed the backward Latin American peons that they should join the United States in the real world, abandoning their "world of magical realism," and should recognize the military coup as Big Brother did.

Obama even broke new ground in support for the military coup. There are two government-funded organizations that claim to support democracy in the world: the International Republican Institute (IRI) and the National Democratic Institute (NDI). The IRI regularly supports military coups to overthrow elected governments, most recently in Venezuela in 2002 and Haiti in 2004. But the NDI had held back, including in these two cases. In Honduras, for the first time, Obama's NDI agreed to observe the elections under military rule, unlike the OAS and the UN, still wandering in the realm of magical realism.[52]

Nevertheless, resort to violence is no longer a readily available option in the face of disobedience in Latin America and popular opposition in the United States. Resort to economic warfare is also more restricted than in the past as one government after another restructures or repays debts, freeing themselves from control by the IMF—basically an arm of the U.S. Treasury Department.

Developments in Latin America should be understood within a broader global perspective. The prospect that Europe and Asia might move toward greater independence has seriously troubled U.S. planners since

World War II, and concerns have significantly increased with the evolution of a "tripolar order" (North America, Europe, East Asia) by the 1970s. It is now expanding beyond, along with new and important interactions in the former colonial world (Brazil, South Africa, India, and others), and rapidly growing Chinese engagement with the EU and the countries of the South.

U.S. intelligence has projected that in the coming decades, the United States, while controlling Middle East oil for the traditional reasons, will itself rely mainly on more stable Atlantic Basin resources (West Africa, Western hemisphere). Control of Middle East oil is now far from a sure thing, especially after the arrogant blundering of the violent Bush clique in Iraq—portrayed as a success, but informed observers know better.[53] These expectations are also threatened by developments in the Western hemisphere, accelerated by Bush administration policies that left the United States remarkably isolated in the global arena. The Bush administration even succeeded in alienating Canada, no small feat. The reason was Washington's rejection of NAFTA decisions favoring Canada that led Canada to establish closer relations with China. Canadian officials said that Canada might shift a significant portion of its trade, particularly oil, from the United States to China; not very likely, but an unusual gesture of independence. In a further blow to Washington's energy policies, the leading oil exporter in the hemisphere, Venezuela, has forged probably the closest relations with China of any Latin American country, and plans to sell increasing amounts of oil to China as part of its effort to reduce dependence on the openly hostile U.S. government. Latin America as a whole is increasing trade and other relations with China, with some setbacks but likely expansion, in particular raw materials exporters such as Brazil, Peru, and Chile. For Brazil, now often called "the farmer of the world," China is now its largest trading partner. The increase is part of the tendencies toward a more diverse and multipolar world that are of considerable concern to American planners, who had long taken global hegemony for granted.[54]

Meanwhile Cuba-Venezuela relations have become close, each relying on its comparative advantage. Venezuela is providing low-cost oil, as it does elsewhere in the Caribbean, while in return Cuba organizes literacy and health programs, sending thousands of highly skilled professionals, teachers and doctors, who work in the poorest and most neglected areas, as they do elsewhere in the third world. Joint Cuba-Venezuela projects are also reported to be having an impact in the Caribbean, where with Venezuelan funding Cuban doctors are providing health care to thousands of people who had no hope of receiving it. Operation Miracle, as it is called, is described by Jamaica's ambassador to Cuba as "an example of integration and south-south co-operation," and appears to be generating enthusiasm among the poor majority. The United States and Mexico toyed with the idea of an oil subsidy to counter Venezuelan petro-diplomacy, but apparently did not pursue it.

Venezuela's entry into Mercosur was described by Argentine president Néstor Kirchner as "a milestone" in the development of this trading bloc, and welcomed as opening "a new chapter in our integration" by Brazilian president Lula da Silva. Venezuela also supplied Argentina with fuel oil to help stave off an energy crisis, and bought almost a third of Argentine debt issued in 2005, one element of a regionwide effort to free the countries from the controls of the IMF after two decades of disastrous effects of conformity to its rules. The IMF has "acted towards our country as a promoter and a vehicle of policies that caused poverty and pain among the Argentine people," President Kirchner said in announcing his decision to pay almost $1 trillion to rid Argentina of the IMF forever. Radically violating IMF rules, Argentina enjoyed a substantial economic recovery from the disaster left by IMF policies.

Steps toward independent regional integration advanced further with the election of Evo Morales in Bolivia in December 2005. Morales moved quickly to reach a series of energy accords with Venezuela. He too committed himself to reversing the neoliberal policies that Bolivia had pursued rigorously for twenty-five years, leaving the country with lower per capita income than at the outset. Adherence to the neoliberal programs was interrupted during this period only when popular uprisings compelled the government to abandon them, as when it followed World Bank advice to privatize water supply and "get prices right"—incidentally depriving the poor of access to water.

Since the election of Morales in 2005, Bolivia's economic performance has been quite impressive. A Center for Economic and Policy Research (CEPR) study found that in the four years since Morales took office, economic growth "has been higher than at any time in the last 30 years, averaging 4.9 percent annually.... Projected GDP growth for 2009 is the highest in the hemisphere and follows its peak growth rate in 2008," along with "several programs targeted at the poorest Bolivians." These are doubtless factors in Morales's election in December 2009 by a majority of 64 percent to 26.4 percent for his right-wing opponent, a gain of 10 percent over his unprecedented victory in 2005.[55]

Throughout most of South America, Washington and elite opinion are compelled to support governments of a kind that might have been harshly condemned and undermined not many years ago, a reflection of the general shift toward independence in Latin America. The indigenous populations have become much more active and influential, particularly in Bolivia and Ecuador, where they want oil and gas to be domestically controlled or, in some cases, oppose production altogether. Many indigenous people apparently do not see any reason their lives, societies, and cultures should be disrupted or destroyed so that northern urbanites can sit in their SUVs in traffic gridlock. Some are even calling for an "Indian nation" in South America. Meanwhile internal economic integration is reversing patterns that trace back to the Spanish conquests, with Latin American elites and economies linked to the imperial powers but not to one another.

It is even possible that Latin America may come to terms with some of its severe internal problems. Latin America is not merely the victim of foreign forces. The region is notorious for the rapacity of its wealthy classes and their freedom from social responsibility. Comparative studies of Latin America and East Asian economic development are revealing in this respect. International economist David Felix writes that consumption patterns and elite "status competition" have been quite different in the two regions: in Latin America, there is "a fervor, approaching in some cases insatiability," for foreign-produced luxury goods for Western-oriented elites, in contrast with the homegrown-goods orientation of Asian societies. Asia concentrated on "building up the physical and human capital base prior to turning to consumer durable production," in contrast to Latin America.

South Korea, for example, raised itself from half the per capita income of Ghana in 1960 to become one of the world's leading industrial societies by radical violation of neoliberal rules, including control over foreign exchange (violation could bring the death penalty), while "spending on anything not essential for industrial development was prohibited or strongly discouraged" through various means, Cambridge University economist Ha-Joon Chang observes. Latin America has followed a radically different course. And not surprisingly, South Korea's economic miracle slowed when Korea began to apply orthodox economic precepts after the crash of the late 1990s. These included the financial liberalization demanded by what Chang calls "the unholy trinity": the World Bank, World Trade Organization, and the IMF, all run by the global rulers.[56]

Latin America has close to the world's worst record for inequality, East Asia the best. The same holds for education, health, and social welfare generally. Imports to Latin America have been heavily skewed toward consumption by the rich; in East Asia, toward productive investment. Capital flight from Latin America has approached the scale of the debt—suggesting a way to overcome this crushing burden. According to Karen Lissakers, U.S. executive director of the IMF, "Bankers contend that there would be no [debt] crisis if flight capital—the money the citizens of the borrowing countries sent abroad for investment and safekeeping—were available for debt payments," although "these same bankers are active promoters of flight capital,"[57] and can confidently expect to be bailed out when borrowers default, the burden being transferred to the poor, who never incurred the debt in the first place, and to northern taxpayers. In East Asia, in contrast, capital flight has been tightly controlled. In Latin America, the wealthy are generally exempt from social obligations. East Asia differs sharply. Latin American economies have also been more open to unregulated foreign investment than Asia.

Any shift in these patterns is highly unwelcome in Washington, for the traditional reasons: The United States has expected to rely on Latin America as a secure resource base, and has feared, as already mentioned, that if it cannot control this hemisphere, then it cannot expect "to achieve a successful order elsewhere in the world."

For many reasons, the system of U.S. global dominance is fragile, even apart from the damage inflicted to it by Bush planners and the deep financial crisis of 2007–8.[58]

Developments in Latin America today are of very great importance in themselves, and the challenge they pose to Washington planners is very real, particularly when the global context is considered. There are opportunities for cooperative development and interchange, and progress toward a better future. The solidarity movements of the 1980s in the United States were something entirely new in hundreds of years of Western imperialism. No one from the imperial societies dreamed of going to live in an Algerian or Vietnamese village to help the victims of imperial assault, or to offer the protection given by a white face. But it did happen in the 1980s, many thousands of people in fact. By now it is extending to a global popular solidarity movement, with roots right in mainstream America, often in churches, including evangelical churches. The exciting internal developments in much of Latin America are strongly influenced by popular organizations that are coming together in the unprecedented international global justice movements, ludicrously called "anti-globalization" because they favor globalization that privileges the interests of people rather than investors and financial institutions. Just where all of this will lead, of course no one can say, and there is sure to be an uneven path ahead. But there are opportunities today for real progress toward freedom and justice, in hemisphere-wide cooperation, even extending beyond. Though the gains are fragile, and face bitter opposition at home and abroad, these are welcome prospects. The critical task for today is to make use of these opportunities, and to carry their promise forward.

THREE

Democracy and Development:
Their Enemies, Their Hopes

The concepts of democracy and development are closely related in many respects. One is that they have a common enemy: loss of sovereignty. In the contemporary world of state capitalist nation-states—a crucial qualification—loss of sovereignty can entail decline of democracy, and decline in ability to conduct social and economic policy and to integrate on one's own terms into international markets. That in turn harms development, an expected conclusion that is well confirmed by centuries of economic history. The same historical record reveals that fairly consistently, loss of sovereignty leads to imposed liberalization, of course in the interests of those with the power to institute this social and economic regime. In recent years, the imposed regime is commonly called "neoliberalism." It is not a very good term: the social-economic regime is not new, and it is not liberal, at least as the concept was understood by classical liberals. With such provisos as these, it is fair to say that a common enemy of democracy and development in the modern period is neoliberalism, though it has earlier guises. The statement is debatable in the case of development, much less so in the case of democracy. The very design of neoliberal principles is a direct attack on democracy. I will return to that, but first let us consider development.

Whether neoliberalism is the enemy of development is debatable, for a simple reason: the economy—particularly the international economy—

is so poorly understood and involves so many variables that even when close correlations are found, one cannot be confident about whether there are causal relations, or if so, in which direction. The founder of the modern theory of economic growth, Nobel laureate Robert Solow, commented that despite the enormous accumulation of data since his pioneering work half a century ago, "the direction of causality" is unknown. It is not clear, he concludes, whether capital investment causes productivity, or productivity leads to capital investment; whether openness to trade improves economic growth, or growth leads to trade; and the same problems arise in other dimensions. One prominent economic historian, Paul Bairoch, argues that protectionism, paradoxically, has commonly increased trade. The reason, he suggests, is that protectionism tends to stimulate growth, and growth leads to trade; while imposed liberalization, since the eighteenth century, has fairly consistently had harmful economic effects. The historical record provides substantial evidence that "historically, trade liberalization has been the outcome rather than the cause of economic development" (Ha-Joon Chang), apart from the "development" of narrow sectors of great wealth and privilege who benefit from resource extraction.[1]

From an extensive review, Bairoch concludes that "It is difficult to find another case where the facts so contradict a dominant theory [as the theory] concerning the negative impact of protectionism." The conclusion holds into the twentieth century, when other forms of market interference become more prominent, to which I will return.

The "dominant theory" is that of the rich and powerful, who have regularly advocated liberalization for others, and sometimes for themselves as well, once they have achieved a dominant position and hence are willing to face competition on a "level playing field"—that is, one sharply tilted in their favor. The stand is sometimes called "kicking away the ladder" by economic historians: first we violate the rules to climb to the top, then we kick away the ladder so that you cannot follow us, and we righteously proclaim: "Let's play fair, on a level playing field."

Until the 1920s, the United States was "the mother country and bastion of protectionism," Bairoch writes, well beyond the rest of the world, and had the fastest growth rate, becoming by far the world's most powerful economy, and after World War II, the dominant global power as well. The basic programs of economic development were established as soon as the United States gained its independence from England. Their author was Alexander Hamilton, the pioneer of import substitution industrialization—an error according to economic doctrine then and now, a regular foundation for development in actual history. Hamilton determined to violate the injunctions of the greatest economists of the day, who urged that Americans should import superior British manufactures and concentrate on their comparative advantage in primary resource and agricultural export. Adam Smith warned that "were the Americans, either by combination or by any other sort of violence, to stop the importation of European manufactures, and, by thus giving a monopoly to such of their own countrymen as could manufacture the like goods, divert any considerable part of their capital into this employment, they would retard instead of accelerating the further increase in the value of their annual produce, and would obstruct instead of promoting the progress of their country towards real wealth and greatness. This would be still more the case were they to attempt, in the same manner, to monopolize to themselves their whole exportation trade."[2] Surely among the most spectacularly refuted predictions in economic history, but solidly based in the abstract theories that continue to be imposed on the weak.

Long before World War II, as noted, the United States already had by far the world's largest economy. The Great Depression set it back substantially, but New Deal measures stabilized the economy and provided many needed institutional correctives. The semi-command wartime economy overcame the depression with deficit spending far beyond what is regarded as lethal today, yielding the most remarkable growth rate in manufacturing in economic history and laying the basis for unprecedented postwar economic growth, while competitors were severely weakened or destroyed. U.S. industrial production more than tripled during the war, and by its end the United States possessed about half the wealth of the world, along with incomparable security. By then, U.S. business and the state that largely caters to its interests were willing to sponsor a limited version of free trade, in part for geostrategic reasons, yet reasonably confident that U.S. firms should be able to prevail in "free competition." But as in the case of the British before them, they made sure that the bet was hedged with many crucial market interventions to ensure that the powerful would prevail. I will return to these mechanisms, generally ignored by free-market enthusiasts.

The United States was not forging a new path. On the contrary, it was following the practice of its predecessor in global dominance: England. England did finally adopt a liberal agenda in 1846, after over a century of intense protectionism and state intervention had left it so far in the lead in industrialization that competition seemed relatively safe. The process can be traced to the Tudor monarchs of the fifteenth and sixteenth centuries, who intervened radically in the economy in violation of market principles to create a textile industry, meanwhile destroying competitors and after a century, gaining enough foreign exchange through exports to fuel the incipient industrial revolution. For English manufacturers, the liberalization of the mid-nineteenth century, allowing agricultural imports, brought the benefits of lowered wages and increased profits, and also helped to "halt the move towards industrialization on the Continent by enlarging the market for agricultural produce and primary materials," economic historian Charles Kindelberger observes. It was not simply the triumph of "sound economic principles," as conventionally portrayed.[3]

Even with its enormous advantages in the mid-nineteenth century, England took few chances, maintaining major protected markets, primarily in India. State violence also created by far the most extensive narco-trafficking industry in world history; much of India was conquered in an effort to monopolize opium production, which did not quite succeed, thanks to the enterprise of Yankee traders. The primary goal was to break into the China market by gunboats and opium, since the Chinese had little interest in British manufactures, finding their own quite adequate. That violent interference with markets succeeded. The China market was opened by the "poison trade" and the "pig trade," as they were called. The poison trade turned China into a nation of opium addicts; the pig trade brought kidnapped Chinese workers to the United States to build railroads and perform other hard labor. Profits from the narcotrafficking racket also covered the costs of the Royal Navy and its imperial role, the administration of India, and the purchase of U.S. cotton, which fueled the early industrial revolution much in the way oil does today. And cotton production of course was also not exactly a free-market miracle: it was based on elimination of the indigenous population by state violence, and on slavery, rather extreme forms of market interference that do not fall within economic history.[4]

In passing, we may note that slavery did not end with the Civil War, despite the Constitutional Amendments that prohibited it in principle. The war was followed by a decade of partial freedom for African Americans, but by 1877, with the end of Reconstruction, slavery was reconstituted in a new and even more sadistic form, as Black life was effectively criminalized and sentencing was rendered permanent by various means, while brutalizing prison labor provided a large part of the basis not only for agricultural production, as under chattel slavery, but also for the American industrial revolution of the late nineteenth and early twentieth centuries. The savagery of the practices lent some shameful support to the claims of slave owners that they were more humane than the northern capitalists who "rented" labor, because those who owned people were concerned to sustain their capital investments. These horrifying practices continued until World War II, when free Black labor was needed, and in the postwar boom there was a window of opportunity for the Black population. The neoliberal turn in the past thirty years substantially closed the window as domestic manufacturing industry was displaced in favor of financialization of the economy and neoliberal globalization. A new form of criminalization was instituted, much of it in the context of the "drug wars," leading to a huge increase in incarceration, mostly targeting minorities, reaching to levels vastly beyond comparable countries—in fact beyond any countries that have meaningful statistics. This form of control of "superfluous populations" also provided a new supply of prison labor in state or private prisons, much of it in violation of international labor conventions. Ever since the first slaves were brought to the colonies, life for most African Americans has scarcely escaped the bonds of slavery, or sometimes worse.[5]

While protectionism and state violence greatly benefited England and the United States, and the rich industrial countries generally, the liberalization that was imposed by the imperial powers pretty much created the third world. "It is no exaggeration to say that the opening of the colonial economies—of course by force—was one of the major reasons for their lack of development," Bairoch concludes, with the support of other economic historians.

A comparison of the United States and Egypt in the early nineteenth century is one of many enlightening illustrations of the role of sovereignty and massive state intervention in economic development. Having freed itself from British rule, the United States was able to disregard economic theory and adopt British-style measures of large-scale state intervention and protectionism, and it developed. Meanwhile British power was able to bar anything of the sort in Egypt, joining with France to impose Lord Palmerston's doctrine that "no ideas therefore of fairness towards [Egypt's modernizing autocrat] Mehemet [Ali] ought to stand in the way of such great and paramount interests" as barring competition with Britain in the eastern Mediterranean. Palmerston expressed his "hate" for the "ignorant barbarian" who dared to undertake economic development, an effort that was beaten down by imperial violence.[6]

Historical memories resonate when today Britain and France, fronting for the United States, demand that Iran suspend all activities related to nuclear and missile programs, including research and development, so that nuclear energy is barred and the country that is perhaps under the greatest threat of any in the world is denied a deterrent against attack by the United States and its Israeli client: U.S. missile defense programs in Eastern Europe and the Gulf region, to which we return, are in part a thinly disguised contribution to these ends. We might also recall that France and Britain played the crucial role in development of Israel's nuclear arsenal, and that U.S. neocons strongly advocated nuclear programs in Iran while it was under the rule of the U.S.-imposed tyrant. Imperial sensibilities are delicate indeed.

Had it enjoyed sovereignty, Egypt might have undergone an industrial revolution in the nineteenth century. It shared many of the advantages of the United States. Egypt had rich agriculture, including cotton, an incipient development of manufacture, and an indigenous labor force that would have avoided the need to rely on extermination and slavery. But it lacked one crucial factor: independence, which allowed the United States to impose very high tariffs to bar superior British goods—first textiles, later steel and others. As already mentioned, the sovereign United States became the world's leader in protectionism, and economic growth. Egypt in contrast stagnated and declined.

Other comparisons suggest similar conclusions about the crucial role of sovereignty and the ability to enter the international system on terms of one's own choosing. One of the leading historians of Africa, Basil Davidson, observes that modernizing reforms in West Africa in the late nineteenth century were similar to those implemented by Japan at the same time, and believes that the potential for development "was in substance no different from the potential realized by the Japanese after 1867." An African historian comments that "the same laudable object was before them both, [but] the African's attempt was ruthlessly crushed and his plans frustrated" by British force. West Africa joined Egypt and India, not Japan and the United States, which were able to pursue an independent path, free from colonial rule and the strictures of economic rationality.[7]

The Haiti-Taiwan case, noted earlier, is another example. And these are not unusual, but more like the norm.

The hazards of what is now called "neoliberalism" were recognized quite early. One prominent example is Adam Smith. The term "invisible hand" appears only once in his classic *Wealth of Nations*. His primary concern was England. He warned that if English merchants and manufacturers were free to import, export, and invest abroad, they would profit while English society would be harmed. But that is unlikely to happen, he argued. The reason is that English capitalists would prefer to invest and purchase in the home country, so as if by an "invisible hand," England would be spared the ravages of economic liberalism. The other leading founder of classical economics, David Ricardo, drew similar conclusions. Using his famous example of English textiles and Portuguese wines, he concluded that his theory of comparative advantage would collapse if it were advantageous to the capitalists of England to invest in Portugal for both manufacturing and agriculture. But, he argued, thanks to "the natural disinclination which every man has to quit the country of his birth and connections," and "fancied or real insecurity of capital" abroad, most men of property would "be satisfied with the low rate of profits in their own country, rather than seek a more advantageous employment for their wealth in foreign nations," feelings that "I should be sorry to see weakened," he added. We need not tarry on the force of their arguments, but the instincts of the classical economists were insightful.[8]

The post–World War II period conforms closely to these conclusions. There have been two phases. The first was under the economic regime established by the United States and Britain at Bretton Woods after the war, negotiated by Harry Dexter White for the United States and John Maynard Keynes for England. They shared the belief that economic sovereignty is a crucial factor in growth. The system they designed was based on capital controls and regulated currencies in order to protect economic sovereignty, and to permit state intervention to carry out social democratic measures. The regime lasted for about twenty-five years, and was extremely successful by historical standards. By the mid-1970s, the system was gradually replaced in parts of the world by neoliberal principles. The outcomes should surprise no one familiar with economic history. Growth slowed and became far more inegalitarian. The effects were most severe in the countries that most rigidly observed the neoliberal rules: Latin America and Africa, in particular. There were exceptions to the generally harmful impact of neoliberal policies: the countries that rejected the rules, notably the "tigers" of East Asia and China. The basic conclusions were summarized by José Antonio Ocampo, the executive secretary of the Economic Commission for Latin America and the Caribbean: "The period of fastest growth in the developing world in the postwar period, and most prolonged episodes of rapid growth (the East-Asian or the most recent Chinese and Indian 'miracles' or, in the past, the periods of rapid growth in Brazil or Mexico), do not coincide with phases or episodes of extensive liberalization, even when they involved a large scale use of the opportunities provided by international markets."[9]

And we may add that the same has been true internally in the industrial societies, though they have means to protect themselves.

Reviewing the neoliberal experience of the preceding quarter century, a study of the Center for Economic and Policy Research finds that it has been accompanied by slower rates of growth and reduced progress on social indicators—the most meaningful measure of social health. That holds for countries from rich to poor. In a detailed analysis, economist Robert Pollin found that "the overall growth pattern is unambiguous…there has been a sharp decline in growth in the neoliberal era relative to the developmental state period" that preceded, a decline of over half, a "downward growth trend [that] is even more dramatic" when measured per capita, with increase in inequality and little or no reduction of poverty (when China, which rejected the neoliberal policies, is excluded), and devastating side effects among the most vulnerable. Political economist Robert Wade observes that "one of the big—and underappreciated—facts of our time [is the] dramatic growth slowdown in developed and developing countries" in the quarter century of neoliberal economic policy, including, probably, increase in poverty and inequality within and between countries when China is removed and realistic poverty measures are used. "What is striking," he writes, is that virtually all countries that developed rapidly "maintained policy regimes that would mark them as serious failures by neoliberal criteria…while many of the best pupils" have done quite poorly.[10]

Similar conclusions have been reached in other studies. To mention one, international economist David Felix shows that trade growth slowed in the neoliberal period in the rich (G-7) societies (with the sole exception of the United States, which had been well below the G-7 average). The same is true of growth of gross fixed investment. Capital flow of course sharply increased, but "the flows have been transferring ownership but little real resources on balance." Furthermore, "the growth of labor, capital, and total factor productivity have all fallen precipitously since the 1960s in the OECD [Organisation for Economic Co-operation and Development] countries."[11]

In brief, the twenty-five years of economic sovereignty, state-coordinated economic growth, and capital controls under the Bretton Woods system led to better social and economic results than the following twenty-five years of neoliberalism, by just about every relevant measure, and by significant margins. It is important to stress that the results include social indicators. In the United States, for example, growth during the Bretton Woods period was not only the highest ever over a lengthy period, but was also egalitarian. Real wages closely tracked increase in productivity, and social indicators closely tracked growth. That continued until the mid-1970s, when neoliberal policies began to be imposed. Growth continued, but gains were heavily skewed toward the rich, spectacularly so for the very rich. Productivity continued to increase, though more slowly, but real wages for the majority stagnated and the profits went into few pockets, increasingly so in the Bush II years. From 1980 to 1995, real wages for average American workers declined about 1 percent, far more sharply for those lower on the income ladder. A tech bubble raised wages in the late '90s, but after it burst, the stagnation and decline continued, worsening in the Bush years, which also left a long-lasting fiscal burden as a result of sharp tax cuts and war spending, greater than the effect of Obama-era stimulus and bailout, contrary to much fevered commentary. From 1975, social indicators began to decline, reaching the level of 1960 by the year 2000, the latest results available.[12]

The facts are sometimes obscured by the observation that conditions have generally improved under the neoliberal regime, but that is uninformative; conditions almost invariably improve over time by gross measures. Another way of obscuring the facts is by muddling export orientation with neoliberalism, so that if a billion Chinese experience high growth with high exports under policies that violate neoliberal principles, then the increase in average global growth rates can be hailed as a triumph of the principles that China violated. The harmful tendencies associated with neoliberal policies are consistent with economic history over a much longer term.

I mentioned that other factors intervene in the twentieth century in the rich industrial societies, to some extent before as well. The most important of them is the role of the state sector in the economy, often under the guise of "defense." Such measures have played a prominent role in technological and industrial development since the early days of the industrial revolution. That included major advances in metallurgy, electronics, machine tools, and manufacturing processes, including the American system of mass production that astounded nineteenth-century competitors and set the stage for the automotive industry and other manufacturing achievements, based in substantial part on many years of investment, research and development, and experience in weapons production within U.S. Army arsenals. Management of the most complex industrial system in the nineteenth century, railroads, was well beyond the capacities of private capital. It was therefore handed to the U.S. Army. A century ago, some of the hardest problems of electrical and mechanical engineering, and metallurgy, had to do with placing a huge gun on a moving platform aimed at another moving object—naval gunnery. In this case England and Germany were in the lead, and the advances made within the state sector soon spun off to private industry.[13]

These processes underwent a qualitative leap forward after World War II, this time primarily in the United States, as defense provided a cover for creation of the core of the modern high-tech economy: that includes computers and electronics generally, telecommunications and the Internet, automation, lasers, the commercial aviation industry (and with it tourism, a huge service industry), containers and therefore contemporary trade, and much else, now extending to pharmaceuticals and biotechnology as well as nanotechnology, neuroengineering, and other new frontiers. Economic historians have pointed out that the technical problems of naval armament a century ago were roughly comparable to manufacture of space vehicles, and the enormous impact on the civilian economy might be duplicated as well, enhanced by current space militarization projects—a major threat to survival, but a stimulus to the advanced economy. Public funding of research and development from the 1950s to the end of the century accounted for 50–70 percent of research and development, often under the guise of defense. The figures underestimate the reality, because they do not take account of the difference in R&D in the public and private sectors, the former typically more fundamental (hence with greater risk and cost and more significant long-

term impact), the latter tending to be more commercially oriented (consumer electronics, copycat drugs, etc.). It is hardly an exaggeration to say
that the much-praised "New Economy" is in large part a product of the
state sector. Nobel laureate Joseph Stiglitz writes that "a report by the
Council of Economic Advisers (conducted when I was its chair) found
that the returns on public investment in science and technology were far
higher than for private investment in these areas...than for conventional
[private] investment in plant and equipment."[14]

One effect of incorporating national security exemptions in the mislabeled "free trade agreements" is that the rich industrial societies, primarily the United States, can maintain the state sector, on which the
economy heavily relies to socialize cost and risk while privatizing profit.
For most of the world, the exemptions mean nothing.

Governments and business understand this very well. Germany at
first was critical of the missile defense programs, recognizing the dangers
they pose to survival. But German chancellor Gerhard Schroeder backed
away from his critical stance because, as he said, Germany would have a
"vital economic interest" in developing ballistic missile defense technology, and must be sure that "we are not excluded" from technological and
scientific work in the field, mostly subsidized by the U.S. taxpayer. Similarly, the U.S. trade organization lobbying for missile defense advised
Japanese officials in 1995 that this may be "the last military business opportunity for this century," so they had better come on board.[15] In the
new century, more advanced military programs provide many other opportunities for private capital to profit from public expenditures. All of
this enhances the threat to decent survival, but that has always been a secondary consideration.

The state sector is central to innovation and development not only
in national laboratories and universities, but also in many other ways:
subsidy to corporations, procurement, guaranteeing monopoly pricing
rights in the "free trade agreements," and other devices. The failure of the
economics profession to attend to these factors is sometimes startling,
perhaps similar to the myths about development that Bairoch and other
economic historians have discussed. Until the crash of the financial mar-

kets he administered in 2007–8, the world's most revered economist, I suppose, was Alan Greenspan, so let us take him as an example. In one of his orations on the miracles of the market, based on entrepreneurial initiative and consumer choice, he went beyond the usual rhetorical flourishes and gave actual examples: the Internet, computers, information processing, lasers, satellites, and transistors. The list is interesting: these are textbook examples of creativity and production taking place substantially in the public sector, mostly the Pentagon, in some cases for decades, with consumer choice approximately zero during the crucial development stages and entrepreneurial initiative mainly at the marketing end, and relying heavily throughout on the state sector to acquire technology and skills. The Internet was largely within the state sector for about thirty years before it was handed over to private capital in 1995. In the 1950s, computers were enormous, with vacuum tubes regularly blowing up, paper flowing all over with programs punched in, hours of wait for the simplest operation. When the Pentagon-financed systems were reaching the stage where they might soon be sold for profit, several of the leading engineers left the main government laboratory and founded DEC (Digital Equipment Corporation), which went on to become a primary driving force in the computer industry into the early 1980s, when personal computers became available. Meanwhile IBM was using Pentagon-funded computer systems to learn how to shift from punched cards to computers. IBM was able to manufacture the world's fastest computer in 1961, but its price tag was too high for the market, so it was sold to the government's Los Alamos laboratory. Procurement has regularly been a successful way for the public to subsidize private industry.[16]

Of the examples that Greenspan gives, the only one that does not come directly from the state sector is transistors. They were developed in a private laboratory, the Bell Telephone Laboratories, which also made major contributions to science over a broad range. But the role of markets in transistor development was slight. The parent corporation AT&T had a government-guaranteed monopoly on telephone service, so it could tax the public through high prices. Furthermore, the lab used wartime technology, again publicly subsidized and state-initiated. And for years high-performance transistors were too expensive for the private sector so they were purchased only by the military. When the AT&T monopoly was terminated, the great laboratory declined because of lack of public subsidy, and its successors now concentrate on short-term projects for profit.[17]

The role of the state is not just to create and protect high-tech industry. It also intervenes to overcome management failures. That became a serious problem again by the 1970s, as it had been during the development of railroads. The business world was becoming concerned over low rates of productivity and investment growth and the failure of U.S. management to keep up with more advanced foreign methods. The business press was calling for "the re-industrialisation of America." The military was once again called up to help. One major Pentagon program of the '70s, MANTECH (manufacturing technology), doubled its outlays as Reagan took over. One of its tasks was to design the "factory of the future," integrating computer technology and automation in production and design and developing flexible manufacturing technology and management efficiency, in an effort to catch up with Europe and Japan. The goal was to boost the market share and industrial leadership of U.S. industry in the traditional way, through state initiative and taxpayer funding. There was also a side benefit: the factory of the future could be designed to control the workforce. That is an old story. For example, automation and computer-controlled machine tools were developed in the public sector for a long period, then finally handed over to private industry. Within the state sector the technology was designed in a specific way: to de-skill workers and enhance management control. That choice was not inherent in the technology and does not appear to have been more profitable. But it is a powerful weapon in class war. The topic was well studied by then–MIT professor David Noble in important work.[18]

These programs expanded under the Reagan administration, which went beyond the norm in violating market principles for the rich, while excelling in elevated rhetoric about the need for market discipline for the poor. Under Reagan, Pentagon-supported research promoted new technologies in many areas, including supercomputers and information technology, further improvement of the Internet (which was initiated under Pentagon funding), and others. The Reagan administration also virtually doubled protective barriers, breaking all postwar records in protectionism. The purpose was to keep out superior Japanese products: steel, automotive, semiconductors, computers, and others. The goal was not only to save domestic industries that could not compete, but also to place them in a dominant position for the 1990s—now called a "triumph of the market," thanks in large measure to public subsidies, public sector innovation and development, protection, straight bailouts, and other devices.

It might be mentioned that Reaganite dedication to state intervention and protectionism also retraced the British experience. When British manufacturers could no longer compete with Japan, Britain abandoned its (partially rhetorical) love for free trade and closed off the empire to Japanese imports, as did the other Western powers in their smaller Asian empires. This is an important part of the background for World War II in the Pacific.

Radical state intervention in the economy continues to the present, now shifting toward the biology-based industries that are the cutting edge of the next phase of the economy and therefore have been receiving rapidly increasing state funding for R&D, though it declined under the Bush II administration, in part because of the administration's relative lack of concern for the health of the society as compared with the much greater imperatives of enriching the rich even further (for example, by huge tax cuts for the rich) and shaking their fist to intimidate the world.

The private sector is assisted by state intervention in other ways. One central component of the World Trade Organization rules, crafted by a few powerful states and the multinational corporations closely linked to them, is an array of provisions (TRIPS—trade-related aspects of intellectual property rights) to guarantee monopoly pricing to huge corporations by means of a patent regime that exceeds anything in history and would have seriously impeded economic development in the rich societies had it existed during their growth period. It serves primarily to enrich private corporations that rely heavily on the state sector for R&D. Economist Dean Baker, one of the few to have investigated the phenom-

enon carefully, concluded that if public funding for R&D for pharmaceuticals was increased to 100 percent and the corporations were compelled to sell at market prices, the savings to consumers would be
colossal—not to speak of the lives saved. But "really existing capitalism"
works in different ways. In recent years, U.S. negotiators have been seeking to extend monopoly pricing rights in bilateral agreements. The director of the World Health Organization in Thailand warned that
hundreds of thousands of Thai citizens would be put at risk if Thailand
accepted U.S. demands. He was abruptly transferred to a lesser position
in India. There are many similar examples.[19]

These are among the many reasons one should avoid such terms as
"free trade agreement." The states that design the agreements and impose
them on others are not in favor of free markets, or other forms of liberalization, except selectively, and for temporary advantage. Another reason
for avoiding the term is that much of what is called "trade" is an ideological
construction. In the old Soviet Union, if parts were produced in Leningrad,
sent to Poland for assembly, and sold in Moscow, borders would have been
crossed, but it was not called "trade" in Western commentary: rather, interactions within a command economy. And the same is true when GM
produces parts in Indiana, sends them to Mexico for assembly, and sells the
cars in New York. Since corporations are largely unaccountable to the public, the scale of such "trade" is unknown, but it is generally estimated at
about 40 percent of trade—higher for U.S.-Mexico—and if we include out-
sourcing and other forms of market distortions the percentage would rise
much higher. The concept of "trade" is further deprived of meaning when
we consider "trade in services," meaning privatization of services, a term
that includes just about anything of concern to people: education, health,
energy, water and other resources, etc. The term "trade" in this case is a euphemism for turning human life over to unaccountable state-supported
private tyrannies. And finally, the "agreements" are not agreements, at least
if people are considered to be part of their societies: the treaties are generally opposed by the populations, and therefore have to be established mostly
in secret, or under "fast track" provisions that provide the state executive
with Kremlin-style controls, with Congress given the right to say yes (and

in principle no, but without serious discussion or information), and with the public virtually excluded, thanks in part to media complicity.[20]

In the phrase "North American free trade agreement," the only accurate words are "North American."

At this point we are reaching the second of the two issues raised at the outset: neoliberalism as an enemy of democracy. While the evidence indicates that imposed liberalization has generally been harmful to development over history, causal relations can be debated even when there are striking correlations, because of limits of understanding and the complexity of factors. Much less so in the case of neoliberalism and democracy, however. Just about every element of the neoliberal package is an attack on democracy. In the case of privatization, that is true by definition: privatization transfers enterprises from the public to the private domain. In the public domain they are under some degree of public control, at least in principle; in more democratic societies, that could be a considerable degree, and in still more democratic societies, which barely yet exist, they would be under the direct control of "stakeholders": workers and communities. But the private domain is virtually unaccountable to the public in principle, except by regulatory mechanisms that are typically quite weak thanks to the overwhelming influence of concentrated private capital on the state.

Of these measures, the most severe attack on democracy is privatization of services. With services privatized, democratic institutions may exist but they will be mostly formalities, because the most important decisions that affect people's lives will have been removed from the public arena.

The argument for privatization is supposed to be efficiency. If the argument were valid, it would pose a conflict of values: efficiency versus freedom. But it is doubtful that the question even arises. As privatization became the mantra of the World Bank and IMF, a number of studies were undertaken to compare performance of private and public enterprises. One major study was carried out under the auspices of the UN Conference on Trade and Development by Cambridge University economists Ha-Joon Chang and Ajit Singh. They found what one might expect: in well-functioning societies, both private and public enterprise tend to be efficient; in societies that are more corrupt and function poorly, the same will be true of private and public enterprises.[21] In some areas the private sector performs much more poorly. In public enterprise in the industrial world, it would be hard to match the extraordinary corruption of Enron and WorldCom, or the extreme inefficiency of the health system in the United States, the only scarcely regulated privatized system among the industrial economies, with twice the per capita costs of others and some of the worst health outcomes, and the only one in which the government is barred by law from negotiating prices with pharmaceutical corporations—a "free market" policy extended by President Obama, bowing to the successful business campaign to undermine reforms that might cut into profit. Infant mortality in the United States has risen in the past few years to the level of Malaysia, just to mention one illustration. Actually "inefficiency" is not the right word. The health system is highly efficient in performing its institutional role of enriching investors.[22]

Chile is often hailed as the model of a free-market economy. It did indeed follow neoliberal rules after the Pinochet coup, when they could be imposed by violence, under the guidance of the famous "Chicago boys." Their mentors collected their Nobel Prizes while the economy collapsed and had to be bailed out by the state, which by 1982 controlled more of the economy than under Allende; the process was called "the Chicago road to socialism," international economist David Felix recalls. Economist Javier Santiso of the OECD Development Center terms it a "paradox" that "able economists committed to laissez-faire showed the world yet another road to a de facto socialized banking system"; no paradox, to those familiar with economic history. Chile did manage to recover, but by a complex mixture of market reliance and state intervention, including a form of capital control (violating the core principle of neoliberalism) and state ownership of the world's largest copper producer, Codelco, another radical violation of neoliberal principles, and the source of much of Chile's export earnings and the state's fiscal revenues. As the *Financial Times* observes, after the "catastrophic banking crisis of 1982, the product in part of economic policies pursued by the radical free-marketers known as the Chicago boys, [Chile] cooled its ideological fervor" and by the 1990s "controlled its exposure to world financial markets and maintained its efficient copper company in public hands," somewhat protecting itself from market disasters by these and other measures.[23]

It remains to look at the central doctrine of neoliberalism: financial liberalization, which began to take off from the early 1970s. Some of its effects are well known. There was a huge increase in speculative capital flows and countries were forced to set aside much larger reserves to protect currencies from attack, in both cases removing capital from productive use. It is striking, and well known, that countries that maintained capital controls avoided some of the worst financial crises (among them India, China, and Malaysia, during the Asian crisis of 1997–8). In the United States, the share of the financial sector in corporate profit rose from a few percent in the 1960s to over 30 percent in 2004. Concentration also sharply increased, thanks substantially to the deregulatory zeal of the Clinton administration, which set the stage for the doubling of the share of banking industry assets held by the twenty largest institutions to 70 percent from 1990 to 2009, helping create the "too big to fail" disaster of 2007–8. Financialization of the economy had a direct effect on the dismantling of the manufacturing sector, along with other policy decisions, such as the "trade agreements" that were designed to set manufacturing workers in competition with low-wage workers without benefits and protections elsewhere, while evading the "free trade" principle of competition in the case of highly educated professionals.[24]

The business press sometimes recognizes the dilemmas of the state-corporate economic policies—and also has few illusions about "free markets." In a cover story on the question "Can the Future Be Built in America?" *Business Week* outlines the basic problem. The United States, it reports, "is at or near the cutting edge in most of the emerging product areas. Indeed, the new wave of high-tech devices hitting the market is the payoff from billions of dollars in taxpayer-funded research at federal and university science labs stretching back to the 1960s." However, "the U.S. is losing its lead in large-scale high-tech manufacturing," because of lack of concern for manufacturing by corporate and state economic managers. The result is the "'invented here, industrialized elsewhere' syndrome," as the United States becomes "a big funnel of R&D for Asia."[25]

These are natural consequences of the financialization of the economy in an era of neoliberal globalization. For the "principal architects of policy," it is entirely reasonable to shift production abroad while the taxpayer funds R&D, and financial manipulations are concentrated at home. The effects on the society at large may be "grievous"—perhaps even long-term effects for the masters—but these are secondary matters at best, in accord with Adam Smith's maxim along with the institutional constraints on decision making in quasi-market systems in which inherent market inefficiencies are magnified by state-provided perverse incentives, matters to which we return.

Among the consequences is probably the greatest inequality in U.S. history. There is also a global analogue: the creation of what is called "plutonomy" in an upbeat analysis by Citigroup, a bank that is once again feeding at the public trough, as it has done regularly for thirty years in a cycle of risky loans, huge profits, crash, bailout. The bank's analysts describe a world that is dividing into two blocs—the plutonomy and the rest. The United States, UK, and Canada are the key plutonomies, economies in which growth is powered by, and largely consumed by, the wealthy few, joined by scattered islands of wealth elsewhere in a global plutonomy. In plutonomies, they write, there are rich consumers, few in number, but disproportionate in the gigantic slice of income and consumption they take. Then there are the "non-rich," the vast majority, who only account for surprisingly small bites of the national pie. Two-thirds of the world's economic growth, they estimate, is driven by consumption, primarily by the plutonomies, who of course monopolize profits as well.

The Citigroup analysts are providing advice to investors: investment strategy, they advise, should focus on the very rich, where the action is. Their "Plutonomy Stock Basket," as they call it, far outperformed the world index of developed markets since 1985, when the Reagan-Thatcher economic programs of enriching the very wealthy were really taking off. This is a substantial extension of the "80-20 rule" that is taught in business schools: 20 percent of your customers provide 80 percent of the profits, and you may be better off without the other 80 percent. The business press explained years ago that modern information technology—in large measure a gift from an unwitting public—allows corporations to identify profitable customers and provide them with grand treatment, while deliberately offering skimpy services to the rest, whose inquiries or complaints can be safely sidetracked, creating a profitable form of "consumer apartheid." The experience is familiar, and carries severe costs—how great when distributed over a large population, we don't know, because they are not included among the highly ideological measures of economic efficiency. Now this principle of economic rationality can be sharpened further and generalized worldwide, Citigroup cheerily proclaims.[26]

Sometimes the effects are surreal. It is finally dawning on the last holdouts in the business sector that the growing environmental crisis is severe. Even the *Wall Street Journal*, one of the most stalwart deniers, ran a supplement with dire warnings about the "climate disaster," urging that none of the options being considered may be sufficient and it may be necessary to undertake more radical measures of geoengineering, "cooling the planet" in some manner.[27] Many also understand that it will be necessary to reverse the vast state-corporate social engineering programs since World War II, designed to promote an energy-wasting and environmentally destructive fossil fuel–based economy, and that a central element of these changes will have to be development of efficient high-speed rail systems. It is revealing to see how the problem is being addressed.

The *Wall Street Journal* reported that "U.S. transportation chief [Ray Lahood] is in Spain meeting with high-speed rail suppliers.... Europe's engineering and rail companies are lining up for some potentially lucrative U.S. contracts for high-speed rail projects. At stake is $13 billion in stimulus funds that the Obama administration is allocating to upgrade existing rail lines and build new ones that could one day rival Europe's fastest.... [Lahood is also] expected to visit Spanish construction, civil engineering and train-building companies."[28]

Spain and other European countries are hoping to get U.S. taxpayer funding for the high-speed rail and related infrastructure that is badly needed in the United States. At the same time, Washington is busy dismantling leading sectors of U.S. industry, ruining the lives of the workforce and communities. It is difficult to conjure up a more damning indictment of the economic system that has been constructed by state-corporate managers. Surely U.S. manufacturing industries could be reconstructed to produce what the country needs, using its highly skilled work force—and what the world needs, and soon, if we are to have some hope of averting major catastrophe. It has been done before, after all. During World War II, industry was converted to wartime production and the semi-command economy not only ended the Depression, but initiated the most spectacular period of growth in economic history as the economy was retooled for war, also laying the basis for the "golden age" that followed.[29]

The state-corporate leadership has other commitments, but there is no reason for passivity on the part of the "stakeholders"—workers and community. With enough popular support they could take over the plants and carry out the task of conversion themselves. That is not a particularly radical proposal. One standard text on corporations points out that "nowhere is it written in stone that the short-term interests of corporate shareholders in the United States deserve a higher priority than all other corporate 'stakeholders.'" There have been some important concrete efforts. One was undertaken thirty years ago in Youngstown, Ohio, where U.S. Steel was about to shut down a major facility that was at the heart of the life of this steel town. There were substantial protests by the workforce and community, then an effort led by labor lawyer and activist Staughton Lynd to bring to the courts the principle that stakeholders should have the highest priority. The effort failed that time, but with enough popular support it could succeed.[30]

It is worth remembering that such ideas have deep roots in American history and culture. In the early days of the industrial revolution in New England, working people took it for granted that "those who work in the mills should own them." They also regarded wage labor as different from slavery only in that it was temporary—Abraham Lincoln's view as well. The leading twentieth-century social philosopher, John Dewey, basically agreed. Much like nineteenth-century working people, he called for elimination of "business for private profit through private control of banking, land, industry, reinforced by command of the press, press agents and other means of publicity and propaganda." Industry must be changed "from a feudalistic to a democratic social order" based on workers' control, free association, and federal organization, in the general style of a range of thought that includes, along with many anarchists, G. D. H. Cole's guild socialism and such left Marxists as Anton Pannekoek, Rosa Luxemburg, Paul Mattick, and others, including the late Seymour Melman, who studied the matter in some depth for many years. Unless those goals are attained, Dewey held, politics will remain "the shadow cast on society by big business, [and] the attenuation of the shadow will not change the substance." He held that without industrial democracy, political democratic forms will lack real content, and people will work "not freely and intelligently," but for pay, a condition that is "illiberal and immoral"—ideals that go back to the Enlightenment and classical liberalism before it was wrecked on the shoals of capitalism, as the anarchosyndicalist thinker Rudolf Rocker put it seventy years ago.[31]

There have been immense efforts to drive these thoughts out of people's heads—to win what the business world has called "the everlasting battle for the minds of men." On the surface, they seem to have succeeded. But such victories for the masters have often proven to be illusory in the past, and they might be again. If they are, then the question raised by *Business Week*—"Can the Future Be Built in America?"—might have an answer that would be part of a very different America, one that might realize promises of freedom and justice that have too long been suppressed.

Advocates of the radical shift toward financialization of the economy claim that there are compensating economic advantages, but again we get into murky areas, as mentioned earlier. However, the effect on democracy is immediately visible.

Financial liberalization creates what some international economists have called a "virtual Senate" of investors and lenders, who "conduct moment-by-moment referendums" on government policies. If the virtual Senate determines that the policies are irrational—meaning that they are designed to benefit people, not profit—then it can exercise its "veto power" by capital flight, attacks on currency, and other means. To mention one recent example, after Hugo Chávez was inaugurated, capital flight escalated to the point where capital held abroad by wealthy Venezuelans equaled one-fifth of Venezuela's GDP, Santiso reports, adding that after the U.S.-backed military coup in 2002 "the response of the markets approached euphoria" and the Caracas Exchange registered huge gains, collapsing when the elected government was restored by popular protests. In general, with capital flow liberalized, governments face a "dual constituency": voters and the virtual Senate. Even in the rich countries, the private constituency tends to prevail.[32]

Financial liberalization therefore serves as an effective curb on democracy. Perhaps it is coincidence, perhaps not, but it is worth noticing that financial liberalization was introduced along with the growing concern of elites over what they called the "crisis of democracy" of the 1960s,[33] when normally passive and obedient sectors of the society, often called the "special interests," began to enter the public arena to put forward their concerns. The result was called "excessive democracy" that was too much of an overload for the state, which could not attend properly to the "national interest." The special interests are women, workers, farmers, the young, the elderly, minorities, majorities—in fact, the general population. The "national interest" is defined by those who own and run the society. I am paraphrasing the liberal internationalist sector of elite opinion, those who staffed the Carter administration in the United States, and their counterparts in Europe and Japan. Farther to the right, and in the business world, the need to overcome the "crisis of democracy" was a still more pressing concern. Many measures have since been employed to purge society of the evil of democracy, right to the present. Financial liberalization made a potent contribution, whether by design or not.

Under powerful public pressure, such measures for undermining democracy were restricted under the Bretton Woods system established after World War II. The Great Depression and the war aroused radical democratic currents, taking many forms, from the antifascist resistance to working-class organization. These pressures made it possible—and from a different point of view, necessary—to permit social democratic policies. The Bretton Woods system was presumably designed in part for that purpose, with the understanding that capital controls and regulated currencies would create a space for government action responding to public will—for some measure of democracy, that is. Keynes considered the most important achievement of Bretton Woods to be establishment of the right of governments to restrict capital movement. In dramatic contrast, in the neoliberal phase that followed, the U.S. Treasury Department now regards free capital mobility as a "fundamental right," unlike such alleged "rights" as those guaranteed by the Universal Declaration of Human Rights: health, education, decent employment, security, and other rights that the Reagan and Bush administrations dismissed as "letters to Santa Claus," "preposterous," mere "myths."[34]

In earlier years the public had not been much of a problem. The reasons are reviewed by economist Barry Eichengreen in his standard history of the international monetary system. He observes that in the nineteenth century, governments had not yet been "politicized by universal male suffrage and the rise of trade unionism and parliamentary labor parties." Therefore the severe costs imposed by the virtual Senate of lenders and investors could be transferred to the general population. But with the radicalization of the general public during the Great Depression and the antifascist war, that luxury was no longer available to private power and wealth. Hence in the Bretton Woods system, "limits on capital mobility substituted for limits on democracy as a source of insulation from market pressures."[35] It is only necessary to add the obvious corollary: with the dismantling of the system from the 1970s, functioning democracy is restricted. It therefore becomes necessary to divert and control the public in some fashion, processes that are particularly evident in the more business-run societies like the United States, a topic that I will have to put to the side despite its extreme importance.

In Latin America, specialists and polling organizations observed for some years that extension of formal democracy was accompanied by increasing disillusionment about democracy and "lack of faith" in democratic institutions. A persuasive explanation for these disturbing tendencies was given by Argentinian political scientist Atilio Boron, who pointed out

that the new wave of democratization in Latin America coincided with neoliberal economic "reforms," which undermine effective democracy. The
phenomenon extends worldwide, in various forms. It appears that the ten-
dency may have reversed in recent years with departures from neoliberal
orthodoxy and other developments discussed earlier.[36]

The annual polls on Latin American opinion by the Chilean polling
agency Latinobarómetro, and their reception in the West, are interesting
in this respect. Few doctrines of reigning Western orthodoxy are upheld
with more fervor than the principle that Hugo Chávez is a tyrant dedicated to destruction of democracy. The polls are therefore a serious annoyance, which have to be overcome by the usual device: suppression.
The November 2007 poll had the same irritating results as in the preceding few years. Venezuela ranked second behind Uruguay in satisfaction
with democracy and third in satisfaction with leaders. It ranked first in
assessment of the current and future economic situation, equality and
justice, and education standards. True, it ranked only eleventh in favoring
a market economy, but even with this flaw, overall it ranked highest in
Latin America on matters of democracy, justice, and optimism, far above
U.S. favorites Colombia, Peru, Mexico, and Chile.

Latin America analyst Mark Turner writes that he "found an almost
total English speaking blackout about the results of this important snapshot of [Latin American] views and opinions," as had been the case in
earlier years. He also found the usual exception: there were reports of the
finding that Chávez is about as unpopular as Bush in Latin America, a
fact that will come as little surprise to those who are familiar with the bitterly hostile coverage to which Chávez is subjected in the media, in the
Venezuelan press as well, an odd feature of this looming dictatorship.[37]

In the United States, faith in institutions has been declining steadily,
and for good reasons. A considerable gulf has developed between public
opinion and public policy, rarely reported, though people can hardly fail
to be aware that their policy choices are disregarded. It is interesting to
compare near-simultaneous recent presidential elections in the richest
country of the world and the poorest country in South America. In the
2004 U.S. presidential election, voters had a choice between two men born

to wealth and privilege, who attended the same elite university, joined the same secret society where privileged young men are trained to take their place in the ruling class, and were able to run in the election because they were supported by pretty much the same conglomerations of private power. Their announced programs were similar, consistent with the needs of their primary constituency: wealth and privilege. Studies of public opinion revealed that on a host of major issues, both parties were well to the right of the general population, the Bush Republicans sharply so. In part for these reasons, party managers generally displace issues from the electoral agenda. Few voters even knew the stand of the candidates on issues. Candidates are packaged and sold like toothpaste and cars and lifestyle drugs, and by the same industries dedicated to delusion and deceit.

Furthermore, the destruction of democracy is highly regarded. In the most liberal daily paper of the country, a leading consultant to the Democratic Party presented his advice for the November 2006 congressional elections. Democrats, he wrote, must realize, as Republicans do, that "politics is not about issues. Politics is about identity. The candidates and parties that win are not those aligning their positions most precisely with a majority of the electorate. The winners are those who form a positive image in the public mind of who they are (and a negative image of who their opponents are)." What is important is "symbolism and narrative to shape what the public thinks about," just as in marketing other commodities.[38]

His advice was followed in the next presidential campaign, a matter to which we return.

Consider in contrast the December 2005 election in the poorest country in South America, Bolivia. Voters were familiar with the issues, and they were very real and important ones: control of resources, cultural rights for the indigenous majority, problems of justice in a complex multiethnic society, and many others. Voters chose someone from their own ranks, not a representative of narrow sectors of privilege. There was real participation, extending over years of intense struggle and organization. Election day was not just a brief interlude for pushing a lever and then retreating to passivity and private concerns, but one phase in ongoing participation in the workings of the society.

The comparison, and it is not the only one, raises some questions about where programs of democracy promotion are needed.

Latin America has real choices, for the first time in its history. The traditional modalities of imperial control—violence and economic strangulation—are much more limited than before. There are lively and vibrant popular organizations providing the essential basis for meaningful democracy. Latin American and other former colonies have enormous internal problems, and there are sure to be many setbacks, but there are promising developments as well. It is in these parts of the world that today's democratic wave finds its basis and its home. That is why the World Social Forum has met in Porto Alegre, Mumbai, Caracas, Nairobi, not in northern cities, though by now the global forum has spawned many regional and local social forums, doing valuable work geared to problems of particular significance in their own regions. The former colonies, in Latin America in particular, have a better chance now than ever before to overcome centuries of subjugation, violence, repression, and foreign intervention, which they have so far survived as dependencies with islands of luxury in a sea of misery. These are exciting prospects for Latin America, and if the hopes can be realized, even partially, the results cannot fail to have a large-scale global impact as well.

FOUR

Latin American and Caribbean Unity

During the past decade, Latin America has become the most exciting region of the world. The dynamic has in part flowed from right where you are meeting at the Social Summit in Caracas, after the election of a leftist president committed to using Venezuela's rich resources for the benefit of the population rather than for wealth and privilege at home and abroad, and to promoting the regional integration that is so desperately needed as a prerequisite for independence, for democracy, and for meaningful development. The initiatives taken in Venezuela have had a significant impact throughout the subcontinent, what has now come to be called "the pink tide." The impact is revealed within the individual countries, most recently with the election of Fernando Lugo in Paraguay; and in the regional institutions that are in the process of formation. Among these are the Banco del Sur, an initiative that was endorsed in Caracas a year ago by Nobel laureate in Economics Joseph Stiglitz; and the ALBA, the Bolivarian Alternative for Latin America and the Caribbean, which might prove to be a true dawn if its initial promise can be realized.

The ALBA is often described as an alternative to the U.S.-sponsored "Free Trade Area of the Americas," though the terms are misleading. It should be understood to be an independent development, not an alternative. And, furthermore, the so-called free trade agreements have only a limited relation to free trade, or even to trade in any serious sense of that term; and they are certainly not agreements, at least among populations. A more accurate term would be "investor-rights arrangements," designed by multinational corporations and banks and the powerful states that cater to their interests, established mostly in secret, without public participation or awareness and often over public opposition.

Another regional organization that is beginning to take shape is UNASUR, the Union of South American Nations. This continental bloc, modeled on the European Union, aims to establish a South American parliament in Cochabamba, Bolivia, a fitting site for the UNASUR parliament. Cochabamba was not well known internationally before the water wars of 2000. But in that year events in Cochabamba became an inspiration for people throughout the world who are concerned with freedom, justice, and elementary human rights, as a result of the courageous and successful popular struggle against privatization of water, which awakened international solidarity and was a fine and encouraging demonstration of what can be achieved by committed activism.

The aftermath has been even more remarkable. Bolivia has forged an impressive path to true democratization in the hemisphere, with large-scale popular initiatives and meaningful participation of the organized majority of the population in establishing a government and shaping its programs on issues of great importance and popular concern, an ideal that is rarely approached elsewhere, surely not in the colossus of the North, despite much inflated rhetoric by doctrinal managers.

Much the same had been true fifteen years earlier in Haiti, the only country in the hemisphere that surpasses Bolivia in poverty—and like Bolivia, was the source of much of the wealth of the West. In 1990, Haiti's first free election took place, a stunning victory for democracy, as already discussed, quickly reversed with U.S. support. Washington finally permitted the elected president to return, but only on the condition that he adhere to harsh neoliberal rules that were guaranteed to crush what remained of the economy, as they did. And in 2004, the imperial powers that had destroyed Haiti, France and the United States, joined to remove the elected president from office once again, launching a new regime of terror, though the people remain unvanquished and the popular struggle continues despite extreme adversity. All of this is familiar in Latin America, not least in Bolivia, the scene of Latin America's most intense confrontation at this moment between popular democracy and traditional U.S.-backed elites.

Sixty years ago, U.S. planners regarded Bolivia and Guatemala as the greatest threats to its domination of the hemisphere. In both cases, Washington succeeded in overthrowing the popular governments, but in different ways.

In Guatemala, Washington resorted to the standard technique of violence, installing one of the world's most brutal and vicious regimes, which extended its criminality to virtual genocide in the highlands during Reagan's terrorist wars of the 1980s.

While in Guatemala the Eisenhower administration overcame the threat of democracy and independent development by violence; in Bolivia, it achieved much the same results by exploiting Bolivia's economic dependence on the United States, particularly for processing Bolivia's tin exports. Stephen Zunes, one of the leading scholarly analysts of these matters, points out that "at a critical point in the nation's effort to become more self-sufficient [in the early 1950s], the U.S. government forced Bolivia to use its scarce capital not for its own development, but to compensate the former mine owners and repay its foreign debts."[1]

The economic policies forced on Bolivia in those years were a precursor of the structural adjustment programs imposed on the continent thirty years later, under the terms of the neoliberal "Washington consensus," which has generally had harmful effects wherever its strictures have been observed. By now, the victims of neoliberal market fundamentalism are coming to include the rich countries, where financial liberalization is bringing about the worst financial crisis since the Great Depression of the 1930s and leading to massive state intervention in a desperate effort to rescue collapsing financial institutions.

We should note that this is a regular feature of contemporary state capitalism, though the scale today is unprecedented. A study by two international economists fifteen years ago found that at least twenty companies in the Fortune 100 would not have survived if they had not been saved by their respective governments, and that many of the rest gained substantially by demanding that governments "socialize their losses." Such government intervention "has been the rule rather than the exception over the past two centuries," they conclude from a detailed analysis. That is apart from the crucial state role, particularly in the post–World War II period, in socializing the costs and risks of R&D while privatizing profit.[2]

We might also take note of the striking similarity between the structural adjustment programs imposed on the weak by the IMF and the huge financial bailout that is on the front pages today in the North. The U.S. executive director of the IMF, adopting an image from the Mafia, described the institution as "the credit community's enforcer."[3] Under the rules of the Western-run international economy, investors make loans to third world tyrannies, and since the loans carry considerable risk, make high profits. Suppose the borrower defaults. In a capitalist economy, the lenders would incur the loss. But existing capitalism really functions quite differently. If the borrowers cannot pay the debts, then the IMF steps in to guarantee that lenders and investors are protected. The debt is transferred to the poor population of the debtor country, who never borrowed the money in the first place and gained little if anything from it. The method is called "structural adjustment." And taxpayers in the rich country, who also gained nothing from the loans, sustain the IMF through their taxes. These doctrines do not derive from economic theory; they merely reflect the distribution of decision-making power.

The designers of the international economy sternly demand that the poor accept market discipline, but they ensure that they themselves are protected from its ravages, a useful arrangement that goes back to the origins of modern industrial capitalism and played a large role in dividing the world into rich and poor societies, the first and third worlds.

This wonderful anti-market system designed by self-proclaimed market enthusiasts is now being implemented in the United States to deal with the very ominous crisis of financial markets. In general, markets have well-known inefficiencies. One is that transactions do not take into account the effect on others who are not party to them. These so-called externalities can be huge. That is particularly so in the case of financial institutions. Their task is to take risks, and if well managed, to ensure that potential losses to themselves will be covered. To themselves. Under capitalist rules, it is not their business to consider the cost to others. Risk is underpriced, because systemic risk is not priced into decisions. That leads to repeated crisis, naturally. This inherent deficiency of markets is well known. Ten years ago, at the height of the euphoria about efficient markets, two prominent economists, John Eatwell and Lance Taylor, wrote an important book in which they spelled out the consequences of these market inefficiencies and suggested means to deal with them. At the same time, international economist David Felix warned that "the increasing frequency of financial crises [during the period of financial liberalization] could terminate in an uncontrollable one."[4] Such voices were unheard during the deregulatory rage that was then consuming the Clinton administration, under the leadership of those whom Obama has now called upon to put Band-Aids on the disaster they helped create.

After the predicted disaster occurred, an "emerging consensus" developed among economists "on the need for macroprudential supervision" of financial markets, that is, "paying attention to the stability of the financial system as a whole and not just its individual parts." Two prominent international economists added that "there is growing recognition that our financial system is running a doomsday cycle. Whenever it fails, we rely on lax money and fiscal policies to bail it out. This response teaches the financial sector: take large gambles to get paid handsomely, and don't worry about the costs—they will be paid by taxpayers" through bailouts and lost jobs, and the financial system "is thus resurrected to gamble again—and to fail again." The system is a "doom loop," in the words of the official of the Bank of England responsible for financial stability.[5]

One might say "better late than never," except that the chances of any meaningful financial regulation appear to be dim, given the grip of the financial industry on the government, matters to which we return.

When crises hit the South, the masters of the international economy turn to the IMF solution. The costs are transferred to the public, which had nothing to do with the risky choices but is now compelled to pay the costs: the poor countries are instructed to raise interest rates, slow the economy, pay their debts (to the rich), privatize (so that the Western corporations can buy their assets), and suffer. The instructions for the rich are virtually the opposite: lower interest rates, stimulate the economy, forget about debts, consume, have the government take over (but don't "nationalize"—the takeover is a temporary measure to hand it back to the owners in better shape). And the public has almost no voice in determining these outcomes, any more than poor peasants have a voice in being subjected to cruel structural adjustment programs.

Others do have a voice, and well-established practice is a good guide as to where to look and listen. The best guide I know of is political economist Thomas Ferguson's "investment theory of politics," mentioned above, the thesis that to a good first approximation, we can understand elections to be occasions in which groups of investors coalesce to control the state, a very good predictor of policy over a long period, as he shows. For 2008, we would therefore anticipate that the interests of the financial industries, the major funders (who preferred Obama to McCain), would be "most peculiarly attended to" by government policy, in accord with Adam Smith's maxim. And so we find.

For the world, there are many very serious crises, such as the food crisis, already mentioned, or the environmental crisis, which threatens real catastrophe for everyone. But for the West in 2008–9, the phrase "the crisis" refers unambiguously to the financial crisis that has its deeper roots in inherent market inefficiencies, neoliberal doctrines about the alleged value of financial liberalization, dogmas about "efficient markets" and "rational expectations,"[6] deregulation, exotic financial instruments that yielded profits beyond the dreams of avarice for a few—all brought to a head by an $8 trillion housing bubble that somehow regulators and economists did not perceive, portending ultimate disaster, as a few warned all along, notably economist Dean Baker.

The costs of underpricing of risk are magnified by the perverse incentives designed by policy makers, primary among them the government insurance policy called "too big to fail." After the bursting of the housing bubble in 2007, Fed chairman Alan Greenspan was criticized because he hadn't followed through on his brief warning about "irrational exuberance" at the height of the late '90s tech bubble. But that is the wrong criticism: it was quite *rational* exuberance, when the taxpayer is there to bail you out under the operative principles of state capitalism. The doctrine has been observed with precision by Obama and his advisers—selected from the leading figures who were largely responsible for creating the crisis, while excluding those, among them Nobel laureates, who had been issuing warnings about it. And the doctrine appears to have worked very well. The big financial institutions that were the immediate culprits have been making out like bandits, bigger than ever, reporting great profits and paying huge bonuses to the culprits, enjoying even a more lavish government insurance policy, and therefore encouraged to set the stage for the next and worse crisis. That is recognized, but the managers who play by the rules cannot really be criticized. These are institutional decisions. Managers either play the game, or someone else replaces them who will.

As for those who are too small to matter, they suffer. That includes the general population, whose real wages have stagnated for thirty years while benefits decline, and now face huge unemployment and loss of their homes. It also includes the banks that serve the public, going under while those that engage in risky investments and reap enormous profits are doing just fine, thanks to the nanny state they largely control.

In theory, inherent market inefficiencies and perverse incentives could be overcome by efficient regulation. But the same deep-seated tendencies that concentrate wealth and power in private tyrannies reduce the likelihood of such steps. In late 2009 there seemed to be one faint hope that Congress might institute some meaningful regulation: proposals by Senator Christopher Dodd, chair of the Senate Banking Committee. But Dodd succumbed to Wall Street pressure and abandoned his proposal in December 2009. One of its components was a new Consumer Financial Protection Agency intended to "crack down on abusive and risky lending practices that helped fuel last year's financial crisis," Michael Kranish commented in a rare press report. "Banks and other financial institutions have fought hard to kill the proposal," he adds. And succeeded. He quotes Elizabeth Warren, the Harvard Law professor who originated the idea for the agency: "When all the dust settles, the real question for the history books will be whether Congress was able to create an independent consumer agency with the tools necessary to end abusive practices and to prevent future crises." The answer appears to be a loud no, in our business-run democracy.

More generally, Kranish observes, "despite being portrayed as responsible for myriad national ills, Wall Street bankers, oil and coal companies, and health industry executives bounced back in Congress this year with remarkable success, stalling or weakening the biggest regulatory threats on President Obama's domestic agenda," after a $1 billion lobbying blitz. The decline of the threat of financial regulation coincided with a "major victory" of the insurance industry "when Democratic leaders scuttled a government insurance option" in the health care reform plan—incidentally, overruling support for the measure by a considerable majority of the population.[7]

In a narrow sense, the financial crisis will presumably be patched up somehow or other, but leaving the institutions that created it pretty much in place. There are many indications. Thus in June 2009, the Treasury Department permitted early repayments of its TARP loans to banking institutions, which reduces their capacity to lend, as was immediately pointed out, though it allows the banks to pour money into pockets of the few who matter. The mood on Wall Street was captured by two Bank of New York Mellon employees, who "predicted their lives—and pay— would improve, even if the broader economy did not."[8]

Financial institutions are exulting that talk of reform has been effectively beaten back. "The likely result" of the huge public bailout, the business press predicts, will be "a package of worthy but lukewarm reforms that leave the global financial system—and taxpayers—exposed to another costly bust some years down the road." The most powerful may in the end gain the most. "The crisis may be turning out very well for many of the behemoths that dominate U.S. finance," the press reports: "A series of federally arranged mergers safely landed troubled banks on the decks of more stable firms. And it allowed the survivors to emerge from the turmoil with strengthened market positions, giving them even greater control over consumer lending and more potential to profit," and with even better opportunities to take risks and gain profits without concern for the consequences of failure, thanks to the government insurance policy.

Martin Wolf of the *Financial Times*, the media's most respected financial commentator, writes that the financial system was saved from "an abyss" only by massive robbery of taxpayers to pay off the financial sector's creditors—a decision that was "quite unbearable," but "also correct," given the alternative. The lesson learned "is that every systemically significant institution must be rescued in a crisis," though "we cannot let stand the doctrine that systemically significant institutions are too big or interconnected to be allowed to fail in the crisis." In brief, a shocking indictment of financial liberalization. This virtual contradiction could, he believes, be overcome by "pre-emptive tightening," the proposal of former chief economist of the Bank of International Settlements, William White: measures to compel the financial institutions to control their profit-seeking in advance. In a socioeconomic system where even mild regulatory measures are easily beaten back, the proposal, however necessary, has about as much chance of realization as significant measures to prevent environmental catastrophe.[9]

The reasons are similar. Business executives understand as well as other educated elites that the world is heading toward environmental catastrophe if no serious steps are taken to avert it. Nevertheless, they are dedicated to bringing about this result. They put huge efforts into convincing the public to reject what they know to be true and ominous. And they are successful, as polls illustrate. An enormous business-backed propaganda campaign is surely a factor in the very sharp decline of concern among Americans over global warming, to the point where by late 2009, barely one-third believe that it is influenced by human activity.[10] The standard explanation for the willingness of business executives to dismiss the fate of their grandchildren and even to destroy what they own is that short-term profits outweigh long-term considerations. That is not false: as noted earlier, institutional structures virtually require conformity to that principle. But the answer is incomplete. Once again, the choice results from fundamental market inefficiencies: the pressure to ignore the impact on others in undertaking transactions, if one wants to stay in the game. In this case, the externalities happen to be the fate of the species, but the logic is the same.

A more general conclusion is that markets may more or less work for a while, but unless sharply constrained they almost necessarily lead to disaster. And constraints are unlikely when major media are often adjuncts of business, the government is largely in its pocket, and the general public is marginalized in one way or another, and susceptible to manipulation.

The success of the health care industry in 2009 in blocking meaningful reform of the notoriously inefficient and expensive U.S. health care system, to which we return, did not pass unnoticed. Within weeks the energy-intensive industries, which had been pouring funds into lobbying against bills that might regulate fossil-fuel use and emissions, adopted the successful model of the insurance industry. They began organizing public rallies with employees bused in by the companies, portrayed as "citizens' movements" that are protesting government efforts to undermine the unconstrained use of oil, a principle that "we hold dear [and is] our future," in the words of a rodeo announcer recruited to express the will of the public—who happen to favor the measures the industries are opposing, but that is another footnote. The campaign is supported by the major business lobbies—the National Association of Manufacturers, the American Petroleum Institute, and the U.S. Chamber of Commerce—which mounted an expensive campaign of ads and rallies to try to win over key senators, particularly the "moderate Democrats," so-called: Republicans reliably follow instructions. In this case the efforts will not just break the bank but may also lead to environmental catastrophe, but profits for the next quarter (leading to huge bonuses for the CEOs) far outrank any such improper thoughts, and institutional structures virtually dictate such outcomes unless an aroused public intervenes.

One of the PR agencies hired to promote the cause, Bonner & Associates, conceded that letters they were sending "purported to be from groups like the National Association for the Advancement of Colored People and Hispanic organizations" were in fact forgeries. The "error" was quickly forgiven. That is quite unlike the treatment of ACORN, which works for the poor and oppressed and was virtually destroyed when some of its poorly paid employees were caught in a scam set up by a right-wing organization. And of course the major corporate brigands, like those ripping off billions of dollars for "reconstructing Iraq," are exempt even from censure.[11]

No less impressive is the assault of the financial institutions on regulation of the practices that led to the near-collapse of the international economy in 2007–8, and are now even better placed for the next chapter of "rational exuberance," with the world's ten largest banks, all "deemed 'too big to fail,'" having increased their share of assets from 18 percent of the top 1,500 banks at the end of 2008 to 26 percent a year later. The measures by which they ensured that the "moderate Democrats"—that is, the "pro-business Democrats" whose "ties to Wall Street are strong"—would join the Republicans in blocking any serious regulation at the behest of the major business lobbies are spelled out in a *Business Week* cover story, aptly entitled "In Wall Street's Pocket: The Inside Story of Who's Really Running Financial Regulation."[12] No one answerable to the public, surely.

Recalling the "dismal truth" that "nothing succeeds like failure," economics correspondent Gretchen Morgenson observes that "even though calamitous lending practices laid waste to the nation's economy, surprisingly little has changed about how the financial arena operates and is supervised. Sure, a couple of venerable brokerage firms have vanished, but many of the same players remain on the scene, in the same positions of power." As for the regulators, the "senior regulators who stood idly by for years as financial firms built their houses of cards have been rewarded with even bigger jobs or are jockeying for increased responsibilities. The Federal Reserve Board, for example, wants to become the financial system's uber-regulator, even though its officials did nothing as banks made deadly decisions to lend recklessly and leverage themselves to the max."[13]

The chair of the prestigious law firm Sullivan & Cromwell is very likely right in predicting that "Wall Street, after getting billions of taxpayer dollars, will emerge from the financial crisis looking much the same as before markets collapsed."[14]

Only the naïve should be surprised.

A basic principle of modern state capitalism is that cost and risk are socialized to the extent possible, while profit is privatized. That principle extends far beyond financial institutions, the current focus after the financial meltdown of 2007–8. But much the same is true for the entire advanced economy, which, as discussed earlier, relies extensively on the state for innovation, R&D, procurement when purchasers are unavailable, direct bailouts, and numerous other benefits. Furthermore, financial liberalization has effects well beyond the economy. It has long been understood that it is a powerful weapon against democracy, for reasons already reviewed.

There are some encouraging signs elsewhere, at least. Germany and Spain are well in the lead in development and use of solar energy, and China, though it remains a very poor country with enormous internal problems, is dedicating substantial resources to a "green revolution" and may soon surpass them. It already makes one-third of the world's solar cells, is in the lead in mass production of electric cars and the latest generation of "clean coal" power stations, and is predicted to surpass the United States as the largest market for wind turbines. China is also providing the most successful model for financial institutions, Martin Wolf concludes: "China has emerged as the most significant winner from the financial and economic crisis" because of its successful management—and not coincidentally, it rejected the financial liberalization of the neoliberal era.[15]

The primary victims of military terror and economic strangulation are the poor and weak, within the rich countries themselves and far more brutally in the South. But there are significant signs of change. In South America and elsewhere there are promising efforts to bring about desperately needed structural and institutional changes. And not surprisingly, these efforts to promote democracy, social justice, and cultural rights are facing harsh challenges from the traditional rulers, at home and internationally.

For the first time in half a millennium, South America is beginning to take its fate into its own hands. There have been attempts before, but they have been crushed by outside force, in cases too numerous and too familiar to review. But there are now significant departures from a long and shameful history. The departures are symbolized by the UNASUR crisis summit in Santiago in September 2008. At the summit, the presidents of the South American countries issued a strong statement of support for the elected Morales government, which was under attack by the traditional rulers: privileged Europeanized elites who bitterly oppose Bolivian democracy and social justice and, routinely, enjoy U.S. backing. The South American leaders gathered at the UNASUR summit declared "their full and firm support for the constitutional government of President Evo Morales, whose mandate was ratified by a big majority"—referring to his overwhelming victory in the recent referendum. Morales thanked UNASUR for its support, observing that "for the first time in South America's history, the countries of our region are deciding how to resolve our problems, without the presence of the United States."[16]

A matter of no slight significance.

The significance of the UNASUR support for democracy in Bolivia is underscored by the fact that the leading media in the United States scarcely reported what happened, or not at all, though editors and correspondents surely knew all about it. Ample information was available on wire services.

That has been a familiar pattern. To cite just one example, the important Cochabamba declaration of South American leaders in December 2006, calling for moves toward integration on the model of the European Union, apparently passed unreported by U.S. media.[17] There are many other cases, all illustrating the same fear among the political class and economic centers in the United States that the hemisphere is slipping from their control.

Current developments in South America are of historic significance for the continent and its people. It is well understood in Washington that these developments threaten not only its domination of the hemisphere, but also its global dominance. Control of Latin America was the earliest goal of U.S. foreign policy, tracing back to the earliest days of the republic, with ambitious expectations already discussed. Though the more extreme aspirations, those of Jefferson, for example, were not achieved, nevertheless control of Latin America has remained a central policy goal, partly for resources and markets, but also for broader ideological and geostrategic reasons.

As already discussed, the Nixon administration regarded control of Latin America as a necessary condition for establishing a "successful order elsewhere in the world," while devoting itself to barring a successful social democracy in Chile that could be a model for others. Nixon's right-hand man Henry Kissinger warned that success for democratic socialism in Chile might have reverberations as far as southern Europe—not because Chilean hordes would descend on Madrid and Rome, but because success might inspire popular movements to achieve their goals by means of parliamentary democracy, an ideal upheld as an abstract value in the West, but with crucial reservations. In Nixon's own words, "Our main concern in Chile is the prospect that [Allende] can consolidate himself and the picture projected to the world will be his success.... If we let the potential leaders in South America think they can move like Chile and have it both ways, we will be in trouble.... No impression should be permitted in Latin America that they can get away with this, that it's safe to go this way. All over the world it's too much the fashion to kick us around." Even mainstream scholarship recognizes that Washington has supported democracy if and only if it contributes to strategic and economic interests, a policy that continues without change through all administrations, to the present.[18]

These pervasive concerns are the rational form of the domino theory, sometimes more accurately called "the threat of a good example." For such reasons, even the tiniest departure from strict obedience is regarded as an existential threat that calls for a harsh response: peasant organizing in remote communities of northern Laos, fishing cooperatives in Grenada, and so on throughout the world. It is necessary to ensure that the "virus" of successful independent development does not "spread contagion" elsewhere, that a "rotten apple" does not "spoil the barrel," in the terminology of the highest-level planners.

Such concerns have motivated U.S. military intervention, terrorism, and economic warfare throughout the post–World War II era, in Latin America and throughout much of the world. These are leading features of the Cold War. The superpower confrontation regularly provided pretexts, mostly fraudulent, much as the junior partner in world control appealed to the threat of the West when it crushed popular uprisings in its much narrower Eastern European domains.

But times are changing. In Latin America, there are important moves toward integration, which has several dimensions. One is regional: moves to strengthen ties among the South American countries of the kind I mentioned. These are now just beginning to reach to Central America, which was so utterly devastated by Reagan's terror wars that it had mostly stayed on the sidelines since, but is now beginning to move—and also eliciting familiar reactions. Of particular significance are recent developments in Honduras, the classic "banana republic" and Washington's major base for its terrorist wars in the region in the 1980s. Washington's ambassador to Honduras, John Negroponte, was one of the leading terrorist commanders of the period, and accordingly was appointed head of counterterrorist operations by the Bush II administration, a choice eliciting no comment. In an unexpected development, President Manuel Zelaya not only raised the minimum wage and carried out other internal reforms, but also declared that U.S. aid does not "make us vassals" or give Washington the right to humiliate the nation, and began to improve ties with Venezuela, joining the Venezuelan-subsidized oil program Petrocaribe, then the ALBA as well.[19]

The elite reaction was not long in coming. In June 2009, the president was ousted in a military coup and expelled to Costa Rica. As observed by economist Mark Weisbrot, an experienced analyst of Latin American affairs, the social structure of the coup is "a recurrent story in Latin America," pitting "a reform president who is supported by labor unions and social organizations against a mafia-like, drug-ridden, corrupt political elite who is accustomed to choosing not only the Supreme Court and the Congress, but also the president."[20] The aftermath we have already reviewed.

Regional integration of the kind that has been slowly proceeding for several years is a crucial prerequisite for independence, making it more difficult to pick off countries one by one. For that reason it is causing considerable distress in Washington, and is either ignored or regularly distorted in commentary.

A second form of integration is global: the establishment of South-South relations, and the diversification of markets and investment, with China a growing and particularly significant participant in hemispheric affairs. Again, these developments undercut Washington's ability to control what Secretary of War Henry Stimson called "our little region over here" at the end of World War II, when he was explaining that other regional systems must be dismantled, while our own must be strengthened.

The third and in many ways most vital form of integration is internal. Latin America is notorious for its extreme concentration of wealth and power, and the lack of responsibility of privileged elites for the welfare of the nation. It is instructive to compare Latin America with East Asia, as already discussed. Needless to say, development of the East Asian style is hardly a model to which Latin America, or any other region, should aspire. The problems of developing truly democratic societies, based on popular control of social, economic, political, and cultural institutions, and overturning structures of hierarchy and domination, remain a serious challenge, posing formidable and essential tasks for the future.

The problems of Latin America and the Caribbean have global roots, and have to be addressed by regional and global solidarity along with internal struggle. The growth of the social forums, first in South America, now elsewhere, has been one of the most encouraging steps forward in recent years. These developments might bear the seeds of the first authentic International, heralding an era of true globalization: international integration in the interests of people, not investors and other concentrations of power. Those taking part in this Social Summit today are right at the heart of these dramatic developments, an exciting opportunity, a difficult challenge, a responsibility of historic proportions.

PART II

North America

FIVE

"Good News," Iraq and Beyond

Not long before the presidential campaign of 2008, it was taken for granted that the Iraq war would be the central issue, as it was in the midterm election of 2006. But it virtually disappeared, eliciting some puzzlement. There should have been none.

Iraq remained a significant concern for the population, but that is a matter of little moment in a modern democracy. The important work of the world is the domain of the "responsible men," who must "live free of the trampling and the roar of a bewildered herd," the general public, "ignorant and meddlesome outsiders" whose "function" is to be "spectators," not "participants." And spectators are not supposed to bother their heads with issues. The *Wall Street Journal* came close to the point in a major front-page article on "Super Tuesday" (February 5, 2008, the day of many primaries), under the heading "Issues Recede in '08 Contest as Voters Focus on Character." To put it more accurately, issues recede as candidates, party managers, and their PR agencies focus on character (qualities, etc.). For sound reasons. The population can be dangerous if they come too close to the political arena. The "participants in action" are surely aware that, on a host of major issues, both political parties are well to the right of the general population and that their positions are quite consistent over time, a matter reviewed in a useful recent study on foreign policy by Benjamin Page and Marshall Bouton; the same is true on domestic policy. It is important, then, for the attention of the herd to be diverted elsewhere.[1]

The quoted admonitions, taken from highly regarded "progressive essays on democracy" by the leading American public intellectual of the twentieth century (Walter Lippmann), capture well the perceptions of intellectual opinion, largely shared across the narrow elite spectrum. The common understanding is revealed more in practice than in words, though some, like Lippmann, do articulate it: President Wilson, for example, who held that an elite of gentlemen with "elevated ideals" must be empowered to preserve "stability and righteousness,"[2] essentially the perspective of the Founding Fathers. In more recent years the gentlemen are transmuted into the "technocratic elite" and "action intellectuals" of Camelot, "Straussian" neocons, or other configurations. But throughout, one or another variant of the doctrine prevails, with its Leninist overtones.

For the vanguard who uphold the elevated ideals and are charged with managing the society and the world, the reasons for Iraq's drift off the radar screen should not be obscure. They were cogently explained by the distinguished historian Arthur Schlesinger forty years earlier (*Bitter Heritage*, 1966), articulating the position of the doves when the U.S. invasion of South Vietnam was in its fourth year and Washington was preparing to add another 100,000 troops to the 175,000 already tearing South Vietnam to shreds—though as Schlesinger and others paying attention surely knew, "what changed the character of the Vietnam war was...*not* the decision to use American ground troops in South Vietnam" in 1965 or to bomb the North, "but the decision to wage unlimited aerial warfare inside [South Vietnam] at the price of literally pounding the place to bits," facts reported prominently by the highly respected and bitterly anticommunist military historian and Indochina specialist Bernard Fall, who was soon to warn that "Vietnam as a cultural and historic entity...is threatened with extinction...[as]...the countryside literally dies under the blows of the largest military machine ever unleashed on an area of this size."

By the time Schlesinger wrote, the invasion launched by Kennedy was facing difficulties and imposing serious costs on the United States, so he and other Kennedy liberals were reluctantly beginning to question their hawkish stance. That even included Robert Kennedy, who a year earlier, when Fall published his bitter account of the war in the South, had condemned withdrawal as "a repudiation of commitments undertaken and confirmed by three administrations" which would "gravely—perhaps irreparably—weaken the democratic position in Asia." But by 1966, RFK, Schlesinger, and some other Camelot hawks began to call for a negotiated settlement—though not withdrawal, never an option, just as withdrawal without victory was never an option for JFK, contrary to many illusions.[3]

While reconsidering his earlier stance, Schlesinger wrote that of course "we all pray" that the hawks are right in thinking that the surge of the day will be able to "suppress the resistance," and if it does, "we may all be saluting the wisdom and statesmanship of the American government" in winning victory while leaving "the tragic country gutted and devastated by bombs, burned by napalm, turned into a wasteland by chemical defoliation, a land of ruin and wreck," with its "political and institutional fabric" pulverized. But escalation probably won't succeed, and will prove to be too costly for ourselves, so perhaps strategy should be rethought.

Attitudes toward the war at the liberal extreme were well illustrated by the concerns of the Massachusetts branch of Americans for Democratic Action. In late 1967, when opposition to the war was finally becoming a mass popular movement, the ADA leadership undertook considerable (and quite comical) efforts to prevent applications for membership from people they feared would speak in favor of an antiwar resolution sponsored by a local chapter that had fallen out of control (Howard Zinn and I were the terrifying applicants). A few months later came the Tet offensive, leading the business world to turn against the war because of its costs to us, while the more perceptive were coming to realize that Washington had already achieved its major war aims: destroying the "virus" of successful independent development that might "spread contagion" throughout the

region, to borrow Kissingerian rhetoric, and inoculating the potential victims by imposing vicious dictatorships.[4]

It soon turned out that everyone had always been a strong opponent
of the war (in deep silence). The Kennedy memoirists sharply revised
their accounts to fit the new requirement that JFK was a secret dove, con-
signing the rich documentary record (including their own earlier version
of events) to the dustbin of history, where the wrong facts wither away
in blessed peace and oblivion.[5] Others preferred silence, assuming correctly that the truth would disappear. The preferred version soon took
hold: the radical and self-indulgent antiwar movement had disrupted the
sober efforts of the responsible "early opponents of the war" to bring it
to an end. By the new millennium, even terminology had reversed. In the
1960s, historical "revisionists" were lambasted for raising the outrageous
idea that intervention in Vietnam was less than pure and noble in intent,
and even going so far as to suggest that perhaps U.S. actions played some
role in instigating and sustaining the Cold War. Forty years later, "revi-
sionism" refers to the doctrine that the United States was on the verge of
victory in Vietnam when it was sabotaged from within, challenging the
mainstream view that the noble cause was unwinnable, an error in judgment. And so the debate rages in scholarship and intellectual discourse.
The terminological shift reflects a shift in the ideological spectrum, a
considerable victory for the guardians of the imperial culture, among educated elites at least.

At the war's end, in 1975, the position of the extreme doves was expressed by Anthony Lewis, the most critical voice in the newspaper of
record, and the media rather generally. He observed that the war began
with "blundering efforts to do good"—the phrase "efforts to do good"
is close to tautology within the doctrinal system; "blundering" because
of costs and failures—though by 1969 it had become "clear to most of
the world—and most Americans— that the intervention had been a disastrous mistake." The argument against the war, Lewis explained, "was
that the United States had misunderstood the cultural and political forces
at work in Indochina—that it was in a position where it could not impose
a solution except at a price too costly to itself."[6]

By 1975, when Lewis wrote, "most Americans" had a radically different view. Some 70 percent regarded the war as "fundamentally wrong and immoral," not as "a mistake." But they are just "ignorant and meddlesome outsiders" whose voices can be dismissed—or on the rare occasions when they are noticed, explained away without evidence by attributing to them self-serving motives lacking any moral basis.[7]

Elite reasoning, and the accompanying attitudes, carry over with little change to critical commentary on the U.S. invasion of Iraq today. And although criticism of the Iraq war is far greater and more far-reaching than in the case of Vietnam at any comparable stage, nevertheless the principles that Schlesinger articulated decades ago remain in force in media and commentary.

It is of some interest that Schlesinger himself took a very different and much more honorable position on the Iraq invasion, virtually alone in his circles. When the bombs began to fall on Baghdad, he wrote that Bush's policies are "alarmingly similar to the policy that imperial Japan employed at Pearl Harbor, on a date which, as an earlier American president said it would, lives in infamy. Franklin D. Roosevelt was right, but today it is we Americans who live in infamy." It would be instructive to determine how Schlesinger's principled objection to U.S. war crimes fared in the tributes to him that appeared when he died, and in the many reviews of his *Journals* (which do not mention Vietnam until the Johnson years, consistent with the early version of his memoirs of Camelot). It is hardly necessary to investigate.[8]

That Iraq is "a land of ruin and wreck" is not in question. There should no longer be any need to review the facts in any detail. The British polling agency Opinion Research Business recently updated its estimate of extra deaths resulting from the war to 1.03 million—that's excluding Karbala and Anbar provinces, two of the worst regions.[9] Whether that is correct, or the true numbers are much lower as some claim, there is no doubt that the toll is horrendous. There are several million internally displaced. Thanks to the generosity of Jordan and Syria, the millions of refugees fleeing the wreckage of Iraq, including most of the professional classes (those who were not assassinated, that is), have not been simply wiped out. But that welcome is fading, for one reason because Jordan and Syria receive no meaningful support from the perpetrators of the crimes in Washington and London; the idea that they themselves might admit their victims, beyond a trickle, is too outlandish to consider. Previously dormant sectarian conflicts that erupted after the invasion, surprising Iraqis who were convinced that it could not happen, have devastated the country. Baghdad and other areas have been subjected to brutal ethnic cleansing and left in the hands of warlords and militias, the primary thrust of the current counterinsurgency strategy developed by General Petraeus, who won his fame by pacifying Mosul, soon to become the scene of some of the most extreme violence.

The truth of the matter does not escape the most knowledgeable and respected observers. David Gardner, Middle East correspondent of the *Financial Times,* describes the wreckage left by Petraeus in Mosul. He also reviews the reasons for the decline of violence at the time of the "surge" and the dramatic contrast between the Pentagon-media version and the "house of cards" exposed by the General Accountability Office (Congress's independent research bureau). He goes on to review as well the post-surge strategic "catastrophe," not only for Iraq but for the region: the sectarian rivalries that have been unleashed along with other threatening forces as "this latest, malign intervention," which the Arab and Muslim worlds perceive as "a modern version of the Crusades," has "buried the idea of democracy in the rubble of Iraq" while "hugely enhancing the influence of Shia Islamist Iran."[10]

We may usefully recall other occasions when enthusiastic partisans of violence were euphoric about the wonders that war would bring; August 1914, for a classic illustration, on all sides, soon followed by misery and despair over the terrible consequences of their patriotic enthusiasm. Not a unique example.

One of the most dedicated and informed journalists who has been immersed in the shocking tragedy, Nir Rosen, recently published an epitaph entitled "The Death of Iraq." He writes that "Iraq has been killed, never to rise again. The American occupation has been more disastrous than that of the Mongols, who sacked Baghdad in the thirteenth century"—a common perception of Iraqis as well. "Only fools talk of 'solutions' now. There is no solution. The only hope is that perhaps the damage can be contained."[11]

After Rosen wrote his epitaph, conditions declined further. By August 2009, the *New York Times* reported that the once-rich agricultural system had been so devastated "during the past few years" (that is, during the U.S. occupation) that "there are increasing doubts about whether it makes much sense to grow dates—or much of anything for that matter." "As recently as the 1980s," the report continues, "Iraq was self-sufficient in producing wheat, rice, fruits, vegetables, and sheep and poultry products. Its industrial sector exported textiles and leather goods, including purses and shoes, as well as steel and cement. But wars, sanctions, poor management, international competition and disinvestment have left each industry a shadow of its former self. Slowly, Iraq's economy has become based almost entirely on imports and a single commodity," oil, now providing 95 percent of the government's revenues, leading to dependence on markets that are highly volatile, in large measure because of speculation in financial markets. The grim situation is "perhaps nowhere more apparent than in the country's once bountiful date orchards…Iraq, which once produced three-quarters of the world's dates and grew 629 different varieties, is now an also-ran, falling behind Egypt, Iran and Saudi Arabia. Last year, the country produced 281,000 tons, according to the Ministry of Agriculture, about half the level of the mid-1980s…. Likewise, the number of date processing factories is down to six today, from 150 before the American-led invasion in 2003. Iraqi dates are now packaged in the United Arab Emirates—865 miles away."[12]

The U.S.-led sanctions also took a brutal toll, as did Washington's strong support for Saddam Hussein through the period of his worst atrocities in the 1980s, when he was so admired in Washington that his most shocking crimes—the murderous slaughter of Kurds—were denied by the Reagan administration and congressional protests were blocked. The excuse offered is that Iran was more dangerous, but apart from the cynicism, such apologetics cannot be taken seriously. Well after Iraq's war with Iran, the United States continued to support Saddam, even to expedite his development of weapons of mass destruction. Nuclear weapons specialist Gary Milhollin testified to Congress in 1992 that "if you look at the nuclear weapon program, you can see that if Saddam Hussein had not invaded Kuwait [in August 1990], Iraq would be very close to making a bomb today with American machine tools, American instruments for controlling the quality of nuclear weapon material, American computers for nuclear design, and Iraqi scientists trained in America in the techniques of nuclear detonation [in 1989, well after the end of the Iraq-Iran war]. Also the UN found American equipment at chemical and ballistic missile sites. The UN early this year sent the U.S. State Department a confidential list of American equipment that had turned up in chemical and ballistic missile programs." In April 1990, President Bush I even sent a high-level congressional delegation, led by Senate majority leader Bob Dole (later the Republican presidential candidate), to convey his personal greetings to his good friend and to assure him that he should disregard criticisms by "the haughty and pampered press," who are out of control.[13]

A few months later Saddam defied or misunderstood orders, and shifted from admired friend to the embodiment of evil. All such matters have been consigned to the usual repository of unwelcome fact.

Though the wreckage of Iraq today is too visible to try to conceal, the assault of the new barbarians is carefully circumscribed in the doctrinal system, often with the agency delicately obscured, and almost always excluding the horrendous effects of the Clinton sanctions, one of the great crimes of the last decade of the millennium—including their crucial role in preventing the threat that Iraqis might gain control of their own country, sending Saddam to the same fate as Ceausescu, Marcos, Suharto, Chun, and many other monsters supported by the United States and UK until they could no longer be maintained. Information about the effect of the sanctions is hardly lacking, in particular about the humanitarian phase of the sanctions regime, the oil-for-peace program initiated when the early impact became so shocking that UN ambassador Madeleine Albright had to mumble on TV that the price was right whatever the parents of hundreds of thousands of dead Iraqi children might think. The humanitarian program, which graciously permitted Iraq to use some of its oil revenues for the devastated population, was administered by highly respected and experienced UN diplomats, who had teams of investigators all over the country and surely knew more about the situation in Iraq than any other Westerners.

The first administrator, Denis Halliday, resigned in protest because he found the policies to be "genocidal." His assessment of the sanctions he administered is that they "were intended, designed and sustained to kill civilians, particularly children" and that "over 1 million people were allowed to die directly due to the impact of UN sanctions."[14] Halliday's successor, Hans von Sponeck, resigned two years later when he concluded that the sanctions violated the Genocide Convention. The Clinton administration barred him from providing information about the impact to the Security Council, which was technically responsible. As Albright's spokesperson James Rubin explained, "this man in Baghdad is paid to work, not to speak."

Von Sponeck does, however, speak; in extensive detail, particularly in his muted but horrifying review of the sanctions regime.[15] But the State Department ruling prevails. One will have to search diligently to find even a mention of these revelations or what they imply. Knowing too much, Halliday and von Sponeck were also barred from the U.S. media during the buildup to the invasion of Iraq, and to my knowledge since.

None of this can ever be mentioned, even in passing, by those who strike heroic poses about the alleged "genocides" perpetrated by official enemies, while scrupulously avoiding or denying our own crimes, a form of depravity that is not unusual among sectors of educated opinion.[16]

The assessments by Halliday and von Sponeck add considerable weight to the judgment by the very knowledgeable correspondent Jonathan Steele, referring to the invasion and its aftermath, on "the appalling horror of what has become the greatest humanitarian catastrophe in the world, undertaken primarily "to secure access to the country's oil reserves and to send a message of dominance across the region."[17]

Returning to the 2008 presidential campaign, it is true that Iraq was a marginal issue. That is natural, given the spectrum of hawk-dove elite opinion. The liberal doves adhere to their traditional reasoning and attitudes, praying that the hawks will be proven right and that the United States will win a victory in the land of ruin and wreck, establishing "stability," a code word for subordination to Washington's will. By and large hawks are encouraged, and doves silenced, by the good news about Iraq.

And there is good news. The U.S. occupying army in Iraq (euphemistically called the Multi-National Force-Iraq) carries out regular studies of popular attitudes, a crucial component of population control measures—or COIN, in the currently favored term for age-old counterinsurgency doctrine. In December 2007, the Pentagon released a study of focus groups, which was uncharacteristically upbeat. The survey "provides very strong evidence" that national reconciliation is possible and anticipated, contrary to prevailing voices of hopelessness and despair, Karen DeYoung reported in the *Washington Post*. The survey, she continues, found that a sense of "optimistic possibility permeated all focus groups…and far more commonalities than differences are found among these seemingly diverse groups of Iraqis." This discovery of "shared beliefs" among Iraqis throughout the country is "good news, according to a military analysis of the results."[18]

The "shared beliefs" were identified in the report. To quote DeYoung, "Iraqis of all sectarian and ethnic groups believe that the U.S. military invasion is the primary root of the violent differences among them, and see the departure of 'occupying forces' as the key to national reconciliation." So according to Iraqis, there is hope of national reconciliation if the invaders, who are responsible for the internal violence, withdraw and leave Iraq to Iraqis.

The conclusions are credible, consistent with earlier polls, and also with the apparent reduction in violence when the British finally withdrew from Basra, having "decisively lost the south—which produces over 90 percent of government revenues and 70 percent of Iraq's proven oil reserves" by 2005, according to Anthony Cordesman, the most prominent (and respectably hawkish) U.S. specialist on military affairs in the Middle East.[19]

The December 2007 report did not mention other good news: Iraqis appear to accept the highest values of Americans, which should be very gratifying. Specifically, they accept the principles of the Nuremberg Tribunal that sentenced Nazi war criminals to hanging for such crimes as supporting aggression and preemptive war—the main charge against Foreign Minister von Ribbentrop, whose position in the Nazi regime corresponded to that of Colin Powell and Condoleezza Rice, also strong supporters of aggression and preemptive war (more accurately, in their case, preventive war, a doctrine that does not even have the limited legitimacy of preemptive war). The tribunal defined aggression clearly enough: "invasion by its armed forces" of one state "of the territory of another state." The invasion of Iraq is a textbook example, if words have meaning; we need not tarry on the pretexts, thoroughly exploded even before the aggression was launched, and decisively shortly after. The tribunal went on to define aggression as "the supreme international crime differing only from other war crimes in that it contains within itself the accumulated evil of the whole": in the case of Iraq, containing within itself the murderous sectarian violence and ethnic cleansing, the destruction of the national culture and the irreplaceable treasures of the origins of Western civilization under the eyes of "stuff happens" Rumsfeld and his associates, and every other crime and atrocity as the inheritors of the Mongols have followed the path of imperial Japan.

Since Iraqis attribute the accumulated evil of the whole primarily to the invasion, it follows that they accept the core principle of Nuremberg. Presumably, they were not asked whether their acceptance of American values extended to the conclusion of the chief prosecutor for the United States, U.S. Supreme Court Justice Robert Jackson, who forcefully insisted that the Tribunal would be mere farce if we do not apply its principles to ourselves.

Needless to say, U.S. elite opinion, shared with Western counterparts generally, rejects with virtual unanimity the lofty American values professed at Nuremberg and adopted by Iraqis, indeed regards them as bordering on obscene. All of this provides an instructive illustration of some of the reality that lies behind the famous "clash of civilizations."

A January 2008 poll by World Learning/Aspen Institute found that "75 percent of Americans believe U.S. foreign policy is driving dissatisfaction with America abroad and more than 60 percent believe that dislike of American values (39 percent) and of the American people (26 percent) is also to blame." The perception is inaccurate, fed by propaganda. There is little dislike of Americans, and dissatisfaction abroad does not derive from "dislike of American values." Rather, from acceptance of these values and recognition that they are rejected by the U.S. government and elite opinion.[20]

Other "good news" had been reported by General Petraeus and Ambassador Ryan Crocker during the extravaganza staged on September 11, 2007, to drum up support for the administration and its impressive achievements. Perhaps we should call the commander "Lord Petraeus," in light of the reverence displayed by the media and commentators on this occasion. Parenthetically, only a cynic might imagine that the date was chosen to insinuate the Bush-Cheney claims of links between Saddam Hussein and Osama bin Laden, so that by committing the "supreme international crime" they were defending the world against terror—which increased sharply as a result of the invasion as anticipated, sevenfold according to an analysis by terrorism specialists Peter Bergen and Paul Cruickshank, using data of the government-linked RAND Corporation.[21]

Petraeus and Crocker provided figures to show that the Iraqi government had greatly accelerated spending on reconstruction, reaching a quarter of the funding set aside for that purpose. Good news indeed— until it was investigated by the Government Accountability Office, which found that the actual figure was one-sixth what Petraeus and Crocker reported, a 50 percent decline from the preceding year.[22]

More good news is the decline in sectarian violence, attributable in part to the success of the ethnic cleansing that Iraqis blame on the invasion; there are simply fewer people to kill in the cleansed areas. But it is also attributable to Washington's decision to support the tribal groups that had previously organized to drive out Iraqi al-Qaeda, to an increase in U.S. troops, and to the decision of Moqtada al-Sadr's Mahdi army to stand down and consolidate its gains[23]—what the press calls "halting aggression." By definition, only Iraqis can commit aggression in Iraq (or Iranians, of course).

Though there are few signs of it several years later, it is not impossible that Petraeus's strategy might some day approach the success of the

Russians in Chechnya, where fighting is now "limited and sporadic, and Grozny is in the midst of a building boom" after having been reduced to rubble by the Russian attack, C. J. Chivers reports, also on September 11, as Petraeus provided the "good news." Perhaps some day Baghdad and Falluja too will enjoy "electricity restored in many neighborhoods, new businesses opening and the city's main streets repaved," as in booming Grozny. Possible, but dubious, in the light of the likely consequence of creating warlord armies that may be the seeds of even greater sectarian violence, adding to the "accumulated evil" of the aggression.[24]

If Russians rise to the moral level of liberal intellectuals in the West, they must be saluting Putin's "wisdom and statesmanship" for his achievements in his murderous campaign in Chechnya.

A few weeks after the Pentagon's "good news" from Iraq, *New York Times* military-Iraq expert Michael Gordon wrote a reasoned and comprehensive review of the options on Iraq policy facing the candidates for the presidential election. One voice is missing: Iraqis. Their preference is not rejected. Rather, it is not worthy of mention. And it seems that there was no notice of the fact. That makes sense on the usual tacit assumption of most discourse on international affairs: we own the world, so what does it matter what others think? They are "unpeople," to borrow the term used by British diplomatic historian Mark Curtis in his work on Britain's crimes of empire—very illuminating work, accordingly deeply hidden. Routinely, Americans join Iraqis in unpeople-hood. Their preferences too provide no options.[25]

To cite another instructive example, consider Gerald Seib's reflections in the *Wall Street Journal* on "Time to Look Ahead in Iraq." Seib is impressed that debate over Iraq is finally beginning to go beyond the "cartoon-like characteristics" of what has come before and is now beginning to confront "the right issue," the "more profound questions":

> The more profound questions are the long-term ones. Regardless of how things evolve in a new president's first year, the U.S. needs to decide what its lasting role should be in Iraq. Is Iraq to be a permanent American military outpost, and will American troops need to be on hand in some fashion to help defend Iraq's borders for a decade or more, as some Iraqi

officials themselves have suggested? Will the U.S. see Iraq more broadly
as a base for exerting American political and diplomatic influence in the
broader Middle East, or is that a mistake? Is it better to have American
troops just over the horizon, in Kuwait or ships in the Persian Gulf? Driving these military considerations is the political question of what kind
of government the U.S. can accept in Iraq.[26]

No soft-headed nonsense here about Iraqis having a voice on the
lasting role of the United States in Iraq or on the kind of government
they would prefer.

Seib should not be confused with the columnists in the *Journal*'s
opinion pages. He is a rational centrist analyst, who could easily be writing in the liberal media or journals of the Democratic Party like *The New
Republic*. And he grasps quite accurately the fundamental principles guiding the political class.

Such reflections of the imperial mentality are deeply rooted. To pick
examples almost at random, shortly after the Petraeus celebration, in December 2007, Panama declared a Day of Mourning to commemorate the
U.S. invasion of 1989, which killed thousands of poor people, so Panamanian human rights groups concluded, when Bush I bombed the El
Chorillo slums and other civilian targets. The Day of Mourning of the
unpeople scarcely merited a flicker of an eyelid here. It is also of no interest that Bush's invasion of Panama, another textbook example of aggression, appears to have been more deadly than Saddam's invasion of Kuwait
a few months later. Similarly unworthy of note is the fact that Washington's greatest fear was that Saddam would imitate its behavior in Panama,
installing a client government and then leaving, the main reason Washington blocked diplomacy with almost complete media cooperation; the
sole serious exception I know of before the war commenced was Knut
Royce in *Long Island Newsday*. Though the December Day of Mourning
passed with little notice, there was a lead story when the Panamanian National Assembly was opened by President Pedro González, who is charged
by Washington with killing American soldiers during a protest against
President Bush's visit two years after his invasion, charges dismissed by
Panamanian courts but still upheld by the owner of the world.[27]

To take another illustration of the depth of the imperial mentality, correspondent Elaine Sciolino writes that "Iran's intransigence [about nuclear enrichment] appears to be defeating attempts by the rest of the world to curtail Tehran's nuclear ambitions." The phrase "the rest of the world," conventional terminology, happens to exclude the large majority of the world: the Non-Aligned Movement, which forcefully endorses Iran's right to enrich uranium as a signer of the Non-Proliferation Treaty (NPT). But they are not part of the world in conventional discourse, since they do not reflexively accept U.S. government orders.[28]

We might tarry for a moment to ask whether there is any solution to the U.S.-Iran confrontation over nuclear weapons. Here is one idea: (1) Iran should have the right to develop nuclear energy, but not weapons, in accord with the NPT. (2) A nuclear weapons–free zone should be established in the region, including Iran, Israel, and U.S. forces deployed there. (3) The United States should accept the NPT. (4) The United States should end threats against Iran and turn to serious diplomacy.

The proposals are not original. These are the preferences of the large majority of Americans, and also Iranians, in polls by World Public Opinion, which found that Americans and Iranians agree on basic issues. At a forum at the Johns Hopkins School of Advanced International Studies when the polls were released, Joseph Cirincione, senior vice president for National Security and International Policy at the Center for American Progress, said the polls showed "the common sense of both the American people and the Iranian people, [who] seem to be able to rise above the rhetoric of their own leaders to find common sense solutions to some of the most crucial questions" facing the two nations, favoring pragmatic, diplomatic solutions to their differences. The results suggest that if the U.S. and Iran were functioning democratic societies, this very dangerous confrontation could probably be resolved peaceably.[29]

The opinions of Americans on this issue too are not regarded as worthy of consideration; they are not options for candidates or commentators. They were apparently not even reported, perhaps considered too dangerous because of what they reveal about the "democratic deficit" in the United States, and about the extremism of the political class across the spectrum. If public opinion were to be mentioned as an option, it would be ridiculed as "politically impossible"; or perhaps offered as another reason why "the public must be put in its place," as Lippmann sternly admonished.

There is more to say about the preference of Americans on Iran. On point (1) above, as noted, American opinion happens to accord with the stand of the large majority of the world. Hence Americans too are not part of "the world," as conventionally defined. With regard to point (2), the U.S. and its allies have accepted it, formally at least. UN Security Council Resolution 687 of April 1991 commits them to "the goal of establishing in the Middle East a zone free from weapons of mass destruction and all missiles for their delivery and the objective of a global ban on chemical weapons" (Article 14). The United States and UK have a particularly strong commitment to this principle, since it was this resolution that they appealed to in their efforts to provide a thin legal cover for their invasion of Iraq, claiming that Iraq had not lived up to the conditions in 687 on disarmament. As for point (3), 80 percent of Americans feel that Washington should live up to its commitment under the NPT to undertake "good faith" efforts to eliminate nuclear weapons entirely, a legal commitment as the World Court determined, explicitly rejected by the Bush administration. Turning to point (4), Americans are calling on the government to adhere to international law, under which the threats of violence that are voiced by all current candidates are a crime, in violation of the UN Charter. The call for negotiations and diplomacy on the part of the American unpeople extends to Cuba, and has for decades, but is again dismissed by both political parties.[30]

The possibility that functioning democracy might alleviate severe dangers is regularly illustrated. To take another current example, of great importance, there is now justified concern about Russian reactions to U.S. aggressive militarism. That includes the extension of NATO to the East by Clinton in violation of pledges to Mikhail Gorbachev, but particularly the vast expansion of offensive military capacity under Bush, and more recently, the plans to place "missile defense" installations in Eastern Europe. Putin is ridiculed for claiming that they are a threat to

Russia. But U.S. strategic analysts recognize that he has a point. The programs, they argue, are designed in a way that Russian planners would have to regard as a threat to the Russian deterrent, hence calling for more advanced and lethal offensive military capacity to neutralize them. A new arms race is feared.[31]

Recent polls under the direction of strategic analysts John Steinbruner and Nancy Gallagher "reveal a striking disparity between what U.S. and Russian leaders are doing and what their publics desire," again indicating that if these countries were functioning democracies, in which the population had a voice, the increasingly fragile U.S.-Russian strategic relationship could be repaired, a matter of species survival in this case.[32]

In a free press, all these matters, and many more like them, would merit regular prominent headlines and in-depth analysis.

Having brought up Iran, we might as well turn briefly to the third member of the famous Axis of Evil, North Korea. The official story is that after having been forced to accept an agreement on dismantling its nuclear weapons facilities, North Korea is again trying to evade its commitments in its usual devious way—"good news" for superhawks like John Bolton, who have held all along that North Korea understands only the mailed fist and will exploit negotiations only to trick us. A *New York Times* headline reads: "U.S. Sees Stalling by North Korea on Nuclear Pact"; the article by Helene Cooper details the charges. In the last paragraph we discover that the U.S. has not fulfilled its pledges. North Korea has received only 15 percent of the fuel that was promised by the United States and others, and the United States has not undertaken steps to improve diplomatic relations, as promised. Several weeks later, McClatchy Newspapers' Kevin Hall reported that the chief U.S. negotiator with North Korea, Christopher Hill, confirmed in Senate hearings that "North Korea has slowed the dismantling of its nuclear reactor because it hasn't received the amount of fuel oil it was promised."[33]

From the specialist literature, and asides here and there, we learn that this is a consistent pattern. North Korea may well have the worst government in the world, but they have been pursuing a pragmatic tit-for-tat policy on negotiations with the United States. When the United

States takes an aggressive and threatening stance, they react accordingly. When the United States moves toward some form of accommodation, so do they. When Bush II came into office, both North Korea and the United States were bound by the Framework Agreement of 1994. Neither was fully in accord with its commitments, but the agreement was largely being observed. North Korea had stopped testing long-range missiles. It had perhaps one or two bombs' worth of plutonium, and was verifiably not making more. After seven Bush years of confrontation, North Korea has eight to ten bombs and long-range missiles, and it is developing plutonium. The Clinton administration, Korea specialist Bruce Cumings reports, "had also worked out a plan to buy out, indirectly, the North's medium and long-range missiles; it was ready to be signed in 2000 but Bush let it fall by the wayside and today the North retains all its formidable missile capability."[34]

What lies behind Bush's achievements is well understood. His Axis of Evil speech, a serious blow to Iranian democrats and reformers as they have stressed, also put North Korea on notice that the United States was returning to its threatening stance. Washington released intelligence reports about North Korea's clandestine program; these were conceded to be dubious or baseless when the latest negotiations began in 2007, probably, commentators speculated, because it was feared that weapons inspectors might enter North Korea and the Iraq story would be repeated. North Korea responded by ratcheting up missile and weapons development.[35]

In September 2005, under international pressure, Washington agreed to turn to negotiations, within the six-power framework. They achieved substantial success. North Korea agreed to abandon "all nuclear weapons and existing weapons programs" and allow international inspections, in return for international aid and a non-aggression pledge from the United States, with an agreement that the two sides would "respect each other's sovereignty, exist peacefully together and take steps to normalize relations." The ink was barely dry on the agreement when the Bush administration renewed the threat of force, also freezing North Korean funds in foreign banks and disbanding the consortium that was to provide North Korea with a light-water reactor. Cumings alleges that "the sanctions were specifically designed to destroy the September pledges [and] to head off an accommodation between Washington and Pyongyang."

After Washington scuttled the promising September 2005 agreements, North Korea returned to weapons and missile development and carried out a test of a nuclear weapon. Again under international pressure, and with its policy in tatters, Washington returned to negotiations, leading to an agreement, though it is now dragging its feet on fulfilling its commitments.

Cumings concludes that "Bush had presided over the most asinine Korea policy in history. These last years, relations between Washington and Seoul have deteriorated drastically. By commission and omission, Bush trampled on the norms of the historic U.S. relationship with Seoul while creating a dangerous situation with Pyongyang."

Charges against North Korea escalated in September 2007, when Israel bombed an obscure site in northern Syria, an "act of war," as at least one prominent American correspondent recognized.[36] Charges at once surfaced that Israel attacked a nuclear installation being developed with the help of North Korea, an attack compared with Israel's bombing of the Osirak reactor in Iraq in 1981—which, according to available evidence, convinced Saddam Hussein to initiate his nuclear weapons program.[37] Seymour Hersh's tentative conclusion after investigation was that the Israeli actions may have been intended as another threat against Iran: the U.S.-Israel have you in their bombsights. However this may be, there is some important background that should be recalled.

In 1993, Israel and North Korea were on the verge of an agreement: Israel would recognize North Korea, and in return, North Korea would end any weapons-related involvement in the Middle East. The significance for Israeli security is clear. Clinton ordered the deal terminated, and Israel had no choice but to obey.[38] Ever since its fateful decision in 1971 to reject peace and security in favor of expansion, maintained since, Israel has been compelled to rely on the United States for protection, hence to obey Washington's commands.

Whether or not there is any truth to current charges about North Korea and Syria, it appears that the threat to the security of Israel, and the region, might have been avoided by peaceful means, had security been a high priority.

Let us return to the first member of the Axis of Evil, Iraq. Washington's war aims were clearly outlined in a U.S.-proposed Declaration of Principles for the U.S. and Iraqi governments, in November 2007. The declaration allows U.S. forces to remain indefinitely to "deter foreign aggression" and for internal security. The only aggression in sight is from the United States, but that is not aggression, by definition. And only the most naïve will entertain the thought that the United States would sustain the government by force if it moved toward independence; going too far in strengthening relations with Iran, for example. The declaration also committed Iraq to facilitate and encourage "the flow of foreign investments to Iraq, especially American investments."[39]

The unusually brazen expression of imperial will was underscored when Bush quietly issued yet another signing statement, expanding his historical record, declaring that he would reject crucial provisions of congressional legislation that he had just signed, including the provision that forbids spending taxpayer money "to establish any military installation or base for the purpose of providing for the permanent stationing of United States Armed Forces in Iraq" or "to exercise United States control of the oil resources of Iraq." Shortly before, the *New York Times* had reported that Washington "insists that the Baghdad government give the United States broad authority to conduct combat operations," a demand that "faces a potential buzz saw of opposition from Iraq, with its...deep sensitivities about being seen as a dependent state."[40]

More third-world irrationality.

In brief, Iraq was to agree to allow permanent U.S. military installations (called "enduring" in the preferred Orwellism), grant the United States the right to conduct combat operations freely and indefinitely, and ensure U.S. control over oil resources of Iraq while privileging U.S. investors. It is of some interest that these official statements and actions did not influence discussion about the reasons for the U.S. invasion of

Iraq. These had never been obscure, but any effort to spell them out was dismissed with ridicule. Now the reasons are openly conceded, eliciting no retraction or even reflection. Or perhaps even report.

Not long after, Bush was compelled to withdraw these demands, the latest step in a record of backtracking that began not long after the invasion, as the U.S. invaders had to abandon their war aims, step by step, in the face of determined nonviolent Iraqi resistance, an impressive achievement that should be better known. Obama has indicated that he will abide by the concessions forced on Bush. We return to the matter.

Iraqis are not alone in lacking proper respect for the invaders, so it appears from polls in Afghanistan and other considerations to which we turn below.

Recent polls in Pakistan also provide "good news" for Washington. Fully 5 percent favor allowing U.S. or other foreign troops to enter Pakistan "to pursue or capture al Qaeda fighters." Nine percent favor allowing U.S. forces "to pursue and capture Taliban insurgents who have crossed over from Afghanistan." Almost half favor allowing Pakistani troops to do so. And only a little over 80 percent regard the U.S. military presence in Asia and Afghanistan as a threat to Pakistan, while an overwhelming majority believe that the United States is trying to harm the Islamic world.[41]

The good news is that these results are a considerable improvement over October 2001, when a Newsweek poll found that "eighty-three percent of Pakistanis surveyed say they side with the Taliban, with a mere 3 percent expressing support for the United States," while over 80 percent described Osama bin Laden as a guerrilla and 6 percent as a terrorist.[42]

Turning elsewhere, major polls are not such good news for conventional Western doctrines. Few are upheld with such passion and unanimity as the thesis that Hugo Chávez is a tyrant bent on destroying freedom and democracy in Venezuela and beyond. The annual polls on Latin American opinion by the respected Chilean polling agency Latinobarómetro, already discussed, are therefore "bad news" that gave the wrong answers, and were accordingly suppressed, very efficiently. As noted, editorial offices are well aware of the polls, as selective citation reveals, but evidently understand what may pass through doctrinal filters.

Also receiving scant notice was a declaration of President Chávez at the year's end granting amnesty to leaders of the U.S.-backed military coup that kidnapped the president, disbanded parliament and the Supreme Court and all other democratic institutions, but was soon over-turned by a popular uprising.[43] That the West would have followed Chávez's model in a comparable case is, to put it mildly, rather unlikely.

Perhaps all of this too provides some further insight into the "clash of civilizations"—a question that should be prominent in our minds, I think.

SIX

Free Elections, Good News and Bad

Events in the Levant in 2008 add further understanding to the "good news" of those days. In January, in a remarkable act of courageous civil disobedience, tens of thousands of the tortured people of Gaza broke out of the prison to which they had been confined by the U.S.-Israel alliance, with the usual timid European support, as punishment for the crime of voting the wrong way in a free election in January 2006. It was instructive at that time to see the front pages with stories reporting the brutal U.S. response to a genuinely free election alongside others lauding the Bush administration for its noble dedication to "democracy promotion," or sometimes gently chiding it because it was going too far in its idealism, failing to recognize that the unpeople of the Middle East are too backward to appreciate democracy.

There are virtually no limits to the soaring rhetoric about the marvels of free elections when they are believed to have come out "the right way." Accordingly, the 2008 election in Lebanon was greeted with euphoria. *New York Times* columnist Thomas Friedman gushed that he is "a sucker for free and fair elections," so "it warms my heart to watch" what happened in Lebanon in an election that "was indeed free and fair—not like the pretend election you are about to see in Iran, where only candidates approved by the Supreme Leader can run. No, in Lebanon it was the real deal, and the results were fascinating: President Barack Obama defeated President Mahmoud Ahmadinejad of Iran." Crucially, "a solid majority of all Lebanese—Muslims, Christians and Druse—voted for the March 14 coalition led by Saad Hariri," the U.S.-backed candidate and son of the murdered ex–prime minister Rafik Hariri, so that "to the extent that anyone came out of this election with the moral authority to lead the next government, it was the coalition that wants Lebanon to be run by and for the Lebanese—not for Iran, not for Syria and not for fighting Israel." We must give credit where it is due for this triumph of free elections: "Without George Bush standing up to the Syrians in 2005—and forcing them to get out of Lebanon after the Hariri killing—this free election would not have happened. Mr. Bush helped create the space. Power matters. Mr. Obama helped stir the hope. Words also matter."

Friedman was echoed by many others, if less effusively. By Elliott Abrams, for example, who also compared Obama's victory in Lebanon with the Iranian elections. Under the heading "Lebanon's Triumph, Iran's Travesty," Abrams compared these "twin tests of [U.S.] efforts to spread democracy to the Muslim world." The lesson is clear: "What the United States should be promoting is not elections, but free elections, and the voting in Lebanon passed any realistic test…the majority of Lebanese have rejected Hezbollah's claim that it is not a terrorist group but a 'national resistance'…. The Lebanese had a chance to vote against Hezbollah, and took the opportunity."

Reactions were similar elsewhere. A few small problems were, however, overlooked.

The most prominent problem, apparently unreported in the United States, is the actual vote. The Hezbollah-based March 8 coalition won handily, by approximately the same figure as Obama vs. McCain in November 2008, about 53 percent of the popular vote, according to Ministry of Interior figures. Hence by the Friedman-Abrams argument, we should be lamenting Ahmadinejad's defeat of President Obama, and the "moral authority" won by Hezbollah, as "the majority of Lebanese…took the opportunity" to reject the charges that Friedman-Abrams and others repeat uncritically from Washington propaganda. [1]

Like others, Friedman and Abrams are referring to representatives in Parliament. These numbers are skewed by the confessional voting system, which sharply reduces the seats granted to the largest of the sects, the Shi'ites, who overwhelmingly back Hezbollah and its Amal ally. Furthermore, as analysts concerned with fact have pointed out, the confessional ground rules undermine "free and fair elections" in even more far-reaching ways than this. Assaf Kfoury observes that they leave no space for non-sectarian parties and erect a barrier to introducing socioeconomic policies and other real issues into the electoral system. They also open the door to "massive external interference," low voter turnout, and "vote-rigging and vote-buying," all features of the June 2008 election, even more so than before. Thus in Beirut, home of more than half the population, less than a fourth of eligible voters could vote without returning to their usually remote districts of origin. The effect is that migrant workers and the poorer classes are effectively disenfranchised in "a form of extreme gerrymandering, Lebanese style," favoring the privileged and pro-Western classes.[2]

Such glaring illustrations of elite hatred and contempt for democracy appear regularly, apparently with no awareness of what they signify—which tells us a good deal about how deeply rooted in the intellectual culture are the sentiments and the doctrines tacitly upheld. To pick another illustration, Cam Simpson reports in the *Wall Street Journal* that despite the harsh U.S.-Israeli punishment of Gaza, and "flooding the West Bank's Western-backed Fatah-led government with diplomatic and economic support [to] persuade Palestinians in both territories to embrace Fatah and isolate Hamas," the opposite is happening: Hamas's popularity is increasing in the West Bank. As Simpson casually explains, "Hamas won Palestinian elections in January 2006, prompting the Israeli government and the Bush administration to lead a world-wide boycott of the Palestinian Authority," along with much more severe measures. The goal, unconcealed, is to punish the miscreants who fail to grasp the essential principle of democracy: "Do what we say, or else."[3]

It is important not to overlook the fact that the U.S.-Israel operate in tandem. Israel relies crucially on U.S. military, economic, diplomatic, and ideological support. It will proceed as far as the United States allows. Its criminal actions are U.S. crimes.

In response to the unfortunate free elections of January 2006, U.S.-Israeli punishment of the people of Gaza sharply increased, peaking with many killings in early June, then escalating sharply after the capture of an Israeli soldier, Gilad Shalit, on June 25. That act was bitterly denounced in the West. Israel's vicious response was regarded as understandable if perhaps excessive. These thoughts were untroubled by the dramatic demonstration, at once, that they were sheer hypocrisy. The day before the capture of Corporal Shalit on the front lines of the army attacking Gaza, Israeli forces entered Gaza City and kidnapped two civilians, the Muamar brothers, taking them to Israel (in violation of the Geneva Conventions), where they disappeared into Israel's prison population, including almost one thousand held without charge, often for long periods. The kidnapping, a far more serious crime than the capture of Shalit, received a few scattered lines of comment, but no noticeable criticism.[4] That is perhaps understandable, because it is hardly news. U.S.-backed Israeli forces have been engaged in such practices, and far more brutal ones like them, for decades. And in any event, as a client state Israel inherits the right of criminality from its master.

Western hypocrisy on this score is stunning. Thus Thomas Friedman, while instructing us on how the lesser breeds must be "educated" by terrorist violence, writes that Israel's invasion of Lebanon in 2006, once again destroying much of southern Lebanon and Beirut while killing another one thousand civilians, was a just act of self-defense, responding to Hezbollah's crime of "launching an unprovoked war across the U.N.-recognized Israel-Lebanon border, after Israel had unilaterally withdrawn from Lebanon." The shocking crime was the capture of Israeli soldiers on the border, with the apparent intention of a prisoner exchange, the first recorded significant border violation by Hezbollah in six years despite Israel's almost daily border violations since the Hezbollah-led resistance forced it to withdraw from its occupation of southern Lebanon in violation of UN Security Council orders.[5]

The veteran Middle East specialist of the *New York Times* surely knows about Israel's criminal practices in Lebanon and on the high seas, which vastly exceed Hezbollah's crime of capturing two soldiers at the border. At least, he knows if he reads his own newspaper: for example, the eighteenth paragraph of a story on prisoner exchange, which observes that thirty-seven of the Arab prisoners "had been seized recently by the Israeli Navy as they tried to make their way from Cyprus to Tripoli," north of Beirut—many held for years as hostages, sometimes in secret prisons reported in Israel and Europe, but not the United States.[6]

Such crimes continue, barely eliciting a yawn. In September 2009, the Israeli army invaded the North Gaza district south of the town of Beit Lahia and kidnapped five Palestinian children on their way home after grazing sheep. Details are reported by the Gaza-based Al Mezan Center for Human Rights. No coverage could be discovered in the English-language press, though the capture of Shalit, a soldier of an attacking army, receives regular wide coverage, and is regularly depicted as a prime obstacle to peace.[7]

Returning to the aftermath of the unacceptable authentic free election in Gaza, U.S.-Israeli atrocities escalated once again in June 2007, after a civil war that left Hamas in control of the territory. That is commonly described as a Hamas military coup, demonstrating again their evil nature. The real world is a little different. The civil war was incited by the United States and Israel, in a crude attempt at a military coup to overturn the elections that brought Hamas to power. That has been public knowledge at least since April 2008, when David Rose published a detailed and documented account of how Bush, Condoleezza Rice, and Deputy National Security Adviser Elliott Abrams "backed an armed force under Fatah strongman Muhammad Dahlan, touching off a bloody civil war in Gaza and leaving Hamas stronger than ever." The account was corroborated by Norman Olsen, who served for twenty-six years in the Foreign Service, including four years working in the Gaza Strip and four years at the U.S. Embassy in Tel Aviv, and then moved on to become associate coordinator for counterterrorism at the Department of State. Olsen and his son detail the State Department shenanigans intended to ensure that their candidate, Abbas, would win in the January 2006 elections—in which case it would have been hailed as a triumph of democracy, warming the hearts of loyalists. After the election-fixing failed, the United States and Israel turned to the punishment of Palestinians for voting the wrong way, and began arming a militia run by Dahlan. But "Dahlan's thugs moved too soon," the Olsens write, and a Hamas preemptive strike undermined the coup attempt.[8]

As U.S.-backed Israeli savagery reached new heights in Gaza, the criminal pair continued their work in the other part of the occupied territories, the West Bank, which they have been systematically isolating from Gaza since the "Oslo peace process" began in 1993.[9] There Israel is carrying forward its U.S.-backed programs to take over valuable territory and resources, breaking up the fragments remaining to Palestinians by settlements and huge infrastructure projects, and hundreds of checkpoints mostly for harassment, imprisoning the whole by takeover of the Jordan Valley, and expanding settlement and development in Jerusalem to ensure that there will be no more than a token Palestinian presence in the historic center of Palestinian cultural, commercial, and social life. All settlement-related activities are illegal but those in Jerusalem are doubly so, in this case, in violation of Security Council orders that go back forty years. Nonviolent reactions by Palestinians and solidarity groups are viciously crushed. There is little notice. Even when Nobel laureate Mairead Corrigan Maguire was shot and gassed by Israeli troops while participating in a vigil protesting the separation wall—now better termed an annexation wall—there was apparently not a word in the English-language print media, outside of Ireland.[10]

It is useful to bear in mind that Israel understood at once that its settlement projects in the occupied territories, and anything related to them, are illegal. Israel's top legal authority on international law, Theodor Meron, a distinguished international lawyer and a leading figure in international tribunals, informed the government in September 1967 "that civilian settlement in the administered [occupied] territories contravenes the explicit provisions of the Fourth Geneva Convention," the core of international humanitarian law. The cabinet had already been informed of that by Justice Minister Ya'akov Shimshon Shapira. A few weeks later Defense Minister Moshe Dayan, who was in charge of the occupied territories, informed his fellow ministers that "we must consolidate our hold so that over time we will succeed in 'digesting' Judea and Samaria [the West Bank] and merging

them with 'little' Israel," meanwhile "dismember[ing] the territorial con-
tiguity" of the West Bank. This would have to be done by expropriating
land from Arab owners, under the pretense "that the step is necessary for
military purposes," a subterfuge that had also worked quite well to deprive
Israeli Arabs of the rights accorded to Jewish citizens, as in the notorious
case of the town of Carmiel. The settlement and dismemberment policies
have since been followed systematically, and still are. Throughout, a leading
role has been played by the official "doves," notably Shimon Peres.

Dayan had no illusions about the criminality of the enterprise he was
recommending. "Settling Israelis in occupied territory contravenes, as is
known, international conventions," he observed, "but there is nothing essentially new in that." He evidently expected the paymaster in Washington
to object formally, but with a wink. That too has been the regular practice,
even as the criminality has been underscored by Security Council resolutions and more recently by the International Court of Justice, with the
basic agreement of U.S. Justice Buergenthal in a separate declaration.[11]

Criminal actions by Palestinians, such as Qassam rockets fired from
Gaza, are angrily condemned in the West. The far more violent and destructive Israeli actions sometimes elicit polite clucking of tongues if they
exceed approved levels of state terror. Invariably Israel's actions—for
which of course the United States shares direct responsibility—are portrayed as retaliation, perhaps excessive. Another way of looking at the
cycle of violence is that Qassam rockets are retaliation for Israel's un-
ceasing crimes in Gaza and the West Bank, which is not separable from
Gaza except by U.S.-Israeli fiat. But standard racist-ultranationalist as-
sumptions exclude that interpretation.

There is almost universal agreement in the West, including the
human rights organizations, that Israeli actions to deter rockets are legitimate self-defense, even if disproportionate, sometimes perhaps even
verging on criminality. The framework was adopted with virtual unanimity once again when Israel carried out a merciless attack on Gaza in
December–January 2008–9. The position is quite clearly untenable, another reflection of the power of the formidable Western propaganda system with its deep roots in imperial mentality.

The facts and principles are quite straightforward and unambiguous. Like other states, Israel has the right of self-defense; that has not been in question. But the operative question is an entirely different one: does Israel have the right of self-defense *by force* in this particular instance? On this matter, international law, including the UN Charter, is unambiguous: it has that right only if it has exhausted peaceful means (among other conditions that must be met). But Israel not only has not exhausted peaceful means, it has refused even to consider them. Putting aside the broader matter of its ending its daily crimes in occupied Palestine, and just keeping to Gaza, Israel refused even to consider accepting a cease-fire. Hamas repeatedly offered a cease-fire, which Israel and the United States had every reason to suppose would end Hamas rocket firing. These facts utterly undermine any justification for the U.S.-Israeli assault on Gaza in December 2008, apparently initiated to carry forward the programs of imposing massive suffering on the animals in the Gaza prison, taking over whatever is valuable in the West Bank, and ensuring that others are properly intimidated by Israeli force.[12]

Given the virtual unanimity of the claim that the 2008–9 attack on Gaza was undertaken in legitimate self-defense, even if disproportionate in means, it is worthwhile to recall the immediate background. In June 2008 Israel and Hamas reached an agreement on a cease-fire, which called for opening the border crossings to "allow the transfer of all goods that were banned and restricted to go into Gaza." Israel formally agreed, but immediately announced that it would not abide by the agreement and open the borders until Hamas released Gilad Shalit.

After immediately rejecting the June 2008 cease-fire it had formally accepted, Israel maintained its siege. We may recall that a siege is an act of war. In fact, Israel has always insisted on an even stronger principle: hampering access to the outside world, even well short of a siege, is an act of war, justifying massive violence in response. Interference with Israel's passage through the Straits of Tiran was a large part of the justification offered for Israel's invasion of Egypt (with France and England) in 1956, and for its launching of the June 1967 war. The siege of Gaza is total, not partial, apart from occasional willingness of the occupiers to relax it slightly to allow bare survival. And it is vastly more harmful to Gazans than closing the Straits of Tiran was to Israel. Supporters of Israeli doctrines and actions should therefore have no problem justifying rocket attacks on Israeli territory from the Gaza Strip.

Of course, again we run into the nullifying principle: This is *us*, that is *them*.

Israel not only maintained the siege after June 2008, but did so with extreme rigor. It even prevented the UN Relief and Works Agency from replenishing its stores, "so when the ceasefire broke down, we ran out of food for the 750,000 who depend on us," UNRWA director John Ging informed the BBC.[13]

Despite the Israeli siege, rocketing was sharply reduced. The spokesperson for the prime minister, Mark Regev, acknowledged that there was not a single Hamas rocket among the few that were launched from the onset of the June 2008 cease-fire until November 4, when Israel violated it still more egregiously with a raid into Gaza, killing six Hamas activists and eliciting a retaliatory barrage of rockets (with no injuries). The Israeli government acknowledged the same on its official website. The November 4 raid was on the evening of the U.S. presidential elections, when attention was focused elsewhere. The pretext for the raid was that Israel had detected a tunnel in Gaza that might have been intended for use to capture another Israeli soldier; a "ticking tunnel" in official communiques. The pretext was transparently absurd, as a number of Israeli commentators noted. If such a tunnel existed, and reached the border, Israel could easily have barred it right there. But as usual, the ludicrous Israeli pretext was deemed credible, and the timing was overlooked.[14]

What was the reason for the Israeli raid? A fair question, since it was evidently not to stop Hamas rockets or other potential attacks. We have no internal evidence about Israeli planning, but we do know that the raid came shortly before scheduled Hamas-Fatah talks in Cairo aimed at "reconciling their differences and creating a single, unified government," British correspondent Rory McCarthy reported. That was to be the first Fatah-Hamas meeting since the June 2007 civil war that left Hamas in control of Gaza, and would have been a significant step toward advancing diplomatic efforts.

There is a long history of Israel provocations to deter the threat of diplomacy, some already mentioned. This may have been another one.[15]

After Israel broke the June 2008 cease-fire (such as it was) in November, the siege was tightened further, with even more disastrous consequences for the population. According to Sara Roy, the leading academic specialist on Gaza, "On Nov. 5, Israel sealed all crossing points into Gaza, vastly reducing and at times denying food supplies, medicines, fuel, cooking gas, and parts for water and sanitation systems…. During November, an average of 4.6 trucks of food per day entered Gaza from Israel compared with an average of 123 trucks per day in October. Spare parts for the repair and maintenance of water-related equipment have been denied entry for over a year. The World Health Organization just reported that half of Gaza's ambulances are now out of order"—and the rest soon became targets for direct Israeli attack. Gaza's only power station was forced to suspend operation for lack of fuel, and could not be started up again because they needed spare parts, which had been sitting in the Israeli port of Ashdod for eight months. Shortage of electricity led to a 300 percent increase in burn cases at Shifaa' hospital in the Gaza Strip, resulting from efforts to light wood fires. Israel barred shipment of chlorine, so that by mid-December in Gaza City and the north access to water was limited to six hours every three days. The human consequences are not counted among Palestinian victims of Israeli terror—or "disproportionate retaliation," to adopt the standard ideological construct.[16]

After the November 4 Israeli attack, both sides escalated violence (all deaths were Palestinian) until the cease-fire formally ended on December 19, and Prime Minister Olmert authorized the full-scale invasion.

A few days earlier Hamas had proposed to return to the original June cease-fire agreement, which Israel had not observed. Historian and former Carter administration high official Robert Pastor passed the proposal to a "senior official" in the Israeli Defense Forces (IDF), but Israel did not respond. The head of Shin Bet, Israel's internal security agency, was quoted in Israeli sources on December 21 as saying that Hamas is interested in continuing the "calm" with Israel, while its military wing is continuing preparations for conflict.

"There clearly was an alternative to the military approach to stopping the rockets," Pastor said, keeping to the narrow issue of Gaza. There was also a more far-reaching alternative: namely, accepting a political settlement including all of the occupied territories.[17]

Israel's senior diplomatic correspondent Akiva Eldar reports that shortly before Israel launched its full-scale invasion on Saturday, December 27, "Hamas politburo chief Khaled Meshal announced on the Iz al-Din al-Qassam Web site that he was prepared not only for a 'cessation of aggression'—he proposed going back to the arrangement at the Rafah crossing as of 2005, before Hamas won the elections and later took over the region. That arrangement was for the crossing to be managed jointly by Egypt, the European Union, the Palestinian Authority presidency and Hamas."[18]

In brief, Israel had no right to fire a single bullet into the Gaza Strip. Furthermore, it is hard to see how the conclusion can even be controversial.

A standard claim of the more vulgar apologists for Israeli violence is that in the case of the 2008–9 Gaza assault, "as in so many instances in the past half century—the Lebanon War of 1982, the 'Iron Fist' response to the 1988 intifada, the Lebanon War of 2006—the Israelis have reacted to intolerable acts of terror with a determination to inflict terrible pain, to teach the enemy a lesson. The civilian suffering and deaths are inevitable; the lessons less so" (*New Yorker* editor David Remnick).[19] The 2006 Lebanon invasion can be justified only on the grounds of appalling cynicism, as already reviewed. The reference to Israel's brutal response to the 1988 intifada is too depraved even to discuss; a sympathetic interpretation might be that it reflects astonishing ignorance. But Remnick's claim about the 1982 invasion, though equally astonishing, is quite common, a remarkable feat of incessant propaganda, which merits a few reminders.

Uncontroversially, the Israel-Lebanon border was quiet for a year before the Israeli invasion, at least from Lebanon to Israel, north to south. Through the year, the PLO scrupulously observed a U.S.-initiated ceasefire, despite constant Israeli provocations, including bombing with many civilian casualties, presumably intended to elicit some reaction that could be used to justify Israel's planned invasion. The best Israel could achieve was two light symbolic responses. It then invaded with a pretext too absurd to be taken seriously.

The invasion had nothing to do with "intolerable acts of terror," though it did have to do with intolerable acts: of diplomacy. That has never been obscure. Shortly after the U.S.-backed invasion began, Israel's leading academic specialist on the Palestinians, Yehoshua Porath—no dove—wrote that Arafat's success in maintaining the cease-fire constituted "a veritable catastrophe in the eyes of the Israeli government," since it opened the way to a political settlement. The government hoped that the PLO would resort to terrorism, undermining the threat that it would be "a legitimate negotiating partner for future political accommodations."

The facts were well understood in Israel, and not concealed. Prime Minister Yitzhak Shamir stated that Israel went to war because there was "a terrible danger.... Not so much a military one as a political one," prompting the fine Israeli satirist B. Michael to write that "the lame excuse of a military danger or a danger to the Galilee is dead. [We] have removed the political danger" by striking first, in time; now, "Thank God, there is no one to talk to." Historian Benny Morris recognized that the PLO had observed the cease-fire, and explained that "the war's inevitability rested on the PLO as a political threat to Israel and to Israel's hold on the occupied territories." Others have frankly acknowledged the unchallenged facts.[20]

In a front-page think piece on the December 2008 Gaza invasion, *New York Times* correspondent Steven Lee Meyers writes that "in some ways, the Gaza attacks were reminiscent of the gamble Israel took, and largely lost, in Lebanon in 1982 [when] it invaded to eliminate the threat of Yasir Arafat's forces." Correct, but not in the sense he has in mind. In 1982, as very likely in 2008, it was necessary to eliminate the threat of political settlement.[21]

The hope of Israeli propagandists has been that Western intellectuals and media would buy the fairy tale that in 1982 Israel was reacting to rockets raining on the Galilee, "intolerable acts of terror." Hence as in Gaza in 2008, they were acting in legitimate self-defense, though perhaps killing some fifteen thousand to twenty thousand Lebanese and Palestinians, and destroying much of southern Lebanon and Beirut, was "disproportionate," however understandable. And those who run the efficient propaganda services have not been disappointed,[22] just as they have not been disappointed by the remarkable unanimity in adopting Israel's utterly indefensible claim of having acted in legitimate self-defense when it attacked Gaza even more ferociously than before in December 2008.

Criticism by human rights organizations and others, including the Goldstone report, has kept to the narrower question of propriety of means, a secondary issue, and a focus welcomed by advocates of U.S.-Israeli violence because of the inevitable uncertainty about evidence under wartime conditions, even though international humanitarian law is explicit. Article 33 of the Fourth Geneva Convention of 1950 states that "no protected person may be punished for an offence he or she has not personally committed. Collective penalties and likewise all measures of intimidation or of terrorism are prohibited.... Reprisals against protected persons and their property are prohibited." Gazans are unambiguously "protected persons" under Israeli military occupation. The Hague Convention of 1907 also declares that "no general penalty, pecuniary or otherwise, can be inflicted on the population on account of the acts of individuals for which it cannot be regarded as collectively responsible" (Article 50). Furthermore, High Contracting Parties to the Geneva Convention are bound to "respect and to ensure respect for the present Convention in all circumstances," including of course Israel and its U.S. partner in crime, which is obligated to prevent, or to punish, the serious breaches of the convention by its own leaders and its client. When the media report, as they regularly do, that "Israel hopes [reducing supplies of fuel and electricity to the Gaza Strip] will create popular pressure to force the Hamas rulers of Gaza and other militant groups to stop the rocket fire,"[23] they are calmly informing us that Israel is in grave breach of international humanitarian law, as is the United States for not ensuring respect for law on the part of its client. The same is true when the Israeli High Court grants legitimacy to these measures, as it has, adding another page to its dismal record of subordination to state power. Israel's leading legal journalist, Moshe Negbi, knew what he was doing when he entitled his despairing review of the record of the courts *We Were Like Sodom*.[24]

International law cannot be enforced against powerful states, except by their own populations. That is always a difficult task, particularly so when articulate opinion declares crime to be legitimate, either explicitly or by tacit adoption of a criminal framework, which is more insidious because it renders the crimes invisible.

The January 2008 Hamas-led prison break allowed Gazans for the first time in years to go shopping in nearby Egyptian towns, at least briefly, plainly an intolerable act because it slightly undermined U.S.-Israeli-Egyptian strangulation of these unpeople. But the powerful quickly recognized that these events too could turn into "good news." Israeli deputy defense minister Matan Vilnai "said openly what some senior Israeli officials would only say anonymously," Stephen Erlanger reported in the *New York Times*: the prison break might allow Israel to rid itself of any responsibility for Gaza after having reduced it to devastation and misery in forty years of brutal occupation, keeping it only for target practice, and of course under full military occupation, its borders sealed by Israeli forces on land, sea, and air, apart from an opening to Egypt (in the unlikely event that Egypt would agree).[25]

That appealing prospect would complement Israel's ongoing criminal actions in the West Bank, carefully designed along the lines already outlined to ensure that there will be no viable future for Palestinians there. At the same time Israel can turn to solving its persistent and deeply troubling "demographic problem," the presence of non-Jews in a self-declared "democratic Jewish state." The ultranationalist right-wing extremist Avigdor Lieberman, now foreign minister, was harshly condemned as a racist in Israel when he advanced the idea of forcing Arab citizens of Israel (in Wadi Ara in the Galilee) into a derisory "Palestinian state," presenting this to the world as a "land swap." As Israel and its paymaster have shifted to the right, Lieberman's proposal has been incorporated into the mainstream. Knesset member Otniel Schneller of Ehud Olmert's Kadima Party, "considered to be one of the people closest and most loyal to Prime Minister Ehud Olmert," proposed a plan that "appears very similar to one touted by Yisrael Beiteinu leader Avigdor Lieberman," though Schneller says his plan would be "more gradual," and the Arabs affected "will remain citizens of Israel even though their territory will belong to the [Palestinian Authority and] they will not be allowed to resettle in other areas of Israel."[26] The right-wing ultranationalist Ariel Sharon had reservations about such actions, but by now his views seem moderate within the U.S.-Israeli spectrum.

In December 2007, Tzipi Livni, the leading figure in Kadima after Olmert's forced resignation under corruption charges and the last hope of many Israeli doves, adopted the same position. An eventual Palestinian state, she suggested, would "be the national answer to the Palestinians" in the territories and those "who live in different refugee camps or in Israel." With Israeli Arabs dispatched to their natural place, Israel would then achieve the long-sought goal of freeing itself from the Arab taint, a stand that is familiar enough in U.S. history.[27]

The Lieberman-Schneller-Livni notions of "soft transfer" were first proposed by democratic socialist political philosopher Michael Walzer, who wrote thirty years before Lieberman that those who are "marginal to the nation" (Palestinians) should be "helped to leave" in the interests of peace and justice. The ideas are praised by *New York Times* Israel correspondent Ethan Bronner, who writes that the left likes Lieberman's "willingness to create two states, one Jewish, one Palestinian, which would involve yielding areas that are now part of Israel" in a land swap— a polite way of saying that Israeli citizens of the wrong ethnicity will be transferred by force, relieving Israel of its "demographic problem."[28]

Of course the unpeople are not consulted, though their views are occasionally reported, including their vociferous objection to being forcefully transferred from a rich first-world country to some barely existing fragment that might graciously be called "a state."[29]

For Israel, this is no small matter. Despite heroic efforts by its apologists, it is not easy to conceal the fact that a "democratic Jewish state" is no more acceptable to liberal opinion than a "democratic Christian state" or a "democratic white state" or an "Islamic democracy." Such notions could be tolerated if the religious/ethnic identification were mostly symbolic, like selecting an official day of rest. But in the case of Israel, it goes far beyond that. The most extreme departure from minimal democratic principles has been the complex array of laws and bureaucratic arrangements designed to vest control of over 90 percent of the land in the hands of the Jewish National Fund (JNF), an organization committed to using charitable funds in ways that are "directly or indirectly beneficial to persons of Jewish religion, race or origin," so its documents explain; "a public institution recognized by the Government of Israel and the World Zionist Organization as the exclusive instrument for the development of Israel's lands," restricted to Jewish use, in perpetuity (with marginal exceptions when useful), and barred to non-Jewish labor (though the principle has often been ignored for imported cheap labor). This radical violation of elementary civil rights, funded by American citizens thanks to the tax-free status of the JNF, finally reached Israel's High Court in 2000, in a case brought by a professional Arab couple who had been barred from the town of Katzir. The Court ruled in their favor, in a narrow decision, which seems to have been barely implemented. After various delays, they were finally permitted to purchase land in Katzir in 2006, and put up for sale their former house in Baka al-Garbiyeh. They expressed their hope that a Jewish family would move in, explaining why: "I'll tell you why my family won't object to Jews living here. It's a known fact that the State of Israel takes care of every Jew, all over the world. As soon as a Jew moves in they'll give us new asphalt roads without potholes. The electricity network will be replaced too, and even the sewer system will be improved. And maybe, just maybe, they'll build a little synagogue, the light from which will finally enable us to see our way at night."[30]

The comment tells us a good deal about significant aspects of Israeli democracy—again, matters hardly unfamiliar here.

A year later, a young Arab couple was barred from the town of Rakefet, on state land, on grounds of "social incompatibility."[31] The Knesset later took steps to undermine the historic court judgment banning the racist land laws. In December 2009, it passed legislation introduced by (centrist) Kadima Knesset members "which states that reception committees of Israeli communities can decide who will reside in their towns. One consequence of that bill is that Israeli Arabs would not be able to live in those towns if the reception committees decide so." The effect is to reverse the High Court decision, though one Likud MK felt that it did not go far enough in overturning the Court decision. "In this way," Avirama Golan writes, "Israel is shutting an entire population group out of the state's life and turning it into an oppressed, bitter, irredentist community." The Ministerial Committee for Legislation also rejected a bill "proposing that the state enforce equal allocation of land to Jews and Arabs." The bill's sponsors observed that the Israel Lands Administration "hasn't approved the building of a new Arab village since 1948," and has allocated state land only to Jews, one of many aspects of the severe discrimination against non-Jewish citizens.[32]

As the year 2010 opens, one Israeli demand holding up negotiations is that Palestinians must not just recognize Israel, but must recognize it as a "Jewish state," that is, a state in which Palestinian citizens reside by sufferance, not by right. And in reaction to the expression of sympathy for Gazans under Israeli attack by Arab parliamentarians, the Knesset passed a law changing the oath taken by members so that instead of swearing loyalty to "the State of Israel and its laws," they will be required to vow loyalty to the State of Israel as a "Jewish democratic state."[33]

The contradiction in terms is not easy to overcome. Americans who pay the bills are expected to look the other way.

For Palestinians, there are now two options. One is that the United States and Israel will abandon their unilateral rejectionism since the 1970s and accept the international consensus on a two-state settlement, in accord with international law. That outcome is not impossible. A settlement along these lines came close in negotiations in Taba, Egypt, in January 2001, and might have been reached, participants reported, had Israeli prime minister Barak not called off the negotiations prematurely. We return to this important exception. There have been unofficial negotiations since that have produced similar proposals. Though possibilities diminish as U.S.-Israeli settlement and infrastructure programs proceed, they have not been eliminated. By now the international consensus is near universal, supported by the Arab League, Iran, Hamas, in fact every relevant actor apart from the United States and Israel.[34]

A second possibility is the one that the United States and Israel are actually implementing, along the lines described earlier. Palestinians will then be consigned to their Gaza prison and to West Bank cantons, perhaps joined by Israeli Arab citizens as well if the Lieberman-Schneller-Livni plans are implemented. For the occupied territories, that will realize the intentions expressed by Defense Minister Moshe Dayan in the early years of the occupation: Israel, he informed his colleagues, should tell the Palestinian refugees in the occupied territories that "we have no solution, you shall continue to live like dogs, and whoever wishes may leave, and we will see where this process leads." He explained to a Palestinian poetess that "the situation today resembles the complex relationship between a Bedouin man and the girl he kidnaps against her will.... You Palestinians, as a nation, don't want us today, but we'll change your attitude by forcing our presence on you."

Not an original thought. When reports arrived of the massacres of Mexican civilians and rapes of local women by U.S. soldiers during what Mexican historians call "the American invasion" of 1846–48, the *New York Herald* thoughtfully observed that "like the Sabine virgins, she will soon learn to love her ravisher."

For the former Palestine, the general conception was articulated by Labor Party leader Haim Herzog, later president, in 1972: "I do not deny the Palestinians a place or stand or opinion on every matter.... But certainly I am not prepared to consider them as partners in any respect in a land that has been consecrated in the hands of our nation for thousands of years. For the Jews of this land there cannot be any partner."[35]

A third possibility would be a binational state.[36] That was a feasible option in the pre-state period, and advocacy of that outcome was regarded as part of the Zionist movement, and had a degree of popular support within it (not just among a few leading intellectuals, as often assumed). It again became a feasible option in the early years of the occupation, perhaps a federal arrangement leading to eventual closer integration as circumstances permit. There was even some support for similar ideas within Israeli military intelligence, but the grant of any political rights to Palestinians was shot down by the governing Labor Party. Proposals to that effect were made (by me in particular), but were either ignored or elicited fury. The opportunity was lost by the mid-1970s, when Palestinian national rights reached the international agenda, and the two-state consensus took shape. The first U.S. veto of a two-state resolution at the Security Council, advanced by the major Arab states, was in 1976, though it explicitly granted Israel all the rights called for in UN 242, which everyone, Israel included, regards as the basic diplomatic document. Washington's rejectionist stance continues to the present, with the exception of Clinton's last month in office. Some form of unitary state remains a distant possibility through agreement among the parties, as a later stage in a process that begins with a two-state settlement. There is no other form of advocacy of such an outcome, if we understand advocacy to include sketching a process leading from here to there; mere proposal, in contrast, is free for the asking.

It is of some interest, perhaps, that when short-term advocacy of a unitary binational state perhaps had some prospects, it was anathema, while today, when it is completely unfeasible except as a long-term goal after many intermediate stages, it is greeted with respect and is put forth in leading journals. The reason for the new tolerance, perhaps, is that the proposal serves to undermine the prospect of a peaceful diplomatic settlement in some tolerable terms, the only form of true advocacy of a unitary outcome that I know of.

It is sometimes argued that Israeli settlement programs have proceeded so far that a two-state outcome has been eliminated—which means that a unitary binational state is barred as well, unless some other form of true advocacy can be devised, which has not so far happened and seems unlikely. The objection is based on the assumption that if the IDF were to try to remove settlements by force, it would lead to civil war. But there is no need to remove settlements at all. It would be enough for the IDF to be withdrawn to Israel's borders, in which case the vast majority of settlers would move from their comfortable subsidized illegal West Bank homes to subsidized homes within Israel. Those who choose to remain should be granted citizenship in a Palestinian state. The Gaza evacuation in 2005 could have been carried out the same way, but Israel preferred what the distinguished Israeli sociologist, the late Baruch Kimmerling, described as the "absurd theater" of a constructed trauma "to demonstrate to everyone that Israel is incapable of withstanding additional evacuations," a farcical replay of what the press had ridiculed as "Operation National Trauma '82," when Israel had to withdraw from its settlements in Egyptian Sinai.[37]

There is of course a possibility that the IDF would refuse orders, which would amount to a military coup, in which case all bets are off.

One can also contemplate what seem to me more favorable outcomes, erasing state boundaries altogether in closer forms of integration. But those are questions for the future.

Those who call for a binational (one-state) settlement argue that on its present course, Israel will become an apartheid state with a large Palestinian population deprived of rights, laying the basis for a civil rights struggle leading to a unitary democratic state. This position is based on the assumption that there are only two options: the international consensus and Israeli takeover of all of the former Palestine. But that is a fallacy. There are three options: the third, which is omitted in these discussions, is what the United States and Israel are now implementing, and will continue to implement unless something approaching the international consensus can be achieved. There is no reason to believe that the United States, Israel, or any other Western state would allow anything like a full takeover of Palestine to happen. Rather, they will proceed exactly as they are now doing in the territories today, taking no responsibility for Palestinians who are left to rot in the various prisons and cantons that may dot the landscape, far from the eyes of Israelis (and tourists) traveling on their segregated superhighways to their well-subsidized West Bank towns and suburbs, controlling the crucial water resources of the region, and benefiting from their close ties with Western powers and the U.S. and other international corporations that are evidently pleased to see a loyal military power at the periphery of the crucial Middle East region, with an advanced high-tech economy and close military, intelligence, and economic links to Washington.

In that way, the "demographic problem" will be resolved, but it is unlikely to retard Israel's descent to the status of a pariah state. In fact, Israel's global status is already coming to resemble that of South Africa forty years ago, particularly after its invasion of Gaza. And it is reacting much the same way as white nationalists did: with "information campaigns" ("hasbara" exercises) to instruct the world on its errors and misunderstanding, arrogant self-righteousness, circling the wagons, defiance, reliance on the United States to protect it no matter what the world thinks, and often with extraordinary paranoia.[38]

Despite many differences, it is worth recalling the history of the Apartheid regime. In 1958, the South African foreign minister informed the American ambassador that strong UN resolutions against South Africa passed by the majority of countries do not matter: "What matters more than...all other votes put together is [the position] of [the] U.S. in view of its predominant position of leadership in [the] Western world." In brief, there is really only one vote at the UN, an observation that gained more force in subsequent years as decolonization proceeded and protests grew more intense.[39]

By the late 1970s, decades of protest against apartheid had expanded to initiatives of boycott, divestment, and sanctions (BDS). Corporations were beginning to abide by the (1977) Sullivan principles of pulling out, and Congress was soon to pass sanctions (over Reagan's veto). But the South African minister's insight into world affairs retained its force. Through the 1980s, U.S. trade with South Africa increased despite the 1985 congressional sanctions (which Reagan evaded), and Reagan continued to back South African depredations in neighboring countries that led to an estimated 1.5 million deaths. As late as 1988 the administration condemned Nelson Mandela's African National Congress as one of the world's "more notorious terrorist groups."[40] The Apartheid regime remained strong, some thought invulnerable. But then U.S. policy shifted, and within a few years, the regime had collapsed.

There are clear lessons here both for Israelis and for those outside who are committed to bringing some measure of peace and justice to the region. As long as U.S. rejectionism remains firm, Israel may feel that it can defy the world, but it is treading on dangerous ground. And tactics of protest should be guided by the recognition that in the current world order, despite growing diversity, the observation of the South African minister remains largely accurate.

SEVEN

Century's Challenges

The primary challenge facing the people of the world is, literally, decent survival. The former head of the U.S. Strategic Command (STRAT-COM), General Lee Butler, put the matter plainly over a decade ago. He wrote that throughout his long professional military career he was "among the most avid of these keepers of the faith in nuclear weapons," but it is now his "burden to declare with all of the conviction I can muster that in my judgment they served us extremely ill," for reasons he outlines. He then raises a haunting question: "By what authority do succeeding generations of leaders in the nuclear-weapons states usurp the power to dictate the odds of continued life on our planet? Most urgently, why does such breathtaking audacity persist at a moment when we should stand trembling in the face of our folly and united in our commitment to abolish its most deadly manifestations?"[1] To our shame, his question not only remains unanswered, but also has taken on greater urgency.

General Butler may have been reacting to one of the most astonishing planning documents in the available record, the 1995 report of STRATCOM, entitled *Essentials of Post-Cold War Deterrence*. The report advised that the military resources directed against the former Soviet Union be maintained, but with an expanded mission. They must now be directed against "rogue states" of the third world, in accord with the

Pentagon view that "the international environment has now evolved from a 'weapon rich environment' [the USSR] to a 'target rich environment' [the Third World]." STRATCOM further advised that the United States should have available "the full range of responses." Nuclear weapons are the most important of these, because "unlike chemical or biological weapons, the extreme destruction from a nuclear explosion is immediate, with few if any palliatives to reduce its effect," and even if not used, "nuclear weapons always cast a shadow over any crisis or conflict," enabling us to gain our ends through intimidation. Nuclear weapons "seem destined to be the centerpiece of U.S. strategic deterrence for the foreseeable future." We must reject a "no first use policy," and should make it clear to adversaries that our "reaction" may "either be response or preemptive." Furthermore, "it hurts to portray ourselves as too fully rational and cool-headed." The "national persona we project" should make clear "that the U.S. may become irrational and vindictive if its vital interests are attacked" and that "some elements may appear to be potentially 'out of control.'"[2]

Forty years earlier, Bertrand Russell and Albert Einstein had warned that we face a choice that is "stark and dreadful and inescapable: Shall we put an end to the human race; or shall mankind renounce war?" They were not exaggerating. An extraterrestrial observer attending to the events of the years since might marvel that the species has survived this long in an era of nuclear weapons, and would not take lightly the warning of "Apocalypse Soon" if we pursue our present course; the words of Robert McNamara, joined by many other sober and respected analysts.

We have known for some time that environmental catastrophe is no less a threat to survival, in a not too distant future. A serious approach would surely move with dispatch toward conservation and renewable energy, along with dedication of substantial resources to technological innovations—harnessing solar energy, many scientists contend. And beyond that, significant socioeconomic changes must be undertaken to reverse the effects of the huge state-corporate social engineering projects of the post–World War II period designed to create a system based on wasteful reliance on fossil fuels.

A related threat is limited access to the basic means of life: water and sufficient food. There are short-term solutions: desalination, for example, in which Saudi Arabia is well in the lead in scale, and Israel in technology— one of many bases for constructive cooperation, if the United States and Israel permit a resolution of the Israel-Palestine conflict in terms of the international consensus on a viable two-state settlement that they have been barring for over thirty years, with rare and brief departures, another critical challenge with broad repercussions. Currently, desalination relies on high energy inputs, and unless some renewable and non-polluting source is developed, the approach is unfeasible on a large scale. And there are other looming threats: one, perhaps not remote, is the possibility of an uncontrollable pandemic, which could be devastating unless careful planning is undertaken in advance, and resources are devoted to deter the threat.

There are many uncertainties about how to address these issues. We can, however, be confident that the longer the delay in confronting them, the greater will be the cost to coming generations.

In contrast, it is clear how the threat of nuclear weapons can be ended: they can be eliminated, a legal obligation of the nuclear powers, as the World Court determined a decade ago. More broadly, there are sensible and feasible plans to restrict all production of weapons-usable fissile materials to an international agency, to which states can apply for nonmilitary uses. The UN Committee on Disarmament has already voted for a verifiable treaty with these provisions, in November 2004. The vote was 147 to 1 (the United States) with two abstentions (Israel and Britain). A negative vote by the reigning global superpower amounts to a veto, in fact a double veto: the proposals cannot be implemented, and are banned from public awareness. But these outcomes are not graven in stone. There are concrete steps that can be taken to progress toward these critically important goals. And an informed and engaged public, worldwide, can act to ensure that the opportunity is not lost.

One important step would be the establishment of nuclear weapons–free zones (NWFZs). There are a number of cases, though as always, their significance depends on the willingness of the great powers to observe the rules. Indian strategic analyst Brahma Chellaney observes that the 1985 South Pacific NWFZ treaty was only accepted more than twenty years later by Britain, France, and the United States (the United States, however, did not ratify it), "long after its original purpose had been lost." It was delayed until "a final round of French nuclear tests in the region were carried out, with British and American logistical and other assistance, despite objections from many Asia-Pacific nations." Furthermore, the Federated States of Micronesia, the Marshall Islands, and Palau, effectively U.S. colonies, are excluded from the NWFZ, and serve as bases for U.S. nuclear submarines. Chellaney adds that "the objectives of the Southeast Asian [NWFZ] are being frustrated by opposition from all five nuclear powers."[3]

Perhaps the most egregious violation of the intent of an NWFZ involves the island of Diego Garcia, a major U.S.-UK base for their military operations in the Middle East and Central Asia, and a storage site for nuclear weapons for future use. The island, from which the population was brutally and illegally expelled by its British overlords to build the huge U.S. military base, is claimed by Mauritius, a signer of the African NWFZ. In theory, much of the Southern hemisphere is covered by such zones, but without great power compliance, they may "provide comfort from the harsh nuclear realities, but not from the perils of nuclear war," Chellaney comments.

In July 2009, the Treaty of Pelindaba, establishing the African NWFZ, entered into force. The treaty explicitly includes Diego Garcia, though a footnote cites British reservations about sovereignty. The African Union (AU) regards the territory as "an integral part of Mauritius," an AU member. Clinton had signed the treaty but did not submit it for ratification. Were the United States to ratify it, it could not store nuclear weapons in its military base there. Russia will not ratify the treaty without assurances that the United States will not use Diego Garcia as a way station for nuclear weapons. The United States claims that the footnote on disputed sovereignty permits it to continue to use Diego Garcia for offensive military operations and for nuclear weapons, despite the unanimous AU stand to the contrary.[4]

On December 1, 2009, the U.S. Navy announced that a submarine tender "will be forward-deployed to its new homeport at Diego Garcia."

That "will provide an expeditionary maintenance capability to the fast-attack submarines (SSNs) and guided missile submarines (SSGNs), particularly those operating in the U.S. 5th Fleet area of responsibility," Middle East and East African waters. The move "demonstrates the Navy's continuing commitment to peace and regional security through maintaining strong capabilities"—as, presumably, does the use of the base for bombing missions and storage of nuclear weapons. Iranians and other actual and potential targets will no doubt be much impressed by the commitment to peace and security.[5]

Despite the obstructionism of the United States and its British subordinate, establishment of NWFZs can be a valuable step, nowhere more than in the Middle East. As noted earlier, in April 1991, the UN Security Council affirmed "the goal of establishing in the Middle East a zone free from weapons of mass destruction and all missiles for their delivery and the objective of a global ban on chemical weapons" (Resolution 687, Article 14), a particularly firm commitment for the United States and UK, for the reasons already discussed. The goal of a Middle East NWFZ has been endorsed by Iran, and is supported by a large majority of Americans and Iranians. It is, however, dismissed by the U.S. government and both political parties, and it is hard to find even a mention in mainstream discussion despite the intense focus on the alleged threat of Iranian nuclear weapons programs. It is also noteworthy that a large majority of Americans and Iranians, along with the developing countries (G-77, now more than 130), agree that Iran has the "inalienable rights" of all parties to the Non-Proliferation Treaty "to develop research, production, and use of nuclear energy for peaceful purposes without discrimination," rights that would also extend to U.S. allies Israel, Pakistan, and India were they to accept the NPT. When Washington and the media assert, as they do regularly, that Iran is defying "the world" by enriching uranium, they are defining "the world" (alternatively, the "international community") to be Washington and whoever happens to agree with it at the moment.[6]

By definition, Washington is part of the world. London too, almost always. It is not entirely clear how to describe the U.S.-British relationship in the post–World War II period. By 1945, the British Foreign Office recognized ruefully that henceforth Britain would be a "junior partner" in global management, and occasional efforts to go beyond have regularly been rebuffed by the global ruler. Tony Blair was ridiculed in the British media as George Bush's poodle. Perhaps the most accurate description of the relationship was given by a senior Kennedy adviser during the Cuban missile crisis, when U.S. planners were treating Britain with utter contempt, not even informing their British ally of plans that might lead to the destruction of Britain in a retaliatory Russian strike. The adviser gave a definition of the "special relationship": Britain serves as "our lieutenant (the fashionable word is partner)."[7] Britain of course prefers the fashionable word.

The distinction helps explain European delight over the election of Obama. Bush and his colleagues, particularly in Bush's first term, simply informed Europe that you are our lieutenants. You are "irrelevant," Washington declared, if you do not go along with our dictates. Obama tells them they are our respected partners, words they like to hear—and then goes on to treat them as lieutenants, but quietly.

A crucial step toward implementing Resolution 687 would be the willingness of Washington and elite sectors to attend to public opinion—what we might call "democracy promotion." Agreement of the countries of the region is also necessary, as well as adequate inspection. These challenges for the future may not be insurmountable. While 80 percent of the population of the United States believes that the government is "run by a few big interests looking out for themselves," not "for the benefit of all the people," the public may not passively accept these conditions forever. They may choose to act, as in the past, to overcome this disenfranchisement—another critical challenge for the future, worldwide. As for inspection, the International Atomic Energy Agency (IAEA) has proven to be highly competent, and with great power support could become more so. One of Israel's leading strategic analysts, Zeev Maoz, has presented solid arguments that Israel's nuclear programs are harmful to its security, and has urged Israel to "seriously reconsider its nuclear policy and explore using its nuclear leverage to bring about a regional agreement for a weapons of mass destruction free zone (WMDFZ) in the Middle East." As noted, Iran has officially supported this outcome for some years. Iran scholar Ervand Abrahamian observes that Iran seems to be the only case "in international politics where a country has actually discussed the pros and cons of building a bomb" in public. He cites "fairly conservative people from the military arguing against having the nuclear option," including a minister of defense.[8]

If these prove to be idle dreams, we may be marching resolutely toward the decision to "put an end to the human race."

Current developments are not encouraging. With its overwhelming power, Washington's stand is of course decisive. The Bush administration in its later years was praised in the West for a perceived shift from its former aggressive militarism toward diplomacy, but the admiration was not universal. Commenting on President Bush's January 2008 visit to the Gulf states, Middle East specialist and former ambassador Chas Freeman writes that "Arabs are notoriously courteous and welcoming to guests, even when they don't like those guests.... Yet, when the American president visited and spoke on the subject of Iran, he drew an editorial in Saudi Arabia's major English language newspaper deploring the fact that 'American policy represents not diplomacy in search of peace, but madness in search of war.'"[9]

Democrats do not offer much of an alternative. The stands of both political parties are commonly far more confrontational than most of public opinion, not only with regard to the Middle East.[10]

Developments in Europe are also fraught with danger. To the NATO leadership, it is the merest truism that they are a force for peace, like the navy in Diego Garcia. Most of the world, which has rather different memories of Western benevolence, sees matters differently. So does Russia, in part because of Clinton's reneging on clear though informal commitments to Gorbachev not to allow NATO to extend to the former East Germany, let alone farther to the east. The United States also rejected the proposal of Russia (with Ukraine and Belarus) to establish a formal NWFZ from the Arctic to the Black Sea, encompassing Central Europe. In response, Russia withdrew the policy of no first use of nuclear weapons that it had adopted after the Bush-Gorbachev agreement, reverting to the first-use policy that NATO had never abandoned.[11]

Tensions mounted rapidly when Bush II took office, with threatening rhetoric, sharp expansion of offensive military capacity, withdrawal from key security treaties, and direct aggression. As predicted, Russia responded by increasing its own military capacity, followed later by China. Ballistic missile defense (BMD) programs are a particular threat. One reason is that they are understood to be a step toward militarization of space. Washington continues to press forward with these plans, against uniform international opposition. In February 2008, the Union of Concerned Scientists reports, "the Bush administration rejected a draft treaty presented at the U.N. Conference on Disarmament that would ban space weapons and prohibit attacking satellites from the ground or space." Of course potential targets will respond to militarization of space, not with an effort to match the colossal U.S. military system, but in ways appropriate to their capacities, raising the threat of destruction, if only by accident. For such reasons, the most respected and sober U.S. strategic analysts warned early on that the Bush administration's military programs and its aggressive stance carry "an appreciable risk of ultimate doom."[12]

BMD is also understood on all sides to be a first-strike weapon, perhaps capable of nullifying a retaliatory strike and thus undermining deterrent capacity. The quasi-governmental RAND Corporation describes BMD as "not simply a *shield* but an *enabler* of U.S. action." Across a broad part of the political spectrum, military analysts write that "missile defense isn't really meant to protect America. It's a tool for global dominance." BMD is "about preserving America's ability to wield power abroad. It's not about defense. It's about offense. And that's exactly why we need it."[13]

Russian and Chinese analysts draw the same conclusions. Russian strategists can hardly fail to regard U.S. BMD installations in Eastern Europe as serious potential threats to their security. They will "rightly conclude that the system might be designed to counter Russia's deterrent in addition to a nuclear attack from Iran," two prominent U.S. specialists conclude in a detailed analysis, in which they also review the reasons Russia regards the alleged Iranian threat as a mere pretext, particularly after Bush's rejection of Putin's proposal to place the installations in

Georgia or Azerbaijan, or eastern Turkey, where they would face Iran instead of Russia.[14] The alleged Iranian military threat can hardly be taken seriously for other reasons. One is that any potential threat could be overcome by Western agreement to pursue efforts to establish a Middle East NWFZ. Beyond that, unless Iranian leaders are dedicated to instant self-immolation, the chances of Iran even arming a missile, let alone using it, are minuscule. If the missile defense system is directed against Iran, as claimed, then it can only be intended to neutralize a possible deterrent to a U.S. first strike.

Russia reacted as expected, developing more destructive offensive weapons, including new submarine-based missile systems with nuclear warheads; withdrawing from the Conventional Forces NATO–Warsaw Pact treaty; and threatening to aim missiles at European participants in the U.S. BMD programs. "We will be obliged to redirect our missiles at installations which we firmly believe pose a threat to our national security," Putin warned: "I am obliged to say this openly and honestly today."[15]

The U.S. determination to extend NATO to the east has other motives as well. From the 1820s, U.S. planners resolved to dominate the Western hemisphere, and during World War II, extended those aspirations to global dominance, intending to exercise control also over the Far East and the former British empire, particularly Western Asia's energy resources. As Russia began to grind down Nazi armies after Stalingrad, and it was realized that Germany would not survive the war as a great power, the goals extended to as much of Eurasia as possible, at least its economic core in Western Europe. In this "Grand Area," as planners called it, the United States would hold "unquestioned power" with "military and economic supremacy," while ensuring the "limitation of any exercise of sovereignty" by states that might interfere with its global designs. It was always understood that Europe might choose to follow an independent course, perhaps the Gaullist vision of a Europe from the Atlantic to the Urals. NATO was partially intended to counter this threat. For similar reasons, Washington strongly favors expansion of NATO to include small states more likely to heed Washington's demands, thus diluting the influence of the "Old Europe" condemned by Donald Rumsfeld, Germany and France, the commercial and industrial heartland. Expansion of NATO, and assigning new tasks to it, also furthers this goal of controlling Europe.[16]

The Grand Area, however, is tottering, even at its core. As discussed earlier, Nixon's National Security Council concluded in 1971 that if the United States cannot control Latin America, it cannot expect "to achieve a successful order elsewhere in the world," a policy problem that is becoming more serious as South America takes steps to escape U.S. control. More generally, for some years, the international economy has been tripolar, with major centers in North America, Europe, and East/Northeast Asia, now increasingly South Asia and Southeast Asia as well. And there are other rising powers, notably Brazil, though they still lag well behind. There is however one dimension in which the United States reigns supreme: means of violence, on which it spends almost as much as the rest of the world combined, and is technologically far more advanced.[17] But in other respects the world is becoming more diverse and complex.

Traditional methods of control have by no means been abandoned. Militarization of Latin America has already been discussed. Resort to economic strangulation continues worldwide: against Cuba (in opposition to U.S. public opinion), to punish Palestinians for voting "the wrong way" in a free election, and increasingly against Iran. In March 2008, the U.S. Treasury Department warned the world's financial institutions against dealings with Iran's major state-owned banks. The warnings have teeth, thanks to a provision of the Patriot Act that enables Washington to bar any financial institution violating U.S. directives from access to the U.S. financial system. That is a threat that few will dare to face, possibly not even China. Economic analyst John McGlynn hardly exaggerates when he describes the March Treasury warning as a declaration of war against Iran, which might substantially isolate Iran from the international economy.[18]

McGlynn's analysis receives support from an unexpected source: a proposal for a militant "new grand strategy" issued in January 2008 by five high-level former NATO commanders, advising that "nuclear weapons— and with them the option of first use—are indispensable, since there is simply no realistic prospect of a nuclear-free world." Among the potential "acts of war" that we must guard against, they include "abusing the leverage" provided by "weapons of finance." To be sure, they adopt the conventional doctrine that brandishing such weapons becomes an "act of war" only when it is in the hands of others. When we brandish such weapons—actually, not potentially—they are transmuted into righteous means of self-defense, as are any aggressive actions of one's own and by favored states, throughout history.[19]

Europe so far has chosen to remain largely subordinate to the United States, Japan as well. China has followed an independent path, much to the discomfiture of Washington hawks, who are restrained because of the reliance of the U.S. economy on China. India has strengthened its alliance with the United States, while also maintaining a somewhat independent stance. China and India have been growing rapidly, but they face very severe internal problems; whether they can be overcome is far from clear. One indication is their ranking on the UN Human Development Index (December 2008): India ranks 132 and China 94, a ranking that is more speculative in the case of China because of less easy access. The Middle East oil producers face even more dire problems despite the great wealth that they are now accumulating. Thirty years ago, French economist Maurice Guernier, one of the founders of the OECD, warned that the region is "heading for tragedy" unless it undertakes a rational investment policy to overcome its reliance on a wasting resource, a brief opportunity that will not return, and that has yet to be properly exploited.[20]

These are only a few of the serious challenges that lie ahead. Failure to confront them seriously may well confirm the speculation of one of the great figures in modern biology, Ernst Mayr, that higher intelligence is an evolutionary error, incapable of survival for more than a passing moment of evolutionary time.

EIGHT

Turning Point?

The Obama-Netanyahu-Abbas meetings in May 2009, followed by Obama's speech in Cairo, have been widely interpreted as a turning point in U.S. Middle East policy, leading to consternation in some quarters, exuberance in others. Fairly typical is Middle East analyst Dan Fromkin of the *Washington Post*, who sees "signs Obama will promote a new regional peace initiative for the Middle East, much like the one championed by Jordan's King Abdullah...[and also] the first distinct signs that Obama is willing to play hardball with Israel."[1] A closer look, however, suggests reservations.

King Abdullah insists that "There is no change to the Arab Peace Initiative, and there is no need to amend it. Any talk about amending it, is baseless."[2] Abbas, the U.S. favorite and regularly described as the president of the Palestinian Authority (his term expired in January 2009), firmly agreed. The Arab Peace Initiative reiterates the long-standing international consensus that Israel must withdraw to the international border, perhaps with "minor and mutual adjustments," to adopt official U.S. terminology before it departed sharply from world opinion in 1971, endorsing Israel's rejection of peace with Egypt in favor of large-scale settlement expansion (then in the northeastern Sinai)—a fateful decision, granting expansion priority over security, and firming up Israel's dependence on the United States. Furthermore, the consensus calls for a Palestinian state to be established in united Gaza and the West Bank after Israel's withdrawal. The Arab Peace Initiative adds that the Arab states should then normalize relations with Israel. The initiative was later adopted by the Organization of Islamic States, including Iran,[3] which had already indicated its willingness to go along with this plan.

Obama has praised the initiative and called on the Arab states to proceed to normalize relations with Israel, scrupulously evading the core of the proposal: reiteration of the international consensus.[4] His studied omission can only be understood as implicit reiteration of the U.S. rejectionist stand that has blocked a diplomatic settlement since the 1970s along with its Israeli client, in virtual isolation, with rare and temporary—and highly instructive—exceptions. There are no signs that Obama is willing even to consider the Arab Peace Initiative, let alone "promote" it. That was underscored in Obama's much heralded address to the Muslim world in Cairo on June 4, 2009, to which I will return.

The U.S.-Israel interactions—with Abbas on the sidelines—turn on two phrases: "Palestinian state" and "natural growth of settlements." Let's consider these in turn.

Obama has indeed pronounced the words "Palestinian state," echoing Bush. In contrast, the (unrevised) 1999 platform of Israel's governing party, Netanyahu's Likud, "flatly rejects the establishment of a Palestinian Arab state west of the Jordan river." The Bush-Obama position could, therefore, be understood as "hardball," if it meant anything. And it is also useful to recall that it was Netanyahu's 1996 government that was the first in Israel to use the phrase "Palestinian state." It agreed that Palestinians can call whatever fragments of Palestine are left to them "a state" if they like—or they can call them "fried chicken."[5]

The contemptuous reference to Palestinian aspirations by the 1996 Netanyahu government was a shift toward accommodation in Israeli policy. As he left office shortly before, Shimon Peres, regarded in the West as a leading dove, forcefully declared that there will never be a Palestinian state.[6]

Peres was reaffirming the official 1989 position of the Israeli coalition government (Shamir-Peres), fully endorsed by Washington (Secretary of State James Baker), that there can be no "additional Palestinian state" between Israel and Jordan—the latter declared to be a Palestinian state by U.S.-Israeli fiat. Furthermore, in the Peres-Shamir-Baker plan, the fate of the occupied territories was to be settled in terms of the guidelines established by the government of Israel, and Palestinians were permitted to take part in negotiations only if they accepted these guidelines, which ruled out Palestinian national rights.[7]

Contrary to much misunderstanding, the Oslo agreements of September 1993—the "Day of Awe," as the press described it—changed little in this regard. The Declaration of Principles that was signed ostentatiously by both parties, with Clinton standing over them, established that the end point of the process would be realization of the goals of UN 242, which accords no rights to Palestinians. And by 1993, the United States had long withdrawn its earlier interpretation of 242 (still held by the world generally, Israel aside), which took the international border to be the pre–June 1967 "green line," with perhaps "minor and mutual adjustments."

The Peres-Shamir-Baker declarations of 1989 were in response to the official Palestinian acceptance of the international consensus on a two-state solution in 1988. That proposal was first formally enunciated in 1976 in a Security Council resolution introduced by the major Arab states with the tacit support of the PLO, vetoed by the United States (again in 1980). Since then U.S.-Israeli rejectionism has persisted unchanged, with one brief but significant exception, in President Clinton's final month in office.

Clinton recognized that the terms he had offered at the failed 2000 Camp David meetings were not acceptable to any Palestinians, and in December, proposed his "parameters," inexplicit but more forthcoming. He then announced that both sides had accepted the parameters, though both had reservations. Israeli and Palestinian negotiators met in Taba, Egypt, to iron out the differences, and made considerable progress. A full resolution could have been reached in a few more days, they announced in their final joint press conference. But Israeli prime minister Barak called off the negotiations prematurely, and they have not been formally resumed.

The single exception suggests that if an American president were willing to tolerate a meaningful diplomatic settlement, it might very well be reached.

The facts are well documented in Hebrew and English sources.[8] But like much of the relevant history, they are regularly reshaped to suit doctrinal needs; for example by Jeffrey Goldberg, who writes that "by December of 2000, Israel had accepted President Bill Clinton's 'parameters,' offering the Palestinians all of the Gaza Strip, 94 percent to 96 percent of the West Bank and sovereignty over Arab areas of East Jerusalem. Arafat again rejected the deal."[9] That is a convenient and conventional fairy tale, demonstrably false or seriously misleading in all particulars, and another useful contribution to U.S.-Israeli rejectionism.

Returning to the phrase "Palestinian state," the crucial question on the U.S. side is whether when Obama produces the words, he means the international consensus or "fried chicken." So far that remains unanswered, except by careful omission, and—crucially—by Washington's steady funding of Israel's programs of settlement and development in the West Bank, recognized on all sides to be illegal, as already discussed. Probably Netanyahu would still accept his 1996 position.

The contours of "fried chicken" are being carved into the landscape daily by U.S.-backed Israeli programs. The general goals were outlined by Prime Minister Olmert in May 2006 in his "Convergence program," later expanded to "Convergence plus." Under "Convergence," Israel was to take over the territory within the illegal separation wall along with the Jordan Valley, thus imprisoning what is left, which is broken into cantons by several salients extending well to the east. The most important of these is the salient extending to the east of the greatly expanded Jerusalem area including the town of Ma'aleh Adumim, whose lands extend virtually to Jericho, effectively bisecting the West Bank. Recently released Israeli documents reveal that it was planned for this purpose in 1974 by the Rabin Labor government, driving out Palestinians. Current Defense Minister Ehud Barak (also Labor) informed the press in February 2009 that "Ma'aleh Adumim will be an inseparable part of Jerusalem and the State of Israel in any permanent settlement."[10] That includes the E-1 corridor between Greater Jerusalem and Ma'aleh Adumim, where Israeli encroachment has been proceeding slowly. The construction of a huge police headquarters in the E-1 corridor—"like a colonial palace in the Third

World"—was completed in 2008, intended to be connected to a new town that is on the drawing boards but has been held up for five years by U.S. objections, which so far have blocked plans to develop the corridor. Press investigation discovered that the bulk of the funding for the colonial palace comes from far-right private donors operating within the Elad Foundation, whose stated purpose is "the strengthening of Jewish ties to historic Jerusalem"—which has nothing to do with the E-1 corridor, intended to bisect the West Bank. The resort to private donors to build a major police headquarters for the West Bank ("Judea and Samaria") is typical of the devious methods Israel has regularly used to conceal encroachment on Arab lands within Israel itself, and in its systematic takeover of the West Bank. The concealment is very shallow, but it works, if the paymaster chooses not to look.

Several other salients to the north carve up the rest of Palestinian territory. Israel has effectively annexed Greater Jerusalem, the site of most of its current construction projects, again driving out many Arabs. These Jerusalem projects not only violate international law, as do all the others, but also Security Council resolutions (at the time, still backed by the United States).

The plans being executed right now are designed to leave Israel in control of the most valuable land in the West Bank, with Palestinians confined to unviable fragments, all separated from Jerusalem, the traditional center of Palestinian life. The separation wall also establishes Israeli control of the crucially important West Bank aquifer. Hence Israel will be able to continue to ensure that Palestinians receive one-fourth as much water as Israelis, as the World Bank reported in April, in some cases below minimum recommended levels. In the other part of Palestine, Gaza, regular Israeli attacks and the merciless siege reduce consumption far below these levels.[11]

Obama continues to support all of these programs, and has even called for substantially increasing military aid to Israel for an unprecedented ten years.[12] It appears, then, that under Obama Palestinians may be offered fried chicken, but nothing more.

Since the Oslo "peace process" was initiated in 1991, Israel has carried out a systematic policy of forced separation of Gaza from the West

Bank, with carefully calculated savagery, and in violation of Israel's repeated commitments. It was intensified with U.S. support after the unacceptable free election of January 2006. All of this too has been ignored
in Obama's "new initiative," thus underscoring his lack of commitment
to any viable Palestinian state.[13]

Gaza's separation from Palestine has been almost entirely consigned
to oblivion, an atrocity to which we should not contribute by tacit consent. Israeli journalist Amira Hass, one of the leading specialists on Gaza,
writes that

> the restrictions on Palestinian movement that Israel introduced in Jan-
> uary 1991 reversed a process that had been initiated in June 1967. Back
> then, and for the first time since 1948, a large portion of the Palestinian
> people again lived in the open territory of a single country—to be sure,
> one that was occupied, but was nevertheless whole.... The total separa-
> tion of the Gaza Strip from the West Bank is one of the greatest achieve-
> ments of Israeli politics, whose overarching objective is to prevent a
> solution based on international decisions and understandings and in-
> stead dictate an arrangement based on Israel's military superiority....
> Since January 1991, Israel has bureaucratically and logistically merely
> perfected the split and the separation: not only between Palestinians in
> the occupied territories and their brothers in Israel, but also between the
> Palestinian residents of Jerusalem and those in the rest of the territories
> and between Gazans and West Bankers/Jerusalemites. Jews live in this
> same piece of land within a superior and separate system of privileges,
> laws, services, physical infrastructure and freedom of movement.[14]

The leading academic specialist on Gaza, Harvard scholar Sara Roy,
adds that

> Gaza is an example of a society that has been deliberately reduced to a
> state of abject destitution, its once productive population transformed
> into one of aid-dependent paupers.... Gaza's subjection began long
> before Israel's recent war against it [December 2008]. The Israeli occu-
> pation—now largely forgotten or denied by the international commu-
> nity—has devastated Gaza's economy and people, especially since
> 2006.... After Israel's December [2008] assault, Gaza's already compro-
> mised conditions have become virtually unlivable. Livelihoods, homes,
> and public infrastructure have been damaged or destroyed on a scale

that even the Israel Defense Forces admitted was indefensible. In Gaza today, there is no private sector to speak of and no industry. 80 percent of Gaza's agricultural crops were destroyed and Israel continues to snipe at farmers attempting to plant and tend fields near the well-fenced and patrolled border. Most productive activity has been extinguished.... Today, 96 percent of Gaza's population of 1.4 million is dependent on humanitarian aid for basic needs. According to the World Food Programme, the Gaza Strip requires a minimum of 400 trucks of food every day just to meet the basic nutritional needs of the population. Yet, despite a 22 March [2009] decision by the Israeli cabinet to lift all restrictions on foodstuffs entering Gaza, only 653 trucks of food and other supplies were allowed entry during the week of May 10, at best meeting 23 percent of required need. Israel now allows only 30 to 40 commercial items to enter Gaza compared to 4,000 approved products prior to June 2006.[15]

It cannot be too often stressed that Israel had no credible pretext for its 2008–9 attack on Gaza, with full U.S. support and illegally using U.S. weapons. Near-universal opinion asserts the contrary, claiming that Israel was acting in self-defense. That is utterly unsustainable, in light of Israel's flat rejection of peaceful means that were readily available, as Israel and its U.S. partner in crime knew very well.[16] That aside, Israel's siege of Gaza is itself an act of war, as Israel of all countries certainly recognizes, having repeatedly justified launching major wars on grounds of partial restrictions on its access to the outside world, nothing remotely like what it has long imposed on Gaza.

One crucial element of Israel's criminal siege, little reported, is the naval blockade. Peter Beaumont reports from Gaza that "on its coastal littoral, Gaza's limitations are marked by a different fence where the bars are Israeli gunboats with their huge wakes, scurrying beyond the Palestinian fishing boats and preventing them from going outside a zone imposed by the warships."[17] According to reports from the scene, the naval siege has been tightened steadily since 2000. Fishing boats have been driven steadily out of Gaza's territorial waters and toward the shore by Israeli gunboats, often violently without warning and with many casualties. As a result of these naval actions, Gaza's fishing industry has virtually collapsed; fishing is impossible near shore because of the contamination caused by Israel's regular attacks, including the destruction of power plants and sewage facilities.

These Israeli naval attacks began shortly after the discovery by the BG (British Gas) Group of what appear to be quite sizeable natural gas fields in Gaza's territorial waters. Industry journals report that Israel is already appropriating these Gazan resources for its own use, part of its commitment to shift its economy to natural gas. The standard industry source reports that

> Israel's finance ministry has given the Israel Electric Corp. approval to purchase larger quantities of natural gas from BG than originally agreed upon, according to Israeli government sources [which] said the state-owned utility would be able to negotiate for as much as 1.5 billion cubic meters of natural gas from the Marine field located off the Mediterranean coast of the Palestinian controlled Gaza Strip. Last year the Israeli government approved the purchase of 800 million cubic meters of gas from the field by the IEC.... Recently the Israeli government changed its policy and decided the state-owned utility could buy the entire quantity of gas from the Gaza Marine field. Previously the government had said the IEC could buy half the total amount and the remainder would be bought by private power producers.[18]

The pillage of what could become a major source of income for Gaza is surely known to U.S. authorities. It is only reasonable to suppose that the intention to appropriate these limited resources, either by Israel alone or together with the collaborationist Palestinian Authority, is the motive for preventing Gazan fishing boats from entering Gaza's territorial waters.

There are some instructive precedents. In 1989, Australian foreign minister Gareth Evans signed a treaty with his Indonesian counterpart Ali Alatas granting Australia rights to the substantial oil reserves in "the Indonesian Province of East Timor." The Indonesia-Australia Timor Gap Treaty, which offered not a crumb to the people whose oil was being stolen, "is the only legal agreement anywhere in the world that effectively recognises Indonesia's right to rule East Timor," the Australian press reported. Asked about his willingness to recognize the Indonesian conquest and to rob the sole resource of the conquered territory, which had been subjected to near-genocidal slaughter by the Indonesian invader with the strong support of Australia (along with the United States and UK, and some others), Evans explained that "there is no binding legal obligation not to recognise the acquisition of territory that was acquired by force," adding that "the world is a pretty unfair place, littered with examples of acquisition by force."

It should, then, be unproblematic for Israel to follow suit in Gaza.[19]

A few years later, Evans became the leading figure in the campaign to introduce the concept "responsibility to protect"—known as R2P—into international law. R2P is intended to establish an international obligation to protect populations from grave crimes. Evans is the author of a major book on the subject and was co-chair of the International Commission on Intervention and State Sovereignty, which issued what is considered the basic document on R2P. In an article devoted to this "idealistic effort to establish a new humanitarian principle," the London *Economist* featured Evans and his "bold but passionate claim on behalf of a three-word expression which (in quite large part thanks to his efforts) now belongs to the language of diplomacy: the 'responsibility to protect.'" The article is accompanied by a picture of Evans with the caption "Evans: a lifelong passion to protect." His hand is pressed to his forehead in despair over the difficulties faced by his idealistic effort. The journal chose not to run a different photo that circulates in Australia, depicting Evans and Alatas exuberantly clasping their hands together as they toast the Timor Gap Treaty that they had just signed.

In passing, we may note that it is common to conflate two crucially different versions of R2P: the one adopted by the UN General Assembly in 2005 and the one proposed by the Evans Commission. The latter grants NATO, and NATO alone, the right to use military force within what it determines unilaterally to be its "area of jurisdiction"—boundless, as NATO has made clear by action and word, matters to which we return. The UN version, in contrast, reiterates positions already taken, with at most a shift of focus, and therefore was accepted with little opposition—at the same time that the countries of the South were bitterly and vociferously condemning "the so-called right of humanitarian intervention," which is scarcely different from the Evans Commission version of R2P. The confusion on this issue—or deception, take your pick—is both remarkable and dangerous.[20]

Though a "protected population" under international law, Gazans do not fall under the jurisdiction of the "responsibility to protect," joining other unfortunates, in accord with the maxim of Thucydides, which holds with its customary precision.

The kinds of restrictions on movement used to destroy Gaza have long been in force in the West Bank as well, less cruelly but with grim effects on life and the economy. The World Bank reports that Israel has established "a complex closure regime that restricts Palestinian access to large areas of the West Bank.... The Palestinian economy has remained stagnant, largely because of the sharp downturn in Gaza and Israel's continued restrictions on Palestinian trade and movement in the West Bank." The World Bank "cited Israeli roadblocks and checkpoints hindering trade and travel, as well as restrictions on Palestinian building in the West Bank, where the Western-backed government of Palestinian president Mahmoud Abbas holds sway."[21] Israel does permit—indeed encourage—a privileged existence for elites in Ramallah and sometimes elsewhere, largely relying on European funding; a traditional feature of colonial and neocolonial practice.

All of this constitutes what Israeli activist Jeff Halper calls a "matrix of control" to subdue the colonized population. These systematic programs over more than forty years aim to establish Defense Minister Moshe Dayan's recommendation to his colleagues shortly after the 1967 conquests, already cited, that we must tell the Palestinians in the territories that "we have no solution, you shall continue to live like dogs, and whoever wishes may leave, and we will see where this process leads."

Turning to the second bone of contention, settlements, there is indeed a confrontation, but it is rather less dramatic than portrayed. Washington's position was presented most strongly in Hillary Clinton's much-quoted statement rejecting "natural growth exceptions" to the policy opposing new settlements. Netanyahu, along with President Peres and in fact virtually the whole Israeli political spectrum, insists on permitting "natural growth" within the areas that Israel intends to annex, complaining that the United States is backing down on Bush's authorization of such expansion within his "vision" of a Palestinian state.

Senior Netanyahu cabinet members have gone further. Transportation Minister Yisrael Katz announced that "the current Israeli government will not accept in any way the freezing of legal settlement activity in Judea and Samaria."[22] The term "legal" in U.S.-Israeli parlance means "illegal, but authorized by the government of Israel with a wink from Washington." In this usage, unauthorized outposts are termed "illegal," though apart from the dictates of the powerful, they are no more illegal than the settlements granted to Israel under Bush's "vision" and Obama's scrupulous omission.

The Obama-Clinton "hardball" formulation is not new. It repeats the wording of the Bush administration draft of the 2003 Road Map, which stipulates that in Phase I, "Israel freezes all settlement activity (including natural growth of settlements)." All sides formally accept the Road Map (modified to drop the phrase "natural growth")—consistently overlooking the fact that Israel, with U.S. support, at once added fourteen "reservations" that render it inoperable.[23]

If Obama were at all serious about opposing settlement expansion, he could easily proceed with concrete measures, for example, by reducing U.S. aid by the amount devoted to this purpose. That would hardly be a radical or courageous move. The Bush I administration did so (reducing loan guarantees), but after the Oslo accord in 1993, President Clinton left calculations to the government of Israel. Unsurprisingly, there was "no change in the expenditures flowing to the settlements," the Israeli press reported: "[Prime Minister] Rabin will continue not to dry out the settlements," the report concludes. "And the Americans? They will understand."[24]

Obama administration officials informed the press that the Bush I measures are "not under discussion," and that pressures will be "largely symbolic."[25] In short, Obama understands, just as Clinton and Bush II did.

At best, settlement expansion is a side issue, rather like the issue of "illegal outposts"—namely those that the government of Israel has not authorized. Concentration on these issues diverts attention from the fact that there are no "legal outposts" and that it is the existing settlements that are the primary problem to be faced.

The U.S. press reports that "a partial freeze has been in place for several years, but settlers have found ways around the strictures...construction in the settlements has slowed but never stopped, continuing at an annual rate of about 1,500 to 2,000 units over the past three years. If building continues at the 2008 rate, the 46,500 units already approved will be completed in about 20 years.... If Israel built all the housing units already approved in the nation's overall master plan for settlements, it would almost double the number of settler homes in the West Bank."[26] The probable source, Peace Now, which monitors settlement activities, estimates further that the two largest settlements would double in size: Ariel and Ma'aleh Adumim, built mainly during the Oslo years in the salients that subdivide the West Bank into cantons.

"Natural population growth" is largely a myth, Israel's leading diplomatic correspondent, Akiva Eldar, points out, citing demographic studies by Colonel (res.) Shaul Arieli, deputy military secretary to former prime minister and incumbent defense minister Ehud Barak. Settlement growth consists largely of Israeli immigrants in violation of the Geneva Conventions, assisted with generous subsidies. Much of it is in direct violation of formal government decisions, but carried out with the authorization of the government, specifically Barak, considered a dove in the Israeli spectrum.[27]

Correspondent Jackson Diehl derides the "long-dormant Palestinian fantasy," revived by Abbas, "that the United States will simply force Israel to make critical concessions, whether or not its democratic government agrees."[28] He does not explain why refusal to participate in Israel's illegal expansion—which, if serious, would "force Israel to make critical concessions"—would be improper interference in Israel's democracy. By his logic we should stop our interference in Iran's internal affairs by refusing to help it develop nuclear weapons.

Diehl also refers to a recent Olmert peace plan of unprecedented generosity offered to Abbas, which he turned down, though it allegedly yielded just about everything to which Palestinians might reasonably aspire. Others have also referred to this mysterious plan and its rejection by Abbas. Efforts to unearth the plan have been unavailing. The only sources detected to date [June 2009] are comments by Palestinians in the Arab media that appear to be part of internal conflict about power sharing. Elliott Abrams dates the alleged plan to January 2009, citing unspecified press reports.[29]

If there were any significance to this tale, it would be trumpeted by Israeli propaganda and its enthusiasts here with credible sources, as a welcome demonstration that Palestinians simply will not accept peace, even the most moderate of them. It is questionable on other grounds. For one thing, Olmert was in no position to offer any credible proposal, certainly, in January 2009, having announced his resignation as he was facing indictment for serious corruption charges. The alleged plan is also hard to reconcile with the steady ongoing expansion of settlement under Olmert, vitiating even far less forthcoming offers.

Returning to reality, all of these discussions about settlement expansion evade the most crucial issue about settlements: what the United States and Israel have already established in the West Bank. The evasion tacitly concedes that the illegal settlement programs already in place are somehow acceptable (putting aside the Golan Heights, annexed in violation of Security Council orders)—though the Bush "vision," apparently accepted by Obama, moves from tacit to explicit support for these violations of law. What is in place already suffices to ensure that there can be no viable Palestinian self-determination. Hence there is every indication that even on the unlikely assumption that "natural growth" will be ended, U.S.-Israeli rejectionism will persist, blocking the international consensus as before.

Subsequently Prime Minister Netanyahu declared a ten-month suspension of new construction, with many exemptions, and entirely excluding Greater Jerusalem, where expropriation in Arab areas and construction for Jewish settlers continues at a rapid pace. Hillary Clinton praised these "unprecedented" concessions on (illegal) construction, eliciting anger and ridicule in much of the world.[30]

It might be different if a legitimate "land swap" were under consideration, a solution approached at Taba and spelled out more fully in the Geneva Accord reached in informal high-level Israel-Palestine negotiations. The accord was presented in Geneva in October 2003, welcomed by much of the world, rejected by Israel, and ignored by the United States.[31]

Obama's June 4 Cairo address to the Muslim world kept pretty much to his well-honed "blank slate" style—with little of substance, but presented in a personable manner that allows listeners to write on the slate what they want to hear. CNN captured its spirit in headlining a report "Obama Looks to Reach the Soul of the Muslim World." Obama had announced the goals of his address in an interview with *New York Times* columnist Thomas Friedman. "'We have a joke around the White House,' the president said. 'We're just going to keep on telling the truth until it stops working and nowhere is truth-telling more important than the Middle East.'" The White House commitment is most welcome, but it is useful to see how it translates into practice.[32]

Obama admonished his audience that it is easy to "point fingers… but if we see this conflict only from one side or the other, then we will be blind to the truth: the only resolution is for the aspirations of both sides to be met through two states, where Israelis and Palestinians each live in peace and security."

Turning from Obama-Friedman Truth to truth, there is a third side, with a decisive role throughout: the United States. But that participant in the conflict Obama omitted. The omission is understood to be normal and appropriate, hence unmentioned: Friedman's column is headlined "Obama Speech Aimed at Both Arabs and Israelis." The front-page *Wall Street Journal* report on Obama's speech appears under the heading "Obama Chides Israel, Arabs in His Overture to Muslims." Other reports are the same. The convention is understandable on the doctrinal principle that though the U.S. government sometimes makes mistakes, its intentions are by definition benign, even noble. In the world of attractive imagery, Washington has always sought desperately to be an honest broker, yearning to advance peace and justice. The doctrine trumps truth, of which there is little hint in the speech or the mainstream coverage.

Obama once again echoed Bush's "vision" of two states, without saying what he means by the phrase "Palestinian state." His intentions are clarified not only by the crucial omissions already discussed, but also by his one explicit criticism of Israel: "The United States does not accept the legitimacy of continued Israeli settlements. This construction violates previous agreements and undermines efforts to achieve peace. It is time for these settlements to stop." That is, Israel should live up to Phase I of the 2003 Road Map, rejected at once by Israel with tacit U.S. support, as noted—though the truth is that Obama has ruled out even steps of the Bush I variety to withdraw from participation in these crimes.

The operative words are "legitimacy" and "continued." By omission, Obama indicates that he accepts Bush's vision: the vast existing settlement and infrastructure projects are "legitimate," thus ensuring that the phrase "Palestinian state" means "fried chicken."

Always even-handed, Obama also had an admonition for the Arab states: they "must recognize that the Arab Peace Initiative was an important beginning, but not the end of their responsibilities." Plainly, it cannot be a meaningful "beginning" if Obama continues to reject its core principles: implementation of the international consensus. But to do so is evidently not Washington's "responsibility" in Obama's vision; no explanation given, no notice taken.

On democracy, Obama said that "we would not presume to pick the outcome of a peaceful election"—as in January 2006, when Washington picked the outcome with a vengeance, turning at once to severe punishment of the Palestinians because it did not like the outcome of the peaceful election, all with Obama's apparent approval judging by his words before and actions since taking office. Obama politely refrained from comment about his host, President Mubarak, one of the most brutal dictators in the region, though he has had some illuminating words about him. As Obama was about to board the plane to Saudi Arabia and Egypt, the two "moderate" Arab states, "Mr. Obama signaled that while he would mention American concerns about human rights in Egypt, he would not challenge Mr. Mubarak too sharply, because he is a 'force for stability and good' in the Middle East.... Mr. Obama said he did not regard Mr. Mubarak as an authoritarian leader. 'No, I tend not to use labels for folks,' Mr. Obama said. The president noted that there had been criticism 'of the manner in which politics operates in Egypt,' but he also said that Mr. Mubarak had been 'a stalwart ally, in many respects, to the United States.'"[33]

When a politician uses the word "folks," we should brace ourselves for the deceit or worse that is coming. Outside of this context, there are "people"; or often "villains," and using labels for them is highly merito-

rious. Obama is right, however, not to have used the word "authoritarian," which is far too mild a label for his friend.

Just as in the past, support for democracy, and for human rights as
well, keeps to the pattern that scholarship has repeatedly discovered, cor-
relating closely with strategic and economic objectives. There should be
little difficulty in understanding why those whose eyes are not closed
tight shut by rigid doctrine dismiss Obama's yearning for human rights
and democracy as a joke in bad taste.

There had been some verbal pressure from the Bush administration
for relaxing Mubarak's harsh despotism, though it amounted to very little,
and as a special report in the *Financial Times* observes, "US pressure
ended after the electoral gains of the Muslim Brotherhood and the Hamas
victory in parliamentary polls in the Palestinian territories," putting an
end to neocon flirtation with democracy rhetoric. Under Obama, however, such U.S. pressure as there was for political reform "dramatically
eased," and the dictatorship has proceeded "to tighten its grip on politics,
harassing opponents and ensuring that no challenges emerge," showing
"that even an experiment with cosmetic reforms can be reversed."[34]

The regime also felt free to unleash the brutality of the security forces
against the nonviolent international activists who arrived in Egypt to
protest the savage siege of Gaza, to which the government of Egypt is
contributing still further by building a steel wall at its border, deep into
the ground to prevent the desperate prisoners from digging tunnels to
obtain some limited sustenance beyond the trickle permitted by their
captors, all of this a remarkable exercise in coordinated sadism, evidently
tolerable to Western elite opinion. The Egyptian actions were barely reported in the United States.[35]

With his endorsement of the brutal Mubarak tyranny, Obama made
clear that he does not intend to depart from the traditional policy of supporting harsh dictatorships for geostrategic ends, a policy of course not
limited to the Middle East, even though often salient there. The consequences of the policy have long been understood, and have been considered acceptable by planners. George W. Bush was probably genuinely
puzzled when he asked, "Why do they hate us?" and his response that "they

hate our freedom" may reflect what he learned at school. But the diplomatic and historical record, and the specialist literature, provide more compelling answers. More than half a century before Bush's plaintive query, President Eisenhower expressed his concern about "the campaign of hatred against us" in the Arab world, "not by the governments but by the people." The reasons for the "campaign of hatred" were outlined by the National Security Council: "In the eyes of the majority of Arabs the United States appears to be opposed to the realization of the goals of Arab nationalism. They believe that the United States is seeking to protect its interest in Near East oil by supporting the status quo and opposing political or economic progress." Furthermore, the perceptions are accurate: "Our economic and cultural interests in the area have led not unnaturally to close U.S. relations with elements in the Arab world whose primary interest lies in the maintenance of relations with the West and the status quo in their countries," blocking democracy and development.[36]

Popular attitudes in the Arab world were particularly striking at that time (1958), shortly after Eisenhower had expelled Israel, Britain, and France from the Sinai. Polls after 9/11 showed that much the same remained true, even among elite elements deeply embedded in the U.S.-dominated "globalized" economic order. By then, of course, there were other reasons for the hatred, among them the murderous Iraq sanctions, unnoticed in the West but taken seriously in the region, and U.S. support for Israeli crimes. The Afghanistan and particularly the Iraq invasion only exacerbated these feelings. Government studies draw the same conclusion. A Pentagon advisory panel, the Defense Science Board, responded to Bush's question by concluding that "Muslims do not 'hate our freedom,' but rather they hate our policies," adding that "when American public diplomacy talks about bringing democracy to Islamic societies, this is seen as no more than self-serving hypocrisy."[37]

The views are conventional among specialists, who also understand that these U.S. policies are a gift to the extremists among the jihadis, whose goal is to incite violent retaliation against the populations that they are seeking to mobilize. As Gardner summarizes the fairly broad specialist consensus, "For so long as the jihadis can rely on the USA to stand by its

Arab allies, such as the House of Saud and President Mubarak.... The Bin Laden franchise's monstrous bet that it can foment a clash of civilizations may be evil but it is not wholly mad.... If we continue to connive in the survival of tyranny, [then] we abet the onward march of the jihadis, for whom western policy is their most consistently reliable ally." If reducing terror had been a high priority after 9/11, Washington would have used the ample opportunities to isolate and eliminate Bin Laden by encouraging the bitter condemnation of his opportunism and violence by the majority even of the jihadis. Instead the Bush administration chose to unify the jihadi movement in support of Bin Laden and to mobilize many others to his cause by supporting his charges, preferring violence for its own purposes. With good reason, the hawkish Michael Scheuer, in charge of tracking Bin Laden for the CIA for many years, concludes that "the United States of America remains bin Laden's only indispensable ally."[38]

Apart from rhetorical flourishes, Obama seems committed to following the same path, as his praise for Mubarak and other policies illustrate.

Obama also had observations on nuclear weapons, a matter of no slight significance in the light of his focus on Iran. Obama repeated his hope for their general abolition and called on all signers of the Non-Proliferation Treaty to abide by the responsibilities it imposes. His comments pointedly excluded Israel, which like India and Pakistan is not a signer of the NPT, all of them supported by the United States in their development of nuclear weapons—Pakistan particularly under Reagan, India under Bush II and Obama. Israel, India, and Pakistan are now escalating their nuclear weapons programs to a level that is highly threatening. But our significant role in this nuclear confrontation, from the outset and continuing, confers no "responsibility."[39]

Small wonder that outside the West few can take U.S. charges against Iran very seriously, not only the alleged concern for human rights, which Obama clarified with regard to Egypt, but also the primary charges: that Iran is concealing something from the International Atomic Energy Agency, as it doubtless is. Others are concealing nothing at all, for example, the three countries that have never signed the NPT, continuing to rely on U.S. support for their nuclear weapons programs. At the peak of the furor about Iran a few months after Obama's trip to Cairo, India announced that it "can now build nuclear weapons with the same destructive power as those in the arsenals of the world's major nuclear powers." This was India's immediate reaction to Security Council Resolution 1887 (September 24, 2009), which called on all states to join the NPT and to resolve any disputes within that framework, without the threat or use of force in violation of the UN Charter (a provision directed solely at the United States and Israel). At the same time, the IAEA passed a resolution calling on Israel to join the NPT and open up its nuclear facilities to inspection. The United States and Europe tried to block the resolution, and when they failed, voted against it. It passed anyway. President Obama immediately assured Israel that the United States would support its rejection of the resolution. The IAEA also overwhelmingly passed a resolution calling for application of the agency safeguards to the Middle East (103-4: United States, Israel, Canada, Georgia opposed). The White House also assured its Indian ally that it can ignore Security Council resolutions on nuclear weapons, most recently Resolution 1887.[40]

These actions provide further evidence about Obama's concerns about proliferation of nuclear weapons.

Obama reacted to Resolution 1887 in a different way as well. Two days after he was awarded the Nobel Prize for his inspiring commitment to peace, the Pentagon announced that it was accelerating delivery of the most lethal weapons in the arsenal short of nuclear weapons, thirteen-ton bombs to be delivered by B-52 stealth bombers, designed to destroy deeply hidden bunkers shielded by ten thousand pounds of reinforced concrete. There is no secret about what they are for. Planning for these "massive ordnance penetrators" began in the Bush years, but languished, until Obama called for developing them rapidly when he came into office.[41]

Obama's assurance to Israel adheres to the unacknowledged "rules" since Nixon: "It is generally believed that [Israeli prime minister Golda] Meir informed Nixon that Israel had already acquired the bomb and pledged to keep it invisible—that is, untested, undeclared, and in low political salience. Nixon agreed to end American annual visits to the nuclear reactor at Dimona and no longer press Israel to sign the Nuclear Non-Proliferation Treaty."[42]

Some who have placed their hopes in Obama have cited remarks of Assistant Secretary of State Rose Gottemoeller: "Universal adherence to the NPT itself—including by India, Israel, Pakistan and North Korea—also remains a fundamental objective of the United States." But the concern that her comment might mean something was quickly allayed by the report of a senior Israeli diplomat that Israel had received assurances that Obama "will not force Israel to state publicly whether it has nuclear weapons...[but will] stick to a decades-old U.S. policy of 'don't ask, don't tell.'" And as the Institute for Public Accuracy reminds us, the Bush administration had also adopted Gottemoeller's stand, calling for "universal adherence to the Non-Proliferation Treaty."[43]

It appears, then, that "universality" applies to Iran's suspected programs, but not to the actual ones of U.S. allies and clients—not to speak of Washington's own obligations under the NPT.

With regard to Iran's nuclear programs, Obama chose his words carefully. He said that "any nation—including Iran—should have the right to access peaceful nuclear power if it complies with its responsibilities under the nuclear Non-Proliferation Treaty." His words again reiterate the Bush administration's position: it too held that Iran could "*access* peaceful nuclear power." But as Obama and his associates know well, the contentious issue has been whether Iran has the rights guaranteed to signers of the NPT under Article IV, which go well beyond "access"—say by the goodwill of outside powers. The words of the NPT are quite clear: "Nothing in this Treaty shall be interpreted as affecting the inalienable right of all the Parties to the Treaty to develop research, production and use of nuclear energy for peaceful purposes without discrimination and in conformity with Articles I and II of this Treaty," which refer to nuclear weapons. There is a considerable difference between research and production, as Article IV permits, and "access," which Bush and Obama have been willing to permit, meaning access from the outside. That has been at the heart of the dispute, and remains so. The Non-Aligned Movement, most of the world's states, has forcefully affirmed Iran's rights under Article IV (which have also been supported by the majority of Americans). The "international community"—a technical term referring to Washington and whoever happens to agree with it—opposes allowing Iran the rights guaranteed to NPT signers, and Obama, with his customary scrupulous choice of misleading words, indicates his continued adherence to this stand.

It is also worth repeating that despite much fevered rhetoric, rational souls understand that the Iranian threat is not the threat of attack—which would be suicidal. Wayne White, former deputy director of the Near East and South Asia Office of State Department intelligence (INR), quite plausibly estimates the likelihood that the Iranian leaders would carry out a nuclear attack against Israel, thus leading to the instant destruction of Iran and themselves, as "down there with that 1 percent possibility." He dismisses the possibility that Supreme Leader Khamenei and the clerical elite, who hold power in Iran, would throw away the "vast amounts of money" and "huge economic empires" they have created for themselves "in some quixotic attack against Israel with a nuclear weapon," even if they had one. Also timely is his confirmation that Israel's 1981 attack on Iraq's nuclear reactor did not end Saddam's nuclear weapons program, but initiated it. U.S. or Israeli bombing of Iranian facilities, White and other specialists observe, might have the same effect. Violence consistently elicits more violence in response.[44]

Among specialists, including rational hawks, it is well understood that if Iran is pursuing a weapons program, it is for deterrence. Israeli military historian Martin van Creveld writes that "the world has witnessed how the United States attacked Iraq for, as it turned out, no reason at all. Had the Iranians not tried to build nuclear weapons, they would be crazy." In the conservative National Interest, former CIA weapons inspector David Kay speculates that Iran might be moving toward "nuclear weapons capability," with the "strategic goal" of countering a U.S. threat that "is real in Tehran's eyes," for good reasons that he reviews. He notes further that "Perhaps the biggest agitator of all in this is the United States, with its abbreviated historical memory and diplomatic ADD." White too agrees that Iran might seek weapons capability (which is not the same as weapons) for deterrence.[45]

These matters are well understood by informed hardliners. The leading neoconservative expert on Iran, Reuel Marc Gerecht, formerly in the

CIA Middle East division, wrote in 2000 that

> Tehran certainly wants nuclear weapons; and its reasoning is not illogical. Iran was gassed into surrender in the first Persian Gulf War; Pakistan, Iran's ever more radicalized Sunni neighbor to the southeast, has nuclear weapons; Saddam Hussein, with his Scuds and his weapons-of-mass-destruction ambitions, is next door; Saudi Arabia, Iran's most ardent and reviled religious rival, has long-range missiles; Russia, historically one of Iran's most feared neighbors, is once again trying to reassert its dominion in the neighboring Caucasus; and Israel could, of course, blow the Islamic Republic to bits. Having been vanquished by a technologically superior Iraq at a cost of at least a half-million men, Iran knows very well the consequences of having insufficient deterrence. And the Iranians possess the essential factor to make deterrence work: sanity. Tehran or Isfahan in ashes would destroy the Persian soul, about which even the most hardline cleric cares deeply. As long as the Iranians believe that either the U.S. or Israel or somebody else in the region might retaliate with nuclear weapons, they won't do something stupid.[46]

Gerecht also understands very well the real "security problem" posed by Iranian nuclear weapons, should it acquire them:

> A nuclear-armed Islamic Republic would of course check, if not checkmate, the United States' maneuvering room in the Persian Gulf. We would no doubt think several times about responding to Iranian terrorism or military action if Tehran had the bomb and a missile to deliver it. During the lead-up to the second Gulf War, ruling clerical circles in Tehran and Qom were abuzz with the debate about nuclear weapons. The mullahs…agreed: if Saddam Hussein had had nuclear weapons, the Americans would not have challenged him. For the "left" and the "right," this weaponry is the ultimate guarantee of Iran's defense, its revolution, and its independence as a regional great power.

With appropriate translations for the doctrinal terms, Gerecht's concerns capture realistically the threat posed by an Iran with a deterrent capacity.

Also generally discounted is the likelihood that Iran might provide nuclear weapons or technology to terrorists or "rogue states," though such transfers have happened, notably by the infamous A. Q. Khan network protected by U.S. ally Pakistan. Such actions would place Iran itself at great risk for no conceivable gain except possibly deterrence, and even that is a very remote contingency.

It is difficult to disagree with strategic analyst Leonard Weiss of the Center for International Security and Cooperation at Stanford and the Lawrence Livermore National Laboratory. The assumption that Iran, if it had nuclear weapons, would attack Israel, he writes, "amounts to assuming that Iran's leaders are insane, [that] the Iranian clerics' hatred of Israel is so intense that in order to destroy it they would launch a nuclear attack that would kill not only Jews but also up to 1.5 million Muslims living in Israel, as well as triggering an Israeli nuclear counterattack [which] would turn back the clock on Iran's development for many decades and reduce its leaders to radioactive dust." As for the speculation that Iran might transfer such weapons to third parties, not only could Iran not "be sure that the transfer will be perfectly secure from discovery or that the weapons will be used as intended," but it "would undoubtedly be treated as if it came from Tehran, again resulting in Iran's utter destruction."[47]

As all eyes were focused on Iran's possible violations of the NPT in late 2009, Obama initiated a reconfiguration of the missile defense systems planned for Eastern Europe, evoking lively controversy as to whether he was selling out to the Russians or providing a better way to protect the world from Iranian aggression. The debate was resolved in January 2010, when Obama decided to place the systems in northern Poland, thirty-five miles from Kaliningrad, thus posing a threat to Russia but without any obvious relation to Iran; and shortly after in Romania, again immediately arousing Russian concerns. The chief of Russia's general staff warned that the perceived threat to Russian security was holding up negotiations on the crucial Strategic Arms Reduction Treaty (START). Throughout, the debate skillfully avoided the central issue: are these systems designed for defense against an Iranian attack, as advertised? That is hardly plausible, for the reasons just discussed. Zbigniew Brzezinski is perceptive in describing these systems as "based on a nonexistent defense technology, designed against a nonexistent threat, and designed to protect West Europeans, who weren't asking for the protection."[48]

We should recall, however, that antimissile systems, were they to become functional, do serve a military purpose: as a first-strike weapon, potentially eliminating a deterrent, in this case ensuring that Iran is open to U.S.-Israeli attack. The same reasoning holds for U.S. delivery to Israel of Patriot antimissile systems, and Obama's decision in January 2010 to place "special ships off the Iranian coast and antimissile systems in at least four Arab countries," not for "defense" as the government professes and the media uncritically repeat. The antimissile systems supplement the more direct first-strike threats: keeping "all options on the table," including the threat of force, in violation of the UN Charter and repeated UN resolutions, most recently Security Council Resolution 1887. Also, training maneuvers that take Iran as the obvious target; development of superweapons aimed just at Iran; and much else, including such actions as dispatch of Israeli warships and Israel's German-made Dolphin class submarines capable of carrying nuclear missiles, virtually undetectable, through the Suez Canal and Red Sea into positions where they can attack Iran, with Egyptian permission though Egypt denies it.[49]

In February 2010 General Petraeus, head of the U.S. Central Command with jurisdiction over the Middle East region, confirmed the near-unanimous view among specialists that "a military strike on Iran could have the unintended consequence of stirring nationalist sentiment to the benefit of Tehran's hard-line government," a significant blow to the democratic movement in Iran, not to speak of the human disaster and the likelihood of Iranian retaliation.[50]

No one wants Iran—or anyone—to develop nuclear weapons, but it should be recognized that the perceived threat is not that they will be used in a suicide mission, but rather the threat of deterrence of U.S.-Israeli actions to extend their own domination of the region. And to repeat, if the concern were Iranian nuclear weapons, there would be sensible ways to proceed—to which, furthermore, the United States is officially committed: namely, to join in the overwhelming international support (including a large majority of Americans) for a nuclear weapons–free zone including Iran, Israel, and U.S. forces deployed there. Adequate verification is by no means impossible. That should mitigate, if not terminate, the regional nuclear weapons threat. Even steps toward that goal would have a positive impact. But it is not on the agenda.

Obama's "new initiative" for the Middle East was spelled out most extensively by John Kerry, chair of the Senate Foreign Relations Committee and a regular emissary to the region, in an important speech at the Brookings Institution on March 4, 2009.[51] In interpreting Kerry's words, we have to recognize that the actual facts of history are irrelevant. What is important in his address is not the contrived picture of past and present, but the plans outlined.

Kerry urges that we face the unpleasant fact that our honorable efforts to bring about a political settlement have failed, primarily because of the unwillingness of the Arab states to make peace. Furthermore, all of our efforts to "to give the Israelis a legitimate partner for peace," for which Israel has always yearned, have foundered on Palestinian intransigence. Now, however, there is a welcome change. With the Arab Peace Initiative of 2006, the Arab states have finally signaled their willingness to accept Israel's presence in the region. Even more promising is the "unprecedented willingness among moderate Arab nations to work with Israel" against our common enemy Iran. "Moderate" here is used in its technical meaning: "willing to conform to U.S. demands," irrespective of the nature of the regime. "This re-alignment can help to lay the groundwork for progress towards peace," Kerry said, as we "re-conceptualize" the problem, focusing on the Iranian threat. This brings the United States into alignment with the wishes of Prime Minister Binyamin Netanyahu, who speaks for the Israeli right wing—which unfortunately means most of the country after the sharp shift to the jingoist right in Israel in the past few years.

Kerry goes on to explain that there is also at last some hope that a "legitimate partner" can be found for our peace-loving Israeli ally: Abbas and the Palestinian Authority. How then do we proceed to support Israel's new legitimate Palestinian partner? "Most importantly, this means strengthening General [Keith] Dayton's efforts to train Palestinian security forces that can keep order and fight terror…. Recent developments have been extremely encouraging: During the invasion of Gaza, Palestinian Security Forces largely succeeded in maintaining calm in the West Bank amidst widespread expectations of civil unrest. Obviously, more remains to be done, but we can help do it."

Routinely, Kerry describes the attack on Gaza as entirely right and just: by definition, since the United States crucially participated in it. It doesn't matter, then, that the pretext lacks any credibility, under principles that we all accept—with regard to others, that is; matters already discussed. Furthermore, it is evidently right and just, indeed admirable, to use force to prevent Palestinians from publicly expressing concern at the slaughter and destruction under way in the other half of Palestine.

Armed and trained in Jordan, or in the occupied West Bank by Jordanian instructors with Israeli participation and supervision, General Dayton's Palestinian Authority Security Forces (PASF) are described by Israeli journalist Gideon Levy as "subcontractors to the Israeli Security." Accurate enough, and from his pen that is not praise. It is, however, a good reason the PASF is so admired by the Israeli army, by the Obama administration, and by U.S. journalists.[52]

Some recognize that not all is going quite as well as Kerry describes. Charles Levinson, like others, reports that "the [PASF] won exceptional praise from Israeli officers for their effectiveness keeping a check on protests in the West Bank during the December–January Gaza War." But there is concern that the PASF "may not have won the battle of public opinion, and were seen as protecting the Israeli army" (quoting the official in charge of the European police-training team). That is, they are seen as Israeli subcontractors. Levinson cites an incident in which "Palestinian forces swept into a West Bank town on the heels of the Israeli army—only to be chased out by angry residents"—and an internal memo of General Dayton's training team warning: "There are growing signs that the local population are increasingly losing respect for the PASF." He also quotes a PASF commander who describes his troops as "disillusioned": "Operations against Hamas and other anti-Israel groups appeared at odds with a Palestinian public that increasingly viewed him and his men as doing Israel's bidding and getting little in return."[53]

The Dayton army is the soft side of population control, under theoretical State Department supervision. According to knowledgeable observers, the tougher and more brutal forces are trained by the CIA: General Intelligence and Preventive Security.[54]

Kerry is right that Washington can do more to ensure that West Bank Palestinians are so effectively controlled that they cannot even protest the atrocities suffered by Palestinians in Gaza—let alone take a step toward meaningful self-determination or even protection of the shreds of Palestine left to them under the U.S.-Israeli encroachment schemes that are constantly under way. To do more to support the Dayton army, and its more brutal associates, the United States can draw on a long history of colonial practice, developed in exquisite detail during the U.S. occupation of the Philippines after the murderous conquest a century ago, then widely applied elsewhere. This sophisticated refinement of traditional imperial practice has been highly successful in U.S. dependencies, while also providing means of population control at home. These matters are spelled out in pathbreaking work by historian Alfred McCoy.[55] The approach relies on a variety of means to dismantle resistance to colonial domination, using rumor, slander, and the highest available technology of surveillance and control; enlisting cooperative domestic elites; and the mailed fist, the Philippine constabulary and U.S. forces, when needed. Kerry is surely familiar with these techniques from his service in South Vietnam. Applying these measures to Palestine, collaborationist paramilitary forces can be employed to subdue the domestic population with the cooperation of privileged elites, granting the United States and Israel free rein to carry forward Bush's "vision" and Olmert's "Convergence plus," and their later versions. Gaza can meanwhile be kept under a strangling siege as a prison and occasional shooting gallery.

Washington's new initiative for Middle East peace, so it is hoped, will integrate Israel among the "moderate" Arab states as a bulwark for U.S. domination of the vital energy-producing regions. It fits well into Obama's broader programs for Afghanistan and Pakistan, where military operations are escalating and huge "embassies" are being constructed on the model of the city-within-a-city called an "embassy" in Baghdad, clearly signaling Obama's longer-term intentions.[56]

The "re-conceptualization" is evidently satisfactory to U.S. high-tech industry, which continues to enhance its intimate relations with Israel. One striking illustration is a gigantic installation that Intel is constructing in its Kiryat Gat facility in Israel to implement a revolutionary reduction in the size of computer chips, expected to set a new industry standard and to supply much of the world with parts.[57] Relations between U.S. and Israeli military industry remain particularly close, so much so that Israel has been shifting development and manufacturing facilities for its advanced military industry to the United States, where access to U.S. military aid is easier; and is also considering transfer of production of armored vehicles to the United States over the objections of thousands of Israeli workers who will lose their jobs.[58] The relations are also very lucrative for U.S. military producers—doubly so, in fact, because U.S. government–funded weapons supplies to Israel, themselves very profitable, also function as "teasers" that induce the rich Arab dictatorships ("moderates") to purchase great amounts of less sophisticated military equipment. Close intelligence cooperation goes back over half a century.

Israel also continues to provide the United States with a strategically located overseas military base for prepositioning weapons and other functions, most recently in January 2010, when the U.S. army moved to "double the value of emergency military equipment it stockpiles on Israeli soil," raising the level to $800 million. "Missiles, armored vehicles, aerial ammunition and artillery ordnance are already stockpiled in the country." The deal also "allows Israel access to a wider spectrum of military ordnance, [aiding] Israel in its effort to bolster its weapons stockpiles for use in an emergency. Israel's stores of aerial and artillery ammunition were depleted during the Second Lebanon War in 2006, nearly reaching levels the IDF considers dangerously low."[59]

The prepositioning goes back to 1990. The quiet announcement that the United States was sending weapons to Israel during the U.S.-Israeli assault on Gaza in December–January 1999–2000 raised a few eyebrows, but the Pentagon explained, probably accurately, that the weapons were not intended for use in Gaza but were being prepositioned for future use by U.S. forces in the region.[60]

These are among the unparalleled services that Israel provides for U.S. militarism and global dominance, as well as for the U.S. high-tech economy. They afford Israel a certain leeway to defy Washington's orders—though it is skating on thin ice if it tries to push its luck too far, as history has repeatedly shown. So far the jingoist extremism of the current government has been constrained by more sober elements. But if Israel goes too far, there might indeed erupt a U.S.-Israel confrontation of the kind that many commentators perceive today, so far with little basis.

NINE

Elections 2008:
Hope Confronts the Real World

The word that immediately rolled off of every tongue after the presidential election was "historic." And rightly so. A Black family in the White House is truly a momentous event.

There were some surprises. One was that the election was not over after the Democratic convention. One might expect that the opposition party would have a landslide victory during a severe economic crisis, after eight years of disastrous policies on all fronts including the worst record on job growth of any postwar president and a rare decline in median wealth, with an incumbent so unpopular that his own party had to disavow him, and a dramatic collapse in U.S. standing in world opinion. The Democrats did win, barely. If the financial crisis had been slightly delayed, they might not have.

A good question is why the margin of victory for the opposition party was so small, given the circumstances. One possibility is that neither party reflects public opinion at a time when 80 percent think the country is going in the wrong direction and that the government is run by "a few big interests looking out for themselves," not for the people, and a stunning 94 percent object that government does not attend to public opinion. As many studies show, both parties are well to the right of the population on many major issues, domestic and international.[1]

It could be argued that no party speaking for the public would be viable in a society that is business-run to an unusual extent. Evidence for that description is substantial. At a very general level, evidence is provided by the predictive success of political economist Thomas Ferguson's "investment theory" of politics, which holds that policies tend to reflect the wishes of the powerful blocs that invest every four years to control the state, an analysis that gains more force from recent events, and is poised to become even more successful with the Supreme Court decision of January 21, 2010, already discussed. More specific illustrations are numerous. To select one enlightening example, for sixty years the United States has failed to ratify the core principle of international labor law, which guarantees freedom of association. Legal analysts call it "the untouchable treaty in American politics," and observe that there has never even been any debate about the matter.[2] And many have noted Washington's dismissal of conventions of the International Labor Organization as contrasted with the intense dedication to enforcement of monopoly pricing rights for corporations ("intellectual property rights").

The weakness of social democratic (welfare state) programs in the United States as compared to Europe is often attributed to the "American character": individualist, liberty-loving, antigovernment (but superpatriotic), firm in the belief that hard work reaps rewards and that those who fall by the wayside are somehow defective, etc. There may be some elements of truth to these common portrayals, but they are hard to square with the historical record, or even with studies of popular attitudes. We return to attitudes toward health care, often misrepresented. More generally, on welfare state measures, public support is quite high. Even among those who identify themselves as "antigovernment" in polls, overwhelming majorities support "maintaining or expanding spending on Social Security, child care, and aid to poor people" and other social welfare measures, though support in these groups "fell off significantly only when it came to aid to blacks and welfare recipients." Half of the "staunchest conservatives believed that spending is too little [on] assistance to the poor." In the population as a whole, according to the 2008 National Opinion Research Center's General Social Survey, "71 percent of respondents thought the government was spending too little to improve and protect the nation's health, 58 percent said spending on Social Security was too little, 58 percent thought we should spend more to deal with drug addiction, and 55 percent thought spending to be too little on programs to assist people to secure child care"—though again, there were exceptions on aid for Blacks and welfare recipients.[3]

The persistence of generally social democratic attitudes is noteworthy in the face of huge propaganda campaigns to efface any such ideas, a prominent feature of a society dominated to an unusual extent by a highly class-conscious business community, dedicated to winning what they call "the everlasting battle for the minds of men" and to beating back threats of "political power of the masses," a serious "hazard to industrialists" and more recently to the increasingly dominant financial institutions. Over the years the campaigns have had two primary enemies: unions (naturally) and government. The antigovernment campaigns have to be nuanced and sophisticated, because the "architects of policy" understand very well the need for a powerful state that intervenes massively in the economy and abroad to ensure that their own interests are "most peculiarly attended to." The goal of sophisticated business propaganda is to engender fear and hatred of government among the population, so that they are not seduced by subversive notions of democracy and social welfare, while maintaining support for the powerful nanny state for the rich—a difficult course, but one that has been maneuvered with considerable skill.[4]

There is much to explore here, but this is not the place.

The two candidates in the 2008 Democratic primary were a woman and an African American. That too was historic. It would have been unimaginable forty years ago. The fact that the country has become civilized enough to accept this outcome is a considerable tribute to the activism of the 1960s and its aftermath, an observation with lessons for the future.

In some ways the election followed familiar patterns. The McCain campaign was honest enough to announce clearly that they would skirt issues. Sarah Palin's hairdresser received twice the salary of McCain's foreign policy adviser, probably an accurate reflection of significance for the campaign.[5] Obama's message of "hope" and "change" offered a virtual blank slate on which supporters could write their wishes. One could search websites for position papers, but correlation of these to policies is hardly spectacular, and in any event, what enters into voters' choices is what the campaign places front and center, as party managers know well.

The Obama campaign greatly impressed the public relations industry, which named Obama "*Advertising Age*'s marketer of the year for 2008," easily beating out Apple computers.[6] A good predictor of the election a few weeks later. The industry's regular task is to create uninformed consumers who will make irrational choices, thus undermining markets as they are conceptualized in economic theory, but benefiting the masters of the economy. And it recognizes the benefits of undermining democracy in much the same way, creating uninformed voters who make often irrational choices between the factions of the business party that amass sufficient support from concentrated private capital to enter the electoral arena, then to dominate campaign propaganda.

The *Financial Times* reported the enthusiasm of the PR industry over the marketing of "brand Obama." Particularly impressed were those who "helped pioneer the packaging of candidates as consumer brands 30 years ago," when they designed the Reagan campaign. Obama, some felt, is likely to "have more influence on boardrooms than any president since Ronald Reagan, [who] redefined what it was to be a CEO" by teaching the lesson that "you had to give them a vision." Reagan's visionary performance led to "the 1980s and 1990s reign of the imperial CEO," an office that registered such towering successes as destroying the financial system and exporting much of the real economy while amassing huge personal fortunes based largely on ability to choose the boards that determine salary and bonuses, thanks to regulations established by the nanny state for the rich.[7]

Obama himself had expressed his admiration for Reagan as a "transformative figure." Obama was not referring to the rivers of blood that that Reagan spilled from Central America to southern Africa and beyond. Nor was he referring to Reagan's great effectiveness in helping transform Pakistan into a nuclear-armed state with powerful radical Islamic forces, with consequences that Obama regards as the major foreign challenge to his administration. So, yes, Reagan was a transformative figure abroad, though not in Obama's sense of the term.

And at home as well, though Obama was not referring to Reagan's crucial role in transforming the United States from the world's leading creditor to the world's leading debtor, or converting it from an industrial society rather resembling Europe to one in which real wages for the majority stagnate and social indicators decline while a few who are favored by government policy gain fabulous wealth, among other forms of social malaise.

Rather, Obama was referring to the colossus whose "spirit seems to stride the country, watching us like a warm and friendly ghost," the semidivinity constructed by a remarkable PR campaign, which anointed Reagan as the high priest of free markets and small government, culminating in a reverential commemoration of the Great Man that was reminiscent of the veneration of Kim Il-Sung, one of the more embarrassing moments of the modern history of Western political culture.

The imagery is untainted by Reagan's breaking modern records in government intervention in the economy, while also somewhat increasing the size of government. Just to mention a few highlights, he was by far the most protectionist president in postwar American history, virtually doubling protectionist barriers in order to try to save the U.S. economy from takeover by more efficient Japanese producers; he carried out the first "too big to fail" bailout (Continental Illinois) while setting the stage for the huge Savings & Loan financial crisis; his "star wars" fantasies were sold to the business world as a huge taxpayer-funded bonanza to high-tech industry; his "out-of-control spending binge is burying our children and grandchildren under a mountain of unsustainable debt," to quote House Republican leader John Boehner—referring, however, to the evil Obama, and omitting to mention, as did the press reporting him, that the projected interest burdens for Reagan and Obama are virtually identical as a proportion of GDP. And on, and on.[8]

Reagan's "vision," like most heralded "visions," is entirely independent of his deeds. The vision that was constructed by the doctrinal institutions is one of dedication to unfettered free markets and "democracy promotion." In the light of the facts, the creation of the "vision" was indeed a marketing triumph, of which those who "helped pioneer the packaging of candidates as consumer brands 30 years ago" should be proud, as they celebrate their greatest triumph yet in 2008.

The Center for Responsive Politics (CRP), which monitors campaign contributions, reports that once again elections were bought: "The best-funded candidates won nine out of 10 contests, and all but a few members of Congress will be returning to Washington." Obama outspent McCain by almost 2 to 1. The executive director of the CRP observed that "The 2008 election will go down in U.S. history as an election of firsts, but this was far from the first time that money was overwhelmingly victorious on Election Day."[9]

Before the conventions, the viable candidates with most funding from financial institutions were Obama and McCain. Preliminary results suggest that by the end, Obama's campaign contributions, by industry, were concentrated among financial institutions and law firms (including lobbyists), favoring him by a considerable margin. The investment theory of politics suggests some conclusions about guiding policies of the new administration, and they were soon verified—with interesting consequences, to which we return, when Obama veered slightly from the path laid out by his sponsors.

As discussed earlier, the power of financial institutions reflects the increasing shift of the economy from production to finance since the liberalization of finance in the 1970s, one of the root causes of the greatest economic crisis since the Great Depression: the financial collapse of 2007–8, deep and ongoing recession in the real economy, and the miserable performance of the economy for the large majority, whose real wages stagnated for thirty years, while benefits and social indicators declined. The steward of this impressive record, Alan Greenspan—"Saint Alan" as he was sometimes called during his glory years—attributed his success to "greater worker insecurity," which led to "atypical restraint on compensation increases," and corresponding increases into the pockets of those who matter.[10] Greenspan's failure even to perceive the $8 trillion housing bubble, following the collapse of the earlier tech bubble that he oversaw, was the immediate cause of the current financial crisis, as he ruefully conceded. But he was not alone in that among the economic profession and regulators.

Reactions to the election from across the spectrum commonly adopted the "soaring rhetoric" of the Obama campaign. Veteran correspondent John Hughes wrote that "America has just shown the world an extraordinary example of democracy at work," while to British historian-journalist Tristram Hunt, the election showed that America is a land "where miracles happen," such as "the glorious epic of Barack Obama" (leftist French journalist Jean Daniel). "In no other country in the world is such an election possible," said Catherine Durandin of the Institute for International and Strategic Relations in Paris. Many others were no less rapturous.[11]

The rhetoric may have some justification if we keep to the West, but elsewhere matters are different. Consider the world's largest democracy, India. The chief minister of Uttar Pradesh, which is larger than all but a few countries of the world and is notorious for horrifying treatment of women, is not only a woman, but a Dalit ("untouchable"), at the lowest rung of India's disgraceful caste system.

Turning to the Western hemisphere, consider its two poorest countries: Haiti and Bolivia. In Haiti's first democratic election in 1990, grassroots movements were organized in the slums and hills, and though without resources, elected their own candidate, the populist priest Jean-Bertrand Aristide. The results astonished observers who expected an easy victory for the candidate of the elite and the United States, a former World Bank official.

True, this victory for democracy was soon overturned by a military coup, followed by years of terror and suffering to the present, with crucial participation of the two traditional torturers of Haiti, France and the United States. But the victory itself was a far more "extraordinary example of democracy at work" than the miracle of 2008.

The same is true of the 2005 election in Bolivia. The indigenous majority, the most oppressed population in the hemisphere, elected a candidate from their own ranks, a poor peasant, Evo Morales. The electoral campaign did not feature soaring rhetoric about hope and change, or body language and fluttering of eyelashes, but was focused on crucial issues, very well known to the voters: control over resources, cultural rights, questions of justice in a complex multiethnic society, and so on. Furthermore, the election went far beyond pushing a lever on election day or even efforts to get out the vote. It was just one stage in long and intense popular struggles in the face of severe repression, which had won major victories, such as defeating the efforts to deprive poor people of water through privatization.

These popular movements did not take instructions from party leaders. Rather, they formulated the policies that their candidates were chosen to implement. That is quite different from the Western model of democracy, as we see quite clearly in the reactions to Obama's victory.

In the liberal *Boston Globe*, the headline of the lead story observed that Obama's "grass-roots strategy leaves few debts to interest groups": labor unions, women, minorities, or other "traditional Democratic constituencies." That is only partially right, because massive funding by concentrated sectors of financial capital is ignored, perhaps not considered an "interest group." But leaving that detail aside, the report is correct in saying that Obama's hands are not tied, because his only debt is to "a grass-roots army of millions"—who took instructions, but contributed essentially nothing to formulating his program.

At the other end of the doctrinal spectrum, a headline in the *Wall Street Journal* reads, "Grass-Roots Army Is Still at the Ready"—namely, ready to follow instructions to "push his agenda," whatever it might turn out to be.[12]

Obama's organizers regard the network they constructed "as a mass movement with unprecedented potential to influence voters," the *Los Angeles Times* reported. The movement, organized around the "Obama brand," can pressure Congress to "hew to the Obama agenda." But they are not to develop ideas and programs and call on their representatives to implement them. These would be among the "old ways of doing politics" from which the new "idealists" are "breaking free,"[13] preferring the model of obedience to the maximal leader.

It is instructive to compare this picture to the workings of a functioning democracy such as Bolivia. The popular movements of the third world do not accept the Western doctrine that the "function" of the "ignorant and meddlesome outsiders"—the population— is to be "specta-tors of action" but not "participants" (Walter Lippmann, articulating a standard progressive view).

In earlier periods of American history, the public refused to keep to its assigned "function." Popular activism has repeatedly brought about substantial gains in freedom and justice. The authentic hope of the Obama campaign is that the "grass-roots army" organized to take instructions from the leader might "break free" and return to "old ways of doing pol-itics," by direct "participation in action."

In Bolivia, as in Haiti, efforts to promote democracy, social justice, and cultural rights, and to bring about desperately needed structural and institutional changes are, naturally, bitterly opposed by the traditional rulers: the Europeanized, mostly white elite in the eastern provinces, the site of most of the natural resources currently desired by the West. Also naturally, their quasi-secessionist movement is supported by Washington, which once again scarcely conceals its reflexive distaste for democracy when outcomes do not conform to strategic and economic interests.

To punish Bolivians for showing "the world [a truly] extraordinary example of democracy at work," the Bush administration canceled trade preferences, threatening tens of thousands of jobs, on the pretext that Bolivia was not cooperating with U.S. counter-narcotic efforts. In the real world, the UN estimates that Bolivia's coca crop increased 5 percent in 2007, as compared with a 26 percent increase in Colombia, the terror state that is Washington's closest regional ally and the recipient of enor-mous military aid. AP reports that "cocaine seizures by Bolivian police working with DEA agents had also increased dramatically during the Morales administration."[14]

As discussed earlier, "drug wars" are curious affairs. The same is true of condemnation (and decertification) for alleged noncompliance with U.S. demands on counter-narcotic efforts. One interesting case is Mexico, probably the leading narco-state in the world after U.S. ally Colombia. In part that seems to be a consequence of NAFTA, which undermined much of the economy and also led to flight of peasants from land that now, according to Mexican journalists, is planted in poppy and guarded by narco-guerrillas and the army. They also say that investigation and reporting on the narcotrafficking industry is so hazardous that little of what they discover appears in print. Some does, however: for example, that over two hundred thousand peasant women work for narcotraffickers because it is the only option for survival under the new liberalized economy. Also published was the report by the respected analyst Edgardo Buscaglia, a UN specialist and professor of law and economy, that the "war on drugs" of U.S. ally Felipe Calderón is a "caricature," which has left untouched the major private economic powers that participate massively in the racket.[15]

Bolivia was "decertified" by the Bush administration, then by Obama, for alleged lack of cooperation with U.S. antidrug efforts. Mexican president Calderón, in contrast, is highly praised. And Mexico is certified, though over the very strong objections of the National Narcotic Officers Association Coalition, which testified to Congress on the failure of Mexico to take even elementary steps to control the plague, which has now penetrated the southwest United States as well. Priorities and criteria are, again, clearly illuminated.[16]

Turning to the future, what could we realistically have expected of the Obama administration as it took office? We have two sources of information: actions and rhetoric.

The most important actions prior to taking office are selection of staff and advisers. The first selection was for vice president: Joe Biden, one of the strongest supporters of the Iraq invasion among Senate Democrats, a longtime Washington insider, who consistently votes with his fellow Democrats—though not always, as when he brought cheer to financial institutions by supporting a measure to make it harder for individuals to erase debt by declaring bankruptcy.[17]

The first post-election appointment was for the crucial position of chief of staff: Rahm Emanuel, one of the strongest supporters of the Iraq invasion among House Democrats and like Biden, a long-term Washington insider. Emanuel is also one of the biggest recipients of Wall Street campaign contributions. The Center for Responsive Politics reports that he "was the top House recipient in the 2008 election cycle of contributions from hedge funds, private equity firms and the larger securities/investment industry." Since being elected to Congress in 2002, he "has received more money from individuals and PACs in the securities and investment business than any other industry"; these are also among Obama's top donors. His task was to oversee Obama's approach to the worst financial crisis since the 1930s, for which his and Obama's funders share ample responsibility.[18]

In an interview with an editor of the *Wall Street Journal*, Emanuel was asked what the incoming Obama administration would do about "the Democratic congressional leadership, which is brimming with left-wing barons who have their own agenda," such as slashing defense spending and "angling for steep energy taxes to combat global warming," not to speak of the outright lunatics in Congress who toy with slavery reparations and even sympathize with Europeans who want to indict Bush administration war criminals for war crimes. "Barack Obama can stand up to them," Emanuel assured the editor. The administration will be "pragmatic," fending off left extremists.[19]

Labor journalist and lawyer Steve Early wrote that "while running for office, Obama said he strongly backed the Employee Free Choice Act, a long-overdue labor law reform measure that should be part of his promised economic stimulus plan." However, when Obama introduced his top economic advisers on taking office "and talked about steps to 'jolt' the economy...the Act was not part of the package," and Chief of Staff Emanuel "declined to say whether the White House will support the Employee Free Choice Act.... [Workers] will be watching closely to see whether their plight merits the same helping hand so quickly extended to Wall Street."[20]

The answer has been sharp and clear, and working people did not have to wait very long to find it out. EFCA quickly vanished. And to make priorities even clearer, a few weeks after taking office, President Obama decided to show his solidarity with workers by giving a talk at a factory in Illinois (February 12, 2009). He chose a Caterpillar plant, over objections of church, peace, and human rights groups, who were protesting Caterpillar's role in providing Israel with the means to devastate the territories it occupies and to destroy the lives of the population—also killing an American volunteer, Rachel Corrie, who tried to block the destruction of a home.[21]

Apparently forgotten, however, was something else. Following Reagan's lead with the dismantling of the air traffic controllers union, the new hardline CEO of Caterpillar, Donald Fites, rescinded the contract with the United Auto Workers in 1991, instituted a lockout, threatened to bring in "permanent replacement workers" (scabs), and later did so, for the first time in generations in manufacturing industry. The practice was illegal in other industrial countries apart from South Africa at the time; now the United States appears to be in splendid isolation. It is hard to imagine that Obama and his advisers purposely chose a corporation that led the way to undermine labor rights. More likely, they were unaware of the facts, which would be an even worse indictment of the business-run doctrinal system.

At the time of Caterpillar's innovation in labor relations, Obama was a community organizer in Chicago and visiting fellow at the University of Chicago Law School. He must have been reading the *Chicago Tribune*, which ran a careful study of these events.[22] They reported that the union was "stunned" to find that unemployed workers crossed the picket line with no remorse, while Caterpillar workers found little "moral support" in their community, one of the many where the union had "lifted the standard of living for entire communities." Wiping out of those memories is another victory in the campaign to destroy workers' rights and democracy that is relentlessly waged by the highly class-conscious American business sector, elementary facts about American society that the union leadership had stubbornly refused to understand. It was only in 1978 that UAW president Doug Fraser recognized what was happening and criticized the "leaders of the business community" for having "chosen to wage a one-sided class war in this country—a war against working people, the unemployed, the poor, the minorities, the very young and the very old, and even many in the middle class of our society," and for having "broken and discarded the fragile, unwritten compact previously existing during a period of growth and progress."[23]

Placing one's faith in a compact with owners and managers is suicidal. The UAW is discovering that again today, as the state-corporate leadership proceeds to eliminate the hard-fought gains of working people while dismantling the productive core of the American economy, with government assistance.

Continuing to run through Obama's appointments, his transition team was headed by John Podesta, Clinton's chief of staff. The leading figures in his initial economic team were Robert Rubin and Lawrence Summers, both enthusiasts for the deregulation that was a major factor in the current financial crisis. As treasury secretary, Rubin worked hard to abolish the Glass-Steagall Act, which had separated commercial banks from financial institutions that incur high risks. Economist Tim Canova comments that Rubin had "a personal interest in the demise of Glass-Steagall." Soon after leaving his position as treasury secretary, he became "chair of Citigroup, a financial-services conglomerate that was facing the possibility of having to sell off its insurance underwriting subsidiary... the Clinton administration never brought charges against him for his obvious violations of the Ethics in Government Act."[24]

Not surprisingly, Citigroup was a leading beneficiary of the Bush-Paulson bailout. That breaks little new ground. Walter Wriston, the CEO of its predecessor Citicorp, followed World Bank/IMF advice and lent so heavily to Latin America that when the debt crisis broke out in 1982, only a bailout (via the IMF) "saved Citicorp from a preemptive run on its interbank deposits, which could have been fatal," international economist David Felix wrote. He adds that Wriston, like the treasury secretaries, was a firm believer in pure laissez-faire: "for others, not themselves." These are the normal workings of state capitalism, for other industries as well.[25]

A curious feature of commentary on the 2008 financial industry bailout is that it was perceived as a radical departure from the norm, raising the threat of "socialism." That is far from true for the economy in general, though the financial industry did adhere more closely to market doctrines, leading to repeated crises, increasing in severity and requiring state intervention to rescue the casualties among the wealthy and powerful.

The bailout of Rubin's Citigroup was necessary, Paul Krugman wrote, but it was done in a manner that was "an outrage: a lousy deal for the taxpayers." That holds of the bailout generally. His fellow Nobel laureate Joseph Stiglitz observed that "as we pour money in, they can pour money right out" if we "don't have a veto." If the government—in a functioning democracy, the public—does not have a degree of control, the banks can pour the public funds into their own pockets for recapitalization or acquisitions or loans to government-guaranteed borrowers, thus undermining the alleged purpose of the bailout. That appears to be what happened, though details are obscure, because the recipients refuse to say what they are doing with the gift from taxpayers. Indeed they regard the question as outrageous, so the AP discovered when it sought answers: "No bank provided even the most basic accounting for the federal money," most ignoring the request or saying that "we're choosing not to disclose that."[26]

Again, the normal workings of state capitalism. The general population is to be satisfied with "necessary illusion" and "emotionally potent oversimplifications," as the distinguished moralist Reinhold Niebuhr advised.

After leaving the government for Citigroup, Rubin was replaced as treasury secretary by Summers, who presided over legislation barring federal regulation of derivatives, the "weapons of mass destruction" (Warren Buffett) that helped plunge financial markets to disaster. He ranks as "one of the main villains in the current economic crisis," according to Dean Baker, one of the few economists to have warned accurately of the impending crisis. Placing financial policy in the hands of Rubin and Summers is "a bit like turning to Osama Bin Laden for aid in the war on terrorism," Baker adds.[27]

Another achievement of Rubin and Summers (together with Greenspan) was to prevent Brooksley Born, the head of the Commodity Futures Trading Commission, from regulating credit default swaps in 1998—more WMD. "The best example of politics thwarting effective regulation," Baker writes.

Obama's appointment for treasury secretary, Timothy Geithner, a close associate of Summers, elicited a favorable reaction from Wall Street, which may be "hoping that little will change with Geithner at Treasury," Tim Canova observes: "Supporters of President-elect Obama will be tempted to embrace the experience argument, and it is true that Geithner and Summers have lots of experience at crisis management and doling out bailout funds to their Wall Street clientele."

As the crisis began to hit, Geithner hinted that he would use the enormous leverage he had as president of the New York Fed to impose some controls on exotic financial instruments, but "there is no evidence," Canova writes, "that there has been much action, even though Geithner has used this time to negotiate multibillion-dollar bailouts and deals associated with the collapse of Bear Stearns, Lehman Brothers, AIG, and now Citigroup." He adds that "the selection of Geithner and Summers to top administrative posts rewards past failure and protects special interests [and] also sends the wrong message to those who thought they were voting for change."[28]

Not much help in "changing" the world of finance could be expected from the Democratic Congress either. Charles Schumer, who led the Democratic Senatorial Campaign Committee, broke records in obtaining contributions from Wall Street, helping the Democrats win Congress and increasing "the industry's clout in the capital," the *New York Times* reported. He also "helped save financial institutions billions of dollars in higher taxes or fees. He succeeded in limiting efforts to regulate credit-rating agencies, sponsored legislation that cut fees paid by Wall Street firms to finance government oversight, pushed to allow banks to have lower capital reserves and called for the revision of regulations to make corporations' balance sheets more transparent," the last a move to which rational business groups would have no objection. He also weakened efforts to regulate bank debt and supervise the credit-rating agencies, also agents of disaster. His personal reward was to collect more campaign contributions from the financial industry than anyone in Congress except for John Kerry. "He built his career in large part based on his ties to Wall Street [and] has given the Street what it wanted," said the director of a leading firm that advises investors on the regulatory system.[29]

The business press reviewed the records of Obama's Transition Economic Advisory Board, which met on November 7, 2008, to determine

how to deal with the financial crisis. Bloomberg News columnist
Jonathan Weil concluded that "many of them should be getting subpoe-
nas as material witnesses right about now, not places in Obama's inner
circle." About half "have held fiduciary positions at companies that, to
one degree or another, either fried their financial statements, helped send
the world into an economic tailspin, or both." Is it really plausible that
"they won't mistake the nation's needs for their own corporate interests?"
He also pointed out that Chief of Staff Emanuel "was a director at Fred-
die Mac in 2000 and 2001 while it was committing accounting fraud."[30]

Dean Baker observes that "Obama faced the same sort of problem
as those hoping to de-Baathify Iraq following the overthrow of Saddam
Hussein. It would have been almost impossible to establish a government
without including members of the Baath party, since membership was a
virtual requirement for holding a position of responsibility under Saddam Hussein. Similarly, it would have been almost impossible to get to
the top echelons of power, or even the middle ranks, during the Clinton-
Bush years without giving lip service to the policies of one-sided financial
deregulation and bubble-driven growth that were so fashionable at the
time." And those leading Obama's economic team gave more than lip
service. They were instrumental in designing the policies that have led
to the present crisis.[31]

Early on, as noted earlier, the chair of the prestigious corporate law
firm Sullivan & Cromwell, predicted "that Wall Street, after getting billions of taxpayer dollars, will emerge from the financial crisis looking
much the same as before markets collapsed." In fact, strengthened, as it
turned out. The reasons were explained by Simon Johnson, former chief
economist of the IMF: "Throughout the crisis, the government has taken
extreme care not to upset the interests of the financial institutions, or to
question the basic outlines of the system that got us here," and the "elite
business interests…[who] played a central role in creating the crisis, making ever-larger gambles, with the implicit backing of the government,
until the inevitable collapse…are now using their influence to prevent
precisely the sorts of reforms that are needed, and fast, to pull the economy out of its nosedive" while "the government seems helpless, or un-

willing, to act against them." Again no surprise, at least to those who remember their Adam Smith.[32]

The outcome was nicely captured by two adjacent front-page stories in the *New York Times*, headlined "$3.4 Billion Profit at Goldman Revives Gilded Pay Packages" and "In Recession, a Bleaker Path for Workers to Slog."[33]

A headline in the *Financial Times* reads, "Applause as Obama Picks All-Star Team." No one is relevantly mentioned who is not on the right. Bush speechwriter David Frum, said, "I cannot recall the last time Republicans felt so positive towards a Democratic presidential figure." Fellow speechwriter Michael Gerson wrote that "Obama's appointments reveal not just moderation but maturity.... Whatever the caveats, Obama is doing something marvellously right"—where the term "right" should be understood in its dual meaning.[34]

Critical choices in foreign affairs followed much the same script, eliciting applause from Henry Kissinger, among others. Even super-hawk Richard Perle felt "relieved.... Contrary to expectations, I don't think we would see a lot of change" from the Bush neocons. Retiring senior Republican senator John Warner, former chair of the Armed Services Committee, said "the triumvirate of Gates, Clinton and Jones to lead Obama's national security team instills great confidence at home and abroad and further strengthens the growing respect for the president-elect's courage and ability to exercise sound judgment in selecting the best and the brightest to implement our nation's security policies."[35]

Hillary Clinton and Robert Gates need no comment. James Jones is less known. Security analyst Robert Dreyfuss describes former marine commandant Jones, Obama's new national security adviser, as "Obama's hawk," who "seems least compatible with Obama" among his hawkish team—though there is little reason beyond "hope" to justify the judgment about compatibility. Jones, Dreyfuss observes, "is a fierce advocate of NATO expansion," Clinton's policy that reneged on gentlemen's agreements with Gorbachev, guaranteeing confrontation with an encircled Russia. Jones urged that NATO should move to the south as well as the east, to expand U.S. control over Middle East energy supplies (in preferred terminology, "safeguarding energy security"). He also advocates a "NATO response force," which will give the U.S.-run military alliance "much more flexible capability to do things rapidly at very long distances." Europe has been reluctant, but will probably succumb to pressure from a militaristic and expansionist administration in Washington.[36]

The new director of national intelligence is Dennis Blair, former head of the U.S. Pacific Command. In that post, he was a strong supporter of U.S. military ties with the murderous Suharto regime in Indonesia, sometimes skirting State Department and congressional objections. In early 1999, Indonesian violence began to increase again in East Timor, surpassing anything officially attributed to Serbia in Kosovo prior to the NATO bombing, and of course the background of atrocities was vastly worse than anything in the Balkans; and incomparably more significant for the West on elementary moral grounds, not only because the U.S./UK–backed Indonesian crimes were in the course of outright aggression (in contrast, the West then insisted that Kosovo must be part of Serbia) but because these were our own crimes, not someone else's. Reactions among the intellectual classes were the opposite of what elementary moral principles would dictate, in conformity to the historical norm. Blair was sent by the National Security Council to urge Indonesian general Wiranto to curb the violence. Instead, "Blair took a cordial approach," the outstanding correspondent Alan Nairn reported. He told Wiranto that he "looks forward to the time Indonesia will resume its proper role as a leader in the region," according to U.S. officials who reviewed a cable written about the trip—which coincided with a particularly brutal slaughter in a church in Liquiça, leaving at least dozens killed. Blair proposed new U.S. training programs for Indonesia, which were implemented, right through the last paroxysms of violence in September 1999 that practically destroyed what was left of the tortured country.[37]

As his special assistant on the Middle East, Obama selected Dan Kurtzer, Clinton-Bush ambassador to Egypt and Israel, respectively. According to Israel's leading diplomatic correspondent, Akiva Eldar, Kurtzer took part in writing Obama's speech to the Israeli lobbying organization AIPAC in June 2008. This remarkable text went well beyond Bush in its obsequiousness, even declaring that "Jerusalem will remain the capital of Israel, and it must remain undivided," a position so extreme that his campaign had to explain that his words didn't mean what they said. Kurtzer is close to Obama adviser Dennis Ross, whose position as a negotiator for the failed Camp David negotiations was that Israel has "needs"—including parts of the occupied territories—while Palestinians only have "wants," which therefore are less significant. His disgraceful book on the negotiations evades the major issue—the illegal Israeli settlements that expanded steadily under Clinton—and terminates conveniently just before the book's major thesis about Arafat's culpability completely collapsed at the Taba negotiations, in Clinton's last month in office.[38]

Like other Obama Middle East advisers, Ross has been closely associated with the Washington Institute for Middle East Policy (WINEP), an offshoot of AIPAC and a barely disguised component of the Israeli lobby. Hillary Clinton's record of support for Israeli extremism is well known.

Asked in a press conference about the recycling of familiar faces, Obama responded that, as the *New York Times* reported, "Americans would be rightly 'troubled' if he overlooked experience simply to create the perception of change." Explaining further, he said: "What we are going to do is combine experience with fresh thinking. But understand where the vision for change comes from first and foremost: It comes from me."[39]

That should satisfy doubters, mesmerized by the "soaring and persuasive rhetoric" about "change" and "hope."

It was hoped, and indeed with some early degree of realism, that Obama would reverse some of the more flagrant abuses of the Bush administration in dismantling the legal system. But it was not easy to be too confident. Obama's choice for attorney general, Eric Holder, had a good reputation in the legal profession. However, he had explained on CNN that we cannot adhere to the Geneva Conventions in interrogation of those accused of terrorism—which seems to mean that torture of suspects is legitimate, in gross violation of the foundations of international humanitarian law, by which the United States is theoretically bound.[40] Those suspicions were unfortunately confirmed, along with much more to which we return in chapter 11.

The primary concern for the administration was to arrest the financial crisis and the simultaneous recession in the real economy. But there is also a monster in the closet: the notoriously inefficient privatized and scarcely regulated health care system, which threatens to overwhelm the federal budget if current tendencies persist. A majority of the public has long favored a national health care system, which should be far less expensive and more effective, comparative evidence indicates (along with many studies).[41] The United States is alone in relying on such a system, which, quite apart from its impact on those who are left out, introduces numerous wasteful inefficiencies (complex billing costs, close surveillance of doctors by insurance company bureaucrats, advertising, profits, the expenses of cherry-picking and denial of treatment on the basis of small print, reliance on expensive emergency room care for the tens of millions of uninsured and underinsured, etc.). Largely for these reasons—and because of the legislation, unique to the United States, that bars government negotiation of drug prices—per capita health care costs in the United States are about twice those of other industrial countries, and outcomes rank low among them.

As recently as 2004, any government intervention in the health care system was described in the press as "politically impossible" and "lacking political support"—meaning: opposed by the insurance industry, pharmaceutical corporations, and others who count, whatever the irrelevant public may think. In 2008, however, first John Edwards, then Obama and Hillary Clinton, advanced proposals that approached what the public has long preferred. These ideas now have "political support." What has changed? Not public opinion, which remains much as before. But by 2008, major sectors of power, primarily manufacturing industry, had come to recognize that they are being severely damaged by the privatized health care system. Hence the public will is coming to have "political support." The shift tells us something about dysfunctional democracy and the struggles that lie ahead.

The aftermath tells us more.

Obama quickly abandoned the popular and sensible single-payer option that he had previously said he favored. He also made a secret deal with drug companies that the government would not "negotiate drug prices and demand additional rebates from drug manufacturers," under pressure from lobbyists and in opposition to a mere 85 percent of the public. A "public option"—essentially an option of Medicare for all—lingered, but came under intense attack on the interesting grounds that private insurers would not be able to compete with a more efficient government plan (more sophisticated pretexts were only marginally less odd). As of June 2009, it was favored by over 70 percent of the population, despite the unremitting and often hysterical attack mostly traceable back to the insurance industry.

Two months later, the cover story of *Business Week* was headlined "The Health Insurers Have Already Won: How UnitedHealth and Rival Carriers, Maneuvering Behind the Scenes in Washington, Shaped Health-Care Reform for Their Own Benefit." The industry has "succeeded in redefining the terms of the reform debate to such a degree that no matter what specifics emerge in the voluminous bill Congress may send to President Obama this fall, the insurance industry will emerge more profitable...insurance CEOs ought to be smiling."[42]

By mid-September, as the committee bills were coming to the floor of the Congress, business groups expressed their support for the version proposed by Senator Max Baucus's Finance Committee, which had worked "in close talks with employer groups," more so than others, they approvingly related. The House proposals they rejected as not sufficiently business-friendly. The chairman of the Business Roundtable described the Senate Finance Committee proposal as "very closely aligned to" its principles, particularly in that it "doesn't call for creation of a public plan."[43]

Of course, no success is enough, another intrinsic property of a market system. Hence as the health care reform struggle virtually paralyzed Congress in late 2009, business lobbies undertook a major campaign to gain even more, and they did. The public option was finally "scuttled" along with a related "Medicare buy-in" that would have permitted people fifty-five or older to join the national health care system. At that point the public favored the public option by a 56 to 38 percent majority, and the Medicare buy-in by an even greater 64 to 30 percent. The poll yielding these results was reported, but with these facts omitted: the heading read, "Polls: Majority Disapprove of Health Care Legislation." The report leaves the impression that the public is joining the right-wing assault against government involvement in health care led by the business classes, contrary to what this very poll reveals, and what polls have shown for decades.

And what polls continued to show into 2010. A CBS poll released on January 11 found that 60 percent of Americans disapprove of how the president and Congress are dealing with health care. The detailed figures show that of those who object to the way the proposal regulates insurance companies, a large majority feel that it does not go far enough (43 percent not far enough, versus 27 percent too far). A Wall Street Journal/NBC poll found that 64 percent of voters disapprove of the Republicans' handling of health care (55 percent disapproved of Obama's handling). Health care was an issue in the January 2010 Massachusetts senatorial election, in which Republican Scott Brown was the victor. Among Democrats who abstained or switched to Brown, 60 percent felt that the health care program did not go far enough (85 percent among those who abstained). Among both abstainers and Democrat Brown voters, about 85 percent favored a public option.[44]

In brief, the evidence indicates that there was indeed growing popular anger about Obama's health care bill, primarily because it was too limited—though there was more, to which we turn directly.

The insurance executives were smiling along with the directors of the major financial institutions, who not only emerged unscathed from the catastrophe they precipitated, but even gained in wealth and power, and were in an improved position to move on to create the next financial crisis, as we have already discussed. The power of the business world to undermine democracy was again revealed very clearly, along with the institutional imperative to rank short-term gain above such externalities as severe consequences for the species not far down the road, as the petroleum industry at once began to mimic the successful tactics of the insurance industry in the manner already described.

While the financial industry had every reason to feel satisfied about the outcome of their efforts to have their man Obama elected, the love affair was turning sour by January 2010, as Obama began to react to rising public anger about the "Gilded Pay Packages" for bankers while they were mired in "a Bleaker Path for Workers to Slog." He adopted "populist rhetoric," criticizing the huge bonuses of those who had been rescued by the public, and even proposed some measures to constrain the excesses of the big banks (including the "Volcker rule," which would partially reinstate Glass-Steagall, preventing commercial banks with government insurance from using depositors' funds for risky investment). The punishment for his deviation was swift.

The major banks announced prominently that they would shift funding to Republicans if Obama's talk about regulation and rhetoric about greedy bankers continued. Leading the charge, the press reported, was Jamie Dimon, chair of JPMorgan Chase, which along with the perennial champion Goldman Sachs, was one of the major beneficiaries of the bailout programs. Chase executives were also big Democratic donors "from Chicago's Democratic dynasty," reportedly close to the White House as well. In reaction to Obama's veering from the approved path, "Chase's political action committee is sending the Democrats a pointed message," the press reported, rebuffing solicitations from the national Democratic House and Senate campaign committees and donating instead to their Republican counterparts, who are "rushing to capitalize on what they call Wall Street's 'buyer's remorse' with the Democrats." Meanwhile "industry executives and lobbyists are warning Democrats that if Mr. Obama keeps attacking Wall Street 'fat cats,' they may fight back by withholding their cash," which had poured into Obama's campaign in record amounts from the securities and investment business. "The shift reflects the hard political edge to the industry's campaign to thwart Mr. Obama's proposals for tighter financial regulations," the press reported, along with his harsh criticism of excessive bonuses.

Obama heard the message. Within days he informed the business press that bankers are fine "guys," singling out Dimon and Goldman Sachs chair Lloyd Blankfein for praise, and assuring the business world that "I, like most of the American people, don't begrudge people success or wealth," such as the huge bonuses and profits that are infuriating the public. "That's part of the free market system," Obama continued; not inaccurately, as "free markets" are interpreted in state capitalist doctrine.[45]

A revealing snapshot of Smith's maxim in action.

In a parallel thrust, there was a massive infusion of funds for Republican Scott Brown from financial executives in the final days of the Massachusetts senatorial campaign, helping to swing the election to Brown, and providing Republicans with a magical "41st seat" in the Senate.[46] The forty-first seat gains its significance from a new development in American politics since the Republicans lost power. By now, the Republican Party scarcely resembles a traditional U.S. political party. With rare exceptions, they vote in a uniform bloc, whatever the issue, under strict party discipline, rather like the old Communist Party. And their most prominent plank is "No," to anything the majority initiates. With the cooperation of right-wing Democrats (called "moderates") they have been able to change the filibuster from a device that had been occasionally used to an automatic mechanism to require a supermajority, 60–40, for any legislation that Obama might propose, even nominations for federal positions. Hence the Brown victory, or a shift by a single Democrat, provides the Republican Party with a mechanism to undermine majority rule on virtually any issue by threatening a filibuster—at least, as long as the Democrats acquiesce to these means of undermining majority rule, or the public tolerates the blows to democracy.

In the Massachusetts vote, the party of "No" took over the seat of the late Edward Kennedy, the "liberal lion" of the Senate for many years, for whom health care reform had been a prime concern throughout his long career. The outcome was depicted as a right-wing revolt of an angry population against the excesses of the liberal elitists who run the government and "are taking our country away from us," and so on. But the data tell a rather different story, not just the flood of funding from the financial institutions in punishment for Obama's belated "populist" rhetoric and proposals. The official data showed that Brown was carried to victory by very high voting and enthusiasm in the "affluent suburbs," alongside low turnout and general apathy in the urban areas that are largely Democratic. Furthermore, "55% of Republican voters said they were 'very interested' in the election," the *Wall Street Journal* reported, "compared with 38 percent of Democrats." The outcome can be construed as an uprising against Obama's policies: for the wealthy, he was not doing enough to enrich them further, while for the poorer sectors, he was doing too much to achieve that end.[47]

Doubtless there was some impact of the populist image crafted by the PR machine ("I'm Scott Brown, this is my truck," "regular guy," nude model, daughter an *American Idol* contestant, etc.). But this appears to have had only a secondary role. The popular anger is quite understandable, with the banks thriving thanks to bailouts while the population remains in deep recession. Official unemployment is at 10 percent and in manufacturing industry at the level of the Great Depression, with one out of six unemployed, as was reported the day of the Massachusetts election; and with few prospects for recovering the kinds of jobs that are lost as a result of the increasing financialization of the economy and concomitant hollowing out of productive industry. The poll results on health care conform to this conclusion, as noted.[48]

There is more to say about the Democrats' compromises on health care. One striking fact about the election was that the majority of union members, Obama's natural constituency, voted for Brown. The reasons were explained in the labor press. Union leaders and activists reported that workers were angered at Obama's record generally, but particularly incensed over his stand on health care. "He didn't insist on a public option nor a strong employer mandate to provide insurance. It was hard not to notice that the only issue on which he took a firm stand was taxing benefits" for health care, contrary to his campaign pledge, a tax that hits unionized workers.[49]

The effects of the election of the forty-first seat were felt at once. Health care reform, such as it was, drifted to the back burner. Congressional efforts to do something about the looming environmental crisis, weak enough to begin with, were immediately scaled back, which means that other countries are unlikely to make the required moves either. Apparently emboldened by the magic forty-one, the Republican minority on the Security and Exchange Commission "accused the agency of placing 'the imprimatur of the commission on the agenda of the social and environmental policy lobby' by issuing guidelines encouraging corporations to disclose the effects of climate change on their businesses." The Republican hold on the nomination of a pro-union lawyer to the National Labor Relations Board, what's left of it, was invigorated as the forty-first vote arrived, another step in carrying forward the determined government assault on unions that took off when Reagan came into office. Republican Senator Richard Shelby carried the obstructionism a long way forward by announcing that he would place a hold on at least seventy Obama nominations (unless he received some special earmarks), paralyzing a good part of the government. Shelby also announced that he would no longer cooperate with Senator Dodd's legislation on financial reform, even though it had been greatly weakened to accommodate Republican demands; the main issue he brought up was the last residue of consumer protection that remained. An administration effort to "take billions of dollars from the profits of private lenders and give it directly to students" stalled thanks to a vigorous lobbying campaign, which picked up steam after the Supreme Court decision and the Brown vote. With business having its reliable forty-first obstructionist seat, and the Court having declared open season on buying elections, the sky's the limit.[50]

The consequences of the undermining of any reasonable environmental legislation are likely to be dire. In the domestic arena, the unwillingness of the political class to allow health care reform to be addressed will also have serious consequences, not only for those who suffer from the rationing of health care by wealth but for the economy generally. Economists David Rosnick and Dean Baker show that "the huge debt numbers that are being used to scare the country—especially the young—are largely projections of how much debt today's young will pass onto future generations" primarily because "per person health care costs are projected to far outpace the rate of per capita GDP growth" unless there is serious reform of the dysfunctional health care system. The more general impact of turning Congress into a comical version of seventeenth-century Poland, with nobles having a right of veto, is also not pleasant to contemplate, however inadequate the government has been from the standpoint of the public good.[51]

The business community can appeal to respectable antecedents in its dedicated campaign to increase its already overwhelming power in the political system. James Madison framed the constitutional order so that power would be in the hands of the Senate, which represents "the wealth of the nation," the "more capable sett of men," who have respect for property owners and their rights and understand the need for government "to protect the minority of the opulent against the majority"— though it was not long before he came to deplore "the daring depravity of the times," as the "stockjobbers will become the pretorian band of the government—at once its tools and its tyrant; bribed by its largesses, and overawing it by clamors and combinations" (1792).[52]

Returning to the Obama programs, internationally, there was never much of substance on the largely blank slate of the political campaign. What there was gave little reason to expect much change from Bush's second term, which stepped back from the radical ultranationalism and aggressive posture of the first term, also discarding some of the extreme figures like Rumsfeld and Wolfowitz; Cheney could not be sent away, because he virtually *was* the administration.

The immediate issues had to do mostly with the Middle East. On Israel-Palestine, rumors began circulating that Obama might depart from the U.S. rejectionism that has blocked a political settlement for over thirty years, with rare exceptions already discussed. The record, however, never provided any basis for taking the rumors seriously.

Before the primaries, I reviewed Obama's formal positions at the time.[53] They gave no reason for any expectations beyond uncritical and in fact enthusiastic support for Israeli crimes. Above, we have seen how his position evolved since he took office (pp. 177f). Even before, he had made them quite clear. Particularly revealing was his reaction to Israel's sharply accelerated assault on Gaza, opening with its violation of the cease-fire on November 4, 2008, as voters were going to the polls to elect Obama, then breaking out in full fury on December 27 after rejection of Hamas initiatives to reinstate the cease-fire. To these crimes Obama's response was silence—unlike, say, the late November terrorist attack in Mumbai, which he was quick to denounce, along with the "hateful ideology" that lay behind it. In the case of Gaza, his staff hid behind the mantra that "there is one president at a time," and repeated his comment when he visited the

Israeli town of Sderot in July 2008: "If missiles were falling where my two daughters sleep, I would do everything in order to stop that" (as it happened, no Hamas missiles were falling, because Hamas was strictly observing the cease-fire, as the government of Israel conceded, even though Israel had not relieved the punishing siege, an act of war). But he was able to do nothing, not even make a statement, when U.S. jets and helicopters with Israeli pilots were causing incomparably worse suffering to Palestinian children. The Israeli attack was carefully timed to end as Obama came into office, so that he could then content himself with familiar rhetoric about how we must move on and put the past behind us—when it's our crimes, that is; the crimes of others can never be forgotten or forgiven.[54]

Israeli president Shimon Peres had informed the press that on his July 2008 trip to Israel, Obama had told him that he was "very impressed" with the Arab League peace proposal that calls for full normalization of relations with Israel along with Israeli withdrawal from the occupied territories—basically, the long-standing international consensus that the United States and Israel have unilaterally blocked (and that Peres always rejected when in office, as noted earlier). That might have suggested a significant change of heart, except that the right-wing Israeli leader Binyamin Netanyahu said that on the same trip, Obama had told him that he was "very impressed" with Netanyahu's plan, which called for indefinite Israeli control of the occupied territories.

The paradox was resolved by Israeli political analyst Aluf Benn, who observed that Obama's "main goal was not to screw up or ire anyone. Presumably he was polite, and told his hosts their proposals were 'very interesting'—they leave satisfied and he hasn't promised a thing." Understandable for a politician, but it leaves us with nothing except his fervent professions of love for Israel and disregard for Palestinian suffering.[55]

On Iraq, Obama has frequently been praised for his "principled opposition" to the war. In reality, as he has made clear, his opposition has been entirely unprincipled throughout. The war, he said, was a "strategic blunder." When Kremlin critics of the invasion of Afghanistan called it a strategic blunder, we did not say that they were taking a principled stand.

After intensive debate, the government of Iraq finally agreed on a Status of Forces Agreement (SOFA) on the U.S. military presence in Iraq. The U.S. position, released by the White House in November 2007, called for "facilitating and encouraging the flow of foreign investments to Iraq, especially American investments" and for a military presence with no specified limits, allegedly to combat terrorism and "deter foreign aggression against Iraq"; "foreign" of course does not include the United States. The talks dragged on, the *Washington Post* reported, because Iraq insisted on (and obtained) "some major concessions, including the establishment of the 2011 withdrawal date instead of vaguer language favored by the Bush administration [and] also rejected long-term U.S. military bases on its soil." Iraqi leaders "consider the firm deadline for withdrawal to be a negotiating victory," Reuters reported: Washington "long opposed setting any timetable for its troops to withdraw, but relented in recent months," unable to overcome Iraqi resistance.[56]

Throughout the negotiations, the press regularly dismissed the obstinate stance of the Maliki government as pandering to public opinion; understandable for reasons of politics, but regrettable—on the assumption that what is decided is no more the business of Iraqis than it is of Americans. U.S.-run polls continued to report that a large majority of Iraqis opposed any U.S. military presence, and believed that U.S. forces make the situation worse, including the "surge." That judgment was supported, among others, by Middle East specialist and security analyst Steven Simon, who wrote in *Foreign Affairs* that the Petraeus counterinsurgency strategy is "stoking the three forces that have traditionally threatened the stability of Middle Eastern states: tribalism, warlordism, and sectarianism. States that have failed to control these forces have ultimately become ungovernable, and this is the fate for which the surge is preparing Iraq. A strategy intended to reduce casualties in the short term will ineluctably weaken the prospects for Iraq's cohesion over the long run." It may lead to "a strong, centralized state ruled by a military junta that would resemble the Baathist regime Washington overthrew in 2003," or "something very much like the imperial protectorates in the Middle East of the first half of the twentieth century" in which the "club of patrons" in the capital would "dole out goods to tribes through favored conduits." In the Petraeus system, "the U.S. military is performing the role of the patrons—creating an unhealthy dependency and driving a dangerous wedge between the tribes and the state," undermining prospects for a "stable, unitary Iraq." As David Gardner observed while reviewing the dismal consequences of "the surge," the Iraq invasion, "seen in the region as the epitome of U.S. unilateralism, powered by a deadly combination of arrogance and ignorance...has both proliferated jihadism and primed a sectarian time bomb in the heart of the Arab world," leaving Arabs "shocked but not so much awed as disgusted and enraged by this bloody fiasco."[57]

Iraqi opposition to the U.S. presence was underscored by reporting from across Iraq after parliamentary approval of the Iraqi version of the SOFA. The *International Herald Tribune*, drawing from interviews by Iraqi journalists from around the country, reported opposition to the pact on grounds that the Iraqi government had been "bullied into a deal by an occupying force," that the United States would not live up to its terms, and that the central government gained too much power. Apart from one voice disturbed by the parliamentary brawl, there was no report of opposition on grounds that U.S. forces were needed to defend Iraqi interests.[58]

The latest Iraqi success culminates a long process of resistance to demands of the U.S. invaders. Washington fought tooth and nail to prevent elections, but was finally forced to back down in the face of popular demands for democracy, symbolized by the Ayatollah Sistani. The Bush administration then managed to install their own choice as prime minister, and sought to control the government in various ways, meanwhile also building huge military bases around the country and an "embassy" that is a virtual city within Baghdad—all funded by congressional Democrats and as noted above, set to expand under Obama along with similar "embassies" in Islamabad and Kabul. If the invaders do live up to the SOFA that they were compelled to accept, it will constitute yet another significant triumph of nonviolent resistance. Insurgents can be killed, but mass nonviolent resistance is much harder to quell. Though the conclusion is unpopular in the United States, it is understood by the most knowledgeable and astute observers of Iraq.[59]

Many comparisons are being drawn between Vietnam and Iraq, most of them untenable. One, which is not being discussed, is of some interest. In both cases, Washington was faced with strong pressure from the invaded countries to withdraw. JFK discovered a few months before his assassination that the U.S. client regime was seeking a peaceful diplomatic settlement that would lead to U.S. withdrawal. To avert this threat, his administration backed a military coup to install a more compliant regime in South Vietnam. As the internal and public record demonstrate, while JFK did contemplate withdrawal (as was accurately reported at the time), he always imposed a crucial condition: only after U.S. victory was assured. The record shows that he remained dedicated to this goal to the end. In the case of Iraq, in contrast, Washington has been unable to resort to such means to get rid of a government that is calling upon it to leave. There are many reasons for the differences. One is that the domestic population today is much less willing to tolerate U.S. aggression than it was in the early '60s. A few years later strong opposition did develop, but only when the U.S. invasion of Vietnam far exceeded the scale of its aggression and crimes in Iraq.[60]

Within the political class and the media it is reflexively assumed that Washington has the right to demand terms for the SOFA in Iraq. No such right was accorded to Russian invaders of Afghanistan, or indeed to anyone except the United States and its clients. For others, we rightly adopt the principle that invaders have no rights, only responsibilities, including the responsibility to attend to the will of the victims, and to pay massive reparations for their crimes. In this case, the crimes include strong support for Saddam Hussein through his worst atrocities on Reagan's watch, then on to Saddam's massacre of Shiites under the eyes of the U.S. military after the first Gulf War; the Clinton sanctions that were termed "genocidal" by the distinguished international diplomats who administered them and resigned in protest, then the invasion and its hideous aftermath. No such thoughts can be voiced in polite society.

The Iraqi government spokesman said that the tentative SOFA "matches the vision of U.S. President-elect Barack Obama."[61] Obama's vision was in fact left somewhat vague, but presumably he would go along in some fashion with the demands of the Iraqi government. If so, that might require modification of U.S. plans to ensure privileged access to Iraq's enormous oil resources while establishing a major military presence in a client state, and thus reinforcing its dominance over the world's major energy-producing region.

Obama's announced "vision" was to shift forces from Iraq to Afghanistan. That stand evoked a lesson from the editors of the *Washington Post*: "While the United States has an interest in preventing the resurgence of the Afghan Taliban, the country's strategic importance pales beside that of Iraq, which lies at the geopolitical center of the Middle East and contains some of the world's largest oil reserves."[62] Increasingly, as Washington has been compelled to accede to Iraqi demands, tales about "democracy promotion" and other self-congratulatory fables have been shelved in favor of recognition of what had been obvious throughout to all but the most doctrinaire ideologists: that the United States would not have invaded if Iraq's exports were asparagus and tomatoes and the world's major energy resources were in the South Pacific.

The NATO command is also coming to recognize reality in public. In June 2007, NATO secretary-general Jaap de Hoop Scheffer informed a meeting of NATO members that "NATO troops have to guard pipelines that transport oil and gas that is directed for the West," and more generally to protect sea routes used by tankers and other "crucial infrastructure" of the energy system. This may turn out to be the sole operative component of the fabled "responsibility to protect." The decision extends the post–Cold War policies of reshaping NATO into a U.S.-run global intervention force, with the side effect of deterring European initiatives toward Gaullist-style independence. Presumably the task includes the projected $7.6 billion TAPI pipeline that would deliver natural gas from Turkmenistan to Pakistan and India, running through Afghanistan's Kandahar province, where Canadian troops are deployed. The goal is "to block a competing pipeline that would bring gas to Pakistan and India from Iran" and to "diminish Russia's dominance of Central Asian energy exports," the Toronto *Globe and Mail* reported, plausibly outlining some of the contours of the new "Great Game."[63]

Obama strongly endorsed the Bush administration policy of attacking suspected al-Qaeda leaders in countries that Washington has not (yet) invaded, disclosed by the *New York Times* shortly after the election. The doctrine was illustrated again on October 26, 2008, when U.S. forces based in Iraq raided Syria, killing eight civilians, allegedly to capture an al-Qaeda leader. Washington did not notify Iraqi prime minister al-Maliki or President Talabani, both of whom have relatively amicable relations with Syria, which has accepted 1.5 million Iraqi refugees and is bitterly opposed to al-Qaeda. Syria protested, claiming, credibly, that if notified they would have eagerly apprehended this common enemy. According to the *Asia Times*, Iraqi leaders were furious, and hardened their stance in the SOFA negotiations, insisting on provisions to bar the use of Iraqi territory to attack neighbors.

The Syria raid was harshly condemned in the Arab world. In progovernment newspapers, the Bush administration was denounced for lengthening its "loathsome legacy" (Lebanon), while Syria was urged to "march forward in your reconciliatory path" and America to "keep going backwards with your language of hatred, arrogance and the murder of innocents" (Kuwait). For the region generally, it was another illustration of what the government-controlled Saudi press condemned as "not diplomacy in search of peace, but madness in search of war." Obama was silent. So were other Democrats. Political scientist Stephen Zunes contacted the offices of every Democrat on the House and Senate Foreign Relations Committees, but was unable to find any critical word on the U.S. raid on Syria from occupied Iraq.[64]

Presumably, Obama also accepts the more expansive Bush doctrine that the United States not only has the right to invade countries as it chooses (unless it is a "blunder," too costly to us), but also to attack others that Washington claims are supporting resistance to its aggression. In particular, Obama is relying more heavily than Bush on the raids by drones that have killed many civilians in Pakistan. Former Petraeus counterinsurgency adviser David Kilkullen reported that drones have killed about fourteen alleged terrorists and seven hundred civilians—"a hit rate of 2 percent."[65]

These raids of course have consequences: people have the odd characteristic of objecting to slaughter of family members and friends. There has been a vicious mini-war waged in the tribal area of Bajaur in Pakistan, adjacent to Afghanistan. BBC described widespread destruction from intense combat, reporting further that "many in Bajaur trace the roots of the uprising to a suspected U.S. missile strike on an Islamic seminary, or madrassa, in November 2006, which killed around 80 people." The attack on the school, killing eighty to eighty-five people, was reported in the mainstream Pakistani press by physicist and dissident activist Pervez Hoodbhoy, but ignored in the United States as insignificant. Events often look different at the other end of the club.[66]

Hoodbhoy observed that the usual outcome of such attacks "has been flattened houses, dead and maimed children, and a growing local population that seeks revenge against Pakistan and the US." Bajaur may be an illustration of the familiar pattern.

On November 3, 2008, General Petraeus, the newly appointed head of the U.S. Central Command that covers the Middle East region, had his first meeting with Pakistani president Asif Ali Zardari, army chief General Ashfaq Parvez Kayani, and other high officials. Their primary concern was U.S. missile attacks on Pakistani territory, which had increased sharply in previous weeks. "Continuing drone attacks on our territory, which result in loss of precious lives and property, are counterproductive and difficult to explain by a democratically elected government," Zardari informed Petraeus. His government, he said, is "under pressure to react more aggressively" to the strikes. These could lead to "a backlash against the U.S.," which is already deeply unpopular in Pakistan.

Petraeus said that he had heard the message, and "we would have to take [Pakistani opinions] on board" when attacking the country. A practical necessity, no doubt, when over 80 percent of the supplies for the U.S.-NATO war in Afghanistan pass through Pakistan.[67]

The United States had generally supported Pakistani dictators since the country's independence. The most extreme case was Reagan. His administration pretended not to see when Pakistan developed nuclear weapons, outside the Non-Proliferation Treaty (NPT), so as to ensure that congressional resolutions would not hinder Reagan's "unstinting support" for the "ruthless and vindictive" dictator Zia ul-Haq, whose rule had "the most long-lasting and damaging effect on Pakistani society, one still prevalent today," Ahmed Rashid observes. With Reagan's firm backing, and Saudi funding, Zia moved to impose "an ideological Islamic state upon the population." These are the immediate roots of many of "today's problems—the militancy of the religious parties, the mushrooming of madrassas and extremist groups, the spread of drug and Kalashnikov culture, and the increase in sectarian violence." Hoodbhoy adds that "radical extremism is the illegitimate offspring of a union between the United States under Ronald Reagan, and Pakistan under General Zia-ul-Haq." Former CIA analyst Bruce Riedel, a specialist on the region, concludes that "all of the nightmares of the 21st century come together in Pakistan," including Lashkar-e-Taiba, the militant group blamed for the terrorist atrocities in Mumbai in November 2008 and other atrocities.[68]

The Reaganites also "built up the [Inter-Services Intelligence Directorate, ISI] into a formidable intelligence agency that ran the political process inside Pakistan while promoting Islamic insurgencies in Kashmir and Central Asia," Rashid continues. "This global jihad launched by Zia and Reagan was to sow the seeds of al Qaeda and turn Pakistan into the world center of jihadism for the next two decades." Meanwhile Reagan's immediate successors left Afghanistan in the hands of the most vicious jihadis, later handing it over to warlord rule under Rumsfeld's direction. The fearsome ISI continues to play both sides of the street, supporting the resurgent Taliban and simultaneously acceding to some U.S. demands.

The United States and Pakistan are reported to have reached "tacit agreement in September [2008] on a don't-ask-don't-tell policy that allows unmanned Predator aircraft to attack suspected terrorist targets" in Pakistan, according to unidentified senior officials in both countries. "The officials described the deal as one in which the U.S. government refuses to publicly acknowledge the attacks while Pakistan's government continues to complain noisily about the politically sensitive strikes."[69]

Once again problems are caused by the annoying population who dislike being bombed by an increasingly hated enemy from the other side of the world.

Shortly before this report on the "tacit agreement" appeared, a suicide bombing in the conflicted tribal areas killed eight Pakistani soldiers, retaliation for an attack by a U.S. Predator drone that killed twenty people, including two Taliban leaders. The Pakistani parliament called for dialogue with the Taliban. Echoing the resolution, Pakistani foreign minister Shah Mehmood Qureshi said, "There is an increasing realization that the use of force alone cannot yield the desired results."[70]

Afghan president Hamid Karzai's first message to President-elect Obama was much like that delivered to General Petraeus by Pakistani leaders: "End U.S. airstrikes that risk civilian casualties." His message was sent shortly after coalition troops bombed a wedding party in Kandahar Province, reportedly killing forty people. There is no indication that his opinion was "taken on board." Karzai has informed the Afghan public that "he is powerless to halt U.S. airstrikes in his country and he would stop American warplanes if he could," the Voice of America reported. He told a UN Security Council delegation visiting Kabul that he has demanded a timeline for withdrawal of foreign forces from his country. But this plea has also not been "taken on board."[71]

The British command has warned that there is no military solution to the conflict in Afghanistan and that there will have to be negotiations with the Taliban, risking a rift with the United States, the *Financial Times* reports. Correspondent Jason Burke, who has long experience in the region, reported that "the Taliban have been engaged in secret talks about ending the conflict in Afghanistan in a wide-ranging 'peace process' sponsored by Saudi Arabia and supported by Britain," and such efforts have apparently been pursued since.[72]

Some Afghan peace activists have reservations about this approach, preferring a solution without foreign interference. A network of activists is calling for negotiations and reconciliation with the Taliban through the National Peace Jirga, a grand assembly of Afghans, formed in May 2008. At a meeting in support of the jirga, three thousand Afghan political figures and intellectuals, mainly Pashtuns, the largest ethnic group, criticized "the international military campaign against Islamic militants in Afghanistan and called for dialogue to end the fighting," Agence France-Presse reported.

The interim chairman of the National Peace Jirga, Bakhtar Aminzai, "told the opening gathering that the current conflict could not be resolved by military means and that only talks could bring a solution. He called on the government to step up its negotiations with the Taliban and Hizb-i-Islami groups." The latter is the party of the extremist radical Islamist warlord Gulbuddin Hekmatyar, a Reagan favorite responsible for many terrible atrocities, now reported to provide core parliamentary support for the Karzai government and to be pressing it toward a form of re-Talibanization.[73]

Aminzai said further that "we need to pressure the Afghan government and the international community to find a solution without using guns." A spokeswoman added that "we are against Western policy in Afghanistan. They should bury their guns in a grave and focus on diplomacy and economic development." A leader of Awakened Youth of Afghanistan, a prominent antiwar group, says that we must end "Afghanicide—the killing of Afghanistan." In a joint declaration with German peace organizations, the National Peace Jirga claimed to represent "a wide majority of Afghan people who are tired of war," calling for an end to escalation and initiation of a peace process.

The deputy director of the umbrella organization of NGOs in the country says that of roughly 1,400 registered NGOs, nearly 1,100 are purely Afghan operations: women's groups, youth groups, and others, many of them advocates of the National Peace Jirga.[74]

Though polling in war-torn Afghanistan is an uncertain process, there are some suggestive results. A Canadian-run poll found that Afghans favor the presence of Canadian and other foreign troops, the result that made the headlines in Canada. The small print suggests some qualifications. Only 20 percent "think the Taliban will prevail once foreign troops leave." Three-fourths support negotiations between the Karzai government and the Taliban, and more than half favor a coalition government. The great majority therefore strongly disagrees with the U.S.-NATO focus on further militarization of the conflict, and appears to believe that peace is possible with a turn toward diplomacy and negotiations.[75]

Though the question was not asked, it is reasonable to surmise that the foreign presence is favored for aid and reconstruction. More evidence in support of this conjecture is provided by reports about the progress of reconstruction in Afghanistan six years after the U.S. invasion. Six percent of the population has electricity, AP reports, primarily in Kabul, which is artificially wealthy because of the huge foreign presence. There, "the rich, powerful, and well connected" have electricity, but few others, in contrast to the 1980s under Russian occupation, when "the city had plentiful power"—and women in Kabul were relatively free under the occupation and the Russian-backed Najibullah government that followed, possibly more so than now, though they did have to worry about attacks from U.S.-backed radical Islamists, like Hekmatyar, who felt it his duty to throw acid in the faces of young women he thought were improperly dressed.[76]

Such considerations suggest that Afghans really would welcome a foreign presence devoted to aid and reconstruction, as we can perhaps read between the lines in the polls. There are, of course, numerous questions about polls in countries under foreign military occupation, particularly in places like southern Afghanistan where the government/NATO presence is limited. But the results conform reasonably well to other evidence, and should not be dismissed.

A study of Taliban foot soldiers carried out by the Toronto *Globe and Mail*, though not a scientific survey as they point out, nevertheless yields considerable insight. All were Pashtuns, from the Kandahar area. They described themselves as mujahideen, following the ancient tradition of driving out foreign invaders. Almost a third reported that at least one family member had died in aerial bombings in recent years. Many said that they were fighting to defend Afghan villagers from air strikes by foreign troops. Few claimed to be fighting a global jihad, or had allegiance to Taliban leader Mullah Omar, who is reported to be in Quetta, Pakistan. Most saw themselves as fighting for principles—an Islamic government—not a particular leader. Again, the results suggest possibilities for a negotiated peaceful settlement, without foreign interference.[77]

A valuable perspective on such prospects is provided by Sir Rodric Braithwaite, a specialist on Afghanistan who was UK ambassador to

Moscow during the crucial 1988–92 period when the Russians withdrew (and the USSR collapsed), then became chair of the British Joint Intelligence Committee. On a fall 2008 visit, Braithwaite spoke to Afghan journalists, former mujahideen, professionals, people working for the U.S.-based coalition—in general, to "natural supporters for [Western] claims to bring peace and reconstruction." He reports that they were "contemptuous of President Hamid Karzai," regarding him as another one of the puppets installed by foreign force. Their favorite was

> Mohammad Najibullah, the last communist president, who attempted to reconcile the nation within an Islamic state, and was butchered by the Taliban in 1996 [having been overthrown in 1992 by the warlords who virtually destroyed Kabul]: DVDs of his speeches are being sold on the streets. Things were, they said, better under the Soviets. Kabul was secure, women were employed, the Soviets built factories, roads, schools and hospitals, Russian children played safely in the streets. The Russian soldiers fought bravely on the ground like real warriors, instead of killing women and children from the air. Even the Taliban were not so bad: they were good Muslims, kept order, and respected women in their own way. These myths may not reflect historical reality, but they do measure a deep disillusionment with the "coalition" and its policies.[78]

These matters were discussed at the time by Rasil Basu, UN Development Program senior adviser to the Afghan government for women's development (1986–88). She reported "enormous strides" for women under the Russian occupation:

> Illiteracy declined from 98% to 75%, and they were granted equal rights with men in civil law, and in the Constitution…. Unjust patriarchal relations still prevailed in the workplace and in the family with women occupying lower level sex-type jobs. But the strides [women] took in education and employment were very impressive…. In Kabul I saw great advances in women's education and employment. Women were in evidence in industry, factories, government offices, professions and the media. With large numbers of men killed or disabled, women shouldered the responsibility of both family and country. I met a woman who specialized in war medicine which dealt with trauma and reconstructive surgery for the war-wounded. This represented empowerment to her.

Another woman was a road engineer. Roads represented freedom—an
escape from the oppressive patriarchal structures.

By 1988, however, Basu "could see the early warning signals" as Russian troops departed and the fundamentalist Islamist extremists favored
by the Reagan administration took over, brushing aside the more moderate mujahideen groups. Saudi Arabian and American arms and am-
munition "have been vital in giving fundamentalist groups an edge over
the moderates," providing them with military hardware used, "according
to Amnesty International, to target unarmed civilians, most of them
women and children." Then followed much worse horrors as the U.S.-
Saudi favorites overthrew the Najibullah government. The suffering of
the population was so extreme that the Taliban were welcomed when
they drove out Reagan's freedom fighters. Another chapter in the triumph of Reaganite reactionary ultranationalism, worshipped today by
those dedicated to defaming the honorable term "conservative."

Basu is a distinguished advocate for women's rights, including a long
career with the UN during which she drafted the World Plan of Action
for Women and the draft Programme for the Women's Decade, 1975–85,
adopted at the Mexico City Conference (1975) and the Copenhagen Conference (1980). But her words on Kabul under Russian occupation were
not welcome in the United States. Her 1988 report was submitted to the
Washington Post, New York Times, and *Ms.* magazine, but rejected.[79] Also
rejected were Basu's recommendation of practical steps that the West,
particularly the United States, could take to protect women's rights.

Highly relevant in this connection is the testimony of the remarkable
young Afghan woman Malalai Joya, who has spoken out with incredible
courage against the torturers of the Afghan people: the Soviet invaders;
the Islamic fundamentalists unleashed by Reagan and the Pakistani intelligence agencies; the medieval Taliban fanatics trained in the U.S./Saudi-
backed madrassas established by Pakistani dictator Zia ul-Haq; and finally
the U.S. forces and their NATO subordinates who restored the rule of the
warlords and are now themselves killing and destroying in the name of
"liberation" and women's rights. The United States lost little time in
demonstrating that the fine words of Colin Powell and others about pro-

tecting women's rights were cynical farce, Joya observes. "It was obvious from the very first days that the United States had compromised the rights of Afghan women by supporting some of the worst enemies of women that our country had ever seen," as she relates in painful detail.[80]

After having been expelled from the "house of warlords" called the Parliament for denouncing the corruption and crimes of the warlord rulers, Joya lives in hiding, moving secretly from place to place, protected by bodyguards and a wide network of supporters. But she continues, relentlessly, to reveal ongoing atrocities from all sides and to call for democracy and justice. In her powerful 2009 memoir and commentary, she writes that "the situation in Afghanistan is getting progressively worse," not just for women but for all Afghans, "caught between two enemies— the Taliban on one side and the U.S./NATO forces and their warlord friends on the other." What Afghans really need is not landmines, bullets, and bombs, but "an invasion of hospitals, clinics and schools for boys and girls." Whatever hope Obama might have aroused at first, his "military build-up will only bring more suffering and death to innocent civilians," and more violence and corruption by his warlord associates. Liberation will not be brought by outsiders, even if they were to try: "These values must be fought for and won by the people themselves. They can only grow and flourish when they are planted by the people in their own soil and watered by their own blood and tears," ideas with a distinguished pedigree in the West but drowned in imperial greed and arrogance.

Apart from the record of her own life and work, perhaps the most captivating part of her powerful memoir, and surely the most uplifting, is the account of how supporters rallied to her side, braving terror and violence, including many women "protesting with empty hands," evidence that "we are not only victims, and that women have the power to make changes in their lives and in their country."

Joya also has advice for the West. "The very first thing that the international community must do is to reject the United-States led war." The next task is to "send real humanitarian aid," most importantly to the "many great, small projects run by democratically minded Afghans," which are almost never reached by Western funds. Then to "put an end to the rule of the warlords" and "withdraw all foreign troops." Joya feels confident, based on her own rich experience and Afghan history prior to the last terrible decades, that "if foreign countries stop meddling in Afghanistan and if we are left free from occupation, then a strong progressive and democratic force will emerge," Afghanistan may recover the path to progress that was brutally reversed by foreign intervention, and may join Latin Americans and others who are escaping from imperial domination and taking steps toward progressive change.

Joya has won many prestigious awards for her impressive work. None will compare in value to careful attention to her eloquent words.

Also highly relevant, from a different point of view, are the investigations by Nikolai Lanine, a former soldier in the Russian army in Afghanistan, bringing out striking comparisons between Russian commentary during the occupation and that of their NATO successors today[81]—a topic that in general merits careful study.

Specialists on the region urge that U.S. strategy should shift from more troops and attacks in Pakistan to a "diplomatic grand bargain—forging compromise with insurgents while addressing an array of regional rivalries and insecurities."[82] They warn that the current military focus "and the attendant terrorism" might lead to the collapse of nuclear-armed Pakistan, with grave consequences. They urge the Obama administration "to put an end to the increasingly destructive dynamics of the Great Game in the region" through negotiations that recognize the interests of the concerned parties within Afghanistan as well as Pakistan and Iran, but also India, China, and Russia, who "have reservations about a NATO base within their spheres of influence" and concerns about the threats "posed by the United States and NATO" as well as by al-Qaeda and the Taliban. The immediate goal should be "lowering the level of violence in the region and moving the global community toward genuine agreement on the long-term goals," thus allowing Afghans to confront their internal problems in relative peace. The then-incoming U.S. president must put an end to "Washington's keenness for 'victory' as the solution to all problems, and the United States' reluctance to involve competitors, opponents, or enemies in diplomacy."

It appears that there may be feasible alternatives to escalation of the cycle of violence, but there was little hint of such possibilities in the electoral campaign or political commentary. Afghanistan and Pakistan did not even appear among foreign policy issues on the Obama campaign's website.

Iran, in contrast, figured prominently on the campaign website—though not of course as compared with effusive support for Israel; Palestinians remained unmentioned, apart from a vague reference to a two-state settlement of some unspecified kind. For Iran, Obama called for tough direct diplomacy "without preconditions" in order "to pressure Iran directly to change their troubling behavior," namely pursuing a nuclear program and supporting terrorism (presumably referring to support for Hamas and Hezbollah, "terrorists" in U.S. doctrine not because of their crimes—others not so designated have much worse records—but because they resist U.S.-backed aggression and violence). If Iran abandons its troubling behavior, the United States might move toward normal diplomatic and economic relations, Obama proposed, but "if Iran continues its troubling behavior, we will step up our economic pressure and political isolation." And as Obama informed the Israeli lobby AIPAC, "I will do everything in my power to prevent Iran from obtaining a nuclear weapon," repeatedly stressing "everything"—up to nuclear war, if he meant what he said.[83]

Furthermore, Obama proceeded, he will strengthen the NPT "so that countries like North Korea and Iran that break the rules will automatically face strong international sanctions." He made no mention of the conclusion of U.S. intelligence that Iran had not had a weapons program for five years, unlike U.S. allies Israel, Pakistan, and India, the three countries that maintain extensive nuclear weapons programs (with direct U.S. support), all unmentioned as well. We have already discussed their current defiance of the Security Council and the IAEA, with Obama's full support.

The final mention of Iran on the website is in the context of Obama's strong support for Israel's "Right to Self Defense" and its "right to protect its citizens." This commitment Obama demonstrated by recalling his co-sponsorship of "a Senate resolution against Iran and Syria's involvement in the war, and insisting that Israel should not be pressured into a cease-fire that did not deal with the threat of Hezbollah missiles." The reference is to Israel's U.S.-backed invasion of Lebanon in 2006, with pretexts that are hardly credible in light of Israel's regular practices of kidnapping, hijacking, and internment in secret prisons, as already discussed.[84]

The invasion that Obama supported so enthusiastically, Israel's fifth, killed over one thousand Lebanese and once again destroyed much of southern Lebanon as well as parts of Beirut.

This is the sole mention of Lebanon among foreign policy issues on Obama's campaign website. Evidently, Lebanon has no right of self-defense. In fact who could possibly have a right of self-defense against the United States or its clients?

While ignored as irrelevant to policy formation, American public opinion at the time was close to that of serious analysts and also to world opinion. As already discussed, large majorities opposed threats against Iran, thus rejecting the Bush-Obama position that the United States must be an outlaw state, violating the UN Charter, which bars the threat of force. The public also joined the majority of the world's states in endorsing Iran's right, as a signer of the NPT, to enrich uranium for nuclear energy (the position endorsed also by Cheney, Rumsfeld, Wolfowitz, Kissinger, and others when Iran was ruled by the tyrant imposed by U.S.-UK subversion). Most important, the public favors establishment of a nuclear weapons–free zone in the Middle East, which would mitigate and perhaps eliminate this highly threatening issue—a plan to which the U.S.-UK have a particularly strong commitment, as already discussed.[85]

Such observations as these suggest an interesting thought experiment. What would be the content of the "Obama brand" if the public were to become "participants" rather than mere "spectators in action"? It is an experiment well worth undertaking, not just in this case, and there is some reason to suppose that the results might point the way to a saner and more decent world.

TEN

Obama on Israel-Palestine

Barack Obama is recognized to be a person of acute intelligence, a legal scholar, careful with his choice of words. He deserves to be taken seriously—both what he says, and what he omits. Particularly significant is his first substantive statement on foreign affairs after assuming office, on January 22, 2009, at the State Department, when introducing George Mitchell to serve as his special envoy for Middle East peace.[1]

Mitchell's assignment was to focus his attention on the Israel-Palestine problem, in the wake of the recent U.S.-Israeli invasion of Gaza. During the murderous assault, Obama and his staff remained silent apart from expressing their deep sympathy with Israeli children who face rocket attacks (because of Israel's refusal to accept a cease-fire, as they failed to mention). As for the hundreds of Palestinian children being butchered by U.S. arms, he unfortunately could not speak, because there was only one president.

On January 22, however, the one president was Barack Obama. He still could not comment, however, because the attack on Gaza had been called off, by coincidence no doubt, just before the inauguration. And we must look forward.

Obama's State Department talk emphasized his commitment to a peaceful settlement. He left its contours vague, apart from one specific

proposal: "The Arab peace initiative," Obama said, "contains constructive elements that could help advance these efforts. Now is the time for
Arab states to act on the initiative's promise by supporting the Palestinian
government under President Abbas and Prime Minister Fayyad, taking
steps towards normalizing relations with Israel, and by standing up to
extremism that threatens us all."

Obama was not directly falsifying the Arab League proposal, but his
carefully framed characterization of it is instructive.

The Arab League peace proposal does indeed call for normalization
of relations with Israel *in the context*—repeat, *in the context*—of a two-
state settlement in terms of the long-standing international consensus,
which the United States and Israel have blocked for thirty-five years. The
core of the Arab League proposal, as Obama and his Mideast advisers
know very well, is its call for a peaceful political settlement in these terms,
which are well known and recognized to be the only basis for the peaceful
settlement to which Obama professes to be committed. The omission of
that crucial fact can hardly be accidental, and signals clearly that Obama
envisions no departure from U.S. rejectionism. His call for the Arab states
to act on a corollary to their proposal, while the United States ignores
even the existence of its central content, which is the precondition for
the corollary, surpasses cynicism.

The most significant acts to undermine a peaceful settlement are
the daily U.S.-backed actions in the occupied territories, all recognized
to be criminal: taking over valuable land and resources and constructing
what the leading architect of the plan, Ariel Sharon, regarded as bantustans for Palestinians.[2] The comparison has been bitterly attacked as
unfair, a charge that has some merit, though not in the sense intended.
The bantustans had to be sustained as relatively viable, unlike the fragments left to Palestinians under Sharon's conception, now being realized. For good reasons: South Africa relied on Black labor, but Israel's
goal is to remove the Palestinians, at least from sight. The United States
and Israel even continue to oppose a political settlement in words, most
recently in December 2008, when the two rejectionist states (and a few
Pacific dependencies) voted against a UN resolution supporting "the

right of the Palestinian people to self-determination" (passed 173 to 5, U.S.-Israel opposed, with evasive pretexts).

Obama had nothing to say about the settlement and infrastructure developments in the West Bank, and the carefully crafted measures to control Palestinian existence, designed to undermine the prospects for a peaceful two-state settlement, as openly conceded decades ago.[3] His silence was an eloquent refutation of his oratorical flourishes about how "I will sustain an active commitment to seek two states living side by side in peace and security."

Also unmentioned was Israel's use of U.S. arms in Gaza in violation not only of international but also U.S. law. Or Washington's shipment of new arms to Israel—allegedly, prepositioning for potential U.S. use— right at the peak of the U.S.-Israeli attack, surely not unknown to Obama's Middle East advisers. They apparently have not deigned to respond to an Amnesty International study released a few weeks later reviewing the arms used illegally in the Gaza attack, almost all from the United States, and calling for an arms embargo on shipments of arms to Israel, that is, for the United States to observe international and domestic law—a "milestone" in the conflict, Norman Finkelstein rightly observes.[4]

Obama was firm, however, that smuggling of arms to Gaza must be stopped. He endorses the agreement of Condoleezza Rice and then–Israeli foreign minister Tzipi Livni that the Egyptian-Gaza border must be closed—a remarkable exercise of imperial arrogance, as the *Financial Times* observed: "As they stood in Washington congratulating each other, both officials seemed oblivious to the fact that they were making a deal about an illegal trade on someone else's border—Egypt in this case. The next day, an Egyptian official described the memorandum as 'fictional.'" Egypt's objections were ignored—and soon overcome, as we shall see.[5]

In referring to the "constructive" Arab League proposal, Obama called for support for the defeated political party in the January 2006 Palestinian election, to which the United States and Israel reacted, as we have seen, by severely punishing Palestinians for their failure to understand what we mean by "democracy." A minor technicality is that Abbas's term had run out on January 9, and that Fayyad was appointed without confirmation by the Palestinian parliament (many of them kidnapped and held in Israeli prisons without credible charge, or any at all). *Haaretz* describes Fayyad as "a strange bird in Palestinian politics. On the one hand, he is the Palestinian politician most esteemed by Israel and the West. However, on the other hand, he has no electoral power whatsoever in Gaza or the West Bank." The report also notes Fayyad's "close relationship with the Israeli establishment," notably his friendship with Sharon's extremist adviser Dov Weisglass. Though lacking popular support, he is regarded as competent and honest.[6]

Obama's insistence that only Abbas and Fayyad exist conforms to the consistent Western contempt for democracy unless it is under control, recognized in scholarship and so well documented that it takes true genius to remain oblivious to the facts.[7]

Obama repeated the familiar reasons for ignoring the elected government led by Hamas. "To be a genuine party to peace," Obama declared, "the Quartet [United States, EU, Russia, UN] has made it clear that Hamas must meet clear conditions: recognize Israel's right to exist; renounce violence; and abide by past agreements." Unmentioned, also as usual, is the inconvenient fact that the United States and Israel firmly reject all three conditions for themselves. In international isolation, they bar a two-state settlement, thus rejecting Palestinian national rights. They of course do not renounce violence. And they reject the Quartet's central proposal, the "Road Map." Israel formally accepted it, but with fourteen reservations that effectively eliminate its contents (tacitly backed by the United States). As already discussed (see p. 302, note 23), it is the great merit of Jimmy Carter's *Palestine: Peace Not Apartheid* to have brought these facts to public attention for the first time—and in the mainstream, the only time, it appears. But even this was quickly effaced.

It follows, by Obama's reasoning, that neither the United States nor Israel is a "genuine party to peace." But that cannot be. It is not even a phrase in the English language.

It is perhaps unfair to criticize Obama for this further exercise of cynicism, because it is close to universal, unlike his evisceration of the core component of the Arab League proposal, which is his original contribution.

Also near-universal are the standard references to Hamas: a terrorist organization, dedicated to the destruction of Israel (or maybe all Jews). Omitted is the fact that the United States and Israel are not only dedicated to the destruction of any viable Palestinian state, but are steadily implementing those policies. Or that unlike the two leading rejectionist states, Hamas has called for a two-state settlement in the terms of the international consensus: publicly and repeatedly.[8] Israel and the United States object that the Hamas proposals do not go far enough. Perhaps so, but they surely go much farther toward the international consensus than the firm and unwavering U.S.-Israeli rejectionist stance, reiterated obliquely by Obama in his State Department talk.

Obama began his remarks by saying, "Let me be clear: America is committed to Israel's security. And we will always support Israel's right to defend itself against legitimate threats."

He had nothing to say about the right of Palestinians to defend themselves against far more extreme threats, such as those being implemented daily, with U.S. support, in the occupied territories. But that again is the norm.

Also normal is the enunciation of the principle that Israel has the right to defend itself, as if that were in question. It is not. So does everyone. But in the context the cliché is worse than vacuous: it is a further exercise in cynical deceit, for reasons already reviewed. As a well-trained specialist in the law, Obama surely is aware that the real issue is whether Israel had the right to defend itself *by force*—after having rejected peaceful means that it has every reason to believe will suffice. It is a useful propaganda technique to stand up heroically in defense of rights that are not contested, while systematically effacing the only issue at stake.

The deceit is particularly striking in this case because the occasion was the appointment of George Mitchell as special envoy. Mitchell's primary achievement was his leading role in bringing about a peaceful settlement in Northern Ireland. The settlement that Mitchell helped to negotiate called for an end to both IRA terror and British violence. There was no question that Britain had the right to defend itself from terror. At issue was whether it had the right to do so by force when there were peaceful alternatives that could be explored: recognition of the legitimate grievances of the Irish Catholic community that were at the roots of IRA terror. When Britain adopted that sensible course, the terror ended. The implications for Mitchell's mission with regard to Israel-Palestine need not be spelled out. And omission of them is, again, a striking indication of the commitment of the Obama administration to traditional U.S. rejectionism and opposition to peace, except on its own extremist terms.

Obama also praised Jordan for its "constructive role in training Palestinian security forces and nurturing its relations with Israel"—which contrasts strikingly with U.S.-Israeli refusal to deal with the freely elected government of Palestine while savagely punishing Palestinians for electing it, with pretexts that do not withstand a moment's scrutiny. It is true that Jordan joined the United States and Israel in arming and training Palestinian security forces, so effectively that they were able to suppress any manifestation of support for the miserable victims of the U.S.-Israeli assault in Gaza, also arresting supporters of Hamas and the prominent journalist Khaled Amayreh. Meanwhile the faction that the United States supports was organizing their own demonstration in support of Abbas and Fatah, in which most participants "were civil servants and school children who were instructed by the [Palestinian Authority] to attend the rally," according to the *Jerusalem Post*. Our kind of democracy.[9]

Obama made one further substantive comment: "As part of a lasting cease-fire, Gaza's border crossings should be open to allow the flow of aid and commerce, with an appropriate monitoring regime." He did not mention that the U.S.-Israel had rejected much the same agreement after the January 2006 election, and that Israel had never observed similar subsequent agreements on opening borders.

Also missing is any reaction to Israel's announcement that it rejected the cease-fire agreement, so that the prospects for a cease-fire to be established, let alone to be "lasting," are not auspicious. The reasons were reported prominently and repeatedly in the press: Israel will not allow border crossings with Gaza to open, and will insist that Gazan life be reduced to a bare minimum, unless Gilad Shalit is released. Furthermore, "the government planned to use the issue to bargain for" his release, another gross violation of core provisions of international humanitarian law.[10]

Shalit's capture is a persistent and prominent issue in the West, another indication of Hamas's criminality. Whatever one thinks about his capture, it is uncontroversial that capture of a soldier of an attacking army is a far lesser crime than kidnapping of civilians, exactly what Israeli forces did one day before the capture of Shalit, invading Gaza City and kidnapping two brothers, the Muamar brothers, then spiriting them across the border where they disappeared into Israel's opaque prison system. Unlike the much less significant case of Shalit, that crime was virtually unreported and was quickly forgotten, along with Israel's regular practice for decades of kidnapping and killing of civilians in Lebanon and on the high seas, often imprisoning them without charge in Israel.[11] But it is the capture of Shalit that bars a cease-fire, under the principles of imperial ideology.

Israel's routine kidnapping of civilians and similar crimes continue unabated, and unnoted. To recall one example cited earlier, the very reliable Gazan human rights organization, Al Mezan Center for Human Rights, reports that on September 6, 2009, the IDF carried out another regular infiltration into Gaza and "kidnapped five Palestinian children who were on their way home after grazing sheep," ages fifteen to seventeen, taking them to Israel under cover of helicopter fire around the Bedouin village from which they were abducted. Their press release provided the names. The crime—needless to say far more severe than the capture of Shalit—passed unnoticed.[12]

Obama's State Department talk about the Middle East continued with "the deteriorating situation in Afghanistan and Pakistan...the central front in our enduring struggle against terrorism and extremism." A few hours later, U.S. planes attacked a remote village in Afghanistan, intending to kill a Taliban commander. "Village elders, though, told provincial officials there were no Taliban in the area, which they described as a hamlet populated mainly by shepherds. Women and children were among the 22 dead, they said, according to Hamididan Abdul Rahmzai, the head of the provincial council."[13]

Afghan president Karzai's first message to Obama after he was elected in November 2008 was a plea to end the bombing of Afghan civilians, reiterated a few hours before Obama was sworn in. This was considered as significant as Karzai's call for a timetable for departure of U.S. and other foreign forces.[14] The rich and powerful have their "responsibilities." Among them, the *New York Times* reported, is to "provide security" in southern Afghanistan, where "the insurgency is homegrown and self-sustaining." All familiar. From *Pravda* in the 1980s, for example.

ELEVEN

The Torture Memos

The torture memos released by the White House elicited shock, indignation, and surprise. The shock and indignation are understandable—particularly the testimony in the Senate Armed Services Committee report on Cheney-Rumsfeld desperation to find nonexistent links between Iraq and al-Qaeda, links that were later concocted out of thin air as justification for the invasion. Former army psychiatrist Major Charles Burney testified that "a large part of the time we were focused on trying to establish a link between Al Qaeda and Iraq. The more frustrated people got in not being able to establish this link...there was more and more pressure to resort to measures that might produce more immediate results"; that is, torture. McClatchy Newspapers reported the comments of a former senior intelligence official familiar with the interrogation issue: "The Bush administration applied relentless pressure on interrogators to use harsh methods on detainees in part to find evidence of cooperation between al Qaida and the late Iraqi dictator Saddam Hussein's regime.... [Cheney and Rumsfeld] demanded that the interrogators find evidence of al Qaida-Iraq collaboration.... 'There was constant pressure on the intelligence agencies and the interrogators to do whatever it took to get that information out of the detainees, especially the few high-value ones we had, and when people kept coming up empty, they were told by Cheney's and Rumsfeld's people to push harder.'"[1]

These were the most significant revelations, barely reported.

While such testimony about the criminality of the Bush administration should indeed be shocking, the surprise at the general picture revealed is nonetheless surprising. A narrow reason is that even without inquiry, it was reasonable to suppose that Guantánamo was a torture chamber. Why else send prisoners where they would be beyond the reach of the law—incidentally, a place that Washington is using in violation of a treaty that was forced on Cuba at the point of a gun? Security reasons are alleged, but they are hard to take seriously. The same expectations held for secret prisons and rendition, and were fulfilled.

A broader reason is that torture has been routine practice from the early days of the conquest of the national territory, and then beyond, as the imperial ventures of the "infant empire"—as George Washington called the new Republic—extended to the Philippines, Haiti, and elsewhere. Furthermore, torture was the least of the many crimes of aggression, terror, subversion, and economic strangulation that have darkened U.S. history, much as in the case of other great powers. Accordingly, it is surprising to see the reactions even by some of the most eloquent and forthright critics of Bush malfeasance: for example, that we used to be "a nation of moral ideals" and never before Bush "have our leaders so utterly betrayed everything our nation stands for."[2] To say the least, that common view reflects a rather slanted version of history.

In the past sixty years, victims worldwide have endured the CIA's "torture paradigm," developed at a cost reaching $1 billion annually, according to historian Alfred McCoy, who shows that the methods resurfaced with little change in Abu Ghraib. There is no hyperbole when Jennifer Harbury entitles her penetrating study of the U.S. torture record *Truth, Torture, and the American Way*. It is highly misleading when investigators of the Bush gang's descent into the gutter lament that "in waging the war against terrorism, America had lost its way."[3]

Bush-Cheney-Rumsfeld et al. did introduce some important innovations. Ordinarily, torture is farmed out to subsidiaries under U.S. supervision, not carried out by Americans directly in their government-established torture chambers. Alain Nairn, who has undertaken some of the most revealing and courageous investigations of torture, points out that "what the Obama [ban on torture] ostensibly knocks off is that small percentage of torture now done by Americans while retaining the overwhelming bulk of the system's torture, which is done by foreigners under U.S. patronage. Obama could stop backing foreign forces that torture, but he has chosen not to do so." Obama did not shut down the practice of torture, Nairn observes, but "merely repositioned it," restoring it to the norm, a matter of indifference to the victims. Since Vietnam, "the U.S. has mainly seen its torture done for it by proxy—paying, arming, training and guiding foreigners doing it, but usually being careful to keep Americans at least one discreet step removed." Obama's ban "doesn't even prohibit direct torture by Americans outside environments of 'armed conflict,' which is where much torture happens anyway since many repressive regimes aren't in armed conflict...his is a return to the status quo ante, the torture regime of Ford through Clinton, which, year by year, often produced more U.S.-backed strapped-down agony than was produced during the Bush/Cheney years."[4]

Sometimes engagement in torture is more indirect. In a 1980 study, Latin Americanist Lars Schoultz found that U.S. aid "has tended to flow disproportionately to Latin American governments which torture their citizens...to the hemisphere's relatively egregious violators of fundamental human rights." That includes military aid, is independent of need, and runs through the Carter years. Broader studies by Edward Herman found the same correlation, and also suggested an explanation. Not surprisingly, U.S. aid tends to correlate with a favorable climate for business operations, and this is commonly improved by murder of labor and peasant organizers and human rights activists, and other such actions, yielding a secondary correlation between aid and egregious violation of human rights.[5] More matters that cannot enter consciousness.

These studies precede the Reagan years, when the topic was not worth studying because the correlations were so clear. And the tendencies continue to the present.

Small wonder that the president advises us to look forward, not backward—a convenient doctrine for those who hold the clubs. Those who are beaten by them tend to see the world differently, much to our annoyance.

An argument can be made that implementation of the CIA's "torture paradigm" does not violate the 1984 UN Torture Convention, at least as Washington interprets it. Alfred McCoy points out that the highly sophisticated CIA paradigm, based on the "KGB's most devastating torture technique," keeps primarily to mental torture, not crude physical torture, which is considered less effective in turning people into pliant vegetables. McCoy writes that the Reagan administration carefully revised the international Torture Convention "with four detailed diplomatic 'reservations' focused on just one word in the convention's 26-printed pages. That word was 'mental.'... [T]hese intricately-constructed diplomatic reservations re-defined torture, as interpreted by the United States, to exclude sensory deprivation and self-inflicted pain—the very techniques the CIA had refined at such great cost." When Clinton sent the UN Torture Convention to Congress for ratification in 1994, he included the Reagan reservations. The president and Congress therefore exempted the core of the CIA torture paradigm from the U.S. interpretation of the Torture Convention; and those reservations, McCoy observes, were "reproduced verbatim in domestic legislation enacted to give legal force to the UN Convention." That is the "political land mine" that "detonated with such phenomenal force" in the Abu Ghraib scandal and in the shameful Military Commissions Act that was passed with bipartisan support in 2006, later effectively restored by Obama. For such reasons, after the first exposure of Washington's resort to torture, constitutional law professor Sanford Levinson commented that it could perhaps be justified in terms of the "interrogator-friendly" definition of torture adopted by Reagan and Clinton in their revision of international human rights law.[6]

Bush, of course, went beyond his predecessors in authorizing prima facie violations of international law, and several of his extremist innovations were struck down by the courts. While Obama, like Bush, eloquently affirms our unwavering commitment to international law (and differs from Bush in that he is familiar with it), he seems intent on substantially reinstating the extremist Bush measures.

In the important case of *Boumediene v. Bush* in June 2008, the Supreme Court rejected as unconstitutional the Bush administration claim that prisoners in Guantánamo are not entitled to the right of habeas corpus. Glenn Greenwald reviews the aftermath. Seeking to "preserve the power to abduct people from around the world" and imprison them without due process, the Bush administration decided to ship them to Bagram, in Afghanistan, treating "the *Boumediene* ruling, grounded in our most basic constitutional guarantees, as though it was some sort of a silly game—fly your abducted prisoners to Guantánamo and they have constitutional rights, but fly them instead to Bagram and you can disappear them forever with no judicial process." Obama adopted the Bush position, "filing a brief in federal court that, in two sentences, declared that it embraced the most extremist Bush theory on this issue." Obama's argument amounts to saying that prisoners flown to Bagram from anywhere in the world—in the case in question, Yemenis and Tunisians captured in Thailand and the UAE—"can be imprisoned indefinitely with no rights of any kind—as long as they are kept in Bagram rather than Guantánamo."

In March, a Bush-appointed federal judge "rejected the Bush/Obama position and held that the rationale of *Boumediene* applies every bit as much to Bagram as it does to Guantánamo." The Obama administration announced that it would appeal the ruling, thus placing Obama's Department of Justice "squarely to the Right of an extremely conservative, pro-executive-power, Bush 43-appointed judge on issues of executive power and due-process-less detentions," in radical violation of Obama's campaign promises and earlier stands.[7]

The case of *Rasul v. Rumsfeld* appears to be following a similar trajectory. The four plaintiffs charged that Rumsfeld and other high officials were responsible for their torture in Guantánamo, where they were sent after they were captured by Uzbeki warlord Rashid Dostum. Dostum is a notorious thug who was then a leader of the Northern Alliance, the Afghan faction supported by Russia, Iran, India, Turkey, and the Central Asian states, joined by the United States as it attacked Afghanistan in October 2001. Dostum then turned them over to U.S. custody, allegedly for bounty money. The plaintiffs claimed that they had traveled to Afghanistan to offer humanitarian relief. The Bush administration sought to have the case dismissed. Obama's Department of Justice filed a brief supporting the Bush position that government officials are not liable for torture and other violations of due process in this case, because the courts had not yet clearly established the rights that prisoners enjoy.[8]

With mostly cosmetic changes, Obama reinstated military commissions, one of the uglier violations of the rule of law during the Bush years. There is a reason. "Officials who work on the Guantánamo issue say administration lawyers have become concerned that they would face significant obstacles to trying some terrorism suspects in federal courts. Judges might make it difficult to prosecute detainees who were subjected to brutal treatment or for prosecutors to use hearsay evidence gathered by intelligence agencies."[9]

A serious flaw in the criminal justice system by Obama's standards, it appears. The right wing in the United States takes much the same stance, demanding that accused terrorists be tried in military courts because the law grants defendants too many rights, a regular theme of talk radio hosts. It is perhaps of interest that this stance of utter contempt for the values that the country has professed to uphold since its earliest days is called "patriotic."

There is much debate about whether torture has been effective in eliciting information—the assumption being, apparently, that if it is effective, then it may be justified. By the same logic, when Nicaragua captured U.S. pilot Eugene Hasenfuss in 1986 after shooting down his plane delivering aid to Reagan's contra forces, they should not have tried him, found him guilty, and then sent him back to the United States, as they did. Rather, they should have applied the CIA torture paradigm to try to extract information about other terrorist atrocities being planned and implemented in Washington, no small matter for a tiny and poor country under terrorist attack by the global superpower. And Nicaragua should certainly have done the same if they had been able to capture the chief terrorism coordinator, John Negroponte, then ambassador to Honduras, later appointed counterterrorism czar, without eliciting a murmur. Cuba too should have done the same if they had been able to lay hands on the Kennedy brothers and their successors in the terrorism racket. There is no need to bring up what victims should have done to Kissinger, Reagan, and other leading terrorist commanders, whose exploits leave al-Qaeda far in the distance, and who doubtless had ample information that could have prevented further "ticking bombs."

Such considerations, which abound, never seem to arise in public discussion. Accordingly, we know at once how to evaluate the pleas about valuable information and "ticking bombs," or the fury about terrorism— by enemies.

There is, to be sure, a response: our terrorism, even if surely terrorism, is benign, emanating as it does from the City on the Hill. Perhaps the most eloquent exposition of this thesis was presented by *New Republic* editor Michael Kinsley, designated at that time by the media as a spokesman of "the left." Americas Watch (then a branch of Human Rights Watch) had protested State Department confirmation of official orders to Washington's terrorist forces to attack "soft targets"—undefended civilian targets— and to avoid the Nicaraguan army, as they could do thanks to CIA control of Nicaraguan airspace and the sophisticated communications systems provided to these rather unusual guerrillas. In a gentle reprimand, Kinsley explained that U.S. terrorist attacks on civilian targets are justified if they satisfy pragmatic criteria: a "sensible policy [should] meet the test of cost-benefit analysis," an analysis of "the amount of blood and misery that will be poured in, and the likelihood that democracy will emerge at the other end"[10]—"democracy" as U.S. elites determine. His thoughts elicited no comment, to my knowledge, apparently deemed acceptable. It would seem to follow, then, that U.S. leaders and their agents are not culpable for conducting such sensible policies in good faith, even if their judgment might sometimes be flawed.

Perhaps culpability would be greater, by prevailing moral standards, if it were discovered that Bush administration torture cost American lives. That is, in fact, the conclusion drawn by U.S. major Matthew Alexander [pseudonym], one of the most seasoned interrogators in Iraq, who elicited "the information that led to the U.S. military being able to locate Abu Musab al-Zarqawi, the head of al-Qa'ida in Iraq," correspondent Patrick Cockburn reports. Alexander expresses only contempt for the harsh interrogation methods: "The use of torture by the U.S.," he believes, not only elicits no useful information but "has proved so counterproductive that it may have led to the death of as many U.S. soldiers as civilians killed in 9/11." From hundreds of interrogations, Alexander discovered that foreign fighters came to Iraq in reaction to the abuses at Guantánamo and Abu Ghraib, and that they and their domestic allies turned to suicide bombing and other terrorist acts for the same reason.[11]

There is also mounting evidence that Cheney-Rumsfeld torture created terrorists even more directly. One carefully studied case is that of Abdallah al-Ajmi, who was locked up in Guantánamo on the charge of "engaging in two or three fire fights with the Northern Alliance." He had come to Afghanistan after having failed to reach Chechnya to fight against the Russian invasion. After four years of brutal treatment in Guantánamo, he was returned to Kuwait. He later found his way to Iraq, and in March 2008 drove a bomb-laden truck into an Iraqi military compound, killing himself and thirteen soldiers—"the single most heinous act of violence committed by a former Guantánamo detainee," the *Washington Post* reports, the direct result of his abusive imprisonment, his Washington lawyer concludes.[12]

All much as a reasonable person would expect—and something we should bear in mind when reading about released prisoners turning to terror.

Another standard pretext for torture is the context: the "war on terror" that Bush declared after 9/11, an atrocity that was a "crime against humanity" carried out with "wickedness and awesome cruelty," as Robert Fisk reported.[13] 9/11 rendered traditional international law "quaint" and "obsolete," Bush was advised by his legal counsel Alberto Gonzales, later appointed attorney general. The doctrine has been widely reiterated in one or another form in commentary and analysis.

The 9/11 attack was doubtless unique, in many respects. One is where the guns were pointing: typically it is in the opposite direction. Another unique feature is the scale of terror by a non-state actor. But horrifying as it was, it could have been worse—as on the first 9/11, already discussed (p. 27). But in that case responsibility traces straight back to Washington, so that the analogy, though clearly appropriate, does not enter consciousness, while the facts are consigned to the "abuse of reality" that the naïve call history.

It should also be recalled that Bush did not declare the "war on terror"; he re-declared it. Twenty years earlier, the Reagan administration came into office declaring that a centerpiece of its foreign policy would be a war on terror, "the plague of the modern age" and "a return to barbarism in our time," to sample the fevered rhetoric of the day. That war on terror has also been expunged from historical consciousness, because the outcome cannot readily be incorporated into the canon: hundreds of thousands slaughtered in the ruined countries of Central America and many more elsewhere, among them an estimated 1.5 million in the terrorist wars sponsored in neighboring countries by Reagan's favored ally, Apartheid South Africa, which had to defend itself from Nelson Mandela's African National Congress, one of the more world's "more notorious terrorist groups," so Washington determined in 1988. In fairness, it should be added that twenty years later Congress voted to remove the ANC from the list of terrorist organizations, so that Mandela is now at last able to enter the United States without obtaining a waiver from the government.[14]

The reigning doctrine is sometimes called "American exceptionalism." It is nothing of the sort. It is probably close to universal among imperial powers. France was hailing its "civilizing mission" while the French minister of war called for "exterminating the indigenous population" of Algeria. Britain's nobility was a "novelty in the world," John Stuart Mill declared, while urging that this angelic power delay no longer in completing its liberation of India. This classic essay on humanitarian intervention was written shortly after the public revelation of Britain's horrifying atrocities in suppressing the 1857 Indian rebellion. The conquest of the rest of India was in large part an effort to gain a monopoly of opium for Britain's huge narcotrafficking enterprise, by far the largest in world history, designed primarily to compel China to accept Britain's manufactured goods.

Similarly, there is no reason to doubt the sincerity of Japanese militarists who were bringing an "earthly paradise" to China under benign Japanese tutelage, and protecting innocents from "Chinese bandits," as they carried out the rape of Nanking and other hideous crimes. History is replete with similar glorious episodes.

As long as such "exceptionalist" theses remain firmly implanted, the occasional revelations of the "abuse of reality" can backfire, serving to efface terrible crimes. The My Lai massacre is an example. It was a mere footnote to the vastly greater atrocities of the post-Tet pacification programs, ignored while indignation focused on this single crime. Watergate was doubtless criminal, but the furor over it displaced incomparably worse crimes at home and abroad—the FBI-organized assassination of Black organizer Fred Hampton as part of the infamous COINTELPRO repression, or the bombing of Cambodia, to mention two egregious examples.[15]

Torture is hideous enough; the invasion of Iraq is a far worse crime. Quite commonly, selective attention to atrocities has this unfortunate function.

Historical amnesia is a dangerous phenomenon, not only because it undermines moral and intellectual integrity, but also because it lays the groundwork for crimes that lie ahead.

TWELVE

1989 and Beyond

The month of November 2009 was marked by the joyous twentieth-anniversary celebration of what British historian Timothy Garton Ash calls "the biggest year in world history since 1945." That remarkable year "changed everything," thanks primarily to Mikhail Gorbachev's reforms within Russia and his "breathtaking renunciation of the use of force…a luminous example of the importance of the individual in history," leading to the partially open Russian elections of March 1989 and culminating in the fall of the Berlin wall on November 9, which opened the way to liberation of Eastern Europe from Russian tyranny. The general mood was captured well by barrister Matthew Ryder, speaking for the "niners," the generation that is now providing global leadership, with Barack Obama in the lead, their conception of history having been "shaped by a world changed without guns" in 1989, events that gave them confidence in the power of dedication to nonviolence and justice.[1]

The accolades for November 9 are deserved, and the events are indeed memorable. And the picture is compelling, as long as we keep rigorously to a dominant principle of imperial culture: focus laser-like on the crimes of enemies, and on our high-minded and courageous condemnation of their crimes. But crucially, make sure never to look at ourselves. The principles apply in the familiar way to the events of November 1989, and the memories that remain twenty years later. Some alternative perspectives may be instructive.

One was provided, unintentionally, by German chancellor Angela Merkel, who called on all of us to "use this invaluable gift of freedom… to overcome the walls of our time."[2] Excellent advice, and we can easily follow it. One good start would be to dismantle the massive wall, dwarfing the Berlin wall in scale and length, which is snaking its way through Palestinian territory in gross violation of international law. Like virtually every state action, the "annexation wall," as it should be termed, is justified in terms of security. But as is commonly the case, the claim lacks any credibility. If security were the concern, it would be built along the border, and could be made impregnable. The purpose of this illegal monstrosity, constructed with decisive U.S. support and European complicity, is to allow Israel to take over valuable Palestinian land and the main water resources of the region, one part of a much broader annexation project, recognized from the start to be in direct violation of international law, an understanding since confirmed by the World Court.

The anniversary celebrations of the fall of the wall had barely subsided when it was announced that the second leading recipient of U.S. aid, the Egyptian dictatorship, had begun constructing a huge steel wall along its border with the Gaza Strip, six to seven miles long and eighteen meters deep, designed by American army engineers to be "impenetrable."[3] That completes the imprisonment of Gaza from land and sea, and cuts off the last lifeline to escape Israeli strangulation.

Those who wish to follow Merkel's good advice need not limit their efforts to the two leading recipients of U.S. aid: they can turn to the United States itself, and the huge construction along the Mexican border to bar the flight of desperate people from the south, many of them victims of U.S. terror in Central America and of NAFTA.

Another perspective on the 2009 celebrations is provided by the work of the leading scholar/advocate of "democracy promotion," neo-Reaganite Thomas Carothers, reviewed earlier. He ruefully concludes that all U.S. leaders have been "schizophrenic," supporting democracy if and only if it conforms to strategic and economic objectives: hence in Soviet satellites but not U.S. client states.[4]

These judgments were once again confirmed by the events that reached their culmination in November 1989, and again on the twentieth anniversary. The fall of the Berlin wall was rightly celebrated in November 2009, but there was virtually no notice of what had happened one week later in El Salvador, on November 16, 1989: the brutal assassination of six prominent Latin American intellectuals, Jesuit priests, along with their housekeeper Julia Elba and her daughter Celina, by the elite Atlacatl battalion, armed and trained by Washington. The battalion had just returned from a several-month refresher course at the JFK Special Warfare School at Fort Bragg, and a few days before the murders underwent a further training exercise run by U.S. Special Forces flown to El Salvador. Heralded as "El Salvador's best," the cream of Washington's terrorist army in El Salvador, the battalion had already left a bloody trail of the usual victims during the horrendous decade of the 1980s, which opened with the assassination of Archbishop Oscar Romero, the "voice for the voiceless," by much the same hands. The story was similar throughout Central America, leaving hundreds of thousands of corpses and general misery during a reign of torture, murder, and destruction led by the Reagan administration under the guise of a war on terror.[5]

It was surmised at the time that the murder of the Jesuits was probably planned by the high command of the Salvadoran army. That was confirmed in November 2009 by publication in the Spanish press of a copy of the document ordering the murders and those of any witnesses, signed by the chief of staff and his associates, all of them so closely connected to the Pentagon and the embassy that it is hard to imagine that Washington was unaware.[6] The revealing discoveries appear to have passed unreported in the United States.

One can easily understand why the consciousness of the "niners" was shaped by dedication to nonviolence and the power of idealism. That's fair enough, if attention is rigorously guided by the culture of imperialism: focused on *their* crimes, with ours far removed from sight or memory.

The contrast through the 1980s between the liberation of Soviet satellites and the violent crushing of hope in U.S. domains is striking and instructive, and becomes even more so when we broaden the perspective. The assassination of the Jesuit intellectuals was a crushing blow to liberation theology, the remarkable revival of Christianity that had its roots in the initiatives of Pope John XXIII and Vatican II, which he opened in 1962, an event that "ushered in a new era in the history of the Catholic Church," in the words of the distinguished theologian Hans Küng, "an epoch-making and irrevocable turning point." Inspired by Vatican II, Latin American bishops adopted "the preferential option for the poor," renewing the radical pacifism of the Gospels that had been put to rest when the Emperor Constantine established Christianity as the religion of the Roman Empire—instituting "a revolution" that in less than a century converted "the persecuted church" to a "persecuting church" (Küng). In the post–Vatican II attempt to revive the Christianity of the pre-Roman period, priests, nuns, and laypersons took the message of the Gospels to the poor and the persecuted, brought them together in "base communities," and encouraged them to take their fate into their own hands and to work together to overcome the misery of survival in the harsh realms of U.S. power.[7]

The "preferential option for the poor," drawn from the Gospels, was recognized by the masters to be a grave and intolerable heresy, and the reaction was swift. In 1964, a military coup, for which the basis was laid by the Kennedy administration, established a neo-Nazi-style national security state in Brazil, overthrowing a mildly social democratic government and instituting a regime of torture and oppression. In the wake of the Brazilian coup, the dominoes began to fall, and a monstrous plague of repression spread through the hemisphere under similar murderous tyrannies. Included was the first 9/11, in Chile—by any objective measure far more severe than the second 9/11 in 2001—and also the regime of the killers and torturers in Argentina, perhaps the worst of all of them and Reagan's special favorite. The plague finally struck Central America in full force throughout the 1980s. In the course of the terror and slaughter, the practitioners of liberation theology were a prime target, among them the martyrs of the Church whose execution in November 1989 was commemorated on the twentieth anniversary with a resounding silence, barely broken. Forgotten almost completely are Julia Elba and Celina Mariset Ramos. The one survivor of the massacre, Father Jon Sobrino, reminds us that they are the symbols of the suffering masses of El Salvador, and the world.[8] Or would remind us if we were willing to listen.

There has been much debate about who deserves the credit for the fall of the Berlin wall. It was also a topic of a meeting of the three presidents most directly involved. Germany's Helmut Kohl concluded the meeting by saying, "I know now how heaven helped us." George H. W. Bush generously praised the East German people, who "for too long had been deprived of their God-given rights." Gorbachev suggested that the United States needs its own perestroika.[9]

There are no such doubts about the demolition of the attempt to revive the church of the Gospels. The School of the Americas (since renamed), famous for its training of Latin American killers, proudly announces as one of its "talking points" that liberation theology was "defeated with the assistance of the U.S. army"[10]—given a helping hand, to be sure, by the Vatican, using the gentler means of expulsion and suppression, particularly under the guidance of the Vatican enforcer, Cardinal Ratzinger, now Pope Benedict XVI.

The bitter campaign to reverse the heresy set in motion by Vatican II received an incomparable literary expression in Dostoyevsky's parable of the Grand Inquisitor. In this tale, set in Seville at "the most terrible time of the Inquisition," Jesus Christ suddenly appeared on the streets, "softly, unobserved, and yet, strange to say, everyone recognized him" and was "irresistibly drawn to him." The Grand Inquisitor, recognizing the grave danger, "bids the guards take Him and lead Him away" to prison, where the old man accuses Christ of coming to "hinder us" in our great work of destroying the subversive ideas of freedom and community. "We have taken the sword of Caesar" and follow him, not Thee, the Inquisitor admonished Jesus. We seek to be rulers of the earth so that we can teach the "weak and vile" multitude that "they will only become free when they renounce their freedom to us and submit to us." Then they will be timid and frightened and happy. So tomorrow "I must burn Thee" and put an end to Thy evil ways. But finally the old man relented, and "let Him out into the dark alleys of the town. The Prisoner went away."

The pupils of Fort Bragg learned a harsher lesson.

In 1977, the highly respected Jesuit priest Rutilio Grande preached in El Salvador of his fears that "very soon the Bible and the Gospel will not be allowed within our country. We'll get the covers and nothing more, because all its pages are subversive... And I fear, my brothers, that if Jesus of Nazareth returned...they would arrest him. They would take him to the courts and accuse him of being unconstitutional and subversive." His insight into policy was all too accurate. A few weeks later he was assassinated, again by much the same hands.[11]

The two events—the collapse of Russian tyranny and the destruction of the evil ways of the Gospels—were linked symbolically when the hero of 1989, Vaclav Havel, came to Washington shortly after the assassination of his Salvadoran counterparts. Speaking before a joint session of Congress, he received thunderous applause when he praised the United States as the "defender of freedom." The intellectual classes were entranced. The *Washington Post* described Havel's message as a "voice of conscience" that speaks "compellingly of the responsibilities that large and small powers owe each other." Others wondered why American intellectuals do not ascend these lofty heights. Commentators were deeply moved by Havel's explanation for the passivity of the Czech security forces when faced with the forces of "love, tolerance, nonviolence, the human spirit and forgiveness."[12] If only the Salvadoran Jesuits had grasped these lofty thoughts when facing the guns of Washington's Atlacatl battalion.

One may imagine the reactions if the circumstances had been reversed—a thought experiment that could teach us a good deal about ourselves.

At the extreme dissident end, Anthony Lewis hailed Havel for teaching us that "we live in a romantic age." Lewis however had in mind another wondrous achievement of "a world changed without guns" in the new era of nonviolence and idealism that shaped the consciousness of the "niners": the victory of the U.S. candidate in the Nicaraguan elections, an "experiment in peace and democracy," Lewis wrote, which gives "fresh testimony to the power of Jefferson's idea: government with the consent of the governed, as Vaclav Havel reminded us the other day.... To say so seems romantic, but then we live in a romantic age."[13]

Others too exulted in the victory of "peace and democracy" in Nicaragua. Headlines in the *New York Times* proclaimed that Americans are "United in Joy," North Korean–style, over this "Victory for U.S. Fair Play." The modalities of "U.S. Fair Play" were not concealed. *Time* magazine praised the methods that were used to bring about the latest of the "happy series of democratic surprises" as "democracy burst forth" in Nicaragua. The methods were to "wreck the economy and prosecute a long and deadly proxy war until the exhausted natives overthrow the unwanted government themselves," with a cost to us that is "minimal," leaving the victim "with wrecked bridges, sabotaged power stations, and ruined farms," and thus providing the U.S. candidate with "a winning issue": ending the "impoverishment of the people of Nicaragua"—and unmentioned, an end to the terrorist war that was destroying the country and would continue, President Bush I instructed Nicaraguans, unless they gave Americans reason to be "United in Joy." The only issue dividing conservatives and liberals, *Time* correctly concludes, is "who should claim credit" for this triumph of democracy, in a free and fair election, without coercion.[14]

Outside of Western intellectual circles, the comparison between U.S. and Soviet satellites was readily perceived. To cite one all too poignant example, the journal *Proceso* of the Jesuit university in El Salvador observed that

> If Lech Walesa had been doing his organizing work in El Salvador, he would have already entered into the ranks of the disappeared—at the hands of 'heavily armed men dressed in civilian clothes'; or have been blown to pieces in a dynamite attack on his union headquarters. If Alexander Dubcek were a politician in our country, he would have been assassinated like Héctor Oquelí [the social democratic leader assassinated in Guatemala, apparently by Salvadoran death squads]. If Andrei Sakharov had worked here in favor of human rights, he would have met the same fate as Herbert Anaya [one of the many murdered leaders of the independent Salvadoran Human Rights Commission CDHES]. If

Ota-Sik or Vaclav Havel had been carrying out their intellectual work in
El Salvador, they would have [wound] up one sinister morning lying on
the patio of a university campus with their heads destroyed by the bullets
of an elite army battalion.[15]

Despite the U.S. triumph of November 1989, the yearning for freedom and justice has proven hard to crush. A year after Washington's victory over the Church of the Gospels in El Salvador, the demon of
liberation theology emerged again in Haiti with the democratic election
of a liberation theology priest, Jean-Bertrand Aristide. As discussed earlier, Washington moved at once to destroy the threat, reinstating the rule
of the military and the traditional ruling elite. A few years later the demon
raised its head again in Honduras. One of the reasons for Obama's indirect but sufficient support for the military coup that overthrew the democratically elected government and restored power to the traditional
rulers was Zelaya's moves toward "alliance with liberation-theologian
priests and other environmental activists protesting mining and biofuel-
induced deforestation." Meanwhile an ex-bishop tainted by association
with liberation theology was elected in Paraguay, overturning decades of
dictatorship and elite rule in what was considered a safe dependency. It
takes constant vigilance to ensure that the rot does not reappear.[16]

There is much to contemplate in all of this, but let us put these
painful topics aside and proceed.

A critical question about "the biggest year in world history since
1945," which "changed everything," is how global policies were affected
by the dawn of the "unipolar moment," as it came to be called, the glorious
"end of history" in the eyes of some prominent intellectuals. The answer
reveals a good deal about the nature of the Cold War, and its aftermath.

The Bush I administration reacted at once by invading Panama, as
already discussed. The event was a minor footnote to a familiar history,
though there were two innovations. One was the pretext: not "the Russians are coming," the reflexive justification of the past, but the threat to
our existence caused by Hispanic narcotraffickers. The second difference
was explained by former high State Department official Elliott Abrams,
who pointed out that for the first time the United States was able to in-

tervene without concern for a Russian reaction somewhere in the world. As other prominent commentators elaborated, the collapse of the Soviet deterrent "makes military power more useful as a United States foreign policy instrument...against those who contemplate challenging important American interests," and makes it easier to resist "manipulation of America by third world nations." We are now more free to resort to force, violence, and subversion to achieve our global aims.[17]

The Bush I administration responded immediately to these opportunities in its Pentagon budget and national security strategy report in early 1990. In brief, nothing would change, apart from pretexts and tactics. We still need a huge military system, but for a new reason: the "technological sophistication" of third world powers. We have to maintain the "defense industrial base"—a euphemism for state-supported high-tech industry. We must also maintain intervention forces directed at the Middle East energy regions—where the significant threats to our interests "could not be laid at the Kremlin's door," contrary to decades of deceit. All of this and much more like it was passed over quietly, barely even reported. But for those who hope to understand the world, it is quite instructive.[18]

As a pretext for intervention, the "war on drugs" was far too narrow. A more sweeping mission was needed. The intellectual community quickly rose to the challenge. They declared a "normative revolution" that granted the United States the right of "humanitarian intervention" as it chose— for the noblest of reasons, by definition. The traditional victims were unimpressed, to put it mildly. Conferences of leaders of the global South bitterly condemned what they called "the so-called right of humanitarian intervention," reacting particularly to the NATO bombing of Serbia in 1999 (which, as anticipated, precipitated a sharp increase in atrocities). Their stand was upheld by a high-level UN panel in 2004 with leading Western figures participating, among them former National Security Adviser Brent Scowcroft and the distinguished Australian diplomat Gareth Evans.

A refinement was therefore necessary, and again, the intellectual classes rose to the occasion, devising a new doctrine, "responsibility to protect," familiarly known as R2P, now the topic of a substantial literature, many conferences, new organizations and journals, and much praise. The praise is justified, at least in one respect. We may recall Gandhi's response to the question of what he thought about Western civilization. He's alleged to have said, "It would be a good idea." And the same holds of R2P. It would be a good idea, if the concept were taken seriously.

As already briefly discussed, there are two quite distinct versions of R2P: the UN General Assembly version, and the Evans Commission version, the latter hardly more than an authorization for NATO to use force at will. Those who pay attention to history will not be surprised to discover that the Western powers exercise their "responsibility to protect" in accord with the Evans version, and in a highly selective manner, adhering closely to the maxims of Thucydides and Smith, and the Jennings corollary. Merely to illustrate, there is no thought of devoting pennies to protect those dying from hunger and lack of health care at twice the level of Rwanda among children alone, and not for one hundred days but every day.[19] Protected populations are also barred from protection, among them the victims of U.S.-Israeli attacks in Gaza, who are protected persons under the Geneva Conventions. Victims who are the direct responsibility of the Security Council have also been unable to appeal to R2P, for example, Iraqis subjected to Clinton's murderous sanctions. Or the victims of the worst massacres of recent years, in eastern Congo, where only the cynical might suspect that the neglect has something to do with the fact that the worst offender is U.S. ally Rwanda, and that multinationals are making a mint from robbing the region's rich mineral resources with the crucial aid of the militias tearing the place to shreds. And on, and on, amply reviewed elsewhere, and just as the rational would expect.

Returning to the dawn of the unipolar moment, another question that came to the fore at once was the fate of NATO. Its traditional justification had been defense against Russian hordes. With the USSR gone, the pretext evaporated. Naïve souls, who had faith in prevailing doctrine, would have expected NATO to disappear as well. Quite the contrary.

As the Soviet Union collapsed, Gorbachev made an astonishing concession: he permitted a unified Germany to join a hostile military alliance run by the global superpower, though Germany alone had almost destroyed Russia twice in the century. There was a quid pro quo, recently clarified. It had been thought that Bush I and his secretary of state James Baker promised not to expand NATO to the East, but in the first careful study of the original documents, Mark Kramer, apparently seeking to refute charges of U.S. duplicity, in fact shows that it went far beyond what had been assumed.[20] It turns out that Bush-Baker promised that NATO would not even fully extend to East Germany (GDR). They told Gorbachev that "no NATO forces would ever be deployed on the territory of the former GDR.... NATO's jurisdiction or forces would not move eastward." They also assured Gorbachev "that NATO would be transforming itself into a more political organization." There is no need to comment on that promise.

Mary Elise Sarotte, the leading academic specialist on these events, writes that German chancellor Helmut Kohl "assured Mr. Gorbachev, as Mr. Baker had done, that 'naturally NATO could not expand its territory' into East Germany.... Mr. Kohl's foreign minister, Hans-Dietrich Genscher, visiting the Kremlin as well, assured his Soviet counterpart, Eduard Shevardnadze, that 'for us, it stands firm: NATO will not expand itself to the East'.... After listening to Mr. Kohl, Mr. Gorbachev agreed that Germany could unify internally," and unification then proceeded. As Sarotte explains, "In summary, Gorbachev had listened to Baker and Kohl suggest to him for two days in a row that NATO's jurisdiction would not move eastward, and at the end he agreed to let Germany unify." He believed Baker's assurance that "NATO's jurisdiction would not shift one inch eastward from its present position," a step that Gorbachev insisted would be "unacceptable."

What Gorbachev did not know, and Kohl and Genscher dismissed, is that President Bush kept to his position that "we prevailed, they didn't," so they can impose no conditions. After Secretary of State Baker's promise to Gorbachev, Sarotte continues, Bush wrote a letter with "language that differed in a subtle but significant way from the language offered by the secretary of state. Instead of a pledge about NATO's borders, Mr. Bush suggested that East German territory be given a 'special military status' within NATO. What that status would consist of was to be negotiated later, but the core assumption was clear. NATO would grow and former East German areas would have a special status within the alliance as it did so."

Gorbachev was "settling for a gentleman's agreement," Sarotte writes—evidently not a wise move when dealing with Washington.[21]

Central Europe analyst Neil Ascherson observes that "at the heart of Sarotte's book [on 1989 and its aftermath] is the story of a historic swindle," as Gorbachev, trusting in Western honesty, accepted the promise by Baker and Kohl that NATO "would not move an inch eastwards," though it "was disingenuous," as the full record reveals. Gorbachev, and Russia generally, of course came to recognize the swindle, which left bitterness and hostility that persists. Gorbachev later referred to the "unending expansion of NATO…set against the background of sweet talk about partnership" while justifying Russia's actions in the Georgian conflict in 2008. Sarotte concludes that the historic swindle "perpetuated the military dividing line between NATO and its biggest strategic threat, Russia, into the post-Cold War world," contributing to the undermining of a Gorbachev proposal, possibly realistic, for a "Common European Home" of cooperation and interchange from the Atlantic to the Urals, in which both NATO and the Warsaw Pact would vanish in favor of a pan-European security system—not unlike the Gaullist vision that has always been anathema to U.S. planners.[22]

What followed the "historic swindle" tells us a lot about the Cold War itself, and the world that emerged from its ending. As soon as Clinton came into office he began the expansion of NATO to the east. By now its declared jurisdiction is far broader, as we have seen, including control of the "crucial infrastructure" of the global energy system. It is also to serve as a U.S. intervention force, while keeping Europe in its place, a task that may or may not be manageable as the global system becomes more diverse.

At this point new questions come into view, which merit much more intensive inquiry, beyond the scope of this review of 1989, its significance and portent.

Notes

One: Year 514: Globalization for Whom?

1. See Raymond Baker, Shereen Ismael, and Tareq Ismail, eds., *Cultural Cleansing in Iraq* (London: Pluto Press, 2010), a shattering scholarly account of the wanton destruction of treasures of early civilization and the Iraqi intellectual class, though as one contributor observes, the United States did provide some funds to train Iraqi scholars in U.S. universities in curatorial expertise, "an offer of lessons in how to be good custodians of your cultural heritage from the country that was responsible for its destruction," (Zainab Bahrani, Professor of Art History and Archaeology at Columbia University).

2. The toll of disease is sometimes invoked to exonerate the conquerors, a feat of apologetics that is not very impressive. Europe suffered vast population decline during the fourteenth century Black Death, but recovered. Native Americans were subjugated, driven from their homes, and slaughtered, hence could not recover.

3. For sources where not cited, and further details on the earlier history, here and below, see my *Year 501* (Cambridge, MA: South End Press, 1993).

4. John Steinbrunner and Nancy Gallagher, and Robert McNamara, respectively. See my *Failed States* (New York: Metropolitan Books, 2006), for sources and discussion.

5. Charles Mann, *1491: New Revelations of the Americas Before Columbus* (New York: Knopf, 2005). His quote.

6. Francis Jennings, *The Invasion of America* (Chapel Hill, NC: University of North Carolina Press, 1975), 306, one of the earliest modern studies to shatter the jingoist consensus.

7. See among others Kenneth Pomeranz, *The Great Divergence* (Princeton, NJ: Princeton University Press, 2000). Britain's crimes in India grew in intensity until post–World War II liberation opened the way to independent development.

281

Much the same was true in China.

8. John Maynard Keynes, *A Treatise on Money*, cited by Sylvia Ann Hewlett, *The Cruel Dilemmas of Development* (New York: Basic Books, 1980).

9. See the penetrating and shocking study by *Wall Street Journal* bureau chief Douglas Blackmon, *Slavery by Another Name* (New York: Anchor Books, 2009). Ecology and France's destruction, see Jared Diamond, *Collapse* (New York: Penguin, 2005). Sophie Perchellet and Eric Toussaint, http://www.cadtm.org/Haiti-Grants-to-repay-an-odious, January 18, 2010, on the shameful reaction of France's Régis Debray Commission to the compensation request. Also, in the wake of the horrendous earthquake of January 2010, on the urgent need to cancel Haiti's huge debt and for "The most industrialized countries, which have systematically exploited Haiti, beginning with France and the United States, [to] pay compensation towards a fund aimed at financing the reconstruction of the country, controlled by the Haitian people's organizations."

10. Thomas Griffin, *Haiti Human Rights Investigation: November 11–21, 2004*, (Center for the Study of Human Rights, University of Miami School of Law, January 2005), http://www.law.miami.edu/cshr/CSHR_Report_02082005_v2.pdf. On the *Lancet* report, ensuing controversy, and resolution, see "Half-Hour for Haiti," blog archive, Institute for Justice and Democracy in Haiti, August 31, 2006, http://ijdh.org/archives/2074.

11. On the CIA and the coup, see Jim Mann, *Los Angeles Times*, November 2, 1993; Tim Weiner, *New York Times*, December 3, 1995. For details of this period, see *Year 501*, chap. 8, my "Democracy Restored," *Z Magazine*, November 1994, http://www.chomsky.info/articles/199411--.htm, and *New Military Humanism* (Monroe, ME: Common Courage Press, 1999), chap. 3. As discussed in "Democracy Restored," the illegal oil shipments authorized by Bush and Clinton were so prominently reported by the AP that they were impossible to miss, but are almost entirely absent from the media, which have been bitterly opposed to Aristide, with rare exceptions.

12. See Peter Hallward, *Damming the Flood: Haiti, Aristide, and the Politics of Containment* (London: Verso, 2007). For brief review of the late '90s events, see *New Military Humanism*.

13. *Financial Times*, July 12, 2009. *New Nation*, October 26, 2008, reprinted from *Al-Ahram Weekly* (Egypt), http://weekly.ahram.org.eg/2008/919/op12.htm. *New York Times*, Reuters, June 13, 2009.

14. Onyebuchi Ezigbo, *All Africa*, June 23, 2009.

15. Michael Glennon, *Christian Science Monitor*, March 20, 1986; Donald Fox and Michael Glennon, "Report to the International Human Rights Law Group and the Washington Office on Latin America," (Washington D.C., April 1985), 21. Referring to U.S.-backed atrocities in Central America in the 1980s and the reaction at home.

16. Irene Khan, *The Unheard Truth* (London: Amnesty International UK, W. W. Norton, 2009).

17. David Johnston, *Montreal Gazette*, "Montreal Summit Tiptoes Around Haiti's Hidden Crises," January 25, 2010. "Chavez Writes Off Haiti's Oil Debt to Venezuela," EFE, January 26, 2010. Venezuela, *Latin American Herald Tribune*, http://www.laht.com/article.asp?ArticleId=351054&CategoryId=10717; *El Universal* (opposition press),

"Haiti's Prime Minister Thanks Venezuela for Support," January 25, 2010; http://english.eluniversal.com/2010/01/25/en_pol_art_haitis-prime-minist_25A3338491.shtml. Cuba's impressive initiatives received a rare mention on CNN, Steve Kastenbaum, January 17, 2010. Several weeks later, after considerable popular pressure, the rich countries (G-7) pledged debt relief, and support for relief was pledged by the international financial institutions. BBC, February 7, 2010.

18. Francis Jennings, *Empire of Fortune* (New York: W. W. Norton, 1988).

19. Cited by Mann, *Los Angeles Times*. See note 11, this chapter.

20. R. W. van Alstyne, *The Rising American Empire* (New York: Oxford University Press, 1960), Reginald Horsman, *Expansion and American Indian Policy, 1783–1812* (East Lansing, MI: Michigan State University Press, 1967). Richard Drinnon, *Facing West* (Minneapolis, MN: University of Minnesota Press, 1980) and *White Savage* (New York: Schocken Books, 1972). See also his "The Metaphysics of Empire-Building," MS, Bucknell University, 1972.

21. Russell Baker, "A Heroic Historian on Heroes," *New York Review of Books*, July 11, 2009. No letters appeared in reaction, though the editors later published a "clarification" (October 8): Baker, it reads, "wrote that in North America at the time of Columbus, 'there may have been scarcely more than a million inhabitants.' However, archaeological evidence and demographic research in recent decades suggest that the number was much larger, with estimates ranging up to 18 million." Baker was not referring to North America—rather, "from tropical jungle...." The research is not recent, but decades old. It was also known long ago that the "sparsely populated...unspoiled world" included advanced civilizations (in the United States too).

22. Knox cited by Horsman, *Expansion and American Indian Policy*. Adams cited by William Earl Weeks, *John Quincy Adams and American Global Empire* (Lexington, KY: University Press of Kentucky, 1992).

23. Story cited by Nicholas Guyatt, *Providence and the Invention of the United States, 1607–1876* (Cambridge: Cambridge University Press, 2007), reviewing the record of Providentialist justifications for the most shocking crimes, and their more general role in forging "the American idea." Monroe cited by Horsman, *Expansion and American Indian Policy*. Roosevelt cited by Blackmon, *Slavery by Another Name*.

24. Rice quoted by Peter Baker, *New York Times*, December 1, 2008.

25. On these matters, see my "'Come Over and Help Us': A History of R2P" ("Responsibility to Protect"), talk delivered at the UN General Assembly conference on R2P (July 23, 2009), http://www.chomsky.info/talks/20090723.htm. And "Human Rights in the New Millennium," talk at the London School of Economics (October 2009); *Z Magazine*, January 2010. See pp. 185f.

26. Roger Cohen, *New York Times Book Review*, April 26, 2009. Morgenthau, pp. 39–40, below.

27. Great Seal, see Jennings, *Invasion*, 229.

28. Martin and Annelise Anderson, *Reagan's Secret War* (New York: Crown, 2009), cited by Paul Boyer, "Burnishing Reagan's Disarmament Credentials," *Arms Control Today*, September 2009. On Reagan and global jihadism, and Pakistani nuclear weapons, see Ahmed Rashid, *Descent into Chaos* (New York: Viking Press, 2008). Below, p. 194. The goal of these projects was not to defend Afghanistan, as com-

monly claimed—the U.S.-Pakistani initiatives may well have delayed Russian withdrawal, some specialists believe. The goal was to "kill Soviet Soldiers," the CIA station chief in Islamabad declared. He boasted that he "loved" this "noble goal," making clear that "the mission was not to liberate Afghanistan." Tim Weiner, *Legacy of Ashes: the History of the CIA* (New York: Doubleday, 2007).

29. Cited by Lars Schoultz, *That Infernal Little Cuban Republic* (Chapel Hill, NC: University of North Carolina Press, 2009), 16.

30. Ibid., for ample details. Below, for further discussion.

31. Ibid. Alfred McCoy, *Policing America's Empire* (Madison, WI: University of Wisconsin Press, 2009).

32. John Lewis Gaddis, *Surprise, Security, and the American Experience* (Cambridge, MA: Harvard University Press, 2004). Matt Bai, *New York Times Magazine*, October 10, 2004. For more extensive discussion, see *Failed States*.

33. Weeks, *John Quincy Adams*.

34. President Bill Clinton, address to the UN (September 27, 1993); Secretary of Defense William S. Cohen, "Annual Report to the President and Congress," 1999. Kennan cited by Walter LaFeber, *Inevitable Revolutions* (New York: W. W. Norton, 1983).

35. David Green, *The Containment of Latin America* (Chicago: Quadrangle Books, 1971). For more discussion and context, see my *Hegemony or Survival* (New York: Metropolitan Books, 2003), chap. 3.

36. Fawaz Gerges, *The Far Enemy* (Cambridge: Cambridge University Press, 2005). See also his *Journey of the Jihadist* (New York: Harcourt Books, 2006).

37. Quoted in Michael Sherry, *The Rise of American Airpower* (New Haven, CT: Yale University Press, 1987).

38. Peter Bergen and Paul Cruickshank, "The Iraq Effect," *Mother Jones*, March 1, 2007. Zbigniew Brzezinski, *The National Interest*, Winter 2003–04.

39. Christopher Swannin, *Financial Times*, April 12, 2006.

40. Quoted in Joseph Nevins, *Operation Gatekeeper* (New York: Routledge, 2002).

41. Estimate of economic power, Justice Stephen Field, cited by Morton Horwitz, *The Transformation of American Law 1870–1960* (New York: Oxford University Press, 1992). Wilson, *The New Freedom*, 1914, cited by Martin Sklar, *The Corporate Reconstruction of American Capitalism* (Cambridge: Cambridge University Press, 1988).

42. Scott Bowman, *The Modern Corporation and American Political Thought* (University Park, PA: Pennsylvania State University Press, 1996). On corporate manslaughter and virtual impunity, see Gary Slapper, *Blood in the Bank* (Aldershot, UK: Ashgate Publishing, 2000), reviewing the long record in England. For some U.S. analogues, see my introduction to Slapper's study.

43. Horwitz, *Transformation of American Law*. For a lucid discussion, see Joel Bakan, *The Corporation* (New York: Free Press, 2004). One major case was Minneapolis & S.L.O. Co. v. Beckwith (1889), in which corporations were considered persons for purposes of the due process clause of the Fourteenth Amendment, enacted to protect rights of freed slaves, but, notoriously, taken over as a device to protect concentrations of private power. See Bowman, *The Modern Corporation and American Political Thought*.

44. Rasul v. Myers, January 2008, Court of Appeals, District of Columbia Circuit.

45. Adam Liptak, "Supreme Court to Revisit 'Hillary' Documentary," *New York Times*,

August 29, 2009. When first argued, the case "seemed an oddity [but] it has turned into a juggernaut with the potential to shatter a century-long understanding about the government's ability to bar corporations from spending money to support political candidates."

46.   Citizens United v. FEC, January 21, 2009. Adam Liptak, "Justices Overturn Key Campaign Limits," *New York Times*, January 21, 2010. Waldman, blog on New York Times online, cited by editors, same day; Waldman is executive director of the Brennan Center for Justice at the NYU School of Law. Technically the decision also applies to unions, facts constantly brought up in commentary. But that is insignificant in comparison with corporate power, quite apart from very different character of unions representing workers and private tyrannies dedicated to wealth maximization, primarily for the very narrow sector of extreme wealth in whose hands ownership is concentrated.

47.   For data on business funding, government policy, and public opinion concerning business dominance, see Anthony Dimaggio, "Corporate Power and the Deregulation of Campaign Finance: Supremely Swindled," *Counterpunch*, January 25, 2010.

48.   Thomas Ferguson, *Golden Rule: The Investment Theory of Party Competition and the Logic of Money-Driven Political Systems* (Chicago: University of Chicago Press, 1995), and regular updating since.

49.   Editorial, *New York Times*, January 22, 2010.

50.   Horwitz, *Transformation of American Law*.

51.   Horwitz, *Transformation of American Law*, 98, citing H. Spellman. *A Treatise on the Principles of Law Governing Corporate Directors* (New York: Prentice-Hall, 1931).

52.   Jess Bravin, "Democrats Divide on Voice of Possible Top-Court Pick," *Wall Strees Journal*, February 8, 2010.

53.   For details and sources, see my *World Orders Old and New* (New York: Columbia University Press, 1994). On consequences, see *NAFTA at Seven* (Washington, DC: Economic Policy Institute, 2001), http://www.epi.org/publications/entry/briefing papers_nafta01_index/.

54.   A secondary benefit, as a number of economists pointed out, was that its highly protectionist features would turn Mexico into "America's preferential market, with Japan and the EC at a disadvantage" (Jagdish Bhagwati, a genuine free trade advocate). See *World Orders*, chap. 2, for discussion and sources.

55.   U.S. National Intelligence Council (NIC), *Global Trends 2015* (2000).

56.   David Schmitz, *Thank God They're on Our Side* (Chapel Hill, NC: University of North Carolina Press, 1999). On Operation Condor, the "transnational criminal operation" established by the coup, employing terror, torture, and murder to protect traditional elites from social and economic reform and ensure U.S. political and economic hegemony, see J. Patrice McSherry, *Predatory States* (Lanham, MD: Rowman & Littlefield, 2005). There may be more to discover after the overthrow of the U.S.-backed Paraguayan dictatorship, where archives were housed. On the events and prospects, see Hugh O'Shaughnessy, *The Priest of Paraguay: Fernando Lugo and the Making of a Nation* (London & New York: Zed Books, 2009).

57.   Greg Grandin, *Empire's Workshop: Latin America, the United States, and the Rise of the New Imperialism* (New York: Metropolitan Books, 2007).

Two: Latin America and U.S. Foreign Policy

1. Hans Morgenthau, *The Purpose of American Politics* (New York: Vintage Books, 1964).
2. Samuel Huntington, *International Security* 17, no. 4 (Spring 1993).
3. Michael Desch, *International Security*, vol. 32, no. 3, Winter 2007/8.
4. Schmitz, *Thank God They're on Our Side*.
5. Augustus Richard Norton, *Middle East Policy*, Spring 2005. For review of polls and public opinion, and much other insight, see Jonathan Steele, *Defeat* (London: I. B. Tauris Publishers, 2008).
6. Jonathan Monten, *International Security*, Spring 2005; Katerina Dalacoura, *International Affairs* 81, no. 5 (October 2005).
7. Thomas Friedman, *New York Times*, January 12, 1992. David Ignatius, *Washington Post Weekly*, November 10, 2003.
8. For details on this revealing episode, see *Hegemony or Survival*, chap. 5; and *Failed States*, chap. 3.
9. See Gilbert Achcar, Noam Chomsky, and Stephen Shalom, *Perilous Power* (Boulder, CO: Paradigm Publishers, 2007), epilogue. Water, John Bohannon, *Science*, August 25, 2006. Below, for further discussion and sources.
10. Thomas Carothers, *Critical Mission: Essays on Democracy Promotion* (Washington, DC: Carnegie Endowment for International Peace, 2004).
11. Thomas Carothers, *In the Name of Democracy* (Berkeley and Los Angeles: University of California Press, 1991). Also his essay in Abraham Lowenthal, ed., *Exporting Democracy* (Baltimore, MD: Johns Hopkins University Press, 1991).
12. Robert Pastor, *Condemned to Repetition* (Princeton, NJ: Princeton University Press, 1987), his emphasis.
13. Lawrence Jacobs and Benjamin Page, *American Political Science Review* 99, no. 1 (February 2005).
14. On Wilson and the DR, see Frank Moya Pons, *The Dominican Republic: A National History* (Princeton, NJ: Markus Wiener Publishers, 1998); Piero Gleijeses, *The Dominican Crisis* (Baltimore, MD: Johns Hopkins University Press, 1978); Bruce Calder, *The Impact of Intervention* (Austin: University of Texas Press, 1984).
15. William Stivers, *Supremacy and Oil* (Ithaca, NY: Cornell University Press, 1982).
16. Hirohito cited by Tsuyoshi Hasegawa, *Racing the Enemy* (Cambridge, MA: Harvard University Press, 2005). Dulles cited by Stephen Rabe, *Eisenhower and Latin America* (Chapel Hill, NC: University of North Carolina Press, 1988). Arthur Schlesinger, Memorandum from the President's Special Assistant (Schlesinger) to the President's Assistant Special Counsel (Goodwin), March 8, 1961; Report to the President on Latin American Mission, *Foreign Relations of the United States, 1961–1963*, vol. XII, American Republics (Washington, DC: Government Printing Office).
17. Ernest May and Philip Zelikow, *The Kennedy Tapes* (Cambridge, MA: Harvard University Press, 1998).
18. Louis Pérez, *The War of 1898* (Chapel Hill, NC: University of North Carolina Press, 1998); Louis Pérez, *Cuba: Between Reform and Revolution* (New York: Oxford University Press, 1996).
19. For details and sources, see *Failed States*, chap. 4, and for a comprehensive study,

see Lars Schoultz, *Human Rights and United States Policy Toward Latin America* (Princeton, NJ: Princeton University Press, 1981). For voices of the victims of U.S. state terror—almost never heard—see Keith Bolender, *The Unknown War* (London: Pluto Press, 2010).

20. Leonard Weinglass, lawyer for the Cuban Five, at the National Lawyers Guild Conference, October 19, 2002, Pasadena, CA, http://www.iacenter.org/Cuba/cuba5 _weinglass.html. Edith Lederer, Associated Press, September 2, 2009.

21. Noah Feldman, *New York Times Book Review,* February 12, 2006. Steven Erlanger, *New York Times,* February 14, 2006.

22. July 1961, cited by Schoultz, *Human Rights and United States Policy Toward Latin America.*

23. John Norris, *Collision Course* (Westport, CT: Praeger Publishers, 2005), a study strongly endorsed in the introduction by Strobe Talbott, the highest Clinton official responsible for East European affairs, who writes that those who want to know "how events looked and felt at the time to those of us who were involved" in the war should turn to Norris's account, written with the "immediacy that can be provided only by someone who was an eyewitness to much of the action, who interviewed at length and in depth many of the participants while their memories were still fresh, and who has had access to much of the diplomatic record." That the plight of Kosovar Albanians could not have been a serious issue is evident from the rich Western documentary record, which shows that the worst atrocities, by far, were the anticipated consequence of the NATO bombing. For review of the record, see my *A New Generation Draws the Line* (London: Verso, 2000). Of the official reasons offered at the time, the only one that is tenable, and was constantly repeated by U.S. and UK governments, is that "the credibility of NATO" was at stake. Ibid., for discussion; and more extensively, David Gibbs, *First Do No Harm* (Nashville, TN: Vanderbilt University Press, 2009), who argues that "credibility of NATO" in the Balkans is shorthand for U.S. domination over Europe, and takes it to be the driving force behind U.S. Balkans policy from the collapse of Yugoslavia. A similar view had been expressed even more strongly by the conservative military historian and analyst Andrew Bacevich, though without evidence. He dismisses any pretense of humanitarian concern and writes that the bombing of Serbia was intended "to provide an object lesson to any European state fancying that it was exempt from the rules of the post-Cold War era" established by Washington: "the war's architects understood" from the outset that "its purpose had been to sustain American primacy" in Europe, and "the workmanlike demolition of Serbia" demonstrated "what a great power did to fend off perceived threats to its preeminence" and "to forestall the intolerable prospect of Europe's backsliding" toward an independent course. *American Empire* (Cambridge, MA: Harvard University Press, 2004), 104f., 196. Dean Baker, *The Conservative Nanny State* (Washington, DC: Center for Economic and Policy Research, 2006), e-book, http://www.conservativenannystate.org/.

24. Stephen Rabe, *The Road to OPEC* (Austin: University of Texas Press, 1982).

25. War-Peace Studies programs of the Council on Foreign Relations and the State Department, 1939–45. The only careful study is Larry Shoup and William Minter, *Imperial Brain Trust* (New York: Monthly Review Press, 1977).

26. See Joyce Kolko and Gabriel Kolko, *The Limits of Power* (New York: Harper & Row, 1972). Berle Papers, May 11, 1951, cited by Lloyd Gardner, *Three Kings* (New York: New Press, 2009). See also Aaron David Miller, *Search for Security* (Chapel Hill, NC: University of North Carolina Press, 1980); Irvine Anderson, *Aramco, the United States and Saudi Arabia* (Princeton, NJ: Princeton University Press, 1981); Michael Stoff, *Oil, War and American Security* (New Haven, CT: Yale University Press, 1980); David Painter, *Oil and the American Century* (Baltimore, MD: Johns Hopkins University Press, 1986).

27. The manic intensity of the assault is reviewed in detail in Schoultz, *That Infernal Little Cuban Republic*. On poll results for the past three decades, showing about 2–1 support for normalization, see Gallup.com, "Two in Three Americans Favor Re-Establishing Ties with Cuba," poll, December 15, 2006, http://www.gallup.com/poll/25912/Two-Three-Americans-Favor-Re-Establishing-Ties-Cuba.aspx. One can only guess what the results would be if the topic could be discussed.

28. LBJ, "Remarks to American and Korean Servicemen at Camp Stanley, Korea," November 1, 1966, http://www.presidency.ucsb.edu/ws/index.php?pid=27974. Bruce Franklin, *War Stars* (New York: Oxford University Press, 1988; expanded 2008). Samuel Huntington, *Who Are We: the Challenges to America's National Identity* (New York: Simon & Schuster, 1985). On the nativist legacy reflected in this and similar scholarship, and contemporary manifestations in the United States and Europe, see Anouar Majid, *We Are All Moors* (Minneapolis, MN: University of Minnesota Press, 2009).

29. Colette Youngers and Eileen Rosin, eds., *Drugs and Democracy in Latin America* (Washington, DC: WOLA, Lynne Rienner Publishers, 2005). Adam Isacson, Jay Olson, and Lisa Haugard, *Blurring the Lines* (Washington, DC: Latin America Working Group, Center for International Policy, and WOLA, September 2004). On the impact of U.S. training over many years, see Martha Huggins, "US-supported State Terror: A History of Police Training in Latin America," in Huggins, ed., *Vigilantism and the State in Modern Latin America* (Westport, CT: Praeger Publishers, 1991).

30. Fourth fleet, see EFE, "El Senado Brasileño Rechaza la Reactivacíon de la IV Flota Naval de EE UU," *El Pais*, September 7, 2008, http://www.elpais.com/articulo/internacional/Senado/brasileno/rechaza/reactivacion/IV/Flota/Naval/EE/UU/elpepuint/20080709elpepuint_24/Tes.

31. Stephan Kuffner, *Time*, May 14, 2009.

32. "Colombia's Uribe Signs Pact with Honduras' Lobo," *Latin American Herald Tribune*. January 31, 2010, http://www.laht.com/article.asp?ArticleId=351380&CategoryId=12393.

33. On the general remilitarization project, and particularly the crucial role of the Colombian terror state, now partially controlled by the paramilitary-narcotrafficking alliance, see Greg Grandin, "Muscling Latin America," *Nation*, February 8, 2010. On the "horrific atrocities" of the successor groups to the paramilitaries, and the increase in the vast displacement in Colombia (second only to Sudan) as their terror and land grabs expand, see Human Rights Watch, "Colombia: Stop Abuses by Paramilitaries' Successor Groups," February 3, 2010. Full report at http://www.hrw.org/en/reports/2010/02/03/paramilitaries-heirs. Simon Romero,

New York Times, February 3, 2010. For background, see among others Doug Stokes, *America's Other War: Terrorizing Colombia* (London: Zed Books, 2005); Forrest Hylton, *Evil Hour in Colombia* (London: Verso, 2006).

34. White Paper, Air Mobility Command, Global en Route Strategy, presented at symposium, Maxwell Air Base, April, 2009. Ethan Vesely-Flad, "U.S. & Colombia discuss major military bases agreement," Associated Press, July 15, 2009. Cited at http://www.forpeace.net/blog/ethan-vesely-flad/us-colombia-discuss-major-military-bases-agreement. Juliana Sojo, *Washington Report on the Hemisphere*, Council on Hemispheric Affairs, August 18 2009.

35. Department of Air Force, *Military Construction Program Fiscal Year (FY) 2010*, Budget Estimates, Justification Data Submitted to Congress, May 2009. The submission was republished in November 2009, softening the wording, presumably in response to the sharply negative response in Latin America. Eva Golinger, "Washington Alters US Air Force Document to Hide Intentions Behind Accord with Colombia," Postcards from the Revolution, November 27, 2009, http://www.chavezcode.com/2009/11/breaking-news-washington-alters-us-air.html. It is reasonable to speculate that the original thinking prevails.

36. "Transparencia Para Pactos Militares Transnacionales Acuerdan Presidentes," Semana.com, August 28, 2009, http://www.semana.com/wf_ImprimirArticulo.aspx?IdArt=127918.

37. Eduardo Mendoza, "Encuentro Martinelli-Clinton: Proponen acceso expedito a EU," *La Prensa* (prensa.com), September 27, 2009.

38. Quoted in Michael Warren, "Uribe Stands Ground on U.S. Military Deal," Associated Press, August 28, 2009.

39. See Stokes, *America's Other War*.

40. Marina Litvinsky, "Latin American Leaders Say 'No' to U.S. Drug War," Inter Press Service, February 12, 2009, http://ipsnews.org/news.asp?idnews=45753. On the expansion of the "drug war" by Obama, along the conventional lines, see Suzanna Reiss, "Beyond Supply and Demand: Obama's Drug Wars in Latin America," *NACLA Report on the Americas*, January–February 2010.

41. See Jerry Kuzmarov, *The Myth of the Addicted Army* (Amherst, MA: University of Massachusetts Press, 2009), from which much of what follows on Nixon's "drug war" is drawn.

42. M. J. Crozier, S. P. Huntington, and J. Watanuki, *The Crisis of Democracy* (New York: NYU Press, 1975), report to the Trilateral Commission. The general tenor of the commission is illustrated by the fact that the Carter administration was heavily drawn from its ranks.

43. Carter, news conference, March 24, 1977. Bush cited by Barbara Crossette, *New York Times*, October 24, 1992.

44. Iraq mega-embassy, Ernesto Londoño, *Washington Post*, August 29, 2009; Pakistan-Afghanistan, Saeed Shah and Warren P. Strobel, McClatchy Newspapers, May 27, 2009. Militarization of the Gulf region, Nick Turse, "Out of Iraq, Into the Gulf," Tomdispatch.com, November 22, 2009. Diego Garcia, see p. 63, below.

45. Katherine McIntire Peters, "Defense Budget Portends Difficult Tradeoffs," Government Executive.com, August 12, 2009, http://www.govexec.com/dailyfed

/0809/081209kp1.htm. Tom Engelhardt, http://www.tomdispatch.com/archive /175196/, January 26, 2010. Editorial, *New York Times*, February 4, 2010. Sanger, *New York Times*, February 2, 2010. Gerald Seib, "Deficit Balloons into National Security Threat," *Wall Street Journal*, February 2, 2010, warning that national security will be harmed by the deficit (noting that the deficit is "twice as large" as the "staggering" defense outlays.) "Imperial overreach," in the familiar locution.

46. Agence France-Presse, June 8, 2009. Jorn Madslien, "In Graphs: Arming the World," June 14, 2009, BBC News, http://news.bbc.co.uk/2/hi/business/8097942.stm. Ali Gharib, Inter Press Service, December 12, 2009. Associated Press, November 1, 2008.

47. Andrea Shalal-Esa, *Christian Science Monitor*, January 27, 2009. Mark Knoller, "White House to Hold Firm on European Missile Shield," CBS News, July 1, 2009, http://www.cbsnews.com/blogs/2009/07/01/politics/politicalhotsheet/entry5128736. shtml. Joseph Gerson, "Dawn of Hope and Nuclear Paradoxes" (special address, Japan Scientists Association, Kobe, Japan August 2, 2009.)

48. Quoted by Ian James, Associated Press, August 26, 2006.

49. James Hodge and Linda Cooper, "U.S. Continues to Train Honduran Soldiers," *National Catholic Reporter*, July 14, 2009, http://ncronline.org/news/global/us-continues-train-honduran-soldiers. Mark Weisbrot, *Guardian, Counterpunch*, September 7, 2009. On the "yawning political and socioeconomic divide" between wealthy coup supporters and opponents, who include the "solidly working-class" supporters of the ousted president, see Ginger Thompson, *New York Times*, August 9, 2009: members of "this country's small upper class…felt threatened by [President Zelaya's] efforts to lift up the poor" with such measures as a 60 percent increase in the minimum wage in a country where 60 percent live in poverty. On possible U.S. complicity and prior knowledge, see among others Michaela D'Ambrosio, "The Honduran Coup: Was It a Matter of Behind-the-Scenes Finagling by State Department Stonewallers?" *Washington Report on the Hemisphere*, Council on Hemispheric Affairs, September 16, 2009. On Obama's foot-dragging and tacit support, see Alexander Main, "'A New Chapter of Engagement': Obama and the Honduran Coup," *NACLA Report on the Americas*, January–February 2010.

50. Amnesty International, *Honduras: Human Rights Crisis Threatens as Repression Increases* (London: Amnesty International Publications: August 2009).

51. Schoultz, *Human Rights*, 7.

52. Llorens and Valenzuela, Alexandra Olson, Associated Press, December 1, 2009. Anselem, Ginger Thompson, *New York Times*, November 11, 2009. Aid, OAS resolution, Mark Weisbrot, Center for Economic and Policy Research (CEPR), Common Dreams, December 16, 2009. IRI-NDI, CEPR, press release, November 23, 2009.

53. Among others, see now *Financial Times* Mideast editor David Gardner, *Last Chance* (London: I. B. Tauris Publishers, 2009).

54. See *Failed States*, Afterword, here and below. Brazil-China, and more generally Brazilian development and trade, see Kenneth Maxwell, "Lula's Last Year," and Riordan Roett, "How Reform Has Powered Brazil's Rise," *Current History*, February 2010.

55. Mark Weisbrot, Rebecca Ray, and Jake Johnston, *Bolivia: The Economy During the Morales Administration* (Washington, DC: Center for Economic and Policy Research, December 2009), http://www.cepr.net/index.php/publications/reports/bolivian-economy-during-morales-administration/. Frank Chávez, "Bolivia: Evo Morales,

the Best Ally of the Middle Class," Inter Press Service, January 8, 2010, http://www.
ipsnews.net/news.asp?idnews=49925.

56. David Felix, *Latin American Research Review*, January 1, 1998. Ha-Joon Chang, *Kicking Away the Ladder* (London: Anthem Press, 2002); *Bad Samaritans* (London: Random House, 2007).

57. Karen Lissakers, *Banks, Borrowers, and the Establishment* (New York: Basic Books, 1991).

58. For insightful accounts of the roots of the crisis, see Dean Baker, *Plunder and Blunder* (Sausalito, CA: PoliPoint Press, 2009); John Bellamy Foster and Fred Magdoff, *The Great Financial Crisis* (New York: Monthly Review Press, 2009).

Three: Democracy and Development: Their Enemies, Their Hopes

1.   Solow, "Interview," *Challenge*, January–February 2000. Bairoch, *Economics and World History* (Chicago: University of Chicago Press, 1993). Chang, *Kicking Away the Ladder*. See also Shahid Alam, *Poverty from the Wealth of Nations* (New York: St. Martin's Press, 2000). An enduring classic is Frederick Clairmonte, *Economic Liberalism and Underdevelopment* (New York: Asia Publishing House, 1960).

2.   The Jacksonian Democrats sought to do just that, to great economic and geopolitical advantage, specifically with cotton. That was a primary goal of the annexation of Texas, then half of Mexico. President Tyler anticipated that "that monopoly, now secured, places all other nations at our feet.... An embargo of a single year would produce in Europe a greater amount of suffering than a fifty years' war. I doubt whether Great Britain could avoid convulsions." That way the United States could overcome the British deterrent as well as dominate the global economy. See Thomas Hietala, *Manifest Design: Anxious Aggrandizement in Late Jacksonian America* (Ithaca, NY: Cornell University Press, 1985); for quotes and discussion, *Year 501*.

3.   Kindelberger cited by Ha-Joong Chang, *Bad Samaritans*.

4.   See Jack Beeching, *The Chinese Opium Wars* (New York: Harcourt Brace Jovanovich, 1975); Jack Gray, *Rebellions and Revolutions* (New York: Oxford University Press, 1990); J. Y. Wong, *Deadly Dreams: Opium, Imperialism, and the Arrow War (1856–1860) in China* (Cambridge: Cambridge University Press, 1998). In a broader context, Carl Trocki, *Opium, Empire and the Global Political Economy* (London: Routledge, 1999). For reservations on the impact on China, see Franz Dikötter, Lars Laamaan, and Zhou Xun, *Narcotic Culture: a History of Drugs in China* (Chicago: University of Chicago Press, 2004).

5.   For a graphic and shocking account of post–Civil War slavery, see Blackmon, *Slavery by Another Name*. On the current scale and character, see Randall Shelden, *Our Punitive Society* (Long Grove, IL: Waveland Press, 2010). On violation of international labor standards by prison labor, see Susan Kang, "Forcing Prison Labor," *New Political Science*, June 2009.

6.   Afaf Lutfi Al-Sayyid Marsot, *Egypt in the Reign of Muhammad Ali* (Cambridge: Cambridge University Press, 1984). For more extensive discussion, on to post–WWII Egypt, see *World Orders*, chap. 2.

7.   Basil Davidson, *The Black Man's Burden: Africa and the Curse of the Nation-State* (New York, London: Times Books, 1992).

8.   Adam Smith, *Wealth of Nations*, bk. IV, chap. II. David Ricardo, *Principles of Political Economy*, cited by Dean Baker, Gerald Epstein, and Robert Pollin, eds., *Globalization and Progressive Economic Policy* (Cambridge: Cambridge University Press, 1998), editors' introduction.

9.   José Antonio Ocampo, "Rethinking the Development Agenda," MS, 2001, based on paper at the American Economic Association annual meeting, January 2001.

10. Mark Weisbrot, Dean Baker, and David Rosnik, "The Scorecard on Globalization 1980–2005; 25 Years of Diminished Progress," Center for Economic and Policy Reseach, September 2005. Robert Pollin, *Contours of Descent* (London: Verso, 2003). Robert Hunter Wade, "Does Inequality Matter?" *Challenge* 48, (September–October 2005); *Foreign Affairs*, (September/October 2006).

11. David Felix, in Baker et al., eds., *Globalization and Progressive Economic Policy.*

12. Baker, *Plunder and Blunder.* Marc Miringoff and Marque-Luisa Miringoff, *The Social Health of the Nation* (New York: Oxford University Press, 1999). The projected Reagan-Bush debt interest burden is virtually identical to the projection for 2019, despite extensive spending to overcome the impact of the 2007–8 financial crash; Dean Baker, Beat the Press, Center for Economic and Policy Research, August 31, 2009. Also John Irons, Kathryn Edwards, and Anna Turner, "The 2009 Budget Deficit," EPI Issue Brief #262, August 20, 2009, http://www.epi.org/publications /entry/ib262/.

13. For references, see *Hegemony or Survival*, chap. 9.

14. Ibid. Joseph Stiglitz, *Foreign Affairs* 84, no. 6 (2005).

15. Tomas Valasek, *Defense Monitor* 30, no. 3 (March 2001). Gordon Mitchell, *Fletcher Forum* 25, no. 1 (Winter 2001), citing Charles Perrow.

16. See references of note 1, this chapter. On the enormous role of military procurement in technology development, see Vernon Ruttan, *Is War Necessary for Economic Growth?* (New York: Oxford University Press, 2006). On corporate reliance on bailout and other forms of state intervention, see Winfried Ruigrok and Rob van Tulder, *The Logic of International Restructuring* (London, New York: Routledge, 1995).

17. For review of Greenspan's examples, and sources, see my *Rogue States* (Cambridge, MA: South End Press, 2000), chap. 13.

18. James Cypher, "Military Spending, Technical Change, and Economic Growth," *Journal of Economic Issues*, March 1987. David Noble, *Forces of Production* (New York: Knopf, 1984); *Progress without People* (Chicago: Charles Kerr, 1993).

19. Baker, "The High Cost of Protectionism: The Case of Intellectual Property Claims," MS, Economic Policy Institute, 1996; *In These Times*, August 22, 1999. Amy Kazmin, Andrew Jack, and Alan Beattie, "How Washington Uses Trade Deals to Protect Drugs," *Financial Times*, August 21, 2006, http://www.ft.com/cms/s /a36e1050-313e-11db-b953-0000779e2340.html.

20. See note 13, this chapter.

21. Ha-Joon Chang and Ajit Singh, "Public Enterprises in Developing Countries and Economic Efficiency," *UNCTAD Review*, no. 4 (1993): 45–81.

22. David Kirkpatrick, *New York Times*, August 6, 2009. Health care reform, see below,

p. 226.

23. Javier Santiso, *Latin America's Political Economy of the Possible* (Cambridge, MA: MIT Press, 2006). Richard Lapper, *Financial Times*, July 30, 2006.

24. See Baker, *Plunder and Blunder*, for succinct review. Concentration, Kansas City Federal Reserve president Thomas Hoenig, August 6, 2009, cited by Zach Carter, "A Master of Disaster," *Nation*, January 4, 2010, http://www.thenation.com/doc/20100104/carter.

25. Pete Engardio, "Can the Future Be Built in America?" *Business Week*, September 21, 2009.

26. Citigroup, "Equity Strategy, Plutonomy: Buying Luxury, Explaining Global Imbalances," October 16, 2005; "Equity Strategy, Revisiting Plutonomy: The Rich Getting Richer," March 5, 2006. "Why Service Stinks," *Business Week*, October 23, 2000.

27. *Wall Street Journal*, June 15, 2009.

28. Thomas Catan and David Gauthier-Villars, *Wall Street Journal*, May 29, 2009.

29. For discussion and illustrations of the state-corporate policies that have systematically undermined the country's industrial base and technological edge, favoring global investors over U.S. manufacturers, see the special report, "Why Nothing Is Made in the USA Anymore," *American Prospect*, January 2010.

30. Paul Doremus, William Keller, and Louis Paulyet, *The Myth of the Global Corporation* (Princeton, NJ: Princeton University Press, 1998). Staughton Lynd, *Living Inside Our Hope* (Ithaca, NY: Cornell University Press, 1997).

31. For discussion and sources, see *World Orders*, chap. 2.

32. James Mahon, *Mobile Capital and Latin American Development* (University Park, PA: Pennsylvania State University Press, 1996). Timothy Canova, *American University International Law Review* 14, no. 6 (1999). Santiso, *Latin America's Political Economy of the Possible*.

33. M. J. Crozier, et al., *The Crisis of Democracy*.

34. Treasury, Robert Wade, *Challenge* (January–February 2004). On the disparagement of the socioeconomic articles of the Universal Declaration of Human Rights by high officials, see *Failed States*, chap. 6. Keynes cited by Timothy Canova, *Brooklyn Law Review* 60, no. 4 (1995).

35. Barry Eichengreen, *Globalizing Capital: A History of the International Monetary System* (Princeton, NJ: Princeton University Press, 1996).

36. Atilio Boron, in Leo Panitch and Colin Leys, eds., *Socialist Register 2006: Telling the Truth* (London: Merlin Press, 2006).

37. Mark Turner, "Vox Populi," Roubini Global Economics, Latin America EconoMonitor, December 6, 2007, http://www.roubini.com/latmmonitor/514/vox-populi.

38. Paul Waldman, *Boston Globe*, September 6, 2006. On the gap between policy and opinion, and the 2004 U.S. election, see references of note 1, chap. 5, below.

Four: Latin American and Caribbean Unity

1. Stephen Zunes, *Foreign Policy in Focus*, September 18, 2008.

2. Ruigrok and van Tulder, *The Logic of International Restructuring*.

3.   Karin Lissakers, *Banks, Borrowers, and the Establishment.*

4.   John Eatwell and Lance Taylor, *Global Finance at Risk* (New York: New Press, 2000). David Felix, "Is the Drive Toward Free-Market Globalization Stalling?" *Latin American Research Review*, January 1, 1998. See also Felix, in Baker et al., *Globalization and Progressive Economic Policy.*

5.   Barry Eichengreen, "Fortifying the Financial Architecture," *Current History, Global Trends 2010*, January 2010. Peter Boone and Simon Johnson, *Financial Times*, January 19, 2010.

6.   Now largely in the background after dramatic empirical refutation in 2007–08, though serious deficiencies were long known. See, for example, David Felix, "The Past as Future? The Contribution of Financial Globalization to the Current Crisis of Neo-Liberalism as a Development Strategy," Political Economy Research Institute, http://www.peri.umass.edu/fileadmin/pdf/working_papers/working_papers_51-100/WP69.pdf, 2003, bringing up the important work of Hyman Minsky on market inefficiencies, now gaining deserved if belated attention.

7.   Michael Kranish, *Boston Globe*, December 21, 2009. Virtually the only report. See below, pp. 226f.

8.   Eric Dash, *New York Times*, June 10, 2009.

9.   Theo Francis and Peter Coy, "No Big Fix for Global Finance," *Business Week*, September 9, 2009. David Cho, "Banks 'Too Big to Fail' Have Grown Even Bigger; Behemoths Born of the Bailout Reduce Consumer Choice, Tempt Corporate Moral Hazard," *Washington Post*, August 28, 2009. Martin Wolf, *Financial Times*, September 15, 2009.

10. "Fewer American See Solid Evidence of Global Warming," Pew survey reports, October 22, 2009, http://people-press.org/report/556/.

11. Clifford Krauss and Jad Mouawad, *New York Times*, August 19, 2009; John Carey, *Business Week*, September 8, 2009.

12. Alison Vekshin and Dawn Kopecki, *Bloomberg Business Week*, January 11, 2010.

13. Gretchen Morgenson, *New York Times*, September 14, 2009.

14. Michael J. Moore and Jamie McGee, "Wall Street Firms Will Revert to Pre-Crisis Model, Cohen Says," Bloomberg, May 5, 2009; http://www.bloomberg.com/apps/news?pid=20601109&sid=aye5Fzy0L_ss.

15. Peter Ford, "China's Green Leap Forward," *Christian Science Monitor*, August 10, 2009, http://www.csmonitor.com/Innovation/Energy/2009/0810/china-s-green-leap-forward. Martin Wolf, "Wheel of Fortune Turns as China Outdoes West," *Financial Times*, September 14, 2009.

16. Eva Vergara, Associated Press, September 16, 2008, http://www.washingtontimes.com/news/2008/sep/16/summit-of-leaders-aims-to-end-crisis-in-bolivia/.

17. Dan Keane, Associated Press, December 9, 2006.

18. Richard M. Nixon, Memorandum, http://cryptome.org/chile-plot.htm, National Security Archive. Democracy promotion, see p. 45.

19. Kristin Bushby, *Washington Report on the Hemisphere*, Council on Hemispheric Affairs, August 19, 2009. See note 49, chap. 2.

20. Mark Weisbrot, "Hondurans Resist Coup, Will Need Help from Other Countries," *Guardian*, July 8, 2009, http://www.cepr.net/index.php/op-eds-&-columns/op-eds-&-columns/hondurans-resist-coup-will-need-help-from-other-countries/.

Five: "Good News," Iraq and Beyond

1.   Benjamin Page with Marshall Bouton, *The Foreign Policy Disconnect* (Chicago: University of Chicago Press, 2006). For many crucial examples, see *Failed States*. See also Jacobs and Page, *American Political Science Review*, February 2005.

2.   Cited by David Foglesong, *America's Secret War Against Bolshevism* (Chapel Hill, NC: University of North Carolina Press, 1995).

3.   On these matters see my *Rethinking Camelot* (Cambridge, MA: South End Press, 1993). Much more material has appeared since, but while adding some interesting nuances, it leaves the basic picture intact.

4.   In retrospect, Kennedy-Johnson national security adviser McGeorge Bundy reflected that the U.S. war could have been wound down by late 1965, after the Suharto coup protected Indonesia from contagion, killing perhaps a million people, mostly landless peasants, destroying the major mass-based political party and so averting the threat of democracy, and opening up the country's rich resources to Western investors. By then South Vietnam had been largely destroyed, as Fall had described. Cited by David Fromkin and James Chace, *Foreign Affairs*, Spring 1985.

5.   See *Rethinking Camelot* for details.

6.   Ibid.

7.   Ibid.

8.   Arthur Schlesinger, *Los Angeles Times*, March 23, 2003. I found no mention.

9.   Opinion Research Business, September 2007, www.opinion.co.uk/newsroom.aspx.

10.   Gardner, *Last Chance*, 61ff. For illuminating inquiry into the roots of the sectarian violence, and much else, see Steele, *Defeat*.

11.   Nir Rosen, *Current History*, December 2007.

12.   Timothy Williams, *New York Times*, August 15, 2009. On the background of Iraq's oil law, and the threats to the economy as it has evolved under the occupation, see Kamil Mahdi, "Iraq's Oil Law: Parsing the Fine Print," *World Policy Journal*, Summer 2007. As matters have evolved, U.S. energy corporations have not gained anything like the privileges that Washington had anticipated as late as early 2008. See below, p. 140.

13.   Gary Milhollin testimony, *United States Export Policy Toward Iraq Prior to Iraq's Invasion of Kuwait, Hearing Before the Committee on Banking, Housing, and Urban Affairs*, U.S. Senate, 102nd, October 27, 1992. Bush's fawning mission, Miron Rezun, *Saddam Hussein's Gulf Wars* (Westport, CT: Praeger Publishers, 1992).

14.   Denis Halliday, "Responsibility to Protect," *Development Dialogue* 53 (November 2009).

15.   Hans Von Sponeck, *A Different Kind of War: The UN Sanctions Regime in Iraq* (New York, Oxford: Berghahn Books, 2006).

16.   For one particularly striking illustration, see note 15, chap. 11, below.

17.   Steele, *Defeat*. On the wanton "cultural destruction of Iraq," including its intellectual class and priceless monuments of the origins of modern civilization, a "shameful, immoral and illegal chapter in modern history" that flows from a commitment to "'ending states' as a policy objective," see Raymond Baker et al., *Cultural Cleansing in Iraq*.

18.   Karen DeYoung, *Washington Post*, December 19, 2007.

19. Quoted in Stephen Fidler, *Financial Times*, August 20, 2007.

20. PRNewswire–USNewswire, Washington, January 28, 2008.

21. Bergen and Cruickshank, "The Iraq Effect."

22. James Glanz, *New York Times*, January 16, 2008.

23. Gardner, *Last Chance*, for review of what followed.

24. C. J. Chivers, *New York Times*, September 11, 2007.

25. Michael Gordon, *New York Times*, January 20, 2008. Mark Curtis, *Unpeople: Britain's Secret Human Rights Abuses* (London: Vintage Books, 2004).

26. Seib, *Wall Street Journal*, February 12, 2008.

27. Associated Press, December 21, 2007, *Boston Globe*, four sentences. The final two are: "US officials downplayed the issue. 'We prefer to look to the future,' said a U.S. Embassy spokesman." Panamanian courts and United States, Mark Lacey, *New York Times*, November 28, 2007. "The next few days Iraq will withdraw [putting] his puppet in. Everyone in the Arab world will be happy," Joint Chiefs of Staff Chairman Colin Powell anticipated at a high-level meeting immediately after Saddam's invasion of Kuwait (Military correspondents Michael Gordon and Bernard Trainor, *New York Times*, October 23, 1994, excerpt from their forthcoming *The General's War* [Boston: Little, Brown & Co., 1995]). Basically what happened in Panama, except that Latin Americans were infuriated, not happy. For details on the invasions, and reactions here, see my *Deterring Democracy* (New York: Hill & Wang, 1992).

28. Elaine Sciolino, *New York Times*, November 30, 2007.

29. "Public Opinion in Iran and America on Key International Issues," poll, World Public Opinion.org, January 24, 2007, http://www.worldpublicopinion.org/pipa/pdf/jan07/Iran_Jan07_rpt.pdf.

30. Ibid. Also "A Majority of Americans Reject Military Threats in Favor of Diplomacy with Iran," survey, World Public Opinion.org, December 7, 2006, http://www.worldpublicopinion.org/pipa/articles/brunitedstatescanadara/286.php.

31. On NATO expansion, the nature of the "pledge," and the context, see chap. 12, below. On Obama's reconfiguration of the missile defense system, see p. 199. See also pp. 172–73. On strong and long-standing popular preference for normalization of relations with Cuba, see note 27, chap. 2.

32. *Arms Control Today*, January/February 2008.

33. Helene Cooper, *New York Times*, January 19, 2008. Kevin Hall, McClatchy Newspapers, February 16, 2008.

34. Bruce Cumings, *Le Monde diplomatique*, October 2007. See also Leon Sigal, *Current History*, November 2006. See my *Interventions* (San Francisco: City Lights, 2007), for discussion.

35. David Sanger and William Broad, *New York Times*, March 1, 2007.

36. Seymour Hersh, *New Yorker*, February 11, 2008.

37. The conclusion, based on on-site inspection by Harvard nuclear physicist Richard Wilson after the bombing and by Iraqi defectors, has been confirmed by Wayne White, Iraq analyst for State Department intelligence at the time, with access to a rich body of evidence: *Middle East Policy*, Fall 2008.

38. Sigal, *Current History*.

39. "Declaration of Principles for a Long-Term Relationship of Cooperation and Friend-

ship Between the Republic of Iraq and the United States of America, White House news release, November 26, 2007, http://georgewbush-whitehouse.archives.gov /news/releases/2007/11/20071126-11.html.

40. Charlie Savage, *Boston Globe*, January 30, 2008. Thom Shanker and Steven Lee Myers, *New York Times*, January 25, 2008.

41. *Pakistani Public Opinion on Democracy, Islamist Militancy, and Relations with the U.S.*, World Public Opinion.org and U.S. Institute for Peace, January 7, 2008.

42. *Newsweek*, October 18, 2001.

43. Ian James, Associated Press, December 31, 2007. Other wire services.

Six: Free Elections, Good News and Bad

1.   Thomas Friedman, op-ed, *New York Times*, June 10, 2009. Elliott Abrams, op-ed, *New York Times*, June 12, 2009. On the vote, and the large-scale efforts to swing the election to the March 14 coalition, see Assaf Kfoury, "The Fourth Estate in the Service of Power: Media Coverage of the Middle East," Znet, December 6, 2009, www.zcommunications.org/znet/viewArticle/23293.

2.   Ibid.

3.   Cam Simpson, *Wall Street Journal*, February 8, 2009.

4.   See *Perilous Power*, Epilogue, note 29, for review.

5.   Thomas Friedman, *New York Times*, January 14, 2009. On Israeli border violations, see Israeli strategic analyst Zeev Maoz, "The War of Double Standards," author's translation from *Haaretz*, July 24, 2006.

6.   David Shipler, *New York Times*, November 25, 1983; also January 26, 1984. Human Rights Watch, *Israel: Without Status or Protection: Lebanese Detainees in Israel* 9, no. 11 (October 1997). See my "Exterminate All the Brutes," January 2009 (revised June 6, 2009), at http://www.chomsky.info/articles/20090119.htm, for discussion and sources, here and below. For much more extensive discussion of the Gaza attack, see Norman Finkelstein, *"This Time We Went Too Far": Truth and Consequences of the Gaza Invasion* (New York: O/R Books, 2010).

7.   Al Mezan press release, "IOF Kidnaps Five Palestinian Children in North Gaza," September 7, 2009. Reference 74/2009, http://www.mezan.org/en/details.php?id=9028 &ddname=&id_dept=9. The media search covered a week.

8.   David Rose, "The Gaza Bombshell," *Vanity Fair*, April 2008. Norman Olsen and Matthew Olsen, op-ed, *Christian Science Monitor*, January 12, 2009.

9.   For a review of the grisly record, and the current state of the programs to block any hope of decent survival for the Palestinians, see Sara Roy, Introduction, *The Gaza Strip: The Political Economy of De-development* (Beirut, Washington, DC: Institute for Palestine Studies, 2010), third edition.

10. "Irish Nobel Peace Laureate Mairead Maguire Shot with Rubber Bullet by Israeli Military at Nonviolent Protest," Democracy Now.org, April 23, 2007, http://www .democracynow.org/article.pl?sid=07/04/23/1350224, April 23, 2007.

11. Gershom Gorenberg, *The Accidental Empire* (New York: Times Books, 2006). On the carefully planned and systematic execution of the project, and the leading role

of Peres and others honored in the West as "moderates" and "peacemakers," see Idith Zertal and Akiva Eldar, *Lords of the Land* (New York: Nation Books, 2007); also on the shameful behavior of the courts, along with Moshe Negbi, *Kisdom Hayinu* (Jerusalem: Keter Publishing House, 2004, Hebrew), the most prominent legal commentator in the Israeli media. For quotes from his harrowing account of what passes for law in Israel, and from other leading Israeli analysts who bring forth similar material, see *Failed States*. Ibid. on the ICJ and Buergenthal.

12. See references of note 16, this chapter.

13. Jeremy Bowen, "Bowen Diary: The Days Before War," BBC News, January 10, 2009, http://news.bbc.co.uk/2/hi/middle_east/7822048.stm.

14. Regev interviewed by David Fuller, Channel 4, UK, http://www.youtube.com/watch?v=N6e-elrgYL0. Editorial, *The Other Israel*, Holon Israel, December–January 2008–9.

15. Rory McCarthy, *Guardian*, November 5, 2008.

16. Sara Roy, *London Review of Books*, January 1, 2009; *Christian Science Monitor*, January 2, 2009. Physicians for Human Rights–Israel, Update December 12, 2008, http://www.phr.org.il/phr/files/articlefile_1230045569593.doc.

17. Gareth Porter, "Israel Rejected Hamas Ceasefire Offer in December," Inter Press Service, January 9, 2009, http://www.ipsnews.net/print.asp?idnews=45350. See also Peter Beaumont, *Observer*, March 1, 2009.

18. Akiva Eldar, "White Flag, Black Flag," *Haaretz*, January 28, 2009, http://www.haaretz.com/hasen/spages/1052621.html.

19. David Remnick, *New Yorker*, January 12, 2009.

20. See my *Fateful Triangle* (Cambridge, MA: South End Press, 1983; updated 2009), 201ff. *Pirates and Emperors,* 56f.

21. Stephen Lee Myers, *New York Times*, January 4, 2009.

22. In Hebrew, there are two words for "propaganda": "ta'amulah," which is the propaganda of others, and "hasbara" ("explanation"), for Israeli propaganda. The tacit assumption is that since we are always right, it is only necessary to explain to the ignorant outsiders. That is standard state practice, for example, Britain's "Ministry of Information" a century ago, which was dedicated to "informing" American intellectuals of the reasons they should support Britain during World War I—succeeding brilliantly—and Wilson's "Committee on Public Information," targeting the whole population, also with outstanding success. For some discussion, see *Deterring Democracy.*

23. Stephen Erlanger, *New York Times*, January 31, 2008.

24. Moshe Negbi, *Kisdom Hayinu.*

25. Stephen Erlanger, *New York Times*, January 25, 2008.

26. *Israel National News*, April 27, 2007.

27. Livni quoted by Scott Wilson, *Washington Post*, December 20, 2007.

28. Michael Walzer, in Irving Howe and Carl Gershman, eds., *Israel, Arabs, and the Middle East* (New York: Quadrangle Press, 1972). In the context of discussion of Israel and its Palestinian population, Walzer writes that the process of nation-building can be difficult for those "marginal to the nation," and that sometimes the "roughness… can only be smoothed by helping people to leave who have to leave." Ethan Bronner, *New York Times*, February 12, 2009.

29. Aluf Benn, *Washington Post*, August 14, 2005.

30. Quoted in Yoav Stern, *Haaretz*, May 1, 2006.

31. Rakefet, Scott Wilson, *Washington Post*, a very rare report. On the laws, see my *Towards a New Cold War* (New York: Pantheon, 1982), and for a much more extensive study, Walter Lehn and Uri Davis, *The Jewish National Fund* (New York: Kegan Paul International, 1988).

32. Jonathan Liss, *Haaretz*, January 3, 2010. Golan, "No entry for Arabs," *Haaretz*, January 13, 2010.

33. Jonathan Lis, *Haaretz*, January 2, 2010.

34. See below, pp. 179f.

35. Yossi Beilin, *Mehiro shel Ihud* (Tel Aviv: Revivim, 1985), 42, 147; the primary source for Israeli cabinet records under the Labor coalition, 1967–77. Dayan's analogy, Gorenberg, *Accidental Empire*, 81–2. For more on these matters, see *Failed States*, chap. 5; my *Middle East Illusions* (Lanham, MD: Rowman and Littlefield, 2003), chap. 6. *Herald* cited by James Bradley, *The Imperial Cruise* (New York: Little, Brown & Co., 2009), 63.

36. Sometimes called a "one-state solution," though there clearly are two groups, each entitled to respect for their own cultural mix, language, and identity.

37. See *Failed States*, 193ff.

38. For an illustration, see economist Sever Plocker ("A Thorn in the World's Side," *Yediot*, November 3, 1999; http://www.ynetnews.com/articles/0,7340,L-3798761 ,00.html), describing with despair how he must cancel a lecture in Oxford because the anti-Israel atmosphere there is so extreme that he would be treated as a leper. Far from true, but illustrative of a spreading sense of injured innocence.

39. Ryan Irwin, "A Wind of Change?" *Diplomatic History*, November 2009.

40. United Nations Inter-Agency Task Force, Africa Recovery Programme/Economic Commission for Africa, *South African Destabilization: The Economic Cost of Frontline Resistance to Apartheid* (New York: United Nations, 1989), 13, cited by Merle Bowen, *Fletcher Forum*, Winter 1991. ANC, Joseba Zulaika, and William Douglass, *Terror and Taboo* (London, New York: Routledge, 1996), 12. On expansion of U.S. trade with South Africa after Congress imposed sanctions in 1985, see Gay McDougall, Richard Knight, in Robert Edgar, ed., *Sanctioning Apartheid* (Trenton, NJ: Africa World Press, 1990). Richard Garfield, Julia Devin, and Joy Fausey, "The Health Impact of Economic Sanctions," *Bulletin of the New York Academy of Medicine* 72, no. 2 (Winter 1995). For review of BDS programs targeting the Israeli occupation, see John Pilger, Znet, January 16, 2010.

Seven: Century's Challenges

1. Lee Butler, "At the End of the Journey: The Risks of Cold War Thinking in a New Era," *International Affairs* 82, no. 4 (June 22, 2006).

2. Hans Kristensen, Appendix 2 of *Nuclear Futures: Proliferation of Weapons of Mass Destruction and U.S. Nuclear Strategy*, British American Security Information Council (BASIC), Basic Research Report 98, no. 2 (March 1998). For extensive

quotes, see *New Military Humanism*, chap. 6.

3. Brahma Chellaney, *International Herald Tribune*, May 7, 1996.

4. Peter Sand, *ASIL [American Society of International Law] Insight* 13, no. 12 (August 28, 2009). On the sordid record, see David Vine, *Island of Shame* (Princeton, NJ: Princeton University Press, 2009). Cole Harvey, *Arms Control Today*, September 2009, journal of the Arms Control Association.

5. Press release (COMSUBPAC Pearl Harbor, NNS 091203-01). I am indebted to Peter Sand for the document.

6. See note 29, chap. 5. These poll results are from January 2007. A huge government-media propaganda blitz since on Iran may have changed perceptions.

7. Cited by Frank Costigliola, in Thomas Paterson, ed., *Kennedy's Quest for Victory* (New York: Oxford University Press, 1989).

8. World Public Opinion.org, surveys, January 18–27, 2008, http://www.worldpublic opinion.org/pipa/pdf/mar08/USGov_Mar08_quaire.pdf. Zeev Maoz, *Defending the Holy Land* (Ann Arbor, MI: University of Michigan Press, 2006). Abrahamian, in David Barsamian, ed., *Targeting Iran* (San Francisco: City Lights Books, 2005).

9. Chas Freeman, *Middle East Policy*, Spring 2008.

10. See references of note 23, chap. 2.

11. NATO, see chap. 12. NWFZ, Michael McGwire, *International Affairs*, 81, no. 1 (2005).

12. Union of Concerned Scientists, "U.S. Attempt to Shoot Down Satellite Undermines Efforts to Ban Space Weapons, Reduces U.S. Security, Science Group Says," press release, February 20, 2008, http://www.ucsusa.org/news/press_release/us-attempt-to-shoot-down-0098.html. John Steinbruner and Nancy Gallagher, *Daedalus*, Summer 2004.

13. Andrew Bacevich, *National Interest*, Summer 2001; Lawrence Kaplan, *New Republic*, March 12, 2001. RAND cited by Kaplan, emphasis in original. For more on the understanding that missile defense is essentially a first-strike weapon, see *Hegemony or Survival*, chap. 9.

14. George Lewis and Theodore Postol, *Arms Control Today*, October 2007.

15. Quoted in Olivier Zajec, *Le Monde diplomatique*, April 2008.

16. Shoup and Minter, *Imperial Brain Trust*. See Gibbs, *First Do No Harm*, on these considerations and specifically their role in the bombing of Serbia in 1999. See above, p. 53 and note 23, chap. 2.

17. According to military/strategic analyst Melvin Goodman of the Center for International Policy, the United States is spending more than the rest of the world combined on its military, intelligence, and homeland security, and is responsible for 70 percent of global arms sales. Truthout, October 20, 2009.

18. John McGlynn, "The US Declaration of War on Iran," *Japan Focus*, March 20, 2008, http://japanfocus.org/-John-McGlynn/2707.

19. Klaus Naumann, John Shalikashvili, et al., *Towards a Grand Strategy for an Uncertain World: Renewing the Transatlantic Partnership*, (Center for Strategic & International Studies, Noaber Foundation), 2007, http://www.worldsecuritynetwork.com /documents/3eproefGrandStrat(b).pdf.

20. HDI, http://en.wikipedia.org/wiki/List_of_countries_by_Human_Development

_Index. Maurice Guernier, *An-Nahar Arab Report and Memo*, Beirut, April 17, 1978. For further quotes see *Towards a New Cold War*.

Eight: Turning Point?

1.   Dan Fromkin, *Washington Post*, May 29, 2009.
2.   Agence France-Presse, May 16, 2009.
3.   Akiva Eldar, *Haaretz*, June 1, 2009.
4.   See chap. 10, below.
5.   The State of Israel, Likud Party Platform, 1999, http://www.knesset.gov.il/elections /knesset15/elikud_m.htm. David Bar-Illan, director of Communications and Policy Planning in the office of the prime minister, interview, *Palestine-Israel Journal*, Summer/Autumn 1996.
6.   Amnon Barzilai, *Haaretz*, October 24, 1995. For more detail, *World Orders*, Epilogue.
7.   For details, see *Deterring Democracy*, Afterword. For general review of the diplomatic and military history, see Norman Finkelstein, *Image and Reality of the Israel-Palestine Conflict* (London: Verso, 2003); Maoz, *Defending the Holy Land*. Also *Hegemony or Survival* and *Failed States*.
8.   Ibid., for review and sources.
9.   Jeffrey Goldberg, *New York Times*, May 24, 2009.
10.   "Chronicle of Annexation Known from the Outset," Bimkom, B'Tselem, December 2009, Hebrew. Barak cited from Amos Harel, *Haaretz*, February 1, 2009, with endorsement by Tzipi Livni and Binyamin Netanyahu, reiterating a long-standing national consensus.
11.   World Bank, BBC, May 20, 2009. Uri Misgav, *Yediot* Friday Political Supplement, January 22, 2008.
12.   Stephen Zunes, *Foreign Policy in Focus*, March 4, 2009.
13.   All of this was clear enough from the website for his presidential campaign. See *Perilous Power*, Epilogue.
14.   Amira Hass, "An Israeli Achievement," BitterLemons.org, April 20, 2009, http://www.bitterlemons.org/previous/bl200409ed15.html#isr2.
15.   Sara Roy, *Harvard Crimson*, June 2, 2009. For extensive review of the ugly details, see Roy's "Before Gaza, After Gaza: Examining the New Reality in Israel/Palestine," to appear in *Palestine & the Palestinians Today*, Center for Contemporary Arab Studies, Georgetown University. Abbreviated version of introduction to third edition of Roy, *Gaza Strip*.
16.   See above, pp. 150f., and sources cited in note 16, chap. 6.
17.   Peter Beaumont, *Guardian*, May 27, 2009.
18.   *Platt's Commodity News*, February 3, 16, 2009.
19.   For sources, and more on Evans's role in this regard, see *Year 501*, chap. 4; *Powers and Prospects*, chaps. 7, 8. Also Australian Southeast Asian specialist and former intelligence officer Clinton Fernandes's review of Evans's record, 2009, MS.
20.   International Commission on Intervention and State Sovereignty, Gareth Evans and Mohamed Sahnoun, Co-chairs, *The Responsibility to Protect: Report of the*

ICISS (Ottawa, Canada: IDRC Books, December 2001). *Economist*, July 23, 2009. See my "Human Rights in the New Millennium," talk at London School of Economics (October 29, 2009), http://www.chomsky.info/talks/20091029.htm; *Z Magazine*, January 2010; www.chomsky.info. Evans-Alatas photo there and at Edward Herman and David Peterson, "The Responsibility to Protest, the International Ciminal Court, and *Foreign Policy in Focus*," MRZine, August 24, 2009, http://mrzine.monthlyreview.org/hp240809.html. On the various versions of R2P and the principles that govern its application, and the unique right of forceful intervention assigned to NATO in the Evans Commission Report but crucially not in the 2005 UN Summit declaration on R2P, see my "The Responsibility to Protect," UN General Assembly, New York, July 23, 2009, and "Human Rights in the New Millennium." For one of many current illustrations of severe misinterpretations, see Sarah Sewall, Director of the Carr Center's National Security and Human Rights Program at the Harvard University Kennedy School of Government, *Boston Review*, September–October 2009. Apart from misinterpretation of R2P, Sewall writes that "NATO's 1999 bombing campaign to stop Serbian persecution of Kosovars," though recognized to be illegal under international law, "was nonetheless forgiven, or at least tolerated, largely on moral grounds." Putting aside the factual claim, uncritically repeating government propaganda that is flatly refuted by the rich record of official documents, it was neither forgiven, nor tolerated, but rather bitterly condemned by the South, repeatedly and forcefully. Furthermore, like others at the Carr Center, Sewall is concerned only with Washington's failure to prevent crimes, while entirely ignoring the shameful simultaneous U.S. record of perpetrating terrible crimes while Western intellectuals bask in self-praise for their "principles and values," "altruism," "nobility," etc. See *New Military Humanism, A New Generation Draws the Line*, Gibbs, *First Do No Harm*.

21. Avi Issacharoff, *Haaretz*, May 6, 2009. Associated Press, May 6, 2009; Reuters, May 7, 2009. For analysis of the harsh and deteriorioating conditions, see Nadim Kawach, International Solidarity Movement, January 17, 2010, http://palsolidarity.org/2010/01/10761.

22. Yisrael Katz, *Haaretz*, May 31, 2009.

23. The first revelation to the general public of Israel's U.S.-backed rejection of the "road map"—it was known and discussed in activist circles—is in Jimmy Carter's book *Palestine: Peace Not Apartheid* (New York: Simon & Schuster, 2006). The "reservations" are given in an appendix. The book aroused a storm of protest. As far as I could determine, this important section—the one revelation new to the general informed public—was not mentioned. There were great efforts to find trivial errors, but the one serious error was also ignored: Carter's repetition of the conventional myth that Israel's 1982 invasion of Lebanon was in defense against PLO rockets, already discussed. See above, pp. 153–54, and note 21, chap. 6.

24. *Hadashot*, October 8, 1993; Yair Fidel, *Hadashot Supplement*, October 29, 1993.

25. Helene Cooper, *New York Times*, June 1, 2009.

26. Isabel Kirshner, *New York Times*, June 2, 2009.

27. Akiva Eldar, *Haaretz*, June 2, 2009.

28. Jackson Diehl, *Washington Post*, May 29, 2009.

29. Elliott Abrams, *Washington Post*, April 8, 2009.

30. Karen DeYoung and Howard Schneider, *Washington Post*, November 1, 2009.

31. Text at http://www.haaretz.com/hasen/pages/ShArt.jhtml?itemNo=351461.

32. Ed Hornick, "Obama Looks to Reach the Soul of the Muslim World," CNN, June 3, 2009, http://edition.cnn.com/2009/POLITICS/06/03/obama.muslim.outreach/. Thomas Friedman, *New York Times*, June 3, 2009.

33. Quoted in Jeff Zeleyna and Michael Slackman, *New York Times*, June 4, 2009.

34. Yolande Knell, Heba Saleh, and Roula Khalaf, *Financial Times Special Report on Egypt*, December 17, 2009. On the timid gestures about democracy in Egypt under Bush, see *Failed States*.

35. Associated Press, January 5, 2010.

36. Douglas Little, "Cold War and Covert Action," *Middle East Journal*, Winter 1990. NSC 5801/1, January 24, 1958. See also Salim Yaqub, "Imperious Doctrines: U.S.-Arab Relations from Dwight D. Eisenhower to George W. Bush," *Diplomatic History* 26, no. 4 (Fall 2002) and his *Containing Arab Nationalism: The Eisenhower Doctrine and the Middle East* (Chapel Hill, NC: University of North Carolina Press, 2004).

37. For sources, and further discussion of U.S. support for Arab tyrannies and the (understood) consequences, see *Hegemony or Survival*, chaps. 3, 8 and *Failed States*, chap. 5. Also Gardner, *Last Chance*, and many other sources.

38. Ibid. 29, xix. Fawaz Gerges, *Journey of the Jihadist* (Orlando: Harcourt Press, 2006), 210ff. On the reactions of moderate Islamists in Egypt and elsewhere, see Raymond Baker, *Islam without Fear* (Cambridge, MA: Harvard University Press, 2003), 266f. Michael Scheuer, *Imperial Hubris: Why the West Is Losing the War on Terror* (Dulles, VA: Brassey's Inc., 2004); at the time anonymous.

39. Jeffrey Smith and Joby Warrick, *Washington Post*, May 28, 2009.

40. Indian nuclear weapons, James Lamont and James Blitz, *Financial Times*, September 27, 2009. IAEA-Israel, wire services, *La Jornada* (Mexico), September 19, 2009; Mark Weiss, *Irish Times*, September 19, 2009, and AP, *Washington Times*, September 19, 2009 (the only English-language press reports). Obama-Israel, Eli Lake, *Washington Times*, October 2, 2009. Agency safeguards, States News Service, September 19, 2009, Associated Press, *Washington Times*, September 19, 2009. White House-India, Indo-Asian News Service, September 26, 2009.

41. *Daily Mail* (London), October 13, 2009; Mitch Potter, *Toronto Star*, October 13, 2009; Jim Wolf, Reuters, August 27, 2009; Tony Capaccio, Bloomberg, July 31, 2009.

42. Avner Cohen and George Perkovich, "Proliferation Analysis," Carnegie Endowment, May 14, 2009, http://www.carnegieendowment.org/publications/index.cfm?fa=view&id=23124.

43. Julian Borger, *Guardian*, May 6, 2009. Reuters, May 21, 2009. "US Keeps Nuclear 'Don't Ask, Don't Tell' - Israel Aide," May 21, 2009, http://www.reuters.com/article/latestCrisis/idUSLL942309. Institute for Public Accuracy, "Israeli Whistleblower Vanunu on Mideast Nukes," news release, September 17, 2004, http://www.accuracy.org/newsrelease.php?articleId=222.

44. White, *Middle East Policy*, Fall 2008. See note 37, chap. 5, above.

45. Martin van Creveld, *International Herald Tribune*, August 21, 2004. David Kay,

"The Iranian Fallout," *National Interest*, September/October 2008.

46. Reuel Marc Gerecht, in Robert Kagan and William Kristol, eds., *Present Dangers: Crisis and Opportunity in American Foreign and Defense Policy* (San Francisco: Encounter Books, 2000).

47. Leonard Weiss, *Middle East Policy*, Fall 2009. He mentions an authentic threat not to Israel but to the Zionist project: that irrational fears might induce people to emigrate. See Ofri Ilani, *Haaretz*, July 21, 2009, reporting poll findings that "1 in 4 Israelis would consider leaving country if Iran gets nukes."

48. Judy Dempsey, *New York Times*, January 22, 2010. Nicholas Kulish and Ellen Barry, *New York Times*, February 5, 2010; Reuters, "Russia Says Concerned at Romania Hosting U.S. Missiles," February 5, 2010. Ellen Barry, *New York Times*, February 6, 10, 2010. The Russian concerns are two: first that they were not consulted, and second that a second generation of interceptors scheduled for 2018 might threaten the Russian deterrent, and the United States accepts no obligation to provide data about the systems. Brzezinski cited by Gerald Posner, "How Obama Flubbed His Missile Message," Daily Beast, September 18, 2009, http://www.thedailybeast.com/blogs-and-stories/2009-09-18/how-obama-flubbed-his-missile-message/.

49. Aluf Benn and Amos Harel, *Haaretz*, September 14, 2008; along with the missiles, the United States delivered "smart bombs" ("bunker busters"), obviously intended as a threat to Iran. Reuters, March 7; *Haaretz* News Service, July 14, 2009. David Sanger and Eric Schmitt, "U.S. Speeding Up Missile Defenses in Persian Gulf," *New York Times*, January 30, 2010.

50. Phil Stewart, "Petraeus Says Strike on Iran Could Spark Nationalism," Reuters, February 3, 2010, http://www.reuters.com/article/idUSTRE6123TN20100203.

51. John Kerry, "Restoring Leadership in the Middle East," speech at Brookings Institution (March 4, 2009), http://www.brookings.edu/~/media/Files/events/2009/0304_leadership/20090304_kerry.pdf.

52. Gideon Levy, *Haaretz*, June 26, 2009. See the admiring accounts by Ethan Bronner, *New York Times*, February 27, 2009, and Karin Laub, Associated Press, June 27, 2009. On Jordanian instructors, see also Avi Issacharoff, *Haaretz*, April 8, 2009.

53. Charles Levinson, "Palestinian Support Wanes for American-Trained Forces," *Wall Street Journal*, http://online.wsj.com/article/SB125547035200183335.html.

54. A leading specialist, anonymous. On CIA collaboration with Palestinian forces, including those engaged in torture, see Ian Cobain, *Guardian*, December 17, 2009.

55. See p. 23, above.

56. See note 44, chap. 2.

57. Shai Gal, http://www.mako.co.il/finances-hitech/tech/Articled2f62cb466441 21006.htm (Hebrew), May 15, 2009. Mako is a news and entertainment portal that works in close cooperation with Israel's Channel 2 TV.

58. Felix Frisch, "No IDF Orders—Rafael Moving to US; the Move Will Enable the IDF to Use U.S. Aid to Buy Rafael Products," *Globes* (Israeli business journal), March 17, 2004. Anshel Feffer, *Haaretz*, February 2, 2009 (Hebrew), http://www.haaretz.co.il/hasite/spages/1062977.html.

59. Amos Harel, *Haaretz*, January 10, 2010.

60. See "Exterminate All the Brutes."

Nine: Elections 2008:
Hope Confronts the Real World

1.   World Public Opinion.org, surveys, January 18–27, 2008, http://www.world public
     opinion.org/pipa/pdf/mar08/USGov_Mar08_quaire.pdf, survey taken January 2008.
     See note 8, chap. 7.
2.   Editorial comment by Steve Charnovitz, "The ILO Convention on Freedom of As-
     sociation and Its Future in the United States," *American Journal of International
     Law* 102 (2008): 90–107.
3.   Greg Shaw, "Changes in Public Opinion and the American Welfare State," *Political
     Science Quarterly* 124, no. 4 (Winter 2009–2010).
4.   On the remarkable scale of these campaigns in the early post–WWII years, see Eliz-
     abeth Fones-Wolf, *Selling Free Enterprise* (Urbana, IL: University of Illinois Press,
     1994); and more generally, the pioneering study by Alex Carey, *Taking the Risks Out
     of Democracy* (Urbana, IL: University of Illinois Press, 1995), among other impor-
     tant investigations.
5.   Edward Luce and Andrew Ward, *Financial Times*, September 3, 2008. "Campaign
     Diary," *Financial Times*, October 28, 2008.
6.   Matthew Creamer, "Obama Wins! … Ad Age's Marketer of the Year," AdAge.com,
     October 17, 2008.
7.   Andrew Edgecliffe-Johnson, *Financial Times*, November 25, 2008.
8.   Dean Baker, "Republicans Complain Obama Will 'Bury' Our Children with Rea-
     gan Era Debt Burdens," Beat the Press, August 31, 2009. See pp. 88–89, above, on
     Reaganite statist enthusiasm.
9.   "Money Wins Presidency and 9 of 10 Congressional Races in Priciest U.S. Election
     Ever," Open Secrets.org, November 5, 2008, http://www.opensecrets.org/news/2008
     /11/money-wins-white-house-and.html.
10. Alan Greenspan, testimony, Senate Banking Committee, February 1997.
11. John Hughes, *Christian Science Monitor*, November 6. Hunt, Daniel, quoted by Ethan
     Bronner, *New York Times*, November 5. Durandin, quoted by Robert Marquand,
     Christian Science Monitor, November 17, 2008.
12. Scott Helman, *Boston Globe*, November 9. Christopher Cooper, *Wall Street Journal*,
     November 8, 2008.
13. Peter Wallsten and Tom Hamburger, *Los Angeles Times*, November 14, 2008.
14. Joshua Partlow, *Washington Post*, October 20, 2008. Carlos Valdez, Associated Press,
     November 2, 2008.
15. *El Universal*, October 21, 2009; Alfredo Valadez Rodríguez, *La Jornada*, September 22,
     2009; Doris Gómora and Francisco Gómez, "Intaca Estructura Financiera del Narco,"
     El Universal, November 15, 2009, http://www.eluniversal.com.mx/notas/640031.html,
     reporting that 78 percent of business sectors are infiltrated by narcotrafficking while
     the government does not report a single case of dismantling of these structures.
16. Andean Information Network, September 16, 2009. Ron Brooks, chair of NNOAC,
     congressional testimony, http://74.125.113.132/search?q=cache:2nTw8wktJ7IJ
     :www.natlnarc.org/papers/Ron%2520Brooks%2520-Mexico%2520Decertification
     .doc+decertification+drugs&cd=4&hl=en&ct=clnk&gl=us&client=firefox-a.

17. On Biden's voting record, see U.S. Congress Votes Database, *Washington Post* online, http://projects.washingtonpost.com/congress/members/b000444/key-votes/.

18. Lindsay Renick Mayer, "Obama's Pick for Chief of Staff Tops Recipients of Wall Street Money," Open Secrets.org, Center for Responsive Politics, November 5, 2008, http://www.opensecrets.org/news/2008/11/obamas-pick-for-chief-of-staff.html.

19. Jason Riley, *Wall Street Journal*, November 8, 2008.

20. Steve Early, "Unions to Obama: Don't Abandon Us," *Boston Globe*, December 6, 2008.

21. Stephen Zunes, "Obama's Caterpillar Visit a Thumb in the Eye for Human Rights Activists," Alternet, February 14, 2009, http://www.alternet.org/story/126994.

22. Peter Kendall and Colin McMahon, *Chicago Tribune*, September 6, 7, 9, 1992.

23. See Isaac Cohen, "The Caterpillar Labor Dispute and the UAW, 1991–98" *Labor Studies Journal* 27, no. 4 (2003): 77–99; http://lsj.sagepub.com/cgi/content/abstract /27/4/77. Cohen questions the standard conclusion that the dispute was a complete debacle for the UAW, going into how the union devised methods to achieve limited gains in the following years. Sources and background, see *Year 501*, chap. 11.

24. Tim Canova, "The Legacy of the Clinton Bubble," *Dissent*, Summer 2008, http://www.dissentmagazine.org/article/?article=1229.

25. David Felix, "Asia and the Crisis of Financial Globalization," in Baker, Epstein, Pollin, eds., *Globalization and Progressive Economics*. See p. 107 above.

26. Paul Krugman, *Huffington Post*, November 24, 2008. Stiglitz, cited in Joe Nocera, *New York Times*, October 25, 2008. Matt Appuzzo, Associated Press, December 22, 2008.

27. Dean Baker, "Missing the Stock Bubble and Housing Bubble Makes You Qualified to Fix the Crisis," Beat the Press, *American Prospect* online, November 8, 2008, http://prospect.org/csnc/blogs/beat_the_press_archive?month=11&year=2008&base _name=missing_the_stock_bubble_and_h&23.

28. Tim Canova, "Change on Economy?" Institute for Public Accuracy, December 1, 2008, http://www.accuracy.org/newsrelease.php?articleId=1873.

29. Eric Lipton and Raymond Hernandez, "A Champion of Wall Street Reaps Benefits," *New York Times*, December 14, 2008.

30. Jonathan Weil, "Obama's Bailout Bunch Brings Us More of the Same," Bloomberg, November 11, 2008, http://www.bloomberg.com/apps/news?pid=20601039&sid =aNCFKvAMUQ6w.

31. Dean Baker, "Geithner at Treasury: Can He Learn?" *Guardian*, November 24, 2008, http://www.guardian.co.uk/commentisfree/cifamerica/2008/nov/24/barack-obama-timothy-geithner-treasury.

32. See p. 113, note 14, chap. 4. Simon Johnson, "The Quiet Coup," *The Atlantic*, May 2009, http://www.theatlantic.com/magazine/archive/2009/05/the-quiet-coup/7364/.

33. *New York Times*, July 15, 2009.

34. Edward Luce, *Financial Times*, December 5, 2008.

35. Henry Kissinger, *Washington Post*, December 5, 2008. Perle, Robert Dreyfuss, "Is Iran Policy Still Up for Grabs?" TomDispatch.com, December 2, 2008, http://www.tomdispatch.com/post/175009/robert_dreyfuss_is_iran_policy_still_up_for_grabs_. Warner, Peter Baker, "Obama's National Security Team, and the Clintons," *New York Times*, November 30, 2008, http://nytimes.com/2008/11/30/world/americas/30iht-transition.4.18270224.html.

36. Robert Dreyfuss, *Nation*, January 5, 2009. NATO expansion, see chap. 12 below.

37. Alan Nairn, *Nation*, September 27, 1999.

38. Akiva Eldar, *Haaretz*, December 2, 2008 (Hebrew). Dennis Ross, *The Missing Peace* (New York: Farrar, Straus and Giroux, 2004). See Norman Finkelstein, *Dennis Ross and the Peace Process* (Beirut: Institute for Palestine Studies, 2007); *Failed States*, 183–4.

39. Quoted in Jeff Zeleny, *New York Times*, November 27, 2008.

40. "Notable and Quotable," *Wall Street Journal*, November 22, 2008.

41. For a sample of polls, see *Failed States*, 225. For more extensive review, Vicente Navarro, *Why the United States Does Not Have a National Health Program* (Amityville, NY: Baywood, 1992); *Dangerous to Your Health* (New York: Monthly Review Press, 1993); *The Politics of Health Policy* (Cambridge, MA: Blackwell Publishers, 1994), 210ff.

42. David Kirkpatrick, *New York Times*, August 6, 2009; Kaiser Health Tracking Poll, April 2009. New York Times/CBS Poll July 24–28, 2009. Kevin Sack and Marjorie Connelly, *New York Times*, June 21, 2009. Chad Terhune and Keith Epstein, *Business Week*, August 6, 2009. On the arguments concocted against the public option, see Dean Baker, "The Public Plan Option and the Big Government Conservatives," Truthout, September 14, 2009, http://www.truthout.org/091409I. For an enlightening account of how the privatized health system punishes patients in the service of its Wall Street masters, see the congressional testimony of former health insurance company senior executive Wendell Potter, July 10, 2009, at http://www.pbs.org/moyers/journal/07102009/profile.htm.

43. Janet Adamy, *Wall Street Journal*, September 16, 2009.

44. Eric Kleefeld, "Poll: Public Still Doesn't Like Health Care Bill--And Still Like Public Option, Medicare Buy-In," Talking Points Memo, December 22, 2009, http://tpmdc.talkingpointsmemo.com/2009/12/poll-public-still-doesnt-like-health-care-bill----and-still-like-public-option-medicare-buy-in.php. Katherine Seelye, *New York Times*, December 22, 2009. CBS News Poll, "The President, Health Care, and Terrorism," January 6–10, 2010, http://www.cbsnews.com/htdocs/pdf/ poll_obama_011110.pdf. Research poll, January 19, 2010, commissioned by pro-Democrat organizations.

45. David Kirkpatrick, "In a Message to Democrats, Wall St. Sends Cash to G.O.P." *New York Times*, February 8, 2010. "Obama, in Interview, Goes Easy on CEOs," *Wall Street Journal*, February 11, 2010; Edward Luce, "Bonuses Are Part of U.S. Free Market, Obama Says," *Financial Times*, February 11, 2010.

46. Casey Ross, "Financial Executives Spent Big on Brown," *Boston Globe*, February 1, 2010.

47. Brian Mooney, *Boston Globe*, January 21, 2010. Peter Wallsten, *Wall Street Journal*, January 20, 2010.

48. Robert Gavin, "Blue-Collar Workers Bear Brunt of Decline, Ratio of Job Losses at Depression Level," *Boston Globe*, January 19, 2010, reporting a study just released by Northeastern University's Center for Labor Market Studies.

49. Jane Slaughter, "Anger Boils over Health Care Bill," *Labor Notes*, February 2010.

50. Kara Scannell, *Wall Street Journal*, February 6, 2010. As the *Journal* notes, endorsement of the chair's proposal is usually routine, though not since Obama took office. Evan McMorris-Santoro, "Shelby Blocks All Earmarks in the Senate Over AL Ear-

marks," Talking Points Memo, February 4, 2010, http://tpmdc.talkingpointsmemo
.com/2010/02/report-shelby-blocks-all-obama-nominations-in-the-senate-over-
al-earmarks.php. Damien Paletta, "Democrats Go It Alone on Revamp of Finance
Regulation," *Wall Street Journal*, February 6, 2010. Eric Lichtblau, *New York Times*,
February 5, 2010.

51. John Broder and Clifford Krauss, "Advocates of Climate Bill Scale Down Their
Goals," *New York Times*, January 27, 2010. Lisa Wangsness and Susan Milligan,
"GOP Seeks to Block Obama's Labor Pick," *Boston Globe*, February 4, 2010. David
Rosnick and Dean Baker, *Taming the Deficit: Saving Our Children from Themselves*
(Center for Economic and Policy Research, December 2009), http://www.cepr.net
/documents/publications/taming-the-deficit-2009-12.pdf. Center for Economic
and Policy Research, "Future Budget Deficits Almost Entirely Due to Rising Private
Sector Health Care Costs," August 12, 2009. Paul Krugman, "The Senate Becomes
a Polish Joke," *New York Times*, February 5, 2010.

52. On Madison's views, see my "Consent without Consent: Reflections on the Theory
and Practice of Democracy," *Cleveland State Law Review* 44, no. 4, (1996): 415–37.
On the conflicting views of Madison and Aristotle on democracy and inequality,
see *Failed States*, chap. 6.

53. *Perilous Power*, Epilogue.

54. On the Gaza events, see references of note 16, chap. 6.

55. Aluf Benn, *Israel News*, November 20, 2008. Peres, Amnon Barzilai, *Haaretz*, October 24, 1995. Background, see *World Orders Old and New*, Epilogue.

56. "Declaration of Principles for a Long-Term Relationship of Cooperation and Friendship Between the Republic of Iraq and the United States of America," White House
news release, November 26, 2007, http://georgewbush-whitehouse.archives.gov
/news/releases/2007/11/20071126-11.html. Mary Beth Sheridan, *Washington Post*,
November 17. Ahmed Rasheed and Aws Qusay, Reuters, November 18, 2008.

57. Steven Simon, *Foreign Affairs*, May/June 2008. Gardner, *Last Chance*, 13.

58. *International Herald Tribune*, see Lauren Drablier, *Nieman Watchdog*, November
28, 2008, http://www.niemanwatchdog.org/index.cfm?fuseaction=background.view
&backgroundid=308.

59. See Patrick Cockburn, "America Concedes," *London Review of Books*, December
18, 2008. Jonathan Steele, "The Total Defeat of the US Plan to Install a Supine Ally
in the Middle East," *Guardian*, November 27, 2008. See Steele's *Defeat* for detailed
and highly informed review of how and why Bush and Blair "lost their war, and
were bound to do so."

60. For review, see *Rethinking Camelot*. As noted, more has appeared since but leaving
the basic picture intact, and as discussed in *RC*, it was clear enough at the time.

61. Quoted in Sheridan, *Washington Post*.

62. Editorial, *Washington Post*, July 23, 2008.

63. De Hoop Scheffer, Associated Press/Novum, June 29, 2007; *Trouw* (Netherlands),
2008. Shawn McCarthy, *Globe and Mail* (Toronto), June 19, 20, 2008. Mriganka
Jaipuriyar and Shiva Lingam, "India Joins TAPI Natural Gas Pipeline Project; Turk-
men Gas Flows Via Afghanistan, Pakistan to Start in 2015," *Platts Oilgram News*,
April 28, 2008. On NATO and control over Europe after the Soviet collapse, see

Gibbs, *First Do No Harm*, focusing on the Balkans wars.

64. Eric Schmitt and Mark Mazzetti, *New York Times*, November 10, 2008. Sami Moubayed, "US's Syrian Raid Sets Iraq on Fire," *Asia Times*, November 1, 2008. Stephen Zunes, "Bush's Unauthorized Attack on Syria Killed Civilians; Dems Silent," Alternet, November 11, 2008, http://www.alternet.org/story/106329/. Arab world, Assaf Kfoury, "'They Couldn't Handle the Donkey So They Beat the Saddle!'" November 11, 2008. Saudi press, Freeman, *Middle East Policy*, Spring 2008.

65. David Kilkullen and Andrew M. Exum, *New York Times*, op-ed, May 17, 2009. The U.S. command disputes these figures. On the futuristic plans of the administration for drone development, and the possibilities they might provide not only for assassination of suspects but far more generally for population control, down to personal dwellings, and world domination on the cheap, see Nick Turse, "The Forty-Year Drone War," Tomgram, January 24, 2010, http://www.tomdispatch.com /archive/175195/.

66. Barbara Plett, BBC News, Bajaur, October 31, 2008. Pervez Hoodbhoy, *Dawn*, March 9, 2008.

67. Stephen Graham, Associated Press, November 3, 2008. Supplies, Bruce Riedel, *Current History*, November 2008.

68. Ahmed Rashid, *Descent into Chaos* (New York: Viking Press, 2008). Hoodbhoy, interviewed by Cristina Otten for *Focus*, http://www.focus.de/politik/ausland/tid-12856 /pakistan-die-menschen-sind-blind-vor-hass_aid_355157.html. Riedel, quoted by Tim Weiner, *New York Times*, December 7, 2008.

69. Karen DeYoung and Joby Warrick, *Washington Post*, November 16, 2008.

70. Ismail Khan and Pir Zubair Shah, *New York Times*, October 28, 2008.

71. Candace Rondeaux, *Washington Post*, November 6, 2008. Barry Newhouse, Voice of America, November 26, 2008. Rondeaux, *Washington Post*, November 27, 2008.

72. Jimmy Burns and Daniel Dombey, *Financial Times*, October 6, 2008. Jason Burke, *Observer*, September 28, 2008.

73. Declan Walsh, *Guardian*, May 22, 2008.

74. Agence France-Presse, May 8, 2008. Joint declaration of the National Peace Jirga of Afghanistan and the Cooperation for Peace (Germany), National Peace-Jirga of Afghanistan, nd. Anand Gopal, *Christian Science Monitor*, October 20, 2008.

75. Environics, *2007 Survey of Afghans*, October 18, 2007.

76. Jason Straziuso, Associated Press, January 27, 2008.

77. "Face to Face with the Foot Soldiers," *Globe and Mail* (Toronto), March 22, 2008.

78. Rodric Braithwaite, *Financial Times*, October 15, 2008.

79. Rasil Basu, *Asian Age*, December 3, 2001; Rasil Basu, MS, Fall 1988.

80. Malalai Joya, *A Woman Among Warlords: The Extraordinary Story of an Afghan Who Dared to Raise Her Voice* (New York: Scribner, 2009).

81. Nikolai Lanine, *Globe and Mail* (Toronto), November 30, 2006; "A Soviet Case for Bombing Iran: Logic of Interference," January 5, 2009, draft. Lanine and MediaLens, "Invasion—a Comparison of Soviet and Western Media Performance," November 24, 2007, Znet.

82. Barnett Rubin and Ahmed Rashid, *Foreign Affairs*, November–December 2008.

83. Senator Barack Obama, speech at AIPAC Policy Conference (June 4, 2008),

http://www.aipac.org/Publications/SpeechesByPolicymakers/PC_08_Obama.pdf.

84. The practice continued. See among many others Al Jazeera, "Israel Stops Aid Ship to Gaza," June 30, 2009; Mel Frykberg, *Christian Science Monitor*, June 30, 2009. Over the years, the practice has occasionally been mentioned in the United States, but only casually, in passing. For references on these long-standing criminal practices, see note 6, chap. 6, above.

85. "Public Opinion in Iran and America on Key International Issues," poll, World Public Opinion.org, January 24, 2007, http://www.worldpublicopinion.org/pipa /pdf/jan07/Iran_Jan07_rpt.pdf. Chicago Council on Global Affairs, "Global Views 2008." It may be that public opinion has shifted under the intense propaganda assault of the years since.

Ten: Obama on Israel-Palestine

1.   "President Obama Delivers Remarks to State Department Employees," *Washington Post* online, transcript, January 22, 2009, http://www.washingtonpost.com/wp-dyn /content/article/2009/01/22/AR2009012202550.html.

2.   See Zertal and Eldar, *Lords of the Land*.

3.   On what he has had to say since, and its intended lack of force, see above, pp. 177f.

4.   Finkelstein, *"This Time We Went Too Far."* Amnesty International called for an arms embargo on Israel and Hamas, the latter irrelevant to the United States of course. New arms during the war, and the Greek refusal to deliver them, see "Exterminate All the Brutes."

5.   Roula Khalaf, *Financial Times*, January 19, 2009. See chap. 12, below.

6.   Barak Ravid, *Haaretz*, January 19, 2009.

7.   See Carothers, *Critical Mission*. It is superfluous to review once again the ample historical record.

8.   Among others, Palestinian National Authority prime minister Ismail Haniyeh (Hamas), *Washington Post*, July 11, 2006. Hamas political leader Khalid Meshal, Zafarul-Islam Khan, *Milli Gazette*, India, September 16, 2007; *Guardian* (Khalid Meshal), February 13, 2007; Avi Issacharoff, *Haaretz*, April 2, 2008; Taghreed el-Khodary and Ethan Bronner, *New York Times*, May 5, 2009; Jay Solomon and Julien Barnes-Dacey, *Wall Street Journal*, Wall Street Journal (online), July 31, 2009. For more general review, Fawaz Gerges, *Nation*, February 3, 2010.

9.   Khaled Abu Toameh, *Jerusalem Post*, January 23, 2009.

10. *Wall Street Journal*, January 2, 2009; Associated Press, January 22, 2009; *Financial Times*, January 23, 2009; *Christian Science Monitor*, January 23, 2009; *Financial Times*, January 23, 2009.

11. Ken Ellingwood, *Los Angeles Times*, June 25, 2006. There were a few other mentions. The only serious coverage in English appears to have been in the *Turkish Daily News*, June 25, 2006. On the regular Israeli practices, see above, pp. 146–47 and note 6, chap. 6.

12. Al Mezan press release, "IOF Kidnaps Five Palestinian Children in North Gaza," Reference 74/2009, September 7, 2009, http://www.mezan.org/en/details.php

?id=9028&ddname=&id_dept=9.

13. M. Karim Faiez and Laura King, *Los Angeles Times*, January 24, 2009.

14. Dexter Filkins, *New York Times*, January 22, 2009. Karzai, see above, p. 242.

Eleven: The Torture Memos

1   Report of the Senate Armed Services Committee, *Inquiry into the Treatment of De-
     tainees in U.S. Custody*, 110th Congress, 2nd Sess., November 28, 2008 (Washington,
     DC: U.S. Government Printing Office, 2008) p. 72, http://documents.nytimes.com
     /report-by-the-senate-armed-services-committee-on-detainee-treatment#p=72.
     Jonathan Landay, "Abusive Tactics Used to Seek Iraq-al Qaida Link," McClatchy
     Newspapers, April 21, 2009. Gordon Trowbridge, "Levin: Iraq Link Goal of Tor-
     ture," *Detroit News*, April 22, 2009.

2.   Paul Krugman, "Reclaiming America's Soul," *New York Times*, April 24, 2009.

3.   Alfred McCoy, *A Question of Torture: CIA Interrogation, from the Cold War to the
     War on Terror* (New York: Metropolitan Books, 2006). Also Alfred McCoy, "The U.S.
     Has a History of Using Torture," http://hnn.us/articles/32497.html. Jennifer Har-
     bury, *Truth, Torture, and the American Way* (Boston: Beacon Press, 2005). Jane
     Mayer, "The Battle for a Country's Soul," *New York Review of Books*, August 14, 2008.

4.   News and Comment, January 24, 2009, www.allannairn.com.

5.   Lars Schoultz, *Comparative Politics*, January 1981. Edward Herman, in Noam
     Chomsky and Edward Herman, *Political Economy of Human Rights*, vol. I, chap.
     2.1.1 (Cambridge, MA: South End Press, 1979); Edward Herman, *Real Terror Net-
     work* (Cambridge, MA: South End Press, 1982), 26ff.

6.   McCoy, "U.S. Has a History." Levinson, "Torture in Iraq & the Rule of Law in
     America," *Daedalus*, Summer 2004.

7.   Glenn Greenwald, "Obama and Habeas Corpus—Then and Now," *Salon*,
     http://www.salon.com/news/opinion/glenn_greenwald/2009/04/11/bagram/index.
     html. Among other examples of backtracking, see Nedra Pickler and Matt Apuzzo,
     "Still No Rights for Bagram Prisoners," Associated Press, *Army Times*, February 20,
     2009, http://www.armytimes.com/news/2009/02/ap_terrordetainees022009/.

8.   Daphne Eviatar, "Obama Justice Department Urges Dismissal of Another Torture
     Case," *Washington Independent*, March 12, 2009, http://washingtonindependent
     .com/33679. Dostum returned to Afghanistan from exile in August 2009, just be-
     fore the elections, where he lent his support to President Karzai. On his past ex-
     ploits, see Joya, *Woman Among Warlords*.

9.   William Glaberson, *New York Times*, May 16, 1, 2009.

10. Michael Kinsley, *Wall Street Journal*, March 26, 1987.

11   Patrick Cockburn, "Torture? It Probably Killed More Americans Than 9/11," *In-
     dependent*, April 6, 2009.

12. Anonymous (Rajiv Chandrasekaran), "From Captive to Suicide Bomber," *Wash-
     ington Post*, February 22, 2009.

13. Robert Fisk, *Independent*, September 12, 2001.

14. Jesse Holland, Associated Press, May 9, 2009. *New York Times*. See above, p. 163
     and note 40, chap. 6.

15. On the horrendous background for My Lai, see *Political Economy of Human Rights*, vol. I, 315–16, based on unpublished notes given to me by *Newsweek* Saigon bureau chief Kevin Buckley. See also Christopher Hitchens, *The Trial of Henry Kissinger* (London: Verso, 2001), 30f., for the same material from the same source. For new and highly important information on the Hampton assassination, see Jeffrey Haas, *The Assassination of Fred Hampton: How the FBI and the Chicago Police Murdered a Black Panther* (Chicago: Lawrence Hill Books, 2010). For new and quite astonishing revelations about the U.S. bombing of Cambodia and its crucial role in creating the Khmer Rouge, see Cambodia specialists Taylor Owen and Ben Kiernan, "Bombs Over Cambodia," *The Walrus* (Canada), October 2006; posted on Znet. The evasion of these revelations by those who deplore Khmer Rouge atrocities, even when specifically brought to their attention, is instructive. It is not a new phenomenon, nor unique to Cambodia, but nevertheless revealing in the light of the intense focus, often with extraordinary deception, on the terrible crimes of the Khmer Rouge, which followed. For review of the dismal record, see *Manufacturing Consent*. It continues since, in much the same vein, often with mounting hysteria and deceit. All of this reflects, in this case quite dramatically, the usual difference between the reaction to *their* crimes, which we can do little if anything about, and *our* crimes, which we can commonly do a great deal about: in this case, terminating them at once, or at least having the decency to remember them. But they are best kept hidden, like much else that is unpalatable.

Twelve: 1989 and Beyond

1. Timothy Garton Ash, *Guardian*, November 4, 2009; Matthew Ryder, *Observer*, November 15, 2009. Glossed over in the celebrations was the bloody downfall of the most vicious of the Eastern European dictators, Nicolae Ceausescu, a special favorite of Reagan and Bush I until the last days of his savage rule, when he was overthrown from within, like other killers and torturers of their entourage.

2. Bertrand Benoit, *Financial Times*, November 9, 2009.

3. BBC, December 9, 2009.

4. Carothers, *Critical Mission*. During the Reagan years, he writes, there was indeed progress toward democracy in Latin America: in the southern cone, where U.S. influence was least and despite Reagan's efforts to impede it by embracing right-wing dictators. Where U.S. influence was strongest, in the regions nearby, progress was least. The reason is that Washington sought to maintain "the basic order of what, historically at least, are quite undemocratic societies." Reagan's "democracy promotion" endeavors would tolerate only "limited, top-down forms of democratic change that did not risk upsetting the traditional structures of power with which the United States has long been allied."

5. Teresa Whitfield, *Paying the Price* (Philadelphia: Temple University Press, 1995).

6. Antonio Rubio, *El Mundo*, November 21, 2009.

7. Hans Küng, *The Catholic Church* (New York: Modern Library, 2001).

8. Talk at a rare commemoration, November 30, 2009, at Boston College (Jesuit). See Father Sobrino's talk at Santa Clara University, California (Jesuit), November 5, 2009, http://www.adital.com.br/site/noticia.asp?lang=ES&cod=42881.

9.   Derek Scally, *Irish Times*, November 2, 2009.

10. Adam Isaacson and Joy Olson, *Just the Facts 1999 Edition* (Washington, DC: Latin America Working Group and Center for International Policy, 1999).

11. Whitfield, *Paying the Price*.

12. Cited with approval by Timothy Garton Ash, *New York Review of Books*, January 18, 1990, and William Luers, *Foreign Affairs*, Spring 1990. For a sample of reactions, see *Deterring Democracy*, chap. 10. See also Matthew Alexander, "How to Turn a Terrorist," *National Interest* no. 106 (March/April 2010).

13. Anthony Lewis, *New York Times*, March 2, 1990.

14. Elaine Sciolino, *New York Times*, February 27, 1990: David Shipler, op-ed, *New York Times*, March 1, 1990. *Time*, March 12, 1990. For more extensive review of the reaction to this stunning triumph of democracy, see *Deterring Democracy*, chap. 10.

15. Quoted by Jon Reed, *Guardian* (New York), May 23, 1990. On the reaction to the killing of one Polish priest (his murderers tried and convicted) and one hundred religious martyrs in Central America at the same time (murdered with impunity), see *Manufacturing Consent*, chap. 2. For one dramatic illustration in May 1986, see my *Necessary Illusions* (Cambridge, MA: South End Press, 1989), appendix 1, comparing the hysterical outrage over the memoirs of one Cuban political prisoner and the silence greeting the simultaneous release of a 160-page report of sworn testimony and videotapes of 430 political prisoners in El Salvador's main torture chamber, an incredible act of courage, smuggled out of the prison, giving precise and extensive details of their torture by the U.S.-backed security forces; in one case, electrical torture by a North American major in uniform. Greeted with the usual silence, scarcely broken.

16. Zelaya, Greg Grandin, "Muscling Latin America."

17. Dimitri Simes, senior associate at the Carnegie Endowment for International Peace, in a year-end think piece on the prospects of the ending of the Cold War; *New York Times*, December 27, 1988. Abrams cited by Stephen Kurkjian and Adam Pertman, *Boston Globe*, January 5, 1990.

18. For details, see *Deterring Democracy*, chap. 1.

19. Oxfam, cited by John Vidal, *Observer*, October 11, 2009, reporting on reduction of food aid by the rich countries in the face of mounting catastrophe.

20. Mark Kramer, *Washington Quarterly*, April 2009.

21. Sarotte, op-ed, *New York Times*, November 30, 2009; "Not One Inch Eastward?" *Diplomatic History* 34, no. 1 (January 2010).

22. Neil Ascherson, *London Review of Books*, January 7, 2010.

Index